All Things Come into Being through Him

A Christology of Creation

— DAVID O. BROWN —

Sacristy
Press

Sacristy Press
PO Box 612, Durham, DH1 9HT

www.sacristy.co.uk

First published in 2023 by Sacristy Press, Durham

Sacristy Limited, registered in England & Wales, number 7565667

British Library Cataloguing-in-Publication Data
A catalogue record for the book is available from the British Library

ISBN 978-1-78959-276-4

This book is dedicated to the memory of Victor Francis Meecham
(1936–2018) and Patricia May Meecham (1938–2020)

Contents

Acknowledgements

When Christianity was young, men and women who sought to come closer to God went out into the desert, seeking God in stillness and solitude. As Christianity expanded, and men and women could not so easily go out into the desert, they sought God in the stillness and solitude of metaphorical deserts. For those men and women, these metaphorical deserts took the form of monasteries and hermitages; for me, that metaphorical desert took the form of a flat in Belfast. My time spent in that Belfast flat may well have been in an academic context (where I spent most of my time as a Research Fellow at Queen's University Belfast) rather than an ecclesial one, but it was no less eremitic. It is in that flat—physically located within society but emotionally and spiritually secluded from it—guided by Beatrice through prayer and theological study—that I wrote this book.

It would be presumptuous of me to think that the fruit of that prayer and study would be entirely pleasing to Beatrice herself. This book starts from a position that neither Beatrice nor those who comprise the path of ascent to God along which Beatrice guides Dante would recognise. Nevertheless, as speculative as it may be, this book is nothing more than the attempt to understand the relationship between perhaps the two most basic ideas to Christian theology: (a) Thomas Aquinas' doctrine of creation (which is necessary to explain how a God who is beyond being and *actus purus* can be that which is ultimately responsible for the universe); and (b) the biblical doctrine that "[a]ll things came into being through him" (John 1:3), who is the incarnate and crucified Word of God.

This thoughtful and prayerful study would not have been possible without the help and support of a number of people. I could not possibly repay them, but I hope that my recognition of their help goes some way to show my gratitude.

Firstly, I would like to thank the John Templeton Society, and Dr Diarmid Finnegan and Prof. David Livingston of Queen's University Belfast for making my time in Belfast as a Research Fellow (and so the time and space to undertake the research in this book) possible. Their comments on various elements of the research that led to this book—and their constant willingness to indulge my theological musings!—have proved invaluable, and I will always be grateful to them.

I would also like to thank Dr Ralph Norman, who read through a draft of this book and whose comments were also invaluable.

I would also like to thank Richard Rutherford Hilton, Natalie Watson, and all at Sacristy Press for continuing to have faith in my work.

Lastly, but by no means least, I would like to thank Luke Underdown and my family, without whose constant support—both emotional and financial—I could not have written this book.

David O. Brown
London, 2023

Introduction

With the scientific revolution that ended the Middle Ages and ushered in the modern period came a new way of thinking about the world. Advancements in science and the new philosophy that accompanied them saw thinkers increasingly able to describe the world in "natural" terms, with fewer and fewer finding a need for God. God was no longer required to explain why things happened the way they did and, importantly, thinkers were able to make successful predictions about what would happen. The world came to be seen as mechanical, and the clock became an attractive image.

Theologians and thinkers committed to a theistic outlook have a number of ways of dealing with this increasing adeptness of explaining and describing the world in "purely natural" terms. One could argue that science is simply incapable of detecting immaterial causes and axiomatically refuses to accept them, and so science cannot comment on the existence of immaterial causes. That is, there are genuine immaterial causes that genuinely cause material effects, but science is too limited in its scope to detect them. Exponents of Intelligent Design (ID) argue for something similar to this approach.[1]

Alternatively, one could argue that science is incapable of detecting immaterial causes because God voluntarily relinquishes God's ability to influence the world and so the apparent absence of divine influence in the world (e.g., why God appears not to "intervene" to alleviate suffering) is the result of a conscious decision on the part of God to respect creaturely freedom and/or to cultivate certain values. Exponents of *kenosis* argue for something similar to this approach.[2]

---

[1]   Michael Behe, *Darwin's Black Box* (New York, NY: Simon & Schuster, 1998).

[2]   See e.g. John Polkinghorne (ed.), *The Work of Love: Creation as Kenosis* (Grand Rapids, MI: William B. Eerdmans, 2001).

Alternatively still, one could argue that science is incapable of detecting immaterial causes because God acts "in, through, and under" the laws of nature,[3] and so there is no "extra" immaterial cause that could (or could not) be detected. Exponents of panentheism argue for something similar to this approach.[4] These do not exhaust ways in which theists have attempted to retain an outlook that continues to include God, but they do represent the most common.

Yet another way, which has become increasingly unpopular in the modern world, is deism, which holds that God is "reduced" to setting the world in motion, and is no longer necessary to explain anything after that. Perhaps, as with Isaac Newton, God is required for occasional maintenance and "actively intervened from time to time to rest or 'restore' the mechanism",[5] but is basically unnecessary. As Ilia Delio writes:

> The rise of natural theology took the form of deism, a belief in a divine creator, a "clockmaker" who created and wound the time piece that is the universe but had no further role operating it; deism rejected revelation, prophecy, scripture, embracing nature and reason instead.[6]

Deism, at least traditionally, becomes a sort of compromise position: God is no longer required for the day-to-day "maintenance" of the universe, but can be offered a small role to keep the religious happy. Thus, it has been suggested that some thinkers professed deism, not because they genuinely believed that God had created the world and left it to run on its own, but because atheism was socially unacceptable and

---

[3] See Paul Davies, "Teleology without Teleology: Purpose Through Emergent Complexity", in Philip Clayton and Arthur Peacocke (eds), *In Whom We Live and Move and Have Our Being: Panentheistic Reflections on God's Presence in a Scientific World* (Grand Rapids, MI: William B. Eerdmans, 2004), p. 99.

[4] E.g., Arthur Peacocke, *Paths from Science Towards God* (Oxford: OneWorld, 2001).

[5] Ilia Delio, *The Unbearable Wholeness of Being* (Maryknoll, NY: Orbis Books, 2013), p. 11.

[6] Delio, *The Unbearable Wholeness of Being*, p. 11.

so thinkers had to pretend some religious beliefs or risk ostracization. Anthony Grayling writes that "functionally, deism is less than a whisker away from atheism, and eighteenth-century deists were by no means religious".[7] He continues, "the word 'atheist' then had the same kind of profoundly negative cachet that 'murderer' and 'rapist' does, as a result of demonization by the church of those who refused to accept its authority".[8] Therefore, those who felt there was no need to invoke a divine agent adopted the most basic position available that allowed them to continue in normal society while still maintaining their insistence that God was unnecessary. Maurice Wiles also agrees that deism "is widely regarded as no different from atheism".[9] Richard Dawkins puts it slightly differently, calling deism "watered-down theism".[10] Deism becomes a sort of "lowest common denominator" position—science, but a bit of God to satisfy a devoutly religious society (although not really acceptable to either).

Once society was ready to accept atheism—or at least ready to tolerate those who professed it—then deism was no longer required. Those that had once hidden themselves behind the cover of deism now flung it off, proud to profess their atheism and no longer in need of any "religious-looking" disguise. One is either religious and so free to endorse full-blown theism, or one feels that science has demonstrated the superfluity of religion and so is free to endorse atheism. Any middle position—deism—is a cop-out.

Subsequent scholarship has questioned whether this dichotomy of science and religion is an accurate portrayal of how the two disciplines should be viewed.[11] However, regardless of the fact that commentators question whether science and religion have ever been in "conflict", it

---

7   Anthony Grayling, "Introduction", *The Britannica Guide to the Ideas that Made the Modern World: The People, Philosophy, and History of the Enlightenment* (London: Robinson, 2008), p. xi.

8   Grayling, "Introduction", p. xi.

9   Maurice Wiles, *God's Action in the World* (London: SCM Press, 1986), p. 2.

10   Richard Dawkins, *The God Delusion* (London: Black Swan, 2006), pp. 39–40.

11   E.g., Peter Harrison, "Introduction", in Peter Harrison (ed.), *The Cambridge Companion to Science and Religion* (Cambridge: Cambridge University Press, 2010), pp. 1–17.

remains a popular outlook. The success of Dan Brown's *Angels and Demons*—a fictional tale of science vs. religion in the twenty-first century—is an indication that the idea that science and religion are warring ways of looking at the world has become a popular way of thinking about them. The general consensus seems to be that science has become a replacement for religion, which comes to represent a more infantile way of conceiving the world.

Of course, others would disagree, and suggest instead that far from being a cop-out position, limiting deism to a disguise worn by atheists has drastically misrepresented the intentions behind what deism seeks to argue. It could be a genuine attempt to take the best of both worlds. One can accept that science is better than the Bible at explaining how the world works, without appeal to the whims of an all-controlling God, but also think that the question about how that world came into existence in the first place is a religious one. Thus, despite the fact that Anthony Grayling avers that "scarcely anyone is a deist today, that is, a believer in there having been a god to get the world started, but who has since vanished from the picture" because "people can now openly report that they have no religious beliefs or commitments without being socially shunned",[12] there are some thinkers (not very many, but more than "scarcely any") who, right into the twenty-first century, affirm deism as a genuine position. More often than not, it takes the form of what Wilson Poon calls the "lowest common denominator god",[13] by which he means a sort of God that is so inoffensive that any theist, irrespective of religious persuasion, could accept it. Deists hold that God—often an Intelligent Designer—can be deduced from the natural world and there is no need for revelation. Deists believe in reason, not religion. Deists agree with Paley that one only has to look at the world from the proverbial armchair to perceive that it is clearly designed, so one can move from "designed" to the existence of a "designer", and one can move from a "designer"

---

to idea that the "designer" must be that who brought the world into existence. Yet, deists disagree that the Intelligent Designer continues to have a personal interest in the world.

However, for the Christian, there are two apparent problems with heading down this path (ignoring for now that most Christians would want to retain the idea that God continues to act in cosmic history after creation). One problem with this deist God—a problem that nearly all theologians recognize—is that the motive for affirming deism reveals a problem with the way that the deist thinks about God in the first place. If one is a theist, then one is free to think of God as something other than the world and not in competition with it. Yet, if one is a deist, then the underlying assumption appears to be that the increasing ability of science to describe the world leads to a decreasing role for God, and that science has become entirely sufficient to do what God was previously required to explain: that is, it points to an underlying assumption that God and the universe are in a zero-sum relationship. If this is correct, then deism appears unable to escape the criticism that it affirms a "God of the gaps". In other words, the deist has apparently traded off theological sophistication for religio-scientific harmony.

Second, as many have noted, if one wishes to apologize for a God who does not "intervene" in the world then, seemingly quite obviously, one has to dismiss the incarnation along with it. Plenty of theologians have noted this. David Brown, for example, writes that the deist, "while committed to belief in God, rejects Jesus Christ and his doctrines" so that "if there is to be a proper incarnation, God the Son cannot stand aloof from the created order but must become interrelated with it".[14] Gerald O'Collins also gives expression to this, writing that "the logic of deism excluded the possibility of any such special sub-acts of God . . . [e.g.,] an incarnation".[15] In other words, the deist has apparently traded off the need for Jesus Christ for religio-scientific harmony.

Deism, therefore, should be abhorrent to the Christian for two distinct reasons: (a) It leads to a "god-of-the-gaps" type of theology (or, in more

---

[14] David Brown, *The Divine Trinity* (London: Duckworth, 1985), p. 14.

[15] Gerald O'Collins, *Christology: A Biblical, Historical, and Systematic Study of Jesus* (Oxford: Oxford University Press, 1995), p. 217.

technical theological language, it leads to the univocality of being); and (b) it obliges the rejection of the incarnation. This book suggests that these conclusions need not follow.

Here, then, is the intention of this book. The particular history of deism, and its role within wider intellectual history, is well known, and this book does not pretend to offer any contribution to the historical question of deism. Rather, it is an apology for the claim that one can be a deist—and so hold that science shows that God is not needed to explain the "natural processes" of the universe—without having this claim lead to (a) a "god of the gaps", or (b) a rejection of the incarnation. This book is an attempt to have one's cake and eat it: to have all the benefits of a deistic theology—one does not have to explain how science and God can exist side by side—without any of the drawbacks or seeing God and the universe in a zero-sum relationship, and retain the incarnation.

However, before that apology is attempted, there are two things to which the reader's attention needs to be drawn that help to lay the groundwork for the following discussion: (a) the motives that draw a person to deism; and (b) those particular doctrines that comprise deism.

The motives for deism: The relationship between science and religion

Despite the fact that some deists (probably) affirmed their subscription to the doctrine because fully-blown atheism would have been academic and social suicide, it is easy to be sympathetic to the deist's motives. The deist wants to embrace the two most important endeavours that humankind has attempted. The deist accepts quite seriously that the universe can be exhaustively explained through scientific methods, but does not want to discard the conclusions of religious thought.

Exactly how the relationship between religion and science should be understood is by no means agreed. Various models are proposed. Perhaps the simplest delineation poses three distinct models: either (a) science and religion are in conflict; (b) science and religion are entirely separate/

independent; or (c) science and religion can engage with one another.[16] John Haught is perhaps the most famous exponent of this distinction. Some maintain this three-fold distinction but point to slightly different criteria.[17] Others add a fourth. Ian Barbour, for example, agrees with the first two of Haught's categories—"conflict" and "independence"—but he splits the third category into two: religion and science are in dialogue or religion and science are integrated.[18] Others suggest that there are as many as nine distinct models.[19] Others still suggest that what people mean by "religion" and "science" has never been agreed, so it is impossible to suggest that any model can accurately describe their relationship.[20] Thus, John Hedley Brooke argues that history is far too complex to delineate a few neatly compartmentalized models.[21] Of course, Brooke is entirely correct in his observation, but, in order to help guide the discussion, the three-fold distinction will be preferred.

Historically, at least, the notion of deism comes about in conjunction with the scientific method. When science becomes a source of knowledge about the world, God is pushed out. This could lead to the "conflict" model: only science *or* religion can be true and so if science is demonstrably true, then religion cannot be. However, most of those who engage in science and religion accept that this "competition/conflict" is a facile, outdated and unhelpful way of arranging science and religion. Nevertheless, as

---

[16] John Haught, *God after Darwin* (Boulder, CO: Westview Press, 2000), pp. 24–5.

[17] William Stoeger, "Contemporary cosmology and its implications for the science–religion dialogue", in Robert J. Russell, William Stoeger, and George Coyne (eds), *Physics, Philosophy, and Theology: A Common Quest for Understanding* (Vatican City: Vatican Observatory, 1988), pp. 238–9.

[18] Ian Barbour, *Religion in an Age of Science* (San Francisco, CA: Harper, 1990), pp. 3–30.

[19] Robert John Russell, "The Relevance of Tillich for the Theology and Science Dialogue, *Zygon: Journal of Religion and Science* 36:2 (2001), pp. 269–308.

[20] John Hedley Brooke, *Science and Religion: Some Historical Perspectives* (Cambridge: Cambridge University Press, 1991), pp. 6ff.

[21] John Hedley Brooke, "Science, Religion, and Historical Complexity", *Historically Speaking* 8:5 (2007), pp. 10–13.

already shown, despite the fact that most reject it outright, this model has historical value, inasmuch as there *are* those who believed (and still some who continue to believe) science and religion to be so related. The New Atheists and Biblical Fundamentalists are two examples. Both genuinely believe that one cannot coherently accept the validity of both religion *and* science simultaneously. Likewise, the popularity of stories such as Dan Brown's *Angels and Demons* (no doubt influenced by the popularity of exponents of both New Atheism and Biblical Fundamentalism) evidences that this model—while dismissed completely by academics—is still a commonly held belief among the general population.

The "conflict" model, then, while enjoying popular assent, is dismissed as being theologically inaccurate and largely irrelevant for present purposes. This leaves two basic options remaining: either (b) science and religion are entirely separate disciplines that have entirely separate subject matter and do not come into contact with one another, or (c) science and religion explain the same thing—the universe, how it "works" and what its history is—and so cannot help but mutually influence one another.

Some philosophical observations
At this juncture, a few further comments are necessary: (i) scientific truth, empiricism, is not self-evident and itself relies on metaphysical assumptions; and (ii) despite the self-confidence of scientists that they are open-minded and curious, the practice of science requires and relies on just as much authority and dogma as does religion, and fosters just as much closed-mindedness as that which they accuse religion of.

The Munchausen Trilemma
It has been widely recognized and commented that modern scientific endeavour is based on Christian values. As many writers acknowledge, "A proposition such as 'the only meaningful statements are those deriving from natural science' is not itself a proposition of natural science,"[22] or, differently, "The truth of the statement 'no statements are true unless

---

[22]   Rupert Shortt, *God Is No Thing: Coherent Christianity* (London: Hurst & Company, 2016), p. 33.

they can be proved scientifically' cannot itself be proved scientifically."[23] Thus, while the scientist might point to empiricism as the philosophical paradigm in which scientific investigation functions, one cannot prove empirically that one must accept empiricism. One cannot provide empirical evidence that the choice of empiricism is appropriate and so must point to something else—something that is not empirical—in order to underpin empiricism. As Michael Heller writes, "All the successes of this method [of empiricism] can be considered as argument revealing the correctness of that choice [of rationality]. However, this does not change the fact that the empirical method cannot prove itself, and that it still remains a moral choice."[24] One can defend on the basis of empiricism that all scientific truth is valid, but one cannot defend the initial choice to accept empiricism in the first place.

This is the Munchausen (or Fries) Trilemma: one must either accept their argument is circular, relies on infinite regression, or rests on dogmatic axioms for which there is no evidence. This provokes the question: why would one be moved to accept empiricism—that the world is rational, logical, and consistent—in the first place? To that question, many philosophers suggest the answer: "No scientist could commence her work unless she had the confidence, born of a theological intuition, that the world she is going out to meet is endowed with intelligibility."[25] Thus, all scientists "live off Judeo-Christian capital, whether they like it or not".[26] Michael Heller writes that "the role of Christianity in the origin of modern science cannot be reduced to sharpening and transmitting the Greek heritage to our times", but "Christianity added to this heritage something substantial, something which doubtless contributed to the fostering of the empirical method". This "something substantial", Heller

---

[23] Gerard Verschuuren, *Aquinas and Modern Science* (Kettering, OH: Angelico Press, 2016), p. 18.

[24] Michael Heller, "Scientific Rationality and Christian Logos", in Robert Russell, William Stoeger, and George Coyne (eds), *Physics, Philosophy, and Theology* (Vatican City: Vatican Observatory, 1988), p. 142.

[25] Robert Barron, *Exploring Catholic Theology* (Grand Rapids, MI: Baker Academic, 2015), p. 70.

[26] Verschuuren, *Aquinas and Modern Science*, p. 87.

claims, is "the Christian teaching on the creation of the world",[27] which, Barron notes, along with Greek philosophy, asserted that the world is both "non-divine"[28] and "orderly and intelligible".[29] It is no surprise, then, that "the modern physical sciences emerged precisely in the universities of the Christian west, that is to say, out of a thought-world in which the doctrine of creation is a structuring element".[30] That is to say, a thought-world in which it was taught that the universe is non-divine (and so open to investigation) and rational, orderly, and intelligible (and so open to repeatable experimentation) precisely because it was created by, and so mirrors, the divine.[31]

Peter Harrison takes this approach one step further, arguing that it is not just Christian values, but specifically *Protestant* values, that underpin the scientific method. Harrison offers an interesting and compelling argument that the classic distinctions between western and eastern theology (i.e., the Christ event as atonement restoring a completely degraded humanity to a previously perfect life vs. the Christ event as deification transforming an infant humanity to a novel future) actually made the west more amenable to the strict scientific method. More specifically, he argues:

---

27   Heller, "Scientific Rationality and Christian Logos", p. 144.

28   Barron, *Exploring Catholic Theology*, p. 225.

29   Barbour, *Religion in an Age of Science*, p. 17.

30   Barron, *Exploring Catholic Theology*, p. 225.

31   No doubt, the reader will want to point to the contribution of Muslim scholars to mathematics, astronomy, and philosophy (to name but a few). This is well known, and it is not the intention of the author to gloss over this outstanding contribution and, perhaps worse, claim that it was solely and uniquely Christian thinkers who made them. Nevertheless, as important as their contribution to western thought was, it could be claimed that it is still this religious sense of creation—that the world is non-divine and intelligible/rational—that fostered that scientific endeavour. That is, while it would be disingenuous to suggest that it is only *Christianity* that drove scientific endeavour forward, it was that religious sensibility that is basic to all Abrahamic faiths, including Christianity, that lay at the heart of any scientific endeavour.

Three related features of Protestant Christianity served to promote a scientific culture in the West: a new, more literal way of reading both the world and the Bible; a strong fall-redemption theology that was harnessed to motivate and legitimize science by identifying it as a redemptive activity; and a theological anthropology that emphasized the fallenness of the human condition and the moral, cognitive, and sensory impairments that resulted from that fall, thus promoting a critical, experimental approach to natural philosophy.[32]

While Peter Harrison points to Protestantism, Brian Davies points to Thomism. Davies argues that "what Aquinas thinks about God may be compared with what we find at the end of Wittgenstein's *Tractatus Logico-Philosophicus*",[33] in which we read that "not *how* the world is, is the mystical, but *that* it is"[34] and so "we feel that even if *all possible* scientific questions be answered, the problems of life have still not been touched at all".[35] Davies claims that this is comparable to how Aquinas thinks, and so "Aquinas seems to be saying something similar when he speaks of *esse* and creation".[36] Albert Einstein's musing that "the fact that [the universe] is comprehensible is a miracle",[37] is also not far behind.

In other words, no matter how competent science is at explaining the world, science can never explain *why* science is so competent. *That* the universe is so rational and intelligible makes science so competent at describing the universe; *why* the universe is so rational and intelligible is a mystery to the scientist.

---

[32] Peter Harrison, "Science, Eastern Orthodoxy, and Protestantism", *Isis* 107:3 (2016), pp. 589–90.

[33] Brian Davies, "Aquinas on What God is Not", *Revue Internationale de Philosophie* 52:204 (1998), p. 225.

[34] Ludwig Wittgenstein, *Tractatus Logico-Philosophicus*, tr. C. K. Ogden (London: Routledge & Kegan Paul, 1933), 6.44.

[35] Wittgenstein, *Tractatus*, 6.52.

[36] Davies, "Aquinas on What God is Not", p. 225.

[37] Albert Einstein, *Out of my Later Years* (Westport, CT: Greenwood, 1970), p. 61.

Scientific dogma and authority

It is often assumed that scientists are open-minded and free to accept whatever thesis can be demonstrated and the religious are closed minded and indoctrinated to believe a false thesis (invariably that is exploited by those in power to secure the submission of the masses). However, it is not hard to demonstrate that science relies on authority and dogma just as much as religion. As scientific endeavour grew and became more sophisticated and specialist, so the number of people who could competently practice it shrank. Nowadays, many years of dedicated study and training are required to conduct scientific investigation, and it usually requires significant financial investment and the use of intricate and specialized machinery, neither of which most people have access to. However, this inevitably means that, as the number of people who can competently *practice* science has shrunk, so has the number of people who can competently *understand* science. As Michael Heller writes, "The point is that the understanding of scientific theories (let alone creative work in science) requires protracted studies and great intellectual effort" so that "proper assessment of scientific theories by an outsider is practically impossible".[38] It does not need much to move from this fact about the decreasing accessibility of science to the fact that the general public must take scientists at their word, without being able to competently question the claims they profess. Gerard Verschuuren writes:

> The enterprise of science relies on the trusting of "eyewitness" reports of observed data, largely in the case of special experiences and experiments. Most of what we know about science and its findings is from hearsay, based on expert reports. The scientists involved must conduct some experiment to gather data, whether the experiment is simple (such as dropping a ball and timing its fall) or complex (such as searching for the infamous and enigmatic Higgs boson). They are essentially eyewitnesses.[39]

---

[38]   Heller, "Scientific Rationality and Christian Logos", p. 146.

[39]   Verschuuren, *Aquinas and Modern Science*, pp. 70–1.

Janice Soskice agrees. She writes:

> I have no immediate personal experience of Napoleon, or of the
> current President of the United States, or of a quasar. I speak
> about them in virtue of my connectedness, through language
> and various structures of communication, to others who do
> have some kind of access to these persons and entities. The
> astrophysicist is, for me, an authoritative other when I want
> to speak about quasars or black holes. In religious matters, of
> course, people come to be seen as authoritative for reasons other
> than what they say—we may know of their great devotion, their
> disciplined life of prayer or their concern for the loveless and
> poor, or we sense a kind of sanctity in what we hear, see, or read
> of them. Pascal, Dr. Johnson or one's great-aunt might all count
> for an individual as authoritative others. Ezekiel or St. Paul might
> count for large groups of people, for whole religious traditions,
> as authoritative others.[40]

What is the difference between the priest in his black cassock and the
scientist in her white lab coat? Both are claiming to have privileged access
to information, and both implore the general public to bow to their
superior knowledge. Importantly, drawing on the first point regarding the
inability to prove empiricism above, neither the priest nor the scientist
can offer irrefutable evidence for why one must accept their authority;
one either accepts it (based on an axiom or moral "feeling" about what
the truth should or might look like) or they do not.

Richard Dawkins himself makes this point in his essay "Prayer to my
Daughter". Here, Dawkins acknowledges that "a bad reason for believing
anything" is "that you are told to believe it by someone important".[41]
There are theists everywhere rubbing their hands at the irony here: no

---

[40]   Janet Soskice, "Knowledge and Experience in Science and Religion: Can
       We Be Realists", in Robert J. Russell, William Stoeger, and George Coyne
       (eds), *Physics, Philosophy, and Theology: A Common Quest for Understanding*
       (Vatican City: Vatican Observatory, 1988), p. 181.

[41]   Richard Dawkins, *A Devil's Chaplain* (London: Phoenix, 2003), p. 287.

one should believe atheism because Dawkins tells them to. Presumably, Dawkins *meant* to say that "a bad reason for believing anything is that you are told to believe it by someone important, unless they are wearing a lab coat, in which case do believe them". Or, "a bad reason for believing anything is that you are told to believe it by someone important, unless it conforms to your pre-analytical moral judgement about what to expect regarding what you think the world should look like, in which case do believe them".[42]

In a similar way, Richard Dawkins hails the Apostle Thomas—doubting Thomas—as the patron saint of scientists. He writes that "if there's evidence, it isn't faith. Doubting Thomas, patron saint of scientists, wanted evidence. Other disciples praised [sic] for not doing so".[43] The story of doubting Thomas—who, upon hearing the apostles' revelations that Jesus had risen, stubbornly exclaimed, "Unless I see the mark of the nails in his hands, and put my finger in the mark of the nails and my hand in his side, I will not believe"[44] —is well known. While usually Thomas is painted in a negative light for not having faith, Dawkins praises him for demanding evidence. It is easy to be sympathetic to Dawkins' take and to view Thomas' demand for evidence as sensible, yet one might also wonder how Dawkins himself would react to his own doubting Thomas.

---

[42]   James Smith (who draws on the thought of Catholic philosopher Charles Taylor), adds an interesting angle to this argument. He argues that "converts" to science more often than not frame that "conversion" in terms of the leaving behind of a childhood or immature superstition and the embracing or accepting of a grown-up and mature recognition that the world is simply not like that. Yet, while they claim to base this "conversion" on data and scientific facts, this is very often simply not the case. It is normally based on some sort of ethic or sentimentality, simply replacing one faith—religion—for another—faith in science's ability (James Smith, "Our Chalcedonian Moment", in Andrew Torrance and Thomas McCall (eds), *Christ and the Created Order Vol. 2* (Grand Rapids, MI: Zondervan, 2018), p. 188).

[43]   Richard Dawkins, 28 September 2012, <https://twitter.com/RichardDawkins/status/251588628248145920>, accessed 24 April 2022; see also Richard Dawkins, *The Selfish Gene* (Oxford: Oxford University Press, 2006), p. 198.

[44]   John 20:25.

How would Dawkins feel if (as plenty do!) someone stubbornly refused to believe that evolution occurred on the basis that Richard Dawkins says it does?

Of course, Dawkins points to the wealth of evidence that supports the claims made by scientists that he would expect his daughter to accept. Yet, as it has just been argued, there is no way of accepting without placing (at least some) faith in the scientists who offer that evidence. As Dawkins himself recognizes, he hasn't seen, with his own eyes, that the speed of light is 186,000 miles per second; he has only read about it in books and believes those books. "This looks like 'authority'," he confesses, "but actually it is much better than authority because the people who wrote the books have seen the evidence and anyone is free to look carefully at the evidence whenever they want".[45] Dawkins has a very optimistic view of "anyone's" grasp of the mathematical ability required to understand *why* the evidence should be *interpreted* to prove the speed of light. Dawkins is certainly correct that anyone can ask to see that evidence, but unless they place faith in the authority of the scientists confirming that the charts on the screen and the formulae being used point to the speed of light, it is useless. Moreover, one would also need to axiomatically accept the empirical world view in which such evidence makes sense: if one does not *believe* that the world is rational (and it must be a belief), then there is no reason to accept that producing the same result from repeatable experimentation is evidence of something being "true", regardless of how much of that evidence the scientist tells you they have and how much they explain its meaning to you.

Dawkins might also very well point to the numerous and well-attested examples of when scientists believed things *despite* the fact that those wearing lab coats (or cassocks) told them they were not true and *despite* the fact that they did not conform to what they expected the world should look like. That is, there are plenty of examples of scientists reacting and pushing against the collected wisdom of their peers on the basis of the evidence of their experiments. Thomas Kuhn's book *The Structure of Scientific Revolution*, in which he points to various "paradigm shifts" where scientific understanding underwent a monumental shift, provides

---

[45] Dawkins, *A Devil's Chaplain*, p. 287.

ample evidence of this. Science does have a tendency to discard ideas that have outlived their use and embrace new and exciting ideas in their place. Yet, a cursory glance at the history of theological endeavour will give ample evidence that theologians and religious are just as likely to do the same. Just as there are plenty of examples of the establishment refusing to accept scientific advancement because it did not fit with their closed, narrow conception of the world, so there are plenty of examples where charismatic "theological geniuses" changed the way that the Church thought about religion. Athanasius' repeated banishment and Maximus the Confessor's severed tongue and right hand are good examples of theologians who were dismissed at the time, but whose theology is now accepted orthodoxy.

Theologians are just as open minded as scientists and scientists are just as close minded as theologians. This should not be taken as criticism of Dawkins' (or Thomas') stance on faith; faith in the authority of others is important, but so is the demand for evidence and explanation that help facilitate understanding what those in authority teach. It is just as reasonable to ask for evidence as it is to place faith in the authority of others. Rather, it should be taken as criticism of Dawkins' suggestion that science is immune from the "problem" of faith, dogma, and authority and is a superior endeavour as a result. Science is just as likely to have dogmatic practitioners who demand authority and the faith of those they speak down to as theology is likely to have innovative thinkers who push the boundaries through novel and creative ways of thinking.

There is more that can be said here regarding the philosophy and epistemology of science, but it is not important to dwell on them here. One could say more about whether science is deductive or inductive, how one uses data and evidence, how one interprets data and evidence, the role that theories play in that interpretation, whether science is positive or whether it can only falsify, and the role of paradigm shifts in interpretation. Space prevents further consideration. In any case, more is not needed to support the underlying point: acceptance of the validity of science as a genuine and legitimate source of truth about the world does not mean that theology itself becomes irrelevant.

Non-overlapping *magisteria*

It would be understandable to consider these two arguments—(i) that science relies on Christianity, and (ii) that science is no different to religion—and think that the "engagement" model is the most appropriate. This would be a mistake. Assuming one accepts the validity of science in the first place, these philosophical observations should point to the conclusion that one must accept that science and theology are authoritative in the domain in which they operate—so that one must take their claims about those domains seriously—but also accept that they are not authoritative in other domains, and so cannot comment on that which is properly the subject of other domains. In this way, despite the fact that the suggestion that science and religion are "engaging" claims is the one most often accepted by theologians, this book will take it that, ultimately, this thesis is left wanting.

There is a precedent for rejecting the thesis that religion and science are mutually engaging. Nicholas Lash, for example, writes that interaction between science and religion "suggests (as, perhaps, does 'dialogue') something approaching parity of reciprocal influence",[46] yet he acknowledges that this does not happen. He questions whether "scientists really expect to have to modify their practices in the light of what they learn from theologians?" and concludes, "Not in my experience. And yet, there is much talk of 'dialogue' between theology and science".[47] William Stoeger, in the same collection of essays, goes even further. He does not just notice that any dialogue between science and religion is one-sided, but affirms that it *should* be this way. Asking whether scientists "*as scientists*" should maintain a receptivity to theology and philosophy, he answers "obviously not".[48] This, Stoeger argues, is due to

---

[46] Nicholas Lash, "Observation, Revelation, and the Prosperity of Noah", in Robert J. Russell, William Stoeger, and George Coyne (eds), *Physics, Philosophy, and Theology: A Common Quest for Understanding* (Vatican City: Vatican Observatory, 1988), p. 204.

[47] Lash, "Observation, Revelation, and the Prosperity of Noah", pp. 204–5.

[48] Stoeger, "Contemporary cosmology and its implications for the science-religion dialogue", p. 242.

a difference in the disciplines. Whereas "philosophy and theology *are* essentially interdisciplinary",[49] science is "just not equipped to receive and integrate such [theological] conclusions".[50] Neither Lash nor Stoeger would (presumably) suggest that science and religion were to be kept entirely and completely separate, but yet, quite clearly, neither want to endorse a sort of facile "engagement" thesis.

Moreover (as will be suggested in the chapter on creation), if suggesting that science and religion are mutually engaging leads to the conclusion that they are "approaching parity of reciprocal influence",[51] then this assumes that religion and science are "equal" or that the object of their study is exactly the same. Thus, it would seem that those theologians who claim to accept the validity of science and who see religion and science as engaging or interacting are forced to apologize for a God who is open to scientific investigation and, more pertinently, that what God does is open to scientific investigation. If religion and science are engaging, then this places the claims of the theologians directly under the remit of the scientist.

Thus, Nicholas Saunders writes that it is essential to most theories of divine activity that "God's action in the world does achieve causal physical effects, be they in the natural world or in the minds of intelligent beings", and, as a result, "as genuine physical phenomena they would surely be epistemologically open to scientific analysis".[52] Others agree. Wesley Wildman writes that "the question of divine action is one of the theological issues that most directly presupposes facts about the natural world and its governing laws" and so "evaluating theories of divine action in relation to our best knowledge of the natural world [is] very likely

---

49   Stoeger, "Contemporary cosmology and its implications for the science–religion dialogue", p. 243.

50   Stoeger, "Contemporary cosmology and its implications for the science–religion dialogue", p. 243.

51   Lash, "Observation, Revelation, and the Prosperity of Noah", p. 204.

52   Nicholas Saunders, *Divine Action and Modern Science* (Cambridge: Cambridge University Press, 2002), p. 129.

to be fruitful".[53] Likewise, Frank Kirkpatrick writes that "[a] God who acts and whose acts decisively change the course of history forever but who can't be known through those acts is a peculiar God and so is an epistemological situation in which knowledge of God through God's own acts is impossible or at least profoundly difficult".[54] In other words, if one wishes to accept that science and religion are in conversation with one another, then one has to accept that the claims of the theologian are open to scientific investigation. If the theologian wishes to make claims about the universe, then those claims can be commented on authoritatively by scientists. Does this then mean that no evidence of activity points to inactivity on the part of God, or, perhaps worse yet for the theologian, that no scientific evidence of divine activity points to the non-existence of God?

Richard Dawkins, with his tongue firmly in his cheek, makes similar comments. He claims that "if God really did communicate with humans that fact would emphatically not lie outside science", so asks "[if] God comes bursting through from whatever other-worldly domain is his natural abode, crashing through into our world where his messages can be intercepted by human brains—[then how has] that phenomenon . . . nothing to do with science?'[55] Dawkins has a point. If science cannot detect God's action it is either because there is no God (or at least, there is no God who acts) or it is because the model of "engagement" is incorrect.

Thus, as Lash, Stoeger, and Dawkins recognize, it is contradictory to subscribe to the "engagement" thesis, but then claim that, on the one hand, scientists do not have to accept what theologians say, and on the other hand, theologians do not have to accept what scientists say about the absence of divine activity. If scientists are not obliged to "maintain a receptivity to theology and philosophy" and theologians are free to

---

53   Wesley Wildman, "The Divine Action Project, 1988–2003", in Robert Russell, Nancey Murphy and William Stoeger (eds), *Scientific Perspectives on Divine Action: Twenty Years of Challenge and Progress* (Vatican City: Vatican Observatory Foundation, 2008), p. 135.

54   Frank Kirkpatrick, *The Mystery and Agency of God: Divine Being and Action in the World* (Minneapolis, MN: Fortress Press, 2014), pp. 136–7.

55   Dawkins, *The God Delusion*, p. 184.

dismiss the scientist's failure to find evidence of divine activity, then what exactly is being *engaged*? In other words, the "separate" thesis is the only one available. That is, it leads to what Stephen Jay Gould called "non-overlapping *magisteria*" (NOMA).

Why deism?

Taking Wildman and Fitzpatrick at their word, one is left with sentiments such as that expressed by Nancey Murphy: "Either God does not act at all within the created world, or else God acts at all times in all things."[56] That is, either deism is correct (God does not act within the created world) or pantheism—or at the very least panentheism—is correct (God acts at all times in all things). Either God is entirely and completely transcendent of the world or God is entirely and completely immanent in the world.

Pan(en)theism has enjoyed much support in the twentieth and early twenty-first centuries. Theologians faced with precisely this lack of scientific evidence of a God who acts take Murphy's second option and see God acting in and through all natural processes. However, this does not solve the issue; if anything, it makes it worse, and only kicks the proverbial can further down the explanatory road. As Sarah Lane Ritchie rightly recognizes, it does not matter to which theology of divine activity one appeals: if one holds that God influences the world then "at some point, the transcendent, immaterial God would have to actually interact with the brute, physical mechanisms explicated by contemporary science".[57] If contemporary science cannot find those interactions then one must take that seriously. In other words, one must accept that God is *ontologically identical* to the material universe, or one is still faced with the problem of how an immaterial God influences material processes.

This leaves deism. In other words, this book takes the absence of any evidence of any sort of divine influence on the world and, rather than

---

56   Nancey Murphy, quoted in Joshua Reichard, "Beyond Causation: A Contemporary Theology of Concursus", *American Journal of Theology & Philosophy* 34:2 (2013), p. 128.

57   Sarah Lane Ritchie, "Dancing around the Causal Joint: Challenging the Theological Turn in Divine Action Theories", *Zygon: Journal of Religion and Science* 52:2 (2017), p. 377.

taking the position that this is because science is incapable of detecting religious activity, it accepts that such activity is not there. That is, it is not (necessarily) that God does not "act" but the content of that "activity" has nothing to do with anything which can be claimed to be the domain of science. This does not mean that religion is relegated to the arena of morality but, as will be seen (especially in Chapter 2), religion is concerned with ontology and metaphysics.

Here, it appears that NOMA and deism are perfect bedfellows: one (NOMA) argues that theology is concerned with something other than that which is the domain of science and subject to the scientific method, and the other (deism) claims that God does not act at all within the created world and so "does" nothing that might be "detected" by that scientific method. That is, science should be taken at face value regarding its claims—there is no divine activity in the universe—but it should also be recognized that science relies upon, and therefore cannot comment upon, metaphysics. NOMA and deism say much the same thing, but they come at it from different perspectives. While it is important to stop short of saying that NOMA and deism are essentially identical, they are mutually complementary positions, and this book will use them as such.

Thus, the motives for deism should be clear. One appeals to deism because one wishes to both accept the validity and competency of science to explain the universe without compromising that competency by claiming science is incapable of detecting immaterial causes that produce real and observable material effects and also accept the validity of theology to answer metaphysical and/or ontological questions.

What is deism?

John Macquarrie writes that, although deism appeared as a new religious belief in the Enlightenment period, "the advocates of deism would not have regarded these beliefs as 'new', for they thought of themselves as returning to 'natural' or 'rational' religion, to fundamental beliefs about God and man that are innate to the human mind and discoverable by reason without the aid of any alleged revelation".[58] Of course, such an attempt to legitimize one's beliefs is commonplace. The above claims about the openness of theology to novelty notwithstanding, very rarely do thinkers explicitly wish to promulgate something entirely new; many of the innovations in theological history have been styled by their progenitors as a "return" to fundamentals or as an interpretation of earlier belief. Continuing this explanation, Macquarrie writes that Edward Herbert, Lord Herbert of Cherbury (1582–1648), brother of famous Anglican poet George Herbert, and who is the supposed "originator" of deism, lists five basic beliefs of the deist: (a) belief in a supreme being; (b) the duty to worship "him"; (c) the identification of such worship with the virtuous life; (d) the need for repentance; and (e) a future life bringing rewards and punishments.[59] Nothing here would be scandalous to the traditional theist. In fact, despite the fact that many characterize deism as "widely regarded [to be] no different from atheism",[60] it does not differ *too much* from classical theism.

Yet, important elements of theism are missing. Macquarrie continues that "as the science of the time, especially Newton's account of the solar system, was exhibiting the universe as a self-regulating mechanism, the deists virtually excluded the possibility of divine intervention in the world, by way of miraculous action of revelation".[61] After creation, "God let the world go its own way in accordance with the laws he [sic] had laid down at the beginning".[62] Here then, are those elements of deism that seem to be at odds with traditional Christianity: the fact that there is no further divine intervention of any sort, so there is no revelation whatsoever—including the Christ event—and, crucially, that the world is independent of God. The deist, if they can arrive at belief in God, must do so totally and exclusively through the power of their own reasoning. However, if the deist thinks that they can *only* arrive at belief in God

---

58   John Macquarrie, *Jesus Christ in Modern Thought* (London: SCM Press, 1990), p. 24.

59   Macquarrie, *Jesus Christ in Modern Thought*, p. 24.

60   Wiles, *God's Action in the World*, p. 2.

61   Macquarrie, *Jesus Christ in Modern Thought*, p. 24.

62   Macquarrie, *Jesus Christ in Modern Thought*, p. 24.

through the power of their own reasoning, the theist would certainly agree with many deists who "accepted the argument from design as the strongest evidence for God's existence".[63] The deist exclusion of "the possibility of divine intervention in the world" leads to another popular characterization of deism: the suggestion of an "impersonal God". John Polkinghorne, for example, criticizes both deism and the "mystic's God" because "neither is the personally purposive God of the Judeo-Christian tradition".[64] While it would be a mistake to suppose that "purpose" and "providence" are entirely synonymous terms, it is clear that, for Polkinghorne, the Judeo-Christian God is a God who is personally invested in the lives of God's creatures and that personal investment is understood in terms of "purposiveness" or "providence". Thus, Polkinghorne writes elsewhere that a God with power but no love would be a "deistic bystander, watching the play of history unfold without any influence upon its course",[65] indicating that he understands personal investment in terms of providential influence. For Polkinghorne (and many others whom Polkinghorne represents), God's providential involvement in the world is proxy for God's personhood and love for the world. For Polkinghorne, God can only be seen as loving and personally interested in God's creatures if God acts decisively in history. The deist God is one who is irrelevant and uninterested in the universe that they have created. One can only be a *Christian* (or, indeed, a subscriber to any of the Abrahamic faiths) if one professes that God remains *personally* interested in the world as a *purposeful agent*.

In this book, then, deism is taken to be: (a) the belief that God is not personal; (b) the belief that God only creates and does nothing more/ further/subsequently; and (c) that science can exhaustively explain and describe the world without appeal to the divine in any sense whatsoever, except for the fact of its own existence.

---

63 Macquarrie, *Jesus Christ in Modern Thought*, p. 24.

64 John Polkinghorne, *Science and Providence* (London: SPCK, 1989), p. 36.

65 John Polkinghorne, "Kenotic Creation and Divine Action", in John Polkinghorne (ed.), *The Work of Love: Creation as Kenosis* (Grand Rapids, MI: William B. Eerdmans, 2001), p. 91.

The problem

Two problems have already been identified for the Christian deist: (a) it leads to a "god-of-the-gaps"-type theology; and (b) it obliges the rejection of the incarnation. To this, then, can be added two further problems: (c) the rejection of providence; and (d) the rejection of a personal God. Thus, assuming that one accepts the argument that there are problems with the "conflict" and "engagement" theses, assent to the "separation" thesis/deism leaves a distinct problem for the Christian.

However, this book will argue that this need not be the case. To begin, as the first chapter in this book will outline, it is not entirely clear that Polkinghorne's characterization of the Judeo-Christian God as "personally purposive" is correct. It is not entirely clear that Christians have viewed or should view God as "personal". Likewise, Chapter 3 of this book will question whether providence can or should be seen as a proxy for God's ongoing interest in/love for the world.

If that is the case, then such a belief in God's causal absence does not oblige the deist to reject a full Chalcedonian definition of Christ. This book will demonstrate this by making two quite simple arguments. First, it will argue that the traditional deist characterization of creation as "a more or less sceptical acceptance that some sort of agency had to be invoked as historically responsible for setting the clockwork of the universe going"[66] is entirely incorrect, and that creation is not an "historical" act that "gets the universe going" but, instead, is a relationship of dependence. The second is that this relationship is exclusively found in Christ—in the Emmanuel, "God with us"—and that this makes "creation" and "incarnation" literally identical and entirely co-incident. If creation is a relationship, then Christ *is* that relationship.

The basic thesis of this book is as follows:

1. God is not a person. Nor is God an individual "thing", "subject", or whatever else one might postulate.
2. If God is not a "subject", then creation is not an act, properly speaking: the universe is not the object of an action of which God

---

[66] Grayling, "Introduction", p. xi.

is "historically responsible". Rather, creation is the relation that
creatures have with God. It is a relation in which all being and
motion depends entirely upon God for its existence and power.

3. This means that the theologian should not seek "gaps" within
   scientific knowledge—even "permanent" or "ontological" gaps,
   such as with quantum mechanics—in which to locate divine
   influence and/or activity, but should rather look for "places"
   where divine/creature relation is the most apparent.

4. This book postulates that the incarnation represents such a
   relation. The incarnation, then, becomes identical with creation.
   That is, the incarnation is that through which dependence upon,
   participation in, and/or imitation of God.

5. Having argued this thesis, this book will then speculate on what
   this means for the cross and resurrection/deification.

God is not a person who "does" things (because God is so utterly
transcendent of and ontologically other to creatures), so creation is
not a thing that God "does"—that is, it is an *ontological relation* rather
than *historical event*—and so (precisely because God is so utterly other)
"something else" is needed to explain how creatures can participate in
God, and the incarnation supplies this "something else": the incarnation
is how creatures can participate in God. Thus, participation in God
"looks like" imitation of Jesus.

One could also read this as an essay on how God can both create
and become incarnate without compromising a full and genuine divine
atemporality and simplicity. Divine atemporality and simplicity, when
taken seriously, lead to the conclusion that God only does one "thing".
Thomas Aquinas writes that "God's activity can be considered either on
the part of the doer or of the done. If on the part of the doer, there is
only one activity in God . . . but considered on the side of what is done,
there are indeed different activities".[67] Noted Thomists Eleanore Stump
and Norman Kretzmann confirm that while there are "various temporal
effects" of God's act, there is still only one "single eternal act identical with

---

[67] Thomas Aquinas, *Selected Writings* (London: Penguin, 1998), *Disputed
      Questions on the Power of God 7* (pp. 294–5).

God, God's action in the strict sense".[68] Junius Johnson, writing about the theology of Bonaventure, also argues that "since the divine essence is simple, it is simple also in its actions . . . The divine creativity is . . . one in its source, many in its relations to things".[69] If deism is simply the claim that God only does one thing—which is the "act" of creation—then it appears that this has more in common with traditional theological categories than might be appreciated. That is, if the deist says that God only does one thing, then so does the scholastic.

However, neither Thomas Aquinas nor Bonaventure, nor those who draw on their theology, subscribe to that core tenet of deism: that God does not intervene in the world *at all*. Quite the opposite, in fact. Indeed, despite the fact that Aquinas quite clearly claims that God only does one thing, his subscription to providence has left him open to the accusation of occasionalism by some of his critics.[70] It is arguably here that the difference between deism and theism is most obvious and is the reason why this book will ultimately present a theology that is deistic, rather than as with traditional scholastic theism. That is, while deism and scholastic theism both hold that there is only one divine act/activity, only deism holds that this single divine activity prevents God from further interaction with/influence on the world, subsequent to being the creator. Nevertheless, it is important to note that what is said in this book on how the deist can genuinely accept Chalcedon without compromising their deism might also be relevant to how the scholastic theist can claim that divine atemporality and simplicity mean that God only does one thing, without compromising a full doctrine of Chalcedon.

---

[68]   Eleonore Stump and Norman Kretzmann, "Absolute Simplicity", *Faith and Philosophy: Journal of the Society of Christian Philosophers* 2:4 (1985), p. 356, p. 366; see also Philip McCosker, "Grace", in Philip McCosker and Denys Turner (eds), *The Cambridge Companion to The Summa Theologiae* (Cambridge: Cambridge University Press, 2016), pp. 208–16.

[69]   Junius Johnson, "The One and the Many in Bonaventure Exemplarity Explained", *Religions* 7:144 (2016), p. 12.

[70]   Ignacio Silva, "Divine Action and Thomism: Why Thomas Aquinas's Thought is Attractive Today", *Acta Philosophica* 25:1 (2016), pp. 79ff.

Thus, this book is not an attempt to claim that theism is incoherent, but to claim that, despite criticism, deism is a perfectly coherent and respectable claim. That is, while it recommends deism, this book does not argue that it is impossible to uphold theism. Rather, it argues that, drawing on Thomism, Scotism, and Tillichism, one can profess deism without having to sacrifice many of those elements as one might traditionally suppose that the deist is required to.

Lastly, although this book is concerned to show how one can be deist and retain a full incarnation, it will not be concerned with the related question of how the deist deals with the Holy Spirit, without simply rejecting a full Trinitarian theology. This "relegation" of the Holy Spirit is not a novel approach. Denis Edwards writes that "one of the characteristics of theology in recent times has been the recognition that in western theology and Church practice there has been a tendency to ignore, or to address only in a minimal way, the theology of the Holy Spirit".[71] This book will not make any attempt to redress that imbalance.

Outline of the book

The first chapter will criticize the increasingly popular modern theological position of "theistic personalism", which takes as its starting point the idea that God is "person" and uses this position as a reason to reject traditional theological categories such as atemporality and simplicity, because persons cannot be atemporal or simple. This chapter will show that while there may be genuinely reasonable reasons why one might wish to support it, "theistic personalism" does not represent traditional theological themes. Drawing on theologians from all periods of theological history and from all traditions—Pseudo-Dionysius, Thomas Aquinas, Gregory Palamas, Friedrich Schleiermacher, Paul Tillich, Erich Przywara—this chapter will show that the idea that God is "impersonal", which is so often seen as a characteristic position of deism, actually conforms to traditional theism.

---

[71] Denis Edwards, *Deep Incarnation: God's Redemptive Suffering with Creatures* (Maryknoll, NY: Orbis Books, 2019), p. 106.

The second chapter continues this train of thought and—drawing heavily on Thomist and scholastic categories—suggests that if God is not a "person" who "does" things, then creation cannot be the object of an act of which God is the subject. Rather, as Thomas Aquinas clearly held, creation is not an "act" or "event" that is performed by God, but a relationship of dependence that the creature has with God. This relationship is called participation (which can be seen as synonymous with imitation) and is the content of the doctrine of creation: to create does not mean to do something at the beginning that causes something to exist; to create means to be that in which creatures participate.

The third chapter explores what this understanding of creation means for other elements of divine activity: providence, omnipotence, and theodicy. This chapter will argue that if creation is a relationship of dependence, then this means that providence and omnipotence must also be understood in terms of relationship.

The fourth chapter, at its core, makes one simple argument: if God is so utterly transcendent of and ontologically other to creatures, then something "else" is needed to explain how it is that creatures can participate in God. This something "else" is the incarnation. In other words, it argues that if creation is a relationship, then it is the incarnation that constitutes that relationship. The hypostatic union is *how* creatures depend on and participate in God.

The fifth chapter explains how this Christology can be reconciled with the cross. Drawing on John Duns Scotus' theology of the primacy of Christ, this chapter will suggest that the cross should not be seen as redemptive, but as creative. If the cross is creative—and creation is understood as a relationship of dependence—then the cross also constitutes that through which creatures participate in God. To further support this interpretation, it will be shown that *kenosis* can be interpreted as identical to participation. That is, if participation indicates what the relationship of dependency looks like from the creature side, so *kenosis* is what the relationship of dependency looks like from the divine side.

The final chapter attempts to show how the incarnational deist should or could understand the relationship between nature and grace, and, by extension, the resurrection. It will be shown that, if there is only one divine "act", then there can be no distinction between "nature" and "grace" for God. That distinction is only real for creatures, and so the distinction between "creation" and "deification" is entirely subjective. Resurrection becomes a "gestalt"; resurrection/deification is a relationship with Christ. This means that what constitutes deification for one creature is entirely different and entirely subjective to any other creature. Grace is given to all equally; it is the response of the creature that differs.

1

God

Deism is an idea that relates to divine activity. The deist disagrees with the theist that God "continues" to act in the world "after", or subsequent to, creation. For the theist, God does "many things" "many times" or, at the very least, "one thing" "many times", whereas the deist holds that God only does "one thing" "one time". Those who disagree with deism do so because of a particular view they hold on divine activity.

However, it is not always the case that the deist and the theist hold identical views about the nature of God and simply disagree about the activity of that God. As already quoted from Polkinghorne, the deist God is often characterized as "impersonal" because that God does not have a personal relationship with the creatures God creates either because God does not "want" to have a continuing relationship with the creatures whom God creates, or God "cannot" engage in personal relationships.

However, this chapter will outline that this distinction is not entirely accurate because it is not necessarily the case that the theist thinks about God as a "person". The view that God is a "person"—in much the same way and with much the same characteristics as human persons—can be termed "theistic personalism", and this chapter will show that not only is this emphatically not how God should be thought of, but it has never been how God has been thought of, and is instead a modern innovation that does not give expression to the treasures of theological endeavour. Moreover, and as a result, this "traditional" God is remarkably more amenable to the "impersonal" God of the deist.

Theistic personalism

In his book *The Coherence of Theism*, Richard Swinburne apologizes for the claim that God is a "person without a body (i.e., a spirit) who is eternal, free, able to do anything, knows everything, is perfectly good, is the proper object of human worship and obedience, the creator and sustainer of the universe".[1] This claim, Swinburne proceeds to explain, "seems the most elementary claim of theism",[2] and he argues that persons can communicate private thoughts, have wants, form theories beyond observation, and form moral judgements, all of which it seems appropriate to apply to God.[3] The reason why Swinburne makes this claim is not difficult to understand: the Christian religion is about a *personal* God, a God who has a *personal* relationship with God's creatures. Indeed, for many, this is precisely the point of creation in the first place: God creates in order to have a relationship with others.

However, the "problem" with this endeavour is that it means applying very human-looking qualities to God. Swinburne does not see this as a problem. He clarifies that, while the theologian uses "ordinary words to denote ordinary properties" when speaking about God, the theologian "claims that the properties cited are manifested in unusual combinations and circumstances and to unusual degrees".[4] Swinburne calls this "analogical", but he defines this to mean that using a word analogically does not change the meaning of the word used; rather that it extends what is normally meant by that word. For example, when humans call dogs "loyal", they mean exactly what they mean when they call humans "loyal", but to a lesser degree.[5] Thus, he concludes that "in giving to words analogical senses the theist must avoid loosening up their meaning too far", and so "unless there is reason to suppose otherwise, clearly we ought

---

[1]   Richard Swinburne, *The Coherence of Theism* (Oxford: Clarendon Press, 1993), p. 1.

[2]   Swinburne, *The Coherence of Theism*, p. 101.

[3]   Swinburne, *The Coherence of Theism*, p. 103.

[4]   Swinburne, *The Coherence of Theism*, p. 52.

[5]   Swinburne, *The Coherence of Theism*, pp. 56–73.

to assume that theists are using words in their ordinary mundane senses".[6] For example, "When the theist says that God is 'good,' 'good' is, I suggest, being used in a perfectly ordinary sense. The only extraordinary thing being suggested is that it exists to a degree in which it does not exist in mundane objects."[7]

This means that when the Swinburne talks about God, he is describing God in exactly the same way that he would describe humans. The only difference between God and humans is that God exemplifies those attributes to a greater degree or extent. While Swinburne accepts that the theologian could be using the words "person" or "brings about" or "knows" analogically "in highly stretched senses", he concludes instead that "the theist has no need to make such an appeal"; it is perfectly reasonable to use these words (and others) in a straightforward manner and so retain the ordinary mundane sense of those words when applied to God.[8] As Jim Holt writes, "The God of the Theologians is defined as the entity—or 'substance' to use the technical term—that possesses every positive attribute to an *infinite* degree. He is infinitely powerful, infinitely knowledgeable, infinitely good, infinitely existing, and so forth."[9] God is only different from humans (and other creatures) by degree (albeit an infinite degree). God is *essentially* the same as humans, just grander, more powerful, and more knowledgeable.

Of course, there is precedence for this. The Bible does nothing if it does not present the reader with a very anthropomorphic God: a God who gets angry, jealous etc. Richard Dawkins has remarked that the God of the Old Testament is "jealous and proud of it; a petty, unjust, unforgiving control-freak; a vindictive, bloodthirsty ethnic cleanser; a misogynistic, homophobic, racist, infanticidal, genocidal, filicidal, pestilential, megalomaniacal, sadomasochistic, capriciously malevolent bully".[10] Swinburne would no doubt think that his Oxford colleague is being unjust in his characterization of God, but, nevertheless, would

---

[6] Swinburne, *The Coherence of Theism*, p. 72.

[7] Swinburne, *The Coherence of Theism*, pp. 72–3.

[8] Swinburne, *The Coherence of Theism*, p. 229.

[9] Jim Holt, *Why Does the World Exist?* (London: Profile Books, 2013), p. 98.

[10] Richard Dawkins, *The God Delusion* (London: Black Swan, 2006), p. 51.

agree that one *can* describe God in such language. Swinburne would disagree that those particular adjectives accurately describe God, but he at least agrees with Dawkins that such adjectives can coherently be applied to God. The point here is not whether Dawkins or Swinburne is correct, but to illustrate that the God of the Bible is a God who looks very human. The only way that God differs from humans is that God does not have a body and so is far less limited in the range of abilities that God possesses. If Swinburne is confident that the claim that God is a "person without a body (i.e., a spirit)"[11] is one that "seems the most elementary claim of theism",[12] then he seems to have the Bible in support.

Langdon Gilkey agrees. He writes that for the biblical theologian, "when God was said to have 'acted,' it was believed that he [sic] had performed an observable act in space and time" and "when he was said to have 'spoken,' it was believed that an audible voice was heard by the person addressed. In other words, the words 'act' and 'speak' were used in the same sense of God as of men [sic]."[13] Importantly, Gilkey means this as a criticism of the biblical authors' primitive theology. However, disagreements aside, the point here is to illustrate that for the "theistic personalist" God is very much like a human, and the biblical account of God seemingly supports this approach. God shares the characteristics of humans and differs from them only in the sense that God does not have a body and is less limited.

Yet, expounding the difference between God and creatures in terms of "degree" rather than "kind" is at the heart of what is wrong with this approach. While Swinburne calls this "analogical", this is not "analogical" in the sense that traditional theology meant it (which Swinburne seems to recognize by calling it "my sense of analogical",[14] and by recognizing that his interpretation of Thomas Aquinas' doctrine of analogy will not

---

[11] Swinburne, *The Coherence of Theism*, p. 1.

[12] Swinburne, *The Coherence of Theism*, p. 101.

[13] Langdon Gilkey, "Cosmology, Ontology, and the Travail of Biblical Language", in Owen Thomas (ed.), *God's Activity in the World: The Contemporary Problem* (Chico, CA: Scholars Press, 1983), p. 32.

[14] Swinburne, *The Coherence of Theism*, p. 71.

be acceptable to everyone[15]) and, importantly, Swinburne argues that "using a word in an analogical sense must be for the theist a last resort to save his [sic] system from a charge of incoherence".[16] As will be argued below, if for Swinburne analogy is a "last resort" that is appealed to by the theologian to "save" their system, then the traditional theologian sees analogy as the lynchpin of all theological endeavour and considers it to form the basis upon which all theological endeavour is attempted.

While that may be the case, the salient point at this juncture is that a crucial—if not *the* crucial—element of "theistic personalism" is that language can be used and applied to God in an "ordinary sense" albeit to an extraordinary degree. To use a technical theological term, this means using language "univocally" of both God and creatures: when we use words like "good", etc., they mean the same when applied to God as they do when applied to humans. However, using language "univocally" of both God and creatures has an important implication: it means that God and creatures are both examples of the same "thing". Swinburne, presumably, does not have a problem with this—God and creatures are both examples of "persons"—but others have reservations. Robert Barron, for example, writes that if God and creatures are univocal then "God and creatures had to be categorized under the same general metaphysical heading as modalities of being" and "though [God] was supreme, infinite, all-powerful, and so on, God, on the Scotist/Occamist [i.e., univocal] reading, was one reality alongside others and hence competitive with them".[17] Elsewhere, Barron argues further that, for the "univocal" approach:

> God and creatures belong to the same basic metaphysical category, the genus of being. Though God is infinite and therefore quantitatively superior to any creature or collectivity of creatures, there is nevertheless no qualitative difference, in the metaphysical sense, between the supreme being, God, and finite beings . . . God

---

[15] Swinburne, *The Coherence of Theism*, p. 81.

[16] Swinburne, *The Coherence of Theism*, p. 72.

[17] Robert Barron, *Exploring Catholic Theology* (Grand Rapids, MI: Baker Academic, 2015), pp. 27–8.

and creatures do belong together to a logical category that, in a real sense, transcends and includes them.[18]

It is crucial to highlight two points: God and creatures are "competitive" and the "logical category [of being] . . . transcends" God. If God can be described using the same language as used to describe humans, then God becomes ontologically or metaphysically identical to humans. Crucially, not only does it make God and humans metaphysically identical, but it makes that which describes them both—either "person" or "being"—more metaphysically primary. If God is univocal with creatures, then God is not ontologically or metaphysically primary; some "thing" else—e.g., "being" or "person"—transcends God.[19]

Theistic personalism and atemporality

If, for the "theistic personalist", God is more or less "human-like" except to different degrees, then this has led them to abandon long-held beliefs about God, such as atemporality. For example, Ernan McMullin writes that recent theologians tend to "strongly challenge" divine atemporality because they "seek a closer affinity between Creator and creature than the traditional account admits".[20] That is, divine atemporality is denied by "theistic personalists" (among others) because it leaves God too different from humans. "Theistic personalists" want God involved in the world.

---

[18]   Robert Barron, *The Priority of Christ: Towards A Postliberal Catholicism* (Grand Rapids, MI: Brazos Press, 2007), p. 13.

[19]   See also Erich Przywara, *Analogia Entis* (Grand Rapids, MI: William B. Eerdmans, 2014), p. 233; Jean-Luc Marion, *God without Being* (Chicago, IL: The University of Chicago Press, 2012), p. 209.

[20]   Ernan McMullin, "Cosmic Purpose and The Contingency of Human Evolution", *Zygon: Journal of Religion and Science* 48:2 (2013), p. 354; see Keith Ward, *Rational Theology and the Creativity of God* (Oxford: Basil Blackwell Ltd., 1982); Oscar Cullmann, *Christ and Time* (London: SCM Press, 1962); J. R. Lucas, "The Temporality of God", in Robert Russell, Nancey Murphy, and Chris Isham (eds), *Quantum Cosmology and the Laws of Nature: Scientific Perspectives on Divine Action* (Vatican City: Vatican Observatory, 1993), pp. 235–46.

"Theistic personalists" want a biblical God, who has a continuing personal relationship with God's creatures and who acts decisively in their lives, and they want to talk about that God using "ordinary language". Yet, God cannot be truly and genuinely involved in the lives of God's creatures if God is not temporal with them. This does not mean that, for "theistic personalists", God is limited by time, as creatures are, but God is temporal nonetheless: i.e., temporal duration and succession are real phenomena experienced by God, but those phenomena do not limit God like they do creatures.

There are many who, especially in recent times, have offered sustained refutations of divine atemporality, arguing variously that it is impossible to reconcile atemporality with any number of other apparently traditional divine attributes. Swinburne, for example, while initially accepting that "eternity" should be taken to mean "atemporality",[21] later changed his mind, and came to see it as a sort of "everlasting duration". In technical language, this position is known as "sempiternal": that is, God is not outside of time, but experiences an infinite and everlasting duration of time. The reason for changing his mind, he writes, is that "the Hebrew Bible shows no knowledge of the doctrine of divine timelessness"[22] and that it seems inconsistent with a God who is in relationship with God's creatures.[23] In the same way that Swinburne thinks it is acceptable to use other words univocally of God, and so retain the ordinary mundane sense of the words, so he thinks that "time" can and should be applied to God more or less univocally.

R. Coburn agrees that "surely it is a necessary condition of anything's being a person that it should be capable (logically) of, among other things, doing at least some of the following: remembering, anticipating, reflecting, deliberating, deciding, intending and acting intentionally". If one wishes God to be a person, even if infinitely greater than humanity, then God cannot be atemporal because so many of the things that persons need to do in order genuinely to be a person require experiencing

---

21 Richard Holland Jr., *God, Time, and the Incarnation* (Eugene, OR: Wipf & Stock, 2012), pp. 87ff.

22 Swinburne, *The Coherence of Theism*, p. 236.

23 Swinburne, *The Coherence of Theism*, p. 242.

the passage of time. God could not exhibit these capacities—such as "deliberating, deciding, intending and acting intentionally"—Coburn argues, if God was not temporal, and so "an eternal being would necessarily lack all of these capacities inasmuch as their exercise by a being clearly requires that the being exist in time".[24]

J. R. Lucas agrees with Coburn. Lucas writes simply that "to deny that God is temporal is to deny that he [sic] is personal in any sense in which we understand personality".[25] Lucas presents two reasons for denying divine atemporality: "To be a person is to be capable of being conscious, and to be conscious is to be aware of the passage of time."[26] and that "to act is to bring about change. Things are different, if we act, from what they would have been otherwise", and, moreover, that "some of God's actions can be dated with a fair degree of precision: some time between 29 and 33 AD God did something remarkable".[27] The questions concerning divine activity and the incarnation will be dealt with in following chapters, so it is not necessary to go into detail here. The important point is that Lucas links acting with personhood. If God were not able to act, if God were not able to have desires and wants and to act in specific ways to realize those desires and wants, then God could not be a person. Intentional activity requires temporality.

What is at issue here is the supposition that God must be personal, and that being conscious is essential to personhood, and that one cannot be conscious without being temporal. Therefore, God must be conscious (and so temporal), because God is a person.

The question then becomes: why must God be conscious? Lucas' answer to this question is that God must be conscious because he is sympathetic with process theology and the claim that "what [God]

24   R. Coburn, quoted in J. L. Tomkinson, "Divine Sempiternity and Atemporality", *Religious Studies* 18:2 (1982), pp. 185–6.
25   Lucas, "The Temporality of God", p. 235; see also Delmas Lewis, "Timelessness and Divine Agency", *International Journal for Philosophy of Religion* 21:3 (1987), pp. 143–59.
26   Lucas, "The Temporality of God", p. 235.
27   Lucas, "The Temporality of God", p. 236.

does is far more important than what [God] is".[28] While he does not go into detail, one expects that Lucas is sympathetic to sentiments such as those expressed by Cobb and Griffin, who situate Process Theology in opposition to the "stoic" Thomistic God (and the conception of divine love as "pure giver"),[29] because "it is essential to [God's] being love that he [sic] can be changed and affected by what his own power permits to be"[30] and so "divine creating activity [is] based upon responsive[ness] to the world".[31] Indeed, Lucas himself argues that one of the aspects of his objection to divine atemporality is that it would mean that God cannot respond. He writes that accounts of divine atemporality "cannot accommodate God's responding to the actions, and especially the petitions, of free human agents".[32] God requires consciousness or God cannot be truly said to respond, and if God cannot respond, then God cannot love. Thus, for example, Brian Davies writes that "we admire people who can be moved by tragic events. We admire people who can become elated when good things happen. And, theistic personalists sometimes say, we can admire God only if he [sic], like admirable people, is suitably affected by the good and the bad which occurs in the world".[33] If God cannot respond then God cannot be a person, and if God is not a person, then God does not seem to be able to do the things that demand respect, admiration, and worship.

---

28 Lucas, "The Temporality of God", p. 235.

29 See Thomas Aquinas, *Summa Theologiae* (New York, NY: Benziger Brothers, 1948) I, q.20, a.2.

30 Ward, *Rational Theology and the Creativity of God*, p. 151; see also John B. Cobb and David Ray Griffin, *Process Theology: An Introductory Exposition* (London: The Westminster Press, 1976), pp. 51–2.

31 Cobb and Griffin, *Process Theology*, pp. 51–2.

32 Lucas, "The Temporality of God", p. 236.

33 Brian Davies, *An Introduction to the Philosophy of Religion* (Oxford: Oxford University Press, 2004), p. 13; Likewise, those who deny other classic attributes, such as impassibility, do so "largely because they think that, if God is impassible and unchangeable, then he [sic] cannot be taken seriously as a person" (Davies, *Introduction to Philosophy of Religion*, pp. 12–13).

Clearly, there are questions of univocality. These theologians assume that "love" applied to God must be applied univocally or it does not make any sense. Thus, God must be conscious, temporal, and able to respond to creatures or God cannot truly be said to love. Polkinghorne has already been quoted saying much the same thing.[34] Yet, as J. L. Tomkinson writes contra R. Coburn, "This extremely popular objection [to divine atemporality] seems to involve the critic in more than a small measure of anthropomorphism."[35] That is, one can only suggest that God cannot be atemporal if God is a person if one is treating God and creatures univocally. J. R. Lucas may very well be entirely correct in his assumption that one cannot be both atemporal and conscious (in fact, this author entirely agrees that one cannot be both atemporal and conscious), but the assertion that God must be conscious points to a way of looking at the world with which Teilhard de Chardin would be impressed: "It is better, no matter what the cost, to be more conscious than less conscious."[36] For these theologians, God must be conscious or God is somehow lesser than creatures. It is consciousness (so many believe, although Chapter 3 will contest this claim) that shows why and how humanity must be superior to other creatures and so, by extrapolation, God must be more conscious, or one must be forced into the strange conclusion that humanity is superior to God. Univocality of being is at the centre of how these theologians do theology and why they reach the conclusions they do.

There is obviously a lot to unpack here, and space prevents a further exploration of some of these themes. In subsequent chapters (particularly in Chapter 3), it will be argued that consciousness, intelligence and rationality are just one particular avenue that evolution has taken and one does not have to place a judgement value on them. That is, one does not, and indeed should not, assume that it is better to be conscious than not. Therefore, there is no reason to suppose that God is somehow

---

[34]   John Polkinghorne, "Kenotic Creation and Divine Action", in John Polkinghorne (ed.), *The Work of Love: Creation as Kenosis* (Grand Rapids, MI: William B. Eerdmans, 2001), p. 91.

[35]   Tomkinson, "Divine Sempiternity and Atemporality", pp. 185–6.

[36]   Pierre Teilhard de Chardin, *Christianity and Evolution* (London: Harvest, 1971), p. 108.

diminished by the claim that God is not conscious. Here it is enough to say that assuming that God must be conscious because humans are conscious is another example of this univocal thinking, and univocal thinking involves bringing God down to the same level as humanity.

Theistic personalism and simplicity

If some theologians question divine atemporality on the basis that it seems to contravene God's personality, then Alvin Plantinga has questioned the coherence of divine simplicity on the basis that it seems to imply that God cannot be a "person" who loves, creates and acts. Again, there is not the room to devote attention to every aspect of this complex argument. There are many subtle nuances to each position, and it would involve much philosophical and theological unpacking to exhaust each element. However, it is important to outline the salient points of Plantinga's objection. He writes that "the basic idea of this doctrine [of simplicity] is that no distinctions can be made in God. We cannot distinguish him [sic] from his nature, or his nature from his existence, or his existence from his other properties; he is the very same thing as his nature, existence, goodness, wisdom, power and the like", calling such a claim "a dark saying indeed".[37] While Plantinga spends a good deal of time questioning the philosophical underpinning of the doctrine of simplicity, perhaps his most straightforward criticism is that, on the one hand, it seems to suggest that "if God is identical with each of his properties, then each of his properties is identical with each of his properties, so that God has but one property", which, he claims, "seems flatly incompatible with the obvious fact that God has several properties; he has both power and mercifulness, say, neither of which is identical with the other".[38] On the other hand, "if God is identical with each of his properties, then, since each of his properties is a property, he is a property—a self-exemplifying property. Accordingly God has just one property: himself". It is here that Plantinga makes the claim most pertinent for the purposes of this chapter. He continues that "this view [that God is himself a property] is subject

---

[37] Alvin Plantinga, *Does God Have a Nature?* (Milwaukee, WI: Marquette University Press, 1980), p. 27.

[38] Plantinga, *Does God Have a Nature?*, p. 47.

to a difficulty both obvious and overwhelming. No property could have created the world; no property could be omniscient, or, indeed, know anything at all. If God is a property, then he isn't a person but a mere abstract object; he has no knowledge, awareness, power, love or life."[39] Likewise, he summarizes, "if God is a living, conscious being who knows, wills and acts—if, in a word, God is a *person*—then God is not a property or state of affairs or set or proposition or any other abstract object".[40]

A full response to Plantinga falls outside the scope of this chapter, and, in many respects (as will be seen below) is unnecessary anyway, since, as with temporality, the logic of Plantinga's position is rather sound.[41] That is, this chapter will not question the claim that it is impossible for God (or anything else) to be *both* a person *and* atemporal and/or simple; rather, it will question the axiom that these "theistic personalists" seem to accept: that God must be personal (in precisely the same way that modern philosophy understands humans to be personal). This chapter accepts that God cannot be both personal and atemporal and/or simple, but questions why it is that personality is the characteristic that trumps all others.

However, that being said, a few comments are necessary here to point out one or two errors in Plantinga's understanding of simplicity, as these will be crucial for understanding creation and incarnation in subsequent chapters.

What Plantinga seems to miss is what is called "the absence of a real relation" or "the mixed relation" between God and creatures. That is, while creatures are really and genuinely related to, and completely dependent on God, God is not really or genuinely related to creatures, but is entirely and completely independent of them. This built on the teaching of the Fourth Lateran Council, which taught that "between creator and creature there can be noted no similarity so great that a

---

39   Plantinga, *Does God Have a Nature?*, p. 47.

40   Plantinga, *Does God Have a Nature?*, p. 57 (italics in original).

41   Although I am inclined to agree with Aquinas that God is necessarily *a se*—that is, that God does not depend on anything for being/existence etc.—and simplicity, lack of parts etc., is necessary for aseity.

greater dissimilarity cannot be seen between them".[42] Andrew Davison writes, "The creature's relation to God is at the heart of what it means for it to exist, and to be what it is, while God's relation to the creature does not lie at the heart of what it means for God to be God". That is, Davison continues, creation "makes [a creature] what it is", whereas creation "does not make God what God is".[43] Frederick Bauerschmidt puts the same point differently, writing that creation "tells us something about creatures . . . but it does not tell us something about God".[44] Bauerschmidt uses a good example to illustrate this fact. He writes:

> If John sees Mary but she does not see him, he has a real relation to her, because possession of the sense image of Mary is now a feature of who John is; Mary, on the other hand, has a logical relation to John, since "being seen" is not a feature of Mary. One can interview John and, by asking the right questions, discover that he has seen Mary, but one could never discover by examining or interviewing Mary that she has been seen by John. Mary is not *unrelated* to John, since once John sees Mary we can now say of her something that we could not say before: "Mary was seen by John." What was previously a false statement about Mary becomes a true statement, but not because of anything about Mary.[45]

While there is a "real relation" between John and Mary, there is an "absence of a real relation" between Mary and John, or, there is a "mixed relation" between John and Mary. To put this differently, Mary remains unchanged by John seeing her—the change happens entirely

---

[42]   *Constitutions of the Fourth Lateran Council* (1215) 2.

[43]   Andrew Davison, *Participation in God* (Cambridge: Cambridge University Press, 2019), p. 29.

[44]   Frederick Bauerschmidt, *Thomas Aquinas: Faith, Reason, and Following Christ* (Oxford: Oxford University Press, 2013), p. 115.

[45]   Bauerschmidt, *Thomas Aquinas: Faith, Reason, and Following Christ*, pp. 114–15.

within John—however, something has happened to John that is entirely concerned with Mary.

Eleonore Stump and Norman Kretzmann make the same point in a different way. They describe the "absence of a real relation" between God and creatures by maintaining that all difference, multiplicity, and complexity are "*extrinsic*" to God. They write that "a change in x's extrinsic properties can occur without a change in x, while a change in x's intrinsic properties is as such a change in x".[46] They continue with this example:

> Ronald Reagan's belief that he is of Irish descent is one of his intrinsic accidental properties; his being mentioned in this article is an extrinsic accidental property of his. The intrinsic properties of numbers are all essential; numbers, like God, cannot have intrinsic accidental properties. But no entity, not even a mathematical or a divine entity, can be exempted from having extrinsic accidental properties.[47]

Thus, to say that a property is "*extrinsic*" is to say the same thing as Bauerschmidt did; "being seen by John" is an "*extrinsic*" accidental property of Mary.

This "absence of a real relation" or "extrinsic property" is central to Thomas Aquinas' theology. In *De veritate*, Thomas Aquinas writes:

> Whenever two things are related to each other in such a way that one depends upon the other but the other does not depend upon it, there is a real relation in the dependent member, but in the independent member the relation is merely one of reason— simply because one thing cannot be understood as being related to it.[48]

---

46   Eleonore Stump and Norman Kretzmann, "Absolute Simplicity", *Faith and Philosophy: Journal of the Society of Christian Philosophers* 2:4 (1985), p. 354.

47   Stump and Kretzmann, "Absolute Simplicity", p. 354.

48   Thomas Aquinas, *Quaestiones Disputatae De Veritate* (Chicago, IL: Henry Regnery Company, 1952), 4.5.

However, perhaps Aquinas' best description of this relation occurs in his *Summa Theologiae*. Here, Aquinas likens the absence of a real relation to someone standing next to a pillar. He writes that "we can say that a pillar has changed from being on my left to being on my right, not through any alteration in the pillar but simply because I have turned around".[49] The pillar has not changed, but the person has. Something different can genuinely be said of the pillar—it has genuinely changed from being on the left to being on the right—but that difference has no real relation to the pillar; the pillar itself has not changed.

When this is applied to the "properties" or "attributes" of God, what creatures *call* God's love, mercy, justice, goodness etc. are not *actually* love, mercy, justice, or goodness etc., but are simply *extrinsic* views of one single "attribute". God has (and is) one simple attribute—like Thomas' pillar—and it is only when creatures see that attribute in different contexts that such an attribute appears to change. That is, the multiplicity and difference in God's attributes—indeed all multiplicity and difference—is *extrinsic* to God. This is what Plantinga seems to have missed, and it is the central aspect of Thomas' doctrine of simplicity (indeed, as will be shown in the following chapter, it is the central and crucial aspect of Thomas' doctrine of creation as well). Plantinga seems to assume that love and mercy (for example) are genuinely distinct *for* God, but they are not. God is neither loving nor merciful; that is just what creatures call the one "thing" that God is in different contexts.[50] That is, Plantinga assumes that "simplicity" is a concrete attribute that is being applied to God in a univocal sense as it might be applied to creatures. In fact, divine simplicity is nothing of the sort; if that is what simplicity means then Plantinga is correct to say that God is not simple. Divine simplicity does not mean that God is literally (or univocally) simple; rather, it is a way of explaining and describing the "absence of a real relation".[51]

---

49   *ST* 1, 13, 7.

50   See also Paul Tillich, *Systematic Theology Vol. 1* (Chicago, IL: The University of Chicago Press, 1957), p. 271; *ST* I, q. 13, a. 7; Davison, *Participation in God*, pp. 29–30; Przywara, *Analogia Entis*, pp. 214–16.

51   Although, as Barry Smith acknowledges, perhaps the suggestion that God is identical to an abstract attribute is not as alien to the traditional theologians

Anselm of Canterbury, writing roughly a century before Thomas, agrees with Thomas. Pondering over the issue of how God can be both genuinely immutable and genuinely merciful (that is, to be genuinely merciful requires that one has genuinely changed from being angry to being merciful, so God cannot genuinely be unchanging and genuinely merciful), he concludes that God is not really merciful, it is just that creatures see it as mercy. Anselm writes:

> How, then, are You merciful and not merciful, O Lord, unless it be that You are merciful in relation to us and not in relation to Yourself? In fact, You are [merciful] according to our way of looking at things and not according to Your way. For when You look upon us in our misery it is we who feel the effect of Your mercy, but You do not experience the feeling.[52]

---

as Plantinga supposes. Smith writes that, while Plantinga is correct that "since God is simple, what appears to be discrete divine attributes distinct from God as their suppositum are really not . . . there can be no distinction between God and any one of God's properties or even between God and all of God's properties", but that "from earliest times, this counterintuitive view has been part of the Christian understanding of God" (Barry Smith, *The Oneness and Simplicity of God* (Eugene, OR: Wipf & Stock, 2014), p. 48). To put this differently, God is not a suppositum to which attributes can be applied. As Smith also writes, referring to Gregory of Nyssa, "even to say that God has only one essential attribute like ingenerateness would mean that God is composite insofar as God would consist of a suppositum or subject and that one predicate" (Smith, *The Oneness and Simplicity of God*, p. 48). Again, in relation to John Damascene, simplicity "means that God has no true attributes or properties", so that "insofar as he [sic] is simple, nothing can be predicated of God, not even his [sic] essence or nature" (Smith, *The Oneness and Simplicity of God*, p. 59). This can be seen as similar to the absence of a real relation, but put in different language: both argue that simplicity does not mean that God has one attribute, but that the attributes are outside of God, so God cannot be a discrete personal subject to which attributes can be applied.

52   Anselm of Canterbury, *Collected Works* (Oxford: Oxford University Press, 1998), *Proslogion* 8.

God does not change. Whatever change occurs in the salvation of humanity, whatever change happens in the "exercise" of divine mercy, that change is only in the creature. Thus, God is not genuinely merciful (if genuine mercy requires change), but whatever happens to creatures leads them to call God merciful. Mercy—and any change that happens as a result—is entirely extrinsic to God.

Importantly, the same must be said for time. Atemporality does not make a positive statement about God's temporality; rather, it means that time is extrinsic to God. That is, God is not simultaneously present to all spatiotemporal points—which would mean that God has a real relation to every spatiotemporal point—but rather all spatiotemporal points are present to God. That is, all spatiotemporal points are extrinsically related to God. In the former—"God is present to all spatiotemporal points"—God would be omnitemporal or "sempiternal", that is, God would be really related to each individual spatiotemporal point. However, in the latter—"all spatiotemporal points are present to God"—God is atemporal, that is, God is not really related to each individual spatiotemporal point. All spatiotemporal points are *extrinsic* to God. The difference is admittedly quite a subtle one, but it is fundamental to the traditional understanding of divine atemporality. Failure to appreciate it leads to misunderstandings about what it means to call God atemporal and/or simple.

While it appears that Plantinga genuinely does not appreciate the importance of the absence of a real relation for understanding divine simplicity, this does not mean that the crux of Plantinga's claim (and those who used the same logic in relation to time) that one cannot be *both* personal *and* simple/temporal is not correct. This book agrees with the logic of their criticisms. However, where the "theistic personalists" differ is that they claim that God being a person is the more theologically valuable claim—they want God to think, decide, have wants and desires, and to act decisively to realize those wants and desires—and they move from this to deny other attributes which they understand to be less theologically valuable. However, this book takes the opposite view: God's personality does not show that divine atemporality/simplicity must be incorrect, but God's atemporality/simplicity show that God cannot be a person. As will now be shown, not only is it not at all clear that the claim that God is a "person without a body (i.e., a spirit)"[53] does indeed "[seem to be] the most elementary claim of theism",[54] but it is not at all clear whether it has ever been a claim of Christian theism (at least, not as "person" is understood by modern philosophers).

"Traditional" theology and "classical" theism

The previous section made one overarching claim: talk of God as personal has become increasingly popular in modern times, but it suffers from the fatal flaw of treating God as nothing more than a super-human. God becomes essentially, ontologically, the same as humanity just infinitely less limited. God becomes essentially no different to the Greek or Roman Pantheon, with the only exception that God is the only one. Those who work from this position to criticize atemporality or simplicity might be entirely correct in their reasoning that "person" and "atemporal/simple" are incompatible terms, but they are incorrect in their assumption that God is a person.

Critics of "theistic personalism" criticize it, then, not on the basis that "theistic personalism" makes some philosophical or logical errors (although there are some who question whether it is philosophically incoherent to apologize for an immaterial, incorporeal person),[55] but on the basis that it is not entirely clear that any past theologians ever held that God was a "person", certainly not in the sense that it is taken to mean to modern readers.[56] Roger Pouivet, for example, notes that the notion that "God is a person" was the result of a "Cartesian and Lockean

---

[53]   Swinburne, *The Coherence of Theism*, p. 1.

[54]   Swinburne, *The Coherence of Theism*, p. 101.

[55]   Helen Oppenheimer, *Incarnation and Immanence* (London: Hodder and Stoughton, 1973), pp. 23ff.

[56]   See John Bishop and Ken Perszyk, "The Divine Attributes and Non-personal Conceptions of God", *Topoi* 36 (2017), pp. 609–21 for overview of the problems with "theistic personalism".

epistemology", and was explicitly condemned as heresy (albeit not by an ecclesial body).[57]

For Pouivet, theologians took a modern sense of the word "person" and applied it, retrospectively, to God. That is, theologians have taken the Chalcedonian approval of the word *hypostasis*, translated it into the English "person", and then assumed that the Chalcedonian Fathers meant exactly what the modern English word "person" means when they so approved "*hypostasis*". Yet, as many have noted, this was by no means the intention behind the conciliar approval of the application of "*hypostasis*" (and the Latin translation of *persona*) to God. The Greek word "*hypostasis*" does not accurately translate to the English word "person", with all its modern philosophical connotations. Many have made this observation. Vladimir Lossky argues that "the preoccupation with the category of personhood is a thoroughly modern pursuit, and any attempt to find a theory of human personhood in the early church would be irresponsible".[58] If there is no *human* personhood in the early Church, then neither is there a *divine* personhood. Likewise, Karl Rahner also questioned whether the word "person" has become too far removed from what the Patristic Fathers intended it to mean and has become misleading, arguing that theologians erroneously attribute the modern philosophical concept of "person" to God, when the Patristic Fathers intended something very different.[59] Further, Paul Tillich also questions the motives behind the use of the word "person" being applied to God, calling talk of a personal God a "confusing symbol".[60]

The fact that the early Church argued for, and rubber-stamped, the idea that Christ had two wills and two energies, and—crucially—so

---

[57]   Brian Davies, *The Reality of God and the Problem of Evil* (London: Continuum, 2006), p. 59, quoted in Roger Pouivet, "Against Theistic Personalism: What Modern Epistemology Does to Classical Theism", *European Journal for Philosophy of Religion* 10:1 (2018), p. 4.

[58]   Vladimir Lossky, *In the Image and Likeness of God* (New York, NY: St Vladimir's Seminary Press, 1974), pp. 112–13.

[59]   Karl Rahner, *The Trinity* (London: Burns & Oates, 1970).

[60]   Tillich, *Systematic Theology Vol. 1*, p. 245; after all, God is *three* hypostases, not *one* person (Tillich, *Systematic Theology Vol. 1*, p. 205).

Christ had two centres of consciousness, also shows that those capacities that modern psychology and philosophy attribute to personhood were not those which the early Church had in mind when they were talking about Christ being one *hypostasis*. Marilyn McCord Adams writes that "'Person' in the [Chalcedonian] context does not mean a centre of thought and choice but—after Boethius—an individual substance; in the hands of schoolmen, more precisely the *supposit* of a rational nature". Drawing on Bonaventure, she continues that "Bonaventure reaffirms the distinction of human and Divine wills in Christ against the twentieth-century style objection that two wills make for two willers, and so two personalities. Bonaventure counters that 'person' does not mark an organ of thought and volition, but the supposit of a rational nature".[61] Dermot Lane agrees, arguing that "this duality of natures in Jesus implies that we acknowledge the existence of a human psychological centre of self-consciousness involved in and related to a divine psychological centre of self-consciousness within the one ontological person of Jesus", thus, "in Jesus there is a fully human centre of self-consciousness and a divine centre of self-consciousness which are hypostatically united in one divine person".[62] Admittedly, Lane seems to be suggesting that God is conscious (which this chapter above suggested might not necessarily be the case if the univocality of being is rejected and divine atemporality is affirmed), nevertheless, the salient point here is that consciousness has nothing to do with *personhood* as understood by modern thought. James Moulder, too, writes that "the standard English translation of *prosopon* and *persona* is *person*. But this is highly misleading. A better translation is *individual thing*, or simply, *individual*, in the sense of *the*

---

61   Marilyn McCord Adams, *What Sort of Nature? Medieval Philosophy and the Systematics of Christology* (Milwaukee, WI: Marquette University Press, 1999), p. 8.

62   Dermot Lane, *The Reality of Jesus* (London: Sheed & Ward, 1975), p. 116; cf. John Macquarrie, who criticizes the doctrine of dythelitism on the basis that the will is personal. Although, as Lane observes, this seems to be the confusion of two senses of person, and so Macquarrie appears to be judging the Patristic doctrine on modern sensibilities (*Jesus Christ in Modern Thought* (London: SCM Press, 1990), p. 166–7).

sort of thing which can be spoken of as existing separately and in its own right." Whereas "the Chalcedonian theologians said that Jesus is a single *prosopon* or *hypostasis*. We can make the same point by saying that he is a single individual".[63] If Swinburne calls God "*a*" "person without a body",[64] then this is emphatically and explicitly anti-Chalcedonian: God is "*three* persons",[65] all of which "share" "one single will, a single power, [and] a single operation".[66]

If this chapter has so far situated the discussion in a modern setting, as modern theologians/philosophers incorrectly applying modern concepts to ancient language, it is by no means a modern problem. In the ninth century, Irish theologian John Scotus Eriugena cautioned that one errs when one thinks that "foreknowledge and predestination are transferred to God by likening him to temporal things".[67] Eriugena, like most medieval theologians both east and west, was heavily influenced by Pseudo-Dionysius. The place to start, then, is with Pseudo-Dionysius. This does not mean that the mystical, negative theology for which Pseudo-Dionysius is famous and which was so influential on all later theology was not done before Pseudo-Dionysius (assuming, of course, that the arguments in favour of Pseudo-Dionysius being a sixth-century Syrian monk, and not the Dionysius whom Paul meets in Athens recorded in the "Acts of the Apostles", are accurate). Most notably, Gregory of Nyssa argued for a view of God that is very "Dionysian". In his *Life of Moses*, Gregory writes that "the soul rises ever higher and will always make its flight higher" and "makes its way upwards without ceasing", so that "once having set foot on the ladder which God set up (as Jacob says), [Moses]

---

[63] James Moulder, "Is a Chalcedonian Christology Coherent?", *Modern Theology* 2:4 (1986), p. 288 (italics in original); see also J. W. C. Wand, *The Four Great Heresies* (London: Mowbray, 1961), pp. 64–6.

[64] Swinburne, *The Coherence of Theism*, p. 1.

[65] See Tillich, *Systematic Theology Vol. 1*, p. 205.

[66] Vladimir Lossky, *The Mystical Theology of the Eastern Church* (Cambridge: James Clarke & Co., 1957), p. 53.

[67] Eriugena, *De Divina Praedestinatione liber*, ed. G. Madec, *Corpus Christianorum Continuatio Mediaevalis* 50 (Turnhout: Brepols, 1978), XI.7 393B.

continually climbed to the step above and never ceased to rise higher, because he always found a step higher than the one he had attained".[68] Thus, Gregory continues, "no limit would interrupt growth in the ascent to God, since no limit to the Good can be found nor is the increasing of desire for the Good brought to an end because it is satisfied".[69] This idea—called *epektasis* or "eternal progress"—clearly assumes an idea of God that is very different to that for which the "theistic personalists" apologized. However, while Nyssa (almost certainly) preceded Pseudo-Dionysius, the wide and deep influence that Pseudo-Dionysius had on later theologians, particularly Thomas Aquinas, makes him the place to start.

Even though only a few of his works survived to the present day, they are astonishingly theologically rich. Of those few extant works we have of Pseudo-Dionysius, the short *The Mystical Theology* is probably the most famous, in which Pseudo-Dionysius argues that one can only talk and think of God in negations. If God is transcendent, above all being and knowing, then one cannot come to God through knowledge, but one must *deny* all things. Thus, Pseudo-Dionysius writes that "as we climb from the last things up to the most primary we deny all things so that we may unhiddenly know that unknowing which itself is hidden from all those possessed of knowing amid all beings so that we may see above being that darkness concealed from all the light among beings".[70] The language is quite dense, but the point is that since all language, conception, and knowing are of created things, one cannot talk about, conceive, or know God because God must be above all created things. One cannot talk about God positively—what God is—one can only talk about God negatively—what God is not.

Moreover, Pseudo-Dionysius continues that "we should not conclude that the negations are simply the opposites of the affirmations, but rather that the cause of all is considerably prior to this, beyond

---

[68]   Gregory Nyssa, *The Life of Moses* (Mahwah, NJ: Paulist Press, 1978), pp. 113–14.

[69]   Gregory Nyssa, *The Life of Moses*, p. 116.

[70]   Pseudo-Dionysius, *The Complete Works* (Mahwah, NJ: Paulist Press, 1987), *The Mystical Theology* 2.

privations, beyond every denial, beyond every assertion". It is not enough simply to say that God is the opposite; one must say that God is beyond even opposition.[71] As Vladimir Lossky writes, "God transcends both affirmation and negation . . . and in the last analysis, it goes beyond the opposition between transcendence and immanence".[72] Likewise, Dionysius continues, God "falls neither within the predicate of nonbeing nor of being" and "is beyond assertion and denial".[73] That is, as is characteristic of Pseudo-Dionysius, one must even "negate the negations"; somewhat confusingly, God is not even what God is not. God neither "is" nor "is not".

This point is perhaps the most important, and it is difficult to overemphasize just how crucial it is for understanding what might be called the "traditional theistic" perspective in contrast to "theistic personalism". To say that God is "beyond the predication of nonbeing and being" is to say that God is not "*a*" being, that is, God is not a concrete, discrete, individual being to whom attributes can be predicated but is "above individual being".[74] God is nothing; God is "no thing".[75] For Pseudo-Dionysius, God is so utterly and completely transcendent that all must be negated along the *via negativa* until, Pseudo-Dionysius argues, one is left with nothing but silence. "The more it climbs," writes Pseudo-Dionysius, "the more language falters, and when it has passed up and beyond the ascent, it will turn silent completely."[76] God is so transcendent that God is not a "thing"—neither "being" nor "person"—to which attributes can be predicated and so cannot be described in *any* language, let alone univocal language.

---

[71]   Pseudo-Dionysius, *The Mystical Theology* 1.2

[72]   Lossky, *In the Image and Likeness of God*, p. 40.

[73]   Pseudo-Dionysius, *The Mystical Theology* 5.

[74]   Pseudo-Dionysius, *The Mystical Theology* 3.

[75]   Pseudo-Dionysius, *The Complete Works* (Mahwah, NJ: Paulist Press, 1987), *The Divine Names* 5.10; see also Frank Kirkpatrick, *The Mystery and Agency of God: Divine Being and Action in the World* (Minneapolis, MN: Fortress Press, 2014), p. 42, p. 45; Simone Weil, quoted by Frances Young, *Can These Dry Bones Live?* (London: SCM Press, 1982), p. 57.

[76]   Pseudo-Dionysius, *The Mystical Theology*, 3

Even if it is qualified, as Jim Holt does, that God is *infinitely* greater than creatures, this cannot be used to mean that God is infinitely different to creatures. God can only be other or distinct from the world if there were something in common from which they could differ, that is, "one thing can differ only from another and for one thing to differ from another it must do so in some common respect".[77] This, as Robert Barron has already been quoted arguing, is the basis of the univocality of being: if God and creatures are both "beings" or are both "persons", then "being" or "person" is a thing that God and creatures have in common for them to differ in respect of it. Yet, this is not what Pseudo-Dionysius thought. For him, "divinity and creaturehood are too different to be opposites",[78] so God cannot "just" be different, but God is different in how God is different. God is different differently. As some theologians have perceptively noted, God is not just "other" but must be "other than other", or "other otherwise",[79] or "otherly other, enjoying a transcendence that is not contrastive to the world".[80] If God is so infinitely transcendent of the world to be "beyond the predication of nonbeing and being" and beyond the distinction between "is" and "is not", then God cannot be different to the world, because there is nothing similar between God and the world, no point of connection on which difference can be hung.

In *The Divine Names*, Pseudo-Dionysius continues this theme, writing that God "is not *a* life, but is, rather, superabundant life" and "is not *a* mind, but is superabundant wisdom"[81] and that "God is not some kind of being".[82] Pseudo-Dionysius again clarifies that "the absolute being underlying individual manifestations of being as their cause is not a divine or angelic *being*, for only transcendent being itself can be the source, the being, and the cause of the being of beings".[83] God is the

---

[77] Denys Turner, *The Darkness of God: Negativity in Christian Mysticism* (Cambridge: Cambridge University Press, 1998), p. 42.

[78] Rupert Shortt, *God Is No Thing* (London: Hurst & Company, 2016), p. 8.

[79] Kirkpatrick, *The Mystery and Agency of God*, p. 42.

[80] Barron, *Exploring Catholic Theology*, p. 8.

[81] Pseudo-Dionysius, *The Divine Names* 4.3.

[82] Pseudo-Dionysius, *The Divine Names* 5.4.

[83] Pseudo-Dionysius, *The Divine Names* 11.6 (italics added).

"Cause of being to all, but Itself *not being*".[84] Again, these passages are quite dense and can be difficult to unpack. However, the crucial message is that if creatures participate in God (see the next chapter)—that is, if God is the absolute being underlying individual manifestations of being—then God cannot Godself be "*a*" being. If God is the source of being, then God cannot be an individual, discrete being. God is not *another* "thing", another infinitely greater, infinitely temporal, infinitely powerful "being". God is nothing, no "thing" and so nothing could be said of God at all, including—paradoxically—that God is no "thing".

The Dionysian legacy

The legacy of Pseudo-Dionysius branches into two quite different interpretations: the eastern Fathers, of which Gregory Palamas is the most important representative, and the western scholastics, of which Thomas Aquinas is undoubtedly the most influential. The former took the approach that since nothing could properly be said of God, the only proper approach to theology is silence and prayer. The latter took the approach that nothing could properly be said of God, but the theologian must say something, so they must speak in analogies. John Meyendorff describes these two interpretations as between one way that "asserts divine transcendence as a property of God, and one which no detachment and no surpassing oneself can vanish"[85] and another way that "conceives the transcendence and unknowability of God as a consequence of the limitations of the created mind".[86] Whereas the first corresponds to Palamism, the second corresponds to Thomism.

Of course, there are other issues that characterize the disagreements that Orthodox and Catholic theologians have had over the years. The argument between Gregory Palamas and Barlaam—Gregory's scholastic interlocutor—was as much an argument over whether philosophy could be used in the service of theology (and whether the particular Aristotelian philosophy that characterized scholasticism was adequate for theological

---

84   Pseudo-Dionysius, *The Divine Names* 1.1 (italics added).

85   John Meyendorff, *A Study of Gregory Palamas* (London: The Faith Press, 1964), p. 203.

86   Meyendorff, *A Study of Gregory Palamas*, p. 203.

discourse) as it was about whether one must stay silent or whether one was permitted to use analogy to speak about God. Whereas in the west theology became increasingly academic (Thomas Aquinas was a lecturer at the University of Paris), in the east, the emphasis on silence meant that Palamas was critical of any attempt to "philosophize" about God.[87] Whereas in the west theology moved increasingly into the universities, in the east it remained in the monasteries. As John Meyendorff writes, Palamas started "not from arguments, but from actual and historical assumptions".[88] Theology was an experience of God that must be lived in communion with the Church, not the university. Theology required prayer, fasting, and asceticism, not academic training. Theology was in the service of salvation, not an academic pursuit in analytical philosophy trying to understand and describe God.

Nevertheless, these arguments noted and set to one side, Gregory Palamas' contribution can be seen as continuing this aspect of Pseudo-Dionysius' thought. For Palamas, God was so utterly transcendent that nothing could be said truly of God. He wrote that "if God is nature, all else is not nature; but if every other thing is nature, he [sic] is not nature, just as he is not a being if all other things are beings, and if he is a being, then all other things are not beings".[89] It is clear how different this sentiment is to that of Swinburne. Of most importance, God is not "*a*" being: God is not an individual, concrete, discrete being. God is not

---

[87]   See Efthymios Nicolaidis, *Science and Eastern Orthodoxy: From the Greek Fathers to the Age of Globalisation* (Baltimore, MD: The Johns Hopkins University Press, 2011), p. 96.

[88]   Meyendorff, *A Study of Gregory Palamas*, p. 210.

[89]   Gregory Palamas (tr. Robert Sinkewicz), *One Hundred and Fifty Chapters* (Toronto: Pontifical Institute of Mediaeval Studies, 1988), p. 78; see Turner, *The Darkness of God*, p. 164; Bernard Montagnes, *The Doctrine of Analogy of Being According to Thomas Aquinas* (Milwaukee, WI: Marquette University Press, 2004), p. 66; Torstein Theodor Tollefsen, *Activity and Participation in Late Antique and Early Christian Thought* (Oxford: Oxford University Press, 2012), pp. 72–3, p. 153; Anselm, *Collected Works* (Oxford: Oxford University Press, 1998), *Monologion* 28.

a "thing" to which attributes can be predicated, least of all those attributes that "theistic personalists" thought so crucial.

In order to emphasize as much as possible the sheer transcendence and utter otherness of God, eastern theologians, following Palamas, distinguish between the "essence" and "energies" of God. If God was "beyond being"—and "since language and thought are confined to the realm of created existence" so that "the only valid affirmation is, strictly speaking, that God is non-being"[90]—then God was ultimately and "eternally" beyond knowledge. That is, the creature will never be able to know the divine "essence". However, the creature can know God through the divine energies, which the creature experiences.

Importantly, Palamas did not think that he was inventing any new distinction. For Palamas, the distinction between the "essence" and "energies" of God was nothing but a conforming to theological categories already found in Maximus the Confessor. Thus, Anna Williams writes that "what Palamas does with the essence-energy distinction is little more than codify such commonly agreed observations and standardize the terminology for talking about them, using language that has been used loosely and informally [since] Irenaeus".[91]

Much more could be said about Palamas' theology, and the profound influence that it had on the neo-Palamites of the twentieth century (Vladimir Lossky, Georges Florovsky, etc.). What is important here is that the crucial element of Palamas' theology is the utter transcendence of God, an emphasis that was taken so seriously that it led to the conclusion that God could not be known at all. The extent to which God could be known is the extent to which God's "energies" can be experienced by the creature through prayer and which communicate God. When it comes to the divine "essence", little more is left to the theologian than reverent silence.

[90]   Bogdan G. Bucur, "The Theological Reception of Dionysian Apophatism in the Christian East and West: Thomas Aquinas and Gregory Palamas, *The Downside Review* 125:439 (2007), p. 132.

[91]   Anna Williams, *The Ground of Union: Deification in Aquinas and Palamas* (Oxford: Oxford University Press, 1999), p. 152.

Aquinas and Lateran IV

Thomas Aquinas was also deeply influenced by Pseudo-Dionysius, but emphasized the use of analogy more than the need for silence. This, Bogdan Bucur notes, is because the west could not accept that the vision of the divine essence would not be granted even to the angels and "pure souls",[92] as Palamas held through his distinction of "essence" and "energy". If the divine "essence" was not ultimately beyond the angels and those who were saved, then it wasn't beyond description either. Nevertheless, if the divine "essence" was "describable", this did not lead them to a univocal understanding of God.

Richard Swinburne, as already briefly noted, claims that despite the fact that Thomas Aquinas professed to expounding a doctrine of analogy, in reality he used language univocally as much as did John Duns Scotus.[93] That is, according to Swinburne, Thomas Aquinas' doctrine of analogy is really just a "species" of univocality; Aquinas, so Swinburne thinks, thought that God was basically the same as humans but just less limited. However, Swinburne recognizes that his interpretation of Aquinas as a sort of nuanced Scotist might not find favour with many theologians,[94]

---

[92]   Bucur, "The Theological Reception of Dionysian Apophatism in the Christian East and West", pp. 133–5.

[93]   Swinburne, *The Coherence of Theism*, p. 81; interestingly, if Swinburne argues that Aquinas was closer to Scotus on the question of univocality because (so Swinburne argues) Aquinas was more of an exponent of univocality of being than is generally acknowledged, Alex Hall also argues that Aquinas and Scotus were closer on this question but because (so Hall argues) Scotus was never really an exponent of univocality (see Alex Hall, "Confused Univocality", *Proceedings of the Society for Medieval Logic and Metaphysics* 7 (2007), pp. 18–31). As interesting as these arguments are, it is irrelevant to the purposes of this chapter whether Scotus genuinely argued for univocality or whether Aquinas genuinely argued for analogy, or whether they are closer together on a sort of spectrum; what is important is that the difference between "univocality" and "analogy" is understood.

[94]   Although Lewis Ford agrees that, for Thomas, "the difference between the finite and the infinite is simply one of degree" (Lewis S. Ford, "Tillich and Thomas: The Analogy of Being", *The Journal of Religion* 46:2 (1966), p. 239).

and we will assume that Aquinas did not accept the use of univocal language.

If "univocal" language is inappropriate to talk about God, then the opposite was just as detrimental to theology. To use Aquinas' language, to say that God was entirely "*equivocal*" to creatures—that about God absolutely nothing could be said whatsoever and all language was entirely meaningless—was to make an *affirmation* about God; it was to pretend to know precisely what God was not. As Rowan Williams writes, "If divine difference were the negation of all finite predicates, God would be the other belonging to a discourse about the finite world. God's life would be subsumed under that of the world."[95] That is, claiming that God is equivocal would still bring God into the same "level" of creation, but just different.[96] More importantly, claiming that God is equivocal is tantamount to denying that God is the creator. For Aquinas, an effect reveals its cause. Thus, for Aquinas, there must be *some* "similarity" between creatures and God (but, crucially, not between God and creatures) because God is the creator. If God were equivocal, then there would be absolutely nothing that connects the effect with its cause, and so God could not be the creator. If God is genuinely the creator, then there must be something, however remote, about God that creatures can say (like with Bauerschmidt's example of John and Mary). Yet, if God is equivocal, then God cannot be the creator, because creatures mirror or reflect the creator, however dimly. (Of course, Palamas accepted this argument as well, but he preferred to use the language of "essence" and "energy"; God's essence was entirely and ultimately unknowable, but, because God is the creator, creatures can know God's "energy".)

Yet, as much as Aquinas denied that God was equivocal, so he was also (despite Swinburne's claims) opposed to the univocality of being. Univocality of being was absolutely incorrect because it implied that there was something—the category of being (and anything else, such

---

[95] Rowan Williams, *Wrestling with Angels: Conversations in Modern Theology* (London: SCM Press, 2007), p. 83; see Oliver Tromans, "The 'Divine Names' and the 'Attributes of Deity': On the (Infinite) Analogical Interval in Forty-Six Aphorisms", *Modern Theology* 36:3 (2020), p. 631.

[96] See *ST* 1, 13, 5.

as "person" or "time")—that was more primary than God, a category more ontologically basic than God and which contained both God and creatures. As already quoted from Robert Barron, treating God and creatures univocally means that "God and creatures . . . belong together to a logical category that, in a real sense, transcends and includes them",[97] or, as Alex Hall puts it, "a concept of being univocal to God and creatures threatens to make being over into a genus above both".[98] In this case, God would no longer be the most primary "being", there would be something—e.g., the abstract category or genus of "being" or "person"—that is more primary and which included both God and creatures. Crucially (especially given the definition of creation that will be central in the next chapter), therefore, the affirmation of univocality would mean that there is something else on which God depends, and so, by definition, God would no longer be the most primary "being"; God would not be independent, but would be dependent upon "being"; God would have God's being from something else (which would be the distinct category or genus of "being").

If God is not univocal with creatures—because this would make God the same "thing" as creatures and dependent upon something else for God's being—and God is not equivocal with creatures—because this would mean that God could not be the creator—then God must be analogical with creatures. However, Aquinas did not mean analogy in the way that Swinburne thinks that he meant it (and certainly not how Swinburne himself uses it)—i.e., as a way of using language "in unusual combinations and circumstances and to unusual degrees"[99]—but as a description of the absence of a real relation or as a description of the mixed relation. Analogy for Thomas means that creatures are really and genuinely like God, but God is completely and utterly unlike creatures. Thus, for Thomas, unlike Swinburne, analogy is not really about the application of language (although, obviously, this is part of it); rather, analogy says something important about the nature of God, namely, following Pseudo-Dionysius, that God is not the sole or unique instance

---

[97]   Barron, *The Priority of Christ*, p. 13.

[98]   Hall, "Confused Univocality", p. 18.

[99]   Swinburne, *The Coherence of Theism*, p. 52.

of a species called God. That is, the divine attributes are not definitions of the sort of thing that God is.

This leads to the conclusion that language used about God is not *descriptive*. That is, language cannot be used to describe the sort of thing that God is. Brian Davies writes that God "is not a good such-and-such. He [sic] is no kind of such-and-such. And he cannot be thought of as a perfect such-and-such regardless of the perfection in question".[100] "God is not an instance of a kind",[101] neither is God "a substance with attributes distinguishable from itself and shareable, in different degrees, with other things".[102] Thus, for Aquinas, "attributes ascribed to [God] are not just present in him somewhat differently from the way in which they are present in creatures", rather, it is "wrong to say that God has a character in any sense we can understand. Or, to put it another way, it will be wrong to assert that God is an individual—in the familiar sense of 'individual' where to call something an individual is to think of it as a member of a class of which there could be more than one member, as something with a nature shared by others but different from that of things sharing natures of another kind".[103]

This is nothing more than what Pseudo-Dionysius meant in *The Divine Names*, that God is not an individual being. The analogy of being is not a way to describe "what" God "is", but a vehicle that points to the "otherly otherness" of God. Put differently, it is not the case that Swinburne, Lucas, and Plantinga apply the term "person" univocally to God and Thomas applies it analogously; rather, it is that for Thomas, God is not an individual being to whom attributes or capacities can correctly be applied at all. Thomas does not apply the term "person" to God analogically; for Thomas, God cannot be a "person" because God cannot be an individual being.

---

[100] Brian Davies, "Aquinas on What God is Not", *Revue Internationale de Philosophie* 52:204 (1998), p. 210; see also John Betz, "Translator's Introduction", in Erich Przywara, *Analogia Entis* (Grand Rapids, MI: William B. Eerdmans, 2014), pp. 42–3.

[101] Davies, "Aquinas on What God is Not", p. 217.

[102] Davies, "Aquinas on What God is Not", p. 219.

[103] Davies, "Aquinas on What God is Not", p. 223.

Analogy and idolatry
In fact, any sense in which God is described at all—especially when God is described as "*an*" individual, particular, infinitely distinct "being"— becomes a contravention of the second commandment, against idolatry. As Frank Kirkpatrick puts it, "a God whom one could conceptualize is no God at all. God must utterly transcend one's conception of God because conceiving of God is a form of idolatry".[104] Frank Kirkpatrick draws on the theology of Jean Luc Marion (through Kevin Hector) in making this observation. Jean Luc Marion was influenced by both Pseudo-Dionysius and Thomas Aquinas, and took the approach that even the very concept of God itself must be considered an idol, and so discarded. He writes that "when a philosophical thought expresses a concept of what it then names 'God', this concept functions exactly as an idol".[105] An idol, Marion explains, "thus acts as a mirror, not as a portrait", and so this "gives the gaze its stopping point".[106] In other words, the idol does not allow the viewer to see beyond the idol; the idol does not point to anything transcendent, it simply reflects that which looks at it. Marion contrasts this with the icon, which "attempts to render visible the invisible as such", and so the icon "always must rebound upon the visible, in order to go back in it up the infinite stream of the invisible".[107]

Even the very concept of "God", then, simply reflects the creature. "God" can only ever be a human invention, a crudely defined concept that points to "something" transcendent, which, by its very definition, can only ever be an idol. Swinburne's God can only ever be an idol, because it seeks to "contain" God or "exhaust" God within or "limit" God to a particular concept. God as "a person without a body" becomes an idol, which is nothing more than a reflection of humanity. As a result, God becomes precisely that about which Ludwig Feuerbach criticized: God becomes nothing more than a projection of humanity, an intellectual/ conceptual idol constructed from those values and attributes—such as

---

104   Kirkpatrick, *The Mystery and Agency of God*, p. 144.
105   Marion, *God without Being*, p. 14.
106   Marion, *God without Being*, p. 12.
107   Marion, *God without Being*, p. 18.

consciousness and sympathy etc.—which humans value most.[108] The fact that it has already been noted by Brian Davies that "theistic personalists" take sympathy and response as being attributes worthy of admiration and so project these onto God only serves to increase the force of Marion's claim. If Feuerbach had lived to read Swinburne's theology, he would find very good evidence of his philosophy.

This leads Marion—following Pseudo-Dionysius and Thomas before him—to argue that any theology that attributes "being" to God is a form of idolatry. He writes that "the proposition 'God is a being' itself appears as an idol, because it only returns the aim that, in advance, decides that every possible 'God', present or absent, in one way or another, has to be". "Undoubtedly," Marion continues this train of thought, "if 'God' is, he is a being; but does God have to be?"[109] The answer, Marion concludes, is "no", but he makes some important arguments that further this conclusion. For example, as already noted above in relation to Pseudo-Dionysius, to "liberate God from Being", as Marion puts it, does not mean that God is characterized by "nonbeing", since "nonbeing" "remains within the dominion of the Being of beings".[110] Thus, Marion continues, there cannot even be "ontological difference" between God and creatures, because that assumes that God and creatures are different with respect to their being, but God has no being.[111] God is otherly other, so to claim that God is not characterized by being is not to say that God is characterized by "non-being"—God as "non-being" would be just as idolatrous as God as "being"—but that God transcends the distinction between being and non-being.

Of course, Marion clarifies, "the icon also can proceed conceptually, provided at least that the concept renounce comprehending the incomprehensible".[112] In other words, Marion takes the Thomist rather

---

[108] Ludwig Feuerbach, *The Essence of Christianity* (New York, NY: Harper Torchbooks, 1957); see also Tromans, "The 'Divine Names' and the 'Attributes of Deity'".

[109] Marion, *God without Being*, p. 44.

[110] Marion, *God without Being*, p. 83.

[111] Marion, *God without Being*, p. 45.

[112] Marion, *God without Being*, p. 22.

than the Palamite position: concepts *can* be used of God, but only when
the reader recognizes that they are markers, inaccurate in themselves but
pointing to something infinitely transcendent, or, as Marion continues,
"It is not a question of using a concept to determine an essence but of
using it to determine an intention."[113] Concepts are not idols—distinct
"things" in themselves that replace God—but icons—mysterious and
vague "things" that do not replace God but point beyond themselves to
the God who cannot be understood. Univocal language is an idol that
places a boundary around, and so limits, God; analogical language is
an icon that acts as a "marker" that points beyond itself to the infinitely
transcendent.

Analogy, the Fourth Lateran Council, and the absence of a real relation
If Thomas Aquinas' doctrine of the analogy of being is an important
elaboration of the Pseudo-Dionysian principle that God is beyond the
distinction of "being" and "non-being", and becomes the language of the
principle of the "mixed relation" between God and creatures, then it was
nothing more than the confirmation of something that had been given the
conciliar seal of approval at the Fourth Lateran Council, a decade before
Thomas Aquinas' birth. Critical of the theology of Joachim of Fiore, the
Fourth Lateran Council taught that "between creator and creature there
can be noted no similarity so great that a greater dissimilarity cannot be
seen between them".[114] This is exactly what Thomas meant by analogy
and the "mixed relation": whatever likeness there might be between
creatures and God, there is no likeness that cannot be overshadowed
by a greater dissimilarity between God and creatures. Andrew Davison
puts it as "likeness in the face of . . . or against the backdrop of yet-greater
unlikeness",[115] or, as Erich Przywara writes, "the greater the similarity,
the greater the dissimilarity".[116] When it is used as a lens through which
theology is done, it means that creatures are permitted to say, for example,

---

[113] Marion, *God without Being*, p. 23.

[114] *Constitutions of the Fourth Lateran Council 2.*

[115] Davison, *Participation in God*, p. 147.

[116] Francesca Murphy, "The Sound of the 'Analogia Entis' Part 1", *New Blackfriars*
74:876 (1993), p. 518.

that "God is good", provided it is accepted that the word "good" is more inappropriate than appropriate; what it means for God to be good is only dimly akin to what it means for creatures to be good. In fact, so dim is that kinship, that it is better to say that God is not good. Or, creatures are good as God is good, but God is not good as creatures are good. While between creatures and God there is a similarity—creatures are similar to God (because they are created by God)—between God and creatures there is a dissimilarity—God is dissimilar to creatures (because God infinitely transcends creatures). If that is what the Fourth Lateran Council taught against Joachim, it is nothing more than a restatement of what Pseudo-Dionysius had taught seven hundred years earlier: "It is the power of the divine similarity which returns all created things toward their Cause, and these things must be reckoned to be similar to God by reason of the divine image and likeness," yet, Pseudo-Dionysius immediately qualifies, "we cannot say that God is similar to them."[117]

Here, a topography of analogy might be helpful. E. J. Ashworth writes that (a) "there are analogical terms which are univocal in a broad sense of 'univocal', by which she means that a human and a donkey are both animals, but are not exactly 'equal'".[118] This appears to be the way in which Swinburne uses the term.[119] There are those who (b) see analogy as a genuinely intermediary term between univocal and equivocal. Lastly, there are those who (c) regard analogy as a "subsidiary of equivocation". It is this latter sense that is clearly in the minds of the Lateran bishops. When analogy is used as a theological principle, it is undoubtedly closer to "equivocality" than "univocality". That is, God is not basically similar but different in degree, as Swinburne argued; rather, God is absolutely transcendent, but creatures can be like God as their creator. God and creatures are not univocal—that would make God similar to creatures— neither are God and creatures equivocal—that would mean creatures

---

[117] Pseudo-Dionysius, *The Divine Names* 9.6.

[118] E. J. Ashworth, "Suárez on the Analogy of Being: Some Historical Background", *Vivarium* 33:1 (1995), p. 60.

[119] See also Davies, "Aquinas on What God is Not", p. 218; Ashworth notes that other medieval thinkers similarly thought that analogy was closer to univocality (Ashworth, "Suárez on the Analogy of Being", p. 65).

cannot be similar to God—rather, God and creatures are analogical, which means creatures are similar to God but God is not similar to creatures—however, the emphasis is still on the dissimilarity.

Differently, and more importantly given the centrality of participation in the next chapter as a description of creation, this understanding of the analogy of being points to and describes participation. In fact, Bernard Montagnes calls analogy "the semantics of participation".[120] Norman Russell also argues that "analogy, imitation, and participation thus form a continuum rather than express radically different kinds of relationship".[121] "Participation" ("imitation") and "analogy of being" are two sides of the same coin, two ways of describing the same relationship. Participation both requires that creatures are like God while God cannot be like creatures, and it requires that God is not an individual "thing" or "being". If God were an individual or a particular "thing/species", then there would be something more basic in which God participates. As already argued, this would mean that God would be univocal with creatures. Thus, the analogy of being (far from being simply a way of using "ordinary" language) requires that God is not a particular "thing", but is that in which creatures participate. Or, to put it differently, analogy means that God is not *a* being, but "is" *being itself*. Thus, Samuel Powell can write that "the world cannot be identified with God", but, "because creatures have their being by participation, therefore there is an analogical relation between them and God".[122] John Mortensen also writes that "analogy [of being] is according as one imitated another insofar as it can, without perfectly approaching it; and this is the analogy of the creature to God".[123]

---

[120] Montagnes, *The Doctrine of Analogy of Being According to Thomas Aquinas*, p. 9.

[121] Norman Russell, *The Doctrine of Deification in the Greek Patristic Tradition* (Oxford: Oxford University Press, 2004), p. 2; see also Lewis Ayres, *Nicaea and its Legacy: An Approach to Fourth-Century Trinitarian Theology* (Oxford: Oxford University Press, 2004), pp. 321ff.

[122] Samuel Powell, *Participation in God* (Minneapolis, MN: Augsburg Fortress Press, 2003), p. 48.

[123] John Mortensen, *Understanding St. Thomas on Analogy* (Rome: Pontifical University of the Holy Cross, 2006), p. 160.

If there was not an analogy between God and creatures then creatures could not participate in God. This means, as Daniel Keating writes, that participation "enables us to grasp how we are genuinely related to God and can partake of his life, without jeopardizing the infinite distance that distinguishes the uncreated Trinity from all creatures".[124] Or, as Elizabeth Castelli writes about imitation, "There exists in the notion of imitation this tension between drive to sameness and the inability to achieve it,"[125] so that imitation "becomes a derivative function, in that it attempts to reproduce an unattainable origin",[126] that is, imitation is about the similarity of one to the other—"drive to sameness"—and the dissimilarity of that other to the one—"inability to achieve ... an unattainable origin". Thus, "participation" and "imitation" (and "analogy of being") are nothing more than other ways of expressing the "absence of a real relation".

In the twentieth century, no writer carried the torch for "analogy of being" more than Erich Przywara. His incredible philosophical sophistication made his works inaccessible for most and so he is by no means the most popular of theologians. Indeed, the original German works have only very recently been translated into English. This is not the occasion to spend time delving into his perceptive theological writings, but a few comments are necessary. For Przywara, analogy was the central theological motif. Everything in theology must be done through the prism of analogy. Analogy of being, then, becomes not so much one doctrine among many, another proposition to sit alongside all of the others: analogy of being *is* theology; analogy of being is a prism through which theology must be viewed. Theology is "analogical" or it is incoherent. Thus, distinguishing "the Fourth Lateran Council and Thomas Aquinas" from "Joachimism of the West and East", Przywara writes that "analogy [i]s the utterly fundamental principle of Catholicism, because analogy is the utterly fundamental principle obtaining between

---

[124] Daniel Keating, *Deification and Grace* (Naples, FL: Sapientia Press, 2007), p. 103.

[125] Elizabeth Castelli, *Imitating Paul: A Discourse of Power* (Louisville, KY: Westminster John Knox Press, 1991), p. 75.

[126] Castelli, *Imitating Paul*, p. 86.

God and the creature".[127] Analogy, Przywara continues, "appears not so much as a principle or form of a new theological possibility, but rather the *self-expression of the position of the church* as regards all possible theologies".[128]

However, perhaps more pertinent to this current discussion is the fact that Przywara attempts to "ground" the doctrine of analogy within the principle of non-contradiction. Here, and in a very Dionysian spirit, Przywara argues that "no matter what is said in common of both God and creature (being, truth-goodness-beauty, etc.), it is not the case that God and creature are not related to something they have in common", but instead is that "everything reduces to the ultimate irreducible *prius* of God ... without any 'possibility of appeal' to a third".[129] It is this "possibility of appeal to a third" that is crucial. He means here that "being" or "truth" are not a third "thing", a third category that exists alongside "God" and "creatures", and in which both God and creatures participate. Rather, God *is* being and truth, and creatures *have* them by participation in God. Przywara continues that this means that even the principle of non-contradiction itself cannot be such a "third" thing to which the theologian appeals, as this contradicts the very thing for which it is being postulated. Drawing on the Lateran formula that "one cannot note any similarity between creator and creature, however great, without being compelled to observe an ever greater dissimilarity between them", Przywara continues that "the intrinsic ground of this 'cannot' is not, however, an objective principle that 'regulates' the relation between God and creature" because "then it would stand above both: that is, it would itself be what is really divine". Rather, Przywara concludes, "the intrinsic ground is God as *Deus semper maior*".[130] In other words, precisely as Pseudo-Dionysius taught, the "cannot" in the "one cannot note" cannot be something that describes the relationship between God and creatures because this then would become a category in which both creatures and God participate.

---

[127]   Przywara, *Analogia Entis*, p. 362.

[128]   Przywara, *Analogia Entis*, p. 374 (italics added).

[129]   Przywara, *Analogia Entis*, p. 233; see also Marion, *God without Being*, p. 209.

[130]   Przywara, *Analogia Entis*, p. 234.

Przywara is saying here with much philosophical sophistication what Pseudo-Dionysius said in simple mystical paradox.

This is *exactly* what was argued above in relation to participation and so demonstrates clearly that the contribution that Przywara makes is to show how the analogy of being is considered the "semantics of participation". Participation and analogy as doctrines strongly suggest that God cannot be thought of as being "anything" at all, certainly not a particular instance, individual, or example of "something", because doing so would make whatever that something is that which is "really divine". In other words, if God is thought of univocally, then God, the creature, and "being" itself would each be three distinct "things" and so both God and creatures would only be understood, as Przywara puts it, by appeal to a "third", which would be "being" itself. As Barron has already been quoted, "God and creatures [would] belong together to a logical category that, in a real sense, transcends and includes them".[131] Both God and creatures would participate in a third thing (either "being" or "person") or, as Alex Hall put it, "being" would become "a genus above both".[132] However, if God is thought of analogically, then God is "being" itself and so there is no "third thing"; creatures would participate in God.

To come full circle, while lacking the philosophical development of Aquinas, Marion, Przywara etc., this is nothing more than the reason why Gregory of Nyssa affirmed his theory of *epektasis*, and the "eternal progress". If God was reachable, if the creature could rise up and eventually reach a point where they could approach God, then this makes God another being with whom the creature can engage. Yet, if God is that in which the creature participates, then God cannot be so reached and approached, because "participation necessarily requires a relation between two things that are unequal and that *remain* unequal and distinct in the act of the one participating in the other"[133] so that participation "enables us to grasp how we are genuinely related to God and can partake of his life, without jeopardizing the infinite distance

[131] Barron, *The Priority of Christ*, p. 13.

[132] Hall, "Confused Univocality", p. 18.

[133] Keating, *Deification and Grace*, p. 97 (italics added).

that distinguishes the uncreated Trinity from all creatures".[134] To put it differently, Gregory of Nyssa's theory of *epektasis* is nothing more than a lived experience of the analogy of being, or the idea of the analogy of being clothed in mystical language. If God is so transcendent that the creature can never approach God—so transcendent because God is not "*a*" being that can be approached but is being itself, the "ground of being" (as Tillich comes to call it) in which the creature participates—then this is because there is always and at every moment an infinitely greater dissimilarity. If God can never be approached, that is because no matter how close the creature comes to God, no matter how deeply the creature participates in God or how closely the creature imitates God, there is always a greater distance separating God from creatures.

The rejection of "theistic personalism", therefore, becomes not a question of how one thinks about God, but a question about whether God is coherent or not. The "traditional" theological position that was started in Gregory and Dionysius and (at least in the west) has become refined by Lateran IV, Thomas Aquinas, and Erich Przywara (to name but a few who have contributed) centres on the idea of participation. Without participation, God is not the "most fundamental" "thing"; without participation, "being" (or "person") becomes a "third" "thing", a "genus" that becomes more ontologically primary and on which both God and creatures depend for their being. Without participation, "being" itself becomes the divine and God becomes nothing more than a super-human, participating in "being" (albeit to a greater extent than humans). However, with participation, with God's dissimilarity infinitely surpassing any similarity enjoyed by the creature, God maintains that transcendence. Participation, described in the language of the analogy of being, is the only way to coherently maintain that God is truly divine, and if this is the only coherent way of maintaining God's divinity, then the position of the "theistic personalists"—that God is a "person without a body"[135]—is nothing more than an intellectual idol which must be cast aside as a univocal projection or raising of the human to the level of the divine.

---

[134] Keating *Deification and Grace*, p. 103.
[135] Swinburne, *The Coherence of Theism*, p. 1.

Protestantism and Paul Tillich

Although Thomas Aquinas was adamant that God was not the name of a specific "thing" of which God was the only example—i.e., it was not the case that the only difference between monotheism and polytheism (or henotheism) is that monotheism posits there is just one individual of the genus "god" rather than many—he was still content to use the language of "person" and "nature". Both "person" and "nature" had been given the conciliar seal of approval and so he was content to talk about "divine nature", despite the fact that he was clear that God was not the unique instance of a divine "species". However, some Protestant scholars became increasingly uncomfortable with the use of the word "nature". While these Protestant theologians were not Thomists of any stripe, they reached a similar conclusion: if God is not a "species" then the category of "nature" cannot apply to God; if God is not a "thing" to which attributes can be posited, then that God cannot rightly have a "nature".

Of course, some of these writers were uncomfortable with the word "nature", not because of the theological implications of its use, but because they saw it as an unacceptable alien Hellenistic import that distorted or diluted the true biblical message. In this way, God did not have a "nature" because the Bible had not endorsed that language. Thus, John Passmore writes that "the great mistake of traditional Christian theology, as Barth sees it, is that it was persuaded to substitute the God of the philosophers, for Yahweh",[136] and so the "simple, absolute being" of Augustine, Anselm, and Aquinas is, for Karl Barth (and others), a "pagan tradition".[137] David Williams, too, notes that it has been "suggested that the traditional view of God's attributes is actually foreign to Christianity, [and] is imported from Greek philosophy".[138]

---

[136] John Passmore, *The Perfectibility of Man* (London: Duckworth, 1970), p. 113.

[137] Passmore, *The Perfectibility of Man*, p. 69.

[138] David Williams, "Kenosis and the Nature of the Persons in the Trinity", *Koers* 69:4 (2004), p. 627.

The German Protestant theologian Friedrich Schleiermacher is also an important exponent of this rejection of the language of "nature".[139] In a discussion of the hypostatic union—the ascription of two "natures" to Jesus Christ—acknowledging that "the New Testament knows nothing of this usage" of the language of "nature",[140] Schleiermacher argued that "nature" could not be applied to God and this led Schleiermacher at least to modify Chalcedon, if not completely reject it.[141] However, more importantly (and in a remarkably Palamite spirit),[142] Schleiermacher questions whether it is appropriate to use the same word—"nature"—to describe both God and creatures. He writes that "far worse" is "that the expression 'nature' is used indifferently for the divine and the human". He continues:

> Any other expression that was used indifferently of both [God and creatures] would lead one to suspect that such a formula was bound to become the source of many confusions. For how can divine and human be thus brought together under any single conception, as if they could both be more exact determinations, coordinated to each other, of one and the same universal? Indeed, even divine spirit and human spirit could not without confusion be brought together in this way. But the word "nature" is particularly ill-adapted for such a common use, even if we leave Latin and Greek etymology completely out of account and simply take our stand on our own use of the word. For in one sense we actually oppose God and nature to one another, and hence in this sense cannot attribute a nature to God.[143]

---

[139] See Mark S. G. Nestlehutt, "Chalcedonian Christology: Modern Criticism and Contemporary Ecumenism", *Journal of Ecumenical Studies* 35:2 (1998), p. 181, p.184; see also Donald Keefe, *Thomism and the Ontological Theology of Paul Tillich* (Leiden: Brill, 1971), pp. 244–7.

[140] Friedrich Schleiermacher, *The Christian Faith* (Berkeley, CA: Apocryphile Press, 2011), p. 392.

[141] See Nestlehutt, "Chalcedonian Christology", p. 181, p. 184.

[142] See e.g., Gregory Palamas, *One Hundred and Fifty Chapters*, p. 78.

[143] Schleiermacher, *The Christian Faith*, p. 392.

In this last sentence, Schleiermacher seems to confuse two senses of the word nature ("nature" as opposed to the "supernatural" and "nature" as the description of what a thing is), but, nevertheless, the general thrust of this complaint is compelling. In many ways, it is nothing more than a re-presentation of what has already been considered: divinity cannot be a universal of which God is the unique exemplar. Indeed, Schleiermacher has said more or less exactly the same thing that was said above regarding the problems with the univocality of being and participation. Thus, Schleiermacher continues that:

> For always, whether we use the word ["nature"] generally, as when we speak of animal and vegetable nature, or of an individual, as when we say that a person has a noble or an ignoble nature, always we use it solely of a limited existence, standing in opposition to something else, an existence in which active and passive are bound up together, and which is revealed in a variety of appearances, in the latter case of individuals, in the former of vital factors.[144]

Again, God cannot have a "nature" if that is to mean precisely the same thing that it means when it is said that there is a "human nature" or "murine nature". For Schleiermacher, it is not so much a case of rejecting "nature" because he was more concerned with keeping a "pure" biblical theology, one that is unpolluted or diluted by alien Hellenistic concepts, as it is a concern that the use of word "nature" brings God down to the level of creatures. Schleiermacher was concerned about those issues that led Pseudo-Dionysius, Aquinas, Marion, and Przywara to take the theological avenue they did.

However, perhaps no Protestant theologian encapsulates this way of thinking about God more than the Lutheran theologian Paul Tillich. In the second volume of *Systematic Theology*, Tillich expresses an attitude towards "nature" that is reminiscent of Schleiermacher when Tillich calls

---

[144] Schleiermacher, *The Christian Faith*, p. 393.

it inadequate to express what one means by "God".[145] In relation to the traditional "two nature" Christology, Tillich, like Schleiermacher, finds the language of "nature" incoherent. When "nature" is "applied to man, it is ambiguous; when applied to God, it is wrong".[146] It is ambiguous when applied to humanity, Tillich explains, because it is unclear whether the Patristic Fathers who gave their seal of approval to the term "nature" meant "man's essential or created nature . . . man's existential or created nature . . . [or] man's nature in the ambiguous unity of the two others".[147] However, it is the use of "divine nature" in relation to the incarnation that is the most important here. Using language that is almost identical to that of Thomas Aquinas, Tillich writes that "the term 'divine nature' can mean only that which makes God into God" and so "in this sense, nature is essence". Yet, Tillich continues, "God has no essence separated from existence, he [sic] is beyond essence and existence".[148] It is not important for present purposes what language Tillich or Schleiermacher use to replace "nature"; what is important is that they essentially follow Thomas Aquinas and Gregory Palamas, who both follow Pseudo-Dionysius: if "nature" is applied to humans/creatures, then it cannot be applied to God.

However, it is what Tillich has to say about "God as person" in the first volume of his *Systematic Theology* that is most important (and explicit) for present purposes. Here Tillich criticizes those who understand God as "person" and, instead, utilizes the language of God as the "ground of being". Crucially, he argues, treating God as "*a*" being—a particular, discrete, concrete individual being, however described—*prohibits* God from being the "ground of being", that which is the "being" of all other beings, that in which all individual beings participate.[149]

---

[145] Paul Tillich, *Systematic Theology Vol. 2* (London: SCM Press, 1978), pp. 142–7.

[146] Tillich, *Systematic Theology Vol. 2*, p. 142.

[147] Tillich, *Systematic Theology Vol. 2*, p. 147.

[148] Tillich, *Systematic Theology Vol. 2*, p. 147; see also Keefe, *Thomism and the Ontological Theology of Paul Tillich*, pp. 244–7.

[149] Tillich, *Systematic Theology Vol. 1*, pp. 244–9.

Much could be said about Tillich's theology, but a few comments will suffice here. Paul Tillich explicitly rejects the term "person" as applied to God, calling the idea of a "personal God" a "confusing symbol".[150] Tillich identifies the "Kantian separation of nature ruled by physical law from personality ruled by moral law" as the moment when theologians began referring to God as "person", reminding his readers that "it should not be forgotten that classical theology employed the term *persona* for the Trinitarian hypostases but not for God himself [sic]".[151] Further, Tillich affirms that not only is God not a person, but God is not a being either; "God is being-itself, not *a* being."[152] "If God is *a* being," Tillich explains, then God "is subject to the categories of finitude, especially to space and substance. Even if he [sic] is called the 'highest being' in the sense of the 'most perfect' and 'most powerful' being, this situation is not changed" because, claims Tillich, it just makes God different from humanity by degree, not by kind.[153] God becomes nothing more than a super-human. Tillich makes the same remarks in reference to omnipotence. God cannot be called "omnipotent" (at least, not how it is normally understood) because "in popular parlance, the concept of 'omnipotence' implies a highest being who is able to do whatever he wants", which serves only to make "God into a being alongside others".[154] Tillich argues that the superlatives—most powerful, most perfect, etc.—become diminutives, because, while elevating God above all creatures, they trap God within the same "level" as creatures.[155] The superlatives become idols: they don't point beyond themselves to a God that is beyond being, but they themselves become God.

Interestingly and illustratively, David Bentley Hart uses the same logic to criticize Anselm's "ontological proof" of the existence of God. He writes that Anselm is incorrect in his ontological proof for the existence of God,

---

150 Tillich, *Systematic Theology Vol. 1*, p. 245.
151 Tillich, *Systematic Theology Vol. 1*, p. 245; see Pouivet, "Against Theistic Personalism", p. 6.
152 Tillich, *Systematic Theology Vol. 1*, p. 237.
153 Tillich, *Systematic Theology Vol. 1*, p. 235.
154 Tillich, *Systematic Theology Vol. 1*, p. 273.
155 Tillich, *Systematic Theology Vol. 1*, p. 235.

not because Anselm's logic contains some incoherence or contradiction (although it may very well do), but because "God is not *a* being who *might* and therefore *must* exist, but is absolute Being as such".[156] David Bentley Hart calls the belief that God is "*a*" being, rather than "being itself" or "ground of being", "monopolytheism", which he defines as "a view of God not conspicuously different from the polytheistic picture of the gods as merely very powerful discrete entities who possess a variety of distinct attributes that lesser entities also possess, if in smaller measure; it differs from polytheism, as far as I can tell, solely in that it posits the existence of only one such being".[157] The God of Swinburne (and others) is nothing more than the God of the Roman or Greek Pantheon, except that there is only one of them.

Phillip Clayton points to this development in the religion of the Old Testament. He argues that the biblical authors held a henotheistic belief because of a residue of polytheism that characterized the earlier thought of the ancient world. The religious thought of the ancient world went through an evolution from polytheism, through henotheism and finally settled on monotheism.[158] It is only when the biblical authors moved through henotheism to monotheism that the idea of *creatio ex nihilo* became an established doctrine. However, "remnants of polytheism [or, more accurately, henotheism] remained in the picture of God and God's action".[159] Thus, Clayton rightly recognizes that theologians "have sometimes failed to be radical enough" in their rejection of, and move away from, polytheistic and henotheistic thinking, so that, although

---

[156] David Bentley Hart, *The Experience of God: Being, Consciousness, Bliss* (London: Yale University Press, 2013), p. 122; see also Tromans, "The 'Divine Names' and the 'Attributes of Deity'"; Robert R. N. Ross, "The Non-Existence of God: Tillich, Aquinas, and the Pseudo-Dionysius", *The Harvard Theological Review* 68:2 (1975), pp. 141–66.

[157] Hart, *The Experience of God*, p. 127.

[158] Phillip Clayton, *God and Contemporary Science* (Edinburgh: Edinburgh University Press, 1997), pp. 83ff.; see also Davison, *Participation in God*, p. 137 and Christopher C. Knight, *The God of Nature: Incarnation and Contemporary Science* (Minneapolis, MN: Fortress Press, 2007), pp. 16–17.

[159] Clayton, *God and Contemporary Science*, p. 86.

Christian theologians "moved away from many gods to one God . . . they have often continued to conceive of God as a being who stands alongside the world, which becomes a 'handiwork' he has crafted".[160] Thus, "a significant part of the theological tradition has not thought through the implications of strict monotheism carefully enough".[161] If this is the case, the fact that theologians who subscribe to theistic personalism point to the Bible as the reason for why they hold the view they do may very well be the source of why that view is problematic. If Clayton is correct, and the Bible represents a primitive theology that still clings to the polytheistic (or henotheistic) cosmology from which it emerged, then it is clear that pointing to the Bible as a theological authority is likely to lead to an unsophisticated God and a theology that has failed to be "radical enough".

To return to Tillich, this leads to perhaps the most important claim that he makes in relation to how God should be understood. While he criticized Thomas Aquinas and did not situate himself within the scholastic tradition, his approach to theology is exactly what one would expect were one following the analogy principle. He writes that "if God is brought into the subject–object structure of being, he [sic] ceases to be the ground of being and becomes one being among others (first of all, a being beside the subject who looks at him as an object). He ceases to be the God who really is God".[162] That is, if God is brought into the "subject-object structure of being" (that is, if God is conceived as standing alongside the world, which becomes God's "handiwork"), then this means that God *has* being, rather than *is* being, and so "being" is set up above God as a "third" category, which is more primary than God and contains both God and creatures. However, if God is not "*a*" being, then God cannot "enter into" a subject–object relationship with anything and so the world, and all creatures within it, would not be an object that exists alongside and/or opposed to God. This will have implications for understanding the act of creation, which will be explored in the following chapter; how can God create if the world cannot be thought of as the object of an act

---

[160]   Clayton, *God and Contemporary Science*, p. 86.

[161]   Clayton, *God and Contemporary Science*, p. 86.

[162]   Tillich, *Systematic Theology Vol. 1*, p. 172.

which has God as the subject? If God is not "*a*" being then God cannot be
the subject of any act, and the universe cannot be the object of anything
that God "does". Tillich does not use the language of "analogy of being"
or "participation", but he is making *exactly* the same argument made by
Aquinas and Przywara as outlined above.

Once again, it is clear that Pseudo-Dionysius is crucial here. John
Macquarrie is clear on this point and argues that the "mystical tradition"
(of which Pseudo-Dionysius is arguably the most important exponent) is
very important for understanding Tillich's theology and that "in this we
can discern a tradition that goes back to Dionysius' treatise, *The Divine
Names*".[163] Pseudo-Dionysius has already been quoted in support of the
argument that God is "above individual being".[164] Pseudo-Dionysius
warned his reader about those he calls "the uninformed", which he
defines as "those caught up with the things of the world, who imagine
that there is nothing beyond instances of individual being and who think
that by their own intellectual resources they can have direct knowledge
of him who has made the shadows his hiding place" and as "those others,
still more uninformed, who describe the transcendent cause of all things
in terms derived from the lowest orders of being, and who claim that it is
in no way superior to the godless, multiformed shapes they themselves
have made".[165] Pseudo-Dionysius could be talking about Swinburne here.
More importantly, Pseudo-Dionysius makes very similar claims to Tillich
in that "the absolute being underlying individual manifestations of being
as their cause is not a divine or angelic being, for only transcendent being
itself can be the source, the being, and the cause of the being of beings".[166]
That is, the "ground of being" cannot be a "being" without ceasing to be
the "ground of being".

So central is this point to Tillich that Lewis Ford suggests that "Tillich's
writings may be regarded as one long polemic against the view that God
is a being".[167] That Ford continues to say that viewing God as Tillich

---

[163] Macquarrie, *Jesus Christ in Modern Thought*, p. 301.

[164] Pseudo-Dionysius, *The Mystical Theology* 3.

[165] Pseudo-Dionysius, *The Mystical Theology* 1.2.

[166] Pseudo-Dionysius, *The Divine Names* 11.6.

[167] Ford, "Tillich and Thomas", p. 243.

does is a "fundamental error" that "runs counter to the monotheistic character of the Judeo-Christian tradition, which conceives of God as a living, personal being" serves to underline the distinction that this chapter has tried to emphasize. It is clear that Ford would place himself on the "theistic personalist" side, against the understanding of God for which this chapter is apologizing, and it seems clear that Ford has not taken into account Pseudo-Dionysius, Aquinas, Palamas, Schleiermacher or any of their adherents.

Moreover, crucially, Tillich sees the idea that God is "*a*" being and the idea that God is the "ground of being" as mutually exclusive; if God is "*a*" being, then God cannot be the "ground of being". For God to be the source of all being, then God cannot be *another* being, whether that being is part of the world and described in univocal language, or exists transcendent of the world. This is nothing more than what Pseudo-Dionysius has already been quoted as saying: "the absolute being underlying individual manifestations of being as their cause is not a divine or angelic being, for only transcendent being itself can be the source, the being, and the cause of the being of beings".[168] God is the "Cause of being to all, but Itself not being".[169] If God is that in which creatures participate, then God cannot also be another "being" alongside others, because this would contradict the fact that God is in fact that in which creatures participate.

In fact, Tillich goes so far as to claim that, in this respect, the Christian must be an atheist and deny the existence of God: "it is as atheistic to affirm the existence of God as it is to deny it".[170] That is, if God is not *a* being, not a subject, then God cannot properly be the subject of any particular verb. To say "God exists" or even that "God is", is to assume that God is a subject to which things can be applied and of which things can be said. Again, the point is that if God is that in which creatures participate, then God cannot exist as "*a*" being. Others have made the same remarks. St. George Mivart makes the same point, writing that "Christianity affirms the truth latent in atheism, namely, that God, as He

---

[168] Pseudo-Dionysius, *The Divine Names* 11.6.

[169] Pseudo-Dionysius, *The Divine Names* 1.1.

[170] Tillich, *Systematic Theology Vol. 1*, p. 237.

is, is unimaginable and inscrutable by us".[171] Mivart does not understand this claim in precisely the same way that Tillich does (not least because Mivart was Catholic, not Lutheran), but there is a consonance in their intentions: God cannot exist because this brings God into the same conception, and so under the same metaphysical category, as creatures.

Perhaps Richard Dawkins would dismiss such statements as unhelpful semantic trickery; word games that are employed by exasperated theologians who are knowingly misrepresenting their position as smoke and mirrors. Perhaps he is right. Perhaps the Christians like Tillich who describe their position as "atheism", while at the same time maintaining the truth of the Christian religion, are being disingenuous. Regardless of how they wish to present themselves, Dawkins might respond, everyone knows the difference between an atheist and a theist. However, that being said, the theist in the Dionysian, Thomist, Tillichian vein can read Dawkins' most famous contribution to modern religion vs. science debates—*The God Delusion*—and assent to nearly every sentiment. The God that Dawkins seeks to disprove is the God in which no "traditional theist" would believe anyway. One could imagine Gregory Palamas, Thomas Aquinas, and Paul Tillich reading Dawkins' book and responding simply, "What's your point?" The fact that Dawkins draws on the theology of Richard Swinburne—and misunderstands Aquinas' theology[172]—only serves to hammer this point home: Dawkins does not distinguish between the "theistic personalist" God and the "traditional theist" God. The God that Richard Dawkins (and others in the New Atheist movement who have popularized religion-bashing) takes great pains to disprove is the God of the "theistic personalist". Perhaps ironically, Dawkins does more to support the position taken by the "traditional theists" than he would care to acknowledge. Dawkins is absolutely correct that Swinburne's God seems to be lacking; Swinburne's God—at least according to the principle of the analogy of being—is no God at all. The God for which Swinburne apologizes and against which Dawkins rallies

---

[171] St. George Mivart, *Contemporary Evolution* (London: Henry S. King & Co., 1876), p. 215.

[172] Hart, *The Experience of God*, pp. 21–2.

is nothing more than a super-human; neither are talking about the God of Pseudo-Dionysius, Aquinas, Palamas, or Tillich.

A compromise?

The Bible presents God as univocal with creatures, yet "traditional" theologians, despite the fact that they drew on biblical language, presented an entirely different picture of God. "Theistic personalists" look at the Bible and see it as a divine seal of approval to talk about God in a way that presents God as univocal with creatures, that God is another person in a world of persons. In that way, the motives behind the "theistic personalist" position are entirely understandable and—Clayton's argument about the henotheistic nature of biblical theology notwithstanding—it is easy to be sympathetic to their intentions. On the other hand, "traditional theists" look at the Bible and see analogy, that is, the Bible must be seen through the lens of philosophical and theological discourse. For them, there is a logical contradiction: one cannot genuinely be the God presented in the Bible and also be that on which all things depend. As Clayton has argued, one must see the biblical God in its place in the evolution of theological thinking and discourse. It appears that one must choose between the God of the Bible and the God of philosophy.

However, this might not necessarily be the case. There are those who argue that one is not forced to choose between these two ways of thinking about God. William Lane Craig is one such theologian who, in his article "Divine Timelessness and Personhood",[173] marshals several arguments to support the claim that God can be both person and atemporal. For example, Craig suggests that in order to be a person God would need to be rational and self-conscious and conscious of others,[174] and none of these capacities require temporal duration and/or succession. That is, he disagrees with Plantinga and Lucas that being atemporal and simple prohibits God from also being conscious, personal, and active. God,

---

[173] William Lane Craig, "Divine Timelessness and Personhood", *International Journal for Philosophy of Religion* 43:2 (1998), pp. 109–24.

[174] Craig, "Divine Timelessness and Personhood", p. 110.

thinks Craig, can be personal—i.e., have desires, wants and the means to realize them—and also be atemporal.

However, as already suggested, it is not entirely clear that Plantinga *et al.* are incorrect. Contra Craig, it appears that Plantinga and Lucas are correct that no "being" (whether God or not) can be genuinely personal and genuinely atemporal/simple without contradiction. For example, one would assume that the possession of certain desires and emotions would be essential for God to be a person, and yet others have argued convincingly that this requires time and mutability. David Blumenfeld and Paul Fiddes have both questioned whether God can genuinely experience panic, fear, dread, embarrassment, etc., without such experiences (regardless of whether God requires a body to feel them or not) conflicting with certain other divine attributes, such as immutability.[175] Paul Fiddes' example of the refugee given aid is an excellent illustration. God cannot genuinely know what it's like to be the refugee on Monday (cold and hungry) because to do so requires that God does not know what it is like to be relieved on Wednesday.[176] For God to be genuinely sympathetic, God necessarily needs to be mutable and temporal.[177] Others, such as Murray MacBeath and Marcel Sarot, question whether a God who "cannot share in our relief that some dreadful episode is over" (because relief that something is over necessarily requires temporality) is unattractive,[178] and not worthy of

---

[175] David Blumenfeld, quoted in Henry Simoni, "Omniscience and the Problem of Radical Particularity: Does God Know How to Ride a Bike?", *International Journal for Philosophy of Religion* 42 (1997), p. 10.

[176] Paul Fiddes, *The Creative Suffering of God* (Oxford: Clarendon Press, 1988), pp. 91–2; see also Simoni, "Omniscience and the Problem of Radical Particularity", p. 11.

[177] Atemporality and immutability are more or less synonyms, so that if God is mutable then God cannot logically be atemporal and if God is atemporal then God cannot change (see Holland Jr., *God, Time, and the Incarnation*, p. 3).

[178] Murray MacBeath and Paul Helm, "Omniscience and Eternity", *Proceedings of the Aristotelian Society, Supplementary Volumes* 63 (1989), pp. 69–70; see also Davies, *An Introduction to the Philosophy of Religion*, pp. 9–14.

human respect and worship.[179] A God who does not have knowledge "feelingly" is "theologically irrelevant" and so God has to be able to "undergo feelings and experiences"[180] or theism becomes incoherent. Brian Davies has already been quoted evidencing the same arguments.[181] These authors make these comments in relation to the question of omniscience, but the point is equally valid here: it would seem that the "theistic personalists" are correct in their arguments that if God is a person, then this necessarily requires God to have certain capacities and attributes that necessitate temporal experience and ontological complexity. Moreover, when Craig seeks to define what he means by "person", he does not choose a theological source, but instead points to Daniel Dennett. Appealing to modern philosophical notions of "personhood", rather than what traditional theological categories might understand by the term, can lead to significant problems, as Rahner and Tillich have already been quoted on. In other words, Craig still seems to assume that God is a person as humans are persons—i.e., univocality of being—the only difference being that God is an atemporal "person". Yet, the present question is whether God is a person or whether God transcends these sorts of questions. For those who argue that God must be able to sympathize with creatures, to have emotions and desires and the ability to realize these, then the idea of personhood is the most important theological value, and those attributes—such as atemporality and simplicity—that point to transcendence are happily sacrificed. If, on the other hand, the transcendence of God above creatures is the more theologically valuable, then this facile, univocal view of God as person is sacrificed. Craig thinks that one can have both, but, even if he is correct that God can be both personal and atemporal (which it does not appear that he is), this still seems alien to the God of Pseudo-Dionysius, Aquinas,

---

[179] See Ben Page, "Wherein Lies the Debate? Concerning whether God is a Person", *International Journal for Philosophy of Religion* 85 (2019), pp. 297–317; see especially pp. 301–2 and pp. 307–11.

[180] Marcel Sarot, "Omniscience and Experience", *International Journal for Philosophy of Religion* 30:2 (1991), p. 90.

[181] Davies, *An Introduction to the Philosophy of Religion*, p. 13.

and Tillich: a God that is so transcendent that even personhood must be sacrificed.

While Craig—the analytical philosopher—might ultimately be in the same category as Plantinga and other theistic personalists, Eleonore Stump—the celebrated Thomist—is not, and is another who thinks that it is not incoherent to suggest that one does not need to choose between the God of the Bible and the God of the philosophers: one can coherently posit that God is both. In her book *The God of the Bible and the God of the Philosophers*, she argues that those theologians who are central for the traditional view of God—Augustine, Anselm, Thomas Aquinas—were quite content to hold that the God of the philosophers was identified with the God of the Bible. Those theologians were adamant that philosophical sophistication was required to understand the God of the Bible, but, nevertheless, they still identified that God with the God of the Bible—a God who had desires and did things.[182]

Drawing specifically on the theology of Thomas, Stump argues that while God is "being-itself", God is also a person. For Stump, God is "irreducibly personal, an *id quod est* with one mind and one will".[183] If God is not a person, then God cannot be personally present to the creature, as God clearly is portrayed in the Bible. If God is not a person, then God cannot be a concrete individual who does things. Pointing to Thomas' doctrine of simplicity, Stump maintains that Aquinas' doctrine of simplicity allows him to say that God is both 'being-itself' (*esse*) and a being (*id quod est*) simultaneously. Thus, Stump argues that "for Aquinas, God is not just *being*, but rather *being* which somehow also subsists as a being or an *id quod est*".[184]

Yet, Stump makes an error here. She writes that "[s]omething X is an image of something else Y only if X resembles Y in some way; but then Y must resemble X in some way",[185] and this leads her to hold that God is like creatures just as creatures are like God. Yet, as this chapter has tried

---

[182] Eleonore Stump, *The God of the Bible and the God of the Philosophers* (Milwaukee, WI: Marquette University Press, 2016).

[183] Stump, *The God of the Bible and the God of the Philosophers*, p. 104.

[184] Stump, *The God of the Bible and the God of the Philosophers*, p. 87.

[185] Stump, *The God of the Bible and the God of the Philosophers*, p. 106.

at length to show, this is *not* what exponents of the "traditional theist" position held. The "Lateran formula" holds that creatures are like God, but God is unlike creatures. This is the point of the "absence of a real relation"; creatures are related to God, but God is not related to creatures. Stump appears to have missed this. Perhaps, then, her suggestion that God can be both *esse* and an *id quod est* simultaneously misses something important.

While it may be true that Augustine, Anselm, and Aquinas identified the God of the Bible with the God described by philosophical endeavour, as this chapter has already expounded, they still found it very difficult to think about God as "*a*" personal being. As already quoted from Pseudo-Dionysius, Erich Przywara and Paul Tillich, the problem with holding that God is *both* "*a*" being *and* the "ground of being" is that it does not sufficiently emphasize the ontological distinction of God from creatures. If God is both, then God is still within the univocal paradigm: that is, God is still a being, just like creatures, but infinitely greater than them.

Nevertheless, seeing this question as a choice between two different ideas of God, the support of one necessarily prohibiting support of the other, might be a rather crude way of understanding the problem that misses something that was crucial to the "traditional theist" position, and one explicitly recognized by Erich Przywara. That is, it is better to think, not that God is *either* the God of the Bible or the God of the philosophers, not that God is *either* "*a*" being or the "ground of being", but that in God the distinction between "being itself" and "*a*" being breaks down. That is, it is not so much that God is *both* "being itself" and "*a*" being simultaneously, but God transcends the distinction between "being itself" and "individual being". If one *affirms* that God is either the God of the Bible or the God of the philosophers, then one is not exercising one of the most important Dionysian distinctions: one must negate the negations.

One might be able to infer such an approach from Aquinas' response to the question of whether "essence" and "existence" are the same in God. Why Aquinas thinks that "essence" and "existence" cannot be the same for God is not important here; what is important is that, for Aquinas,

"[God's] essence is His existence".[186] This does not mean, however (as one can infer from Aquinas' very next question), that God's "genus" is existence, of which God is a member; God does not have/belong to a genus. Rather, it means that God transcends the distinction between them. Normally (at least for the scholastic), all creatures are thought of as a combination of "essence" and "existence"; yet God cannot be a singular "instance" of a "thing"—i.e. a particular existence of an essence—because this would violate God's simplicity, so God must transcend that distinction. As previously quoted from Paul Tillich, God "is beyond essence and existence".[187]

This points to the possibility of a third option. Arthur Peacocke understood that God cannot be "*a*" person, and so argued that God was "*supra*person". He writes that "God is more coherently thought of as 'at least personal', indeed as 'more than personal' . . . Perhaps we could even say that God is 'suprapersonal' or 'transpersonal', for there are many essential aspects of God's nature which cannot be subsumed under the categories applicable to human persons".[188] Peacocke seems to be saying all the right things here. He understands that God must be entirely ontologically other than creation, but still identified with the God of the Bible. Peacocke continues that, while the term "suprapersonal" is somewhat awkward, it "indicate[s] that, while wanting to emphasize that the nature of human personhood, with its transcendence-in-immanence, was the 'least misleading' pointer to the nature of God the Creator as the source of all-that-is, yet we recognized that any extension of the language of human personhood inevitably, like all analogies based on

---

[186]   *ST* 1a q.3 a.4; see also *ST* 1a q.6 a.3, *ST* 1a q.12 a.2.

[187]   Tillich, *Systematic Theology Vol. 2*, p. 147.

[188]   Arthur Peacocke, "Articulating God's Presence in and to the World Unveiled by the Sciences", in Philip Clayton and Arthur Peacocke (eds), *In Whom We Live and Move and Have Our Being: Panentheistic Reflections on God's Presence in a Scientific World* (Grand Rapids, MI: William B. Eerdmans, 2004), p. 151.

created realities, must remain inadequate as a *description* of the nature of that ineffable, ultimate Reality which is God".[189]

However, as much as Peacocke seems to be saying the right things here, his position must still be criticized. Although Peacocke recognizes that personal language is inadequate, he still maintains that "the traditional model of *personal* agency for God's interaction with the world as a whole" is still appropriate.[190] That is, while Peacocke recognizes—quite rightly— that God cannot be a "person" in the same way that humans are persons, he still approves of the use of *personal* language when describing God's relationship with creatures. A more detailed discussion of precisely why "personal agency" must be rejected as a model for God's interaction is properly the subject of the next chapter, so it will be left out here. It is enough to acknowledge here that Peacocke seems to be moving in the right direction, but must ultimately be rejected.

There is a further problem with Peacocke's idea. As he notes, the notion that God is *supra*-personal has to take as its starting point that God is *more* than personal. The implication is that were God to be *non*-personal or *un*-personal, then this would seem to imply that God is ontologically inferior to "persons". However, this makes two important mistakes: (a) it assumes that God can be compared with creatures—that God and creatures can be placed in a "spectrum of being"—and that God is *"more"* than whatever creatures are, thereby making God univocal with creatures; and (b), it assumes that persons are objectively ontologically superior to non-persons, and so the possession of those capacities that point to personhood makes the possessor ontologically superior to those who do not, a position of which (as Chapter 3 will argue) philosophers and biologists are increasingly sceptical. In other words, while Peacocke seems to be transcending the distinction between "non-person" and "person"—which must be correct—actually, he is doing nothing more than setting up God as what might be termed "infinitely personal".

---

[189] Arthur Peacocke, *Theology for a Scientific Age* (Minneapolis, MN: Fortress Press, 1993), pp. 303–4.

[190] Peacocke, *Theology for a Scientific Age*, p. 191 (italics added); see also Peacocke, "Articulating God's Presence in and to the World Unveiled by the Sciences", pp. 144–5.

That is, for Peacocke (who ultimately endorses "personal agency" as an appropriate model for divine activity, God does not *transcend* the personal, but is *infinitely* personal, i.e., God is personal in the same way that humans are personal, but to an infinite degree. Peacocke still appears to be in the "univocality of being" category.

In this way, Stump, Craig, and Peacocke are all fumbling around for the right answer, but none of them quite reach it. Stump is surely on the right track when she says that God is both "being-itself" and "*id quod est*", but she must ultimately fall short: God is not *both* "being-itself" and "*a* being", rather God is *beyond* the distinction between them. Likewise, Peacocke is surely on the right track when he talks of God being "supra-personal", but he must ultimately fall short: to say that God is *more* personal because God is *beyond* the distinction between "being-itself" and "*id quod est*" is incoherent. It is like saying that "something" (whatever "something" means in this context) that is beyond "whiteness-itself" and "a-white-thing" is *more* white because it transcends that distinction. This is certainly not what Pseudo-Dionysius meant when he urged his readers to "negate the negations", and (as already noted above), it seems to stray into the univocality of being—God is not truly *beyond* the distinction, but is rather the same kind of "thing" but infinitely more so or less limited.

The biblical God
However, if, following Clayton, theologians need to be "radical" in transcending more and more distinctions and negating more and more negations until one is left with paradox and silence, Stump is at least correct in that, regardless of how much the God of the Bible is rejected as being an infantile idol and a Feuerbachian projection of the human onto God, the God of Pseudo-Dionysius, Palamas, Przywara, and Tillich *is* identified as the God of Israel. As much as the God presented in the Bible may be a narrative device, Yahweh *is* Tillich's "ground of being" on which all creatures depend.

Thus, rejecting the "facile" description of God in the Bible does not mean that the Bible needs to be rejected in every possible way. One is not forced to choose between the God of the philosophers and the God of the Bible and so reject completely everything in the Bible. As will become apparent, this book will still want to rely on the Bible as authority, it will still want to identify the God of the philosophers with the God revealed in the Bible and—most importantly—it will still want to identify Christ with that God.

If one accepts the validity of scientific and historical investigation, then one is already committed to a certain degree of allegorization; one cannot accept science and history and maintain that the Bible is literally true. All that is being claimed here is that philosophical investigation must also provoke a need for allegory. Why cannot one accept the God revealed in the Bible and also accept that an atemporal and simple God cannot be "person"? That is, if one accepts what science says regarding the age of the universe, then one is committed to an allegorical interpretation of the six days of creation. Likewise, one cannot read the four Gospels without accepting that a certain amount of allegorical interpretation is required to deal with the fact that they flatly contradict one another in their presentation of the history of Jesus. So, if the reader of the Bible is already prepared to read it allegorically because of scientific and historical investigation, then why should there not be a similar commitment to the allegorization of the "nature" of God based on *philosophical* investigation? Or, better, why should there not be a similar commitment to the *analogization* of God? That is, if analogy means that creatures are similar to God but God is dissimilar to creatures then, while the Bible presents God as a person, that is only analogical, which is to say, just because creatures are related to God as creator, this does not mean that God is a person who actually does something; the universe is not the object of an action of which God is the subject.

Pseudo-Dionysius cautions his reader that, as God is so transcendent of creation, "we must not dare to apply words or conceptions to this hidden and transcendent God", but rather "we can use only what scripture has disclosed".[191] Yet, Pseudo-Dionysius clarifies, this does not mean "to look at words rather than at the power of the meanings". Those who do, Pseudo-Dionysius criticizes, "do not wish to know what a particular phrase means or how to convey its sense through equivalent but more effective phrases".[192] In other words, Pseudo-Dionysius argues that one

---

[191]   Pseudo-Dionysius, *The Divine Names* 1.2.

[192]   Pseudo-Dionysius, *The Divine Names* 4.11.

can use the language of Scripture to talk about God—indeed, the language of Scripture is the *only* language we can use to speak of God—but this should not be taken as an indication that this biblical language is in any way an accurate or true description; it is simply that this is the best we have. Scriptural language is the only language that can be used of God, but this does not mean that such language is not analogical.

It is not a case of employing a certain amount of intellectual sleight-of-hand to argue that the atemporal, simple, and immutable God can also display the wild emotions and whimsy of the Old Testament God. That is the source of Plantinga's confusion that Aquinas must be wrong to hold that God can be both personal and simple. Simplicity does not mean that one forces together two views of God—the philosophical and the biblical—into one and the same "thing". Simplicity means the absence of a real relation. It means that every distinction, every attribute, every "thing", every "being" is entirely and completely *extrinsic* to God. It means that God is above all "things" and cannot be a discrete individual who is the subject of activities that have the universe—or other beings—as its object. This can truly be identical to the God revealed in the pages of the Bible and in the person of Jesus Christ, but one must be prepared to do much analogizing. One can certainly identify the God of the Bible with the God of the philosophers, but this does not mean that one has to accept that God is *both* the "ground of being" and "*a*" personal being; God transcends such a distinction.

Conclusion: "Traditional theism" and Deism

It is not important for the purposes of this book to accurately define "what" God is. Indeed, to a large extent the point is precisely that God cannot be defined at all. What is important is that it is recognized that the idea that God is a person, or "*a*" being, has significant problems and, moreover, is not what traditional/classical theology claimed to begin with. As commentators have noted, the idea that God is a person is a rather modern idea that emerged in theological currents under the influence of a particular (Kantian) philosophy.

The overriding point of this chapter, then, is to show that if one subscribes to "theistic personalism", then one is forced into emphasizing the "immanence" of God. By that is meant that it simply does not matter to what infinite degree God is different to creatures, God is still brought into the same category as creatures (or at least humans), which is then placed above God and creatures as a "third", more ontologically primary category than both God and creatures. On the other hand, if one agrees with the "traditional theists", then one is forced into emphasizing the "transcendence of God". By that is meant that God is so completely "otherly other" to creatures that nothing about God can be said with any certainty, not because God is so alien, but because God is no "thing" at all. Creatures have their being because they participate in God, who is the "ground of being" and "being itself". "Theistic personalism" posits that God is another person alongside others; "traditional theism" posits that God is not another being, but is "being itself", in which all beings participate.

There are legitimate reasons why one might want to subscribe to "theistic personalism"; conformity to the way the Bible talks about God is entirely understandable. It is difficult not to be sympathetic to a theological position that seriously attempts to remain as faithful as possible to the God revealed in the Bible. However, this picture of God does not seem "radical enough" and appears to be exactly what Feuerbach criticized. Rather, this chapter has attempted to show that the traditional position is the better theology. The crucial aspect of this theology is that God is not an individual, discrete, personal being. This leads to two important implications: (a) it shows that the "impersonal God of deism",[193] far from being incompatible with the "God of the Judeo-Christian tradition", is actually far more compatible with traditional, classical Judeo-Christian theology than is the "personally purposive God" that Polkinghorne supports;[194] and, if that is the case, then (b) it shows that God is not an individual subject who has particular desires and who "does" things to realize them, i.e., God is not the subject of any activity whose object or effect is, or is within, the universe.

---

[193] Jeffrey Koperski, *Divine Action, Determinism, and the Laws of Nature* (Abingdon: Routledge, 2020), p. 32.

[194] John Polkinghorne, *Science and Providence* (London: SPCK, 1989), p. 36.

The first implication should be apparent from what has been expounded in this chapter, the main concern of which is to show that the deist is not contrary to the Christian tradition when they point to a God who cannot be "personally involved" with the universe (whatever "personally involved" is taken to mean); they are only contrary to a small number of recent theologians who are influenced by certain modern philosophical categories. In fact, the deist, who emphasizes an "infinitely" transcendent God who cannot be "personally involved" has much more in common with traditional, classical theological categories.

Importantly, however, this does not mean that (traditional) deists (such as Isaac Newton) were *obliged* to argue in favour of an atemporal, simple, and immutable God, simply because they were less likely to be concerned about apologizing for a *personal* God. After all, as the following chapter will argue, the problem with traditional deism (such as that expounded by Newton) is that *it was expounded* in a "theistic personalist" paradigm, that is, God was seen to do something discrete and identifiable at an identifiable time (the beginning), which, at the very least violates atemporality (at a particular time) and immutability (God does something and then does not do anything). However, it should be clear that, if the deist subscribes to an impersonal deity who does not have a personal relationship with creation, then this is closer to the classical position than that of the "theistic personalist" one.

The second implication will form the subject of the next chapter, where it will be argued that creation cannot be understood as an "act" or "activity" that God "does" or "performs" but is rather a relation—a "mixed relation"—that creatures have with God. If the "*analogia entis*" position is correct, then creatures must participate in God as their creation, and if that is the case, then as much as creatures are like God because they participate in God, then God is infinitely more radically different from them. Thus, the question that this chapter leaves the reader is this: if God is not a discreet, identifiable, individual "thing" (person or otherwise), then what does this mean for divine activity? That is, if God is not a particular "thing", then how can it be understood that this "non-thing" exercises agency in realizing particular "things", including the very existence of the universe?

2

Creation

If theistic personalists are committed, however unwittingly (although most of them are quite happy to be), to applying univocal language to God—so that God is "good" in exactly the same way that humans are "good", and/or "rational" in the same way that humans are "rational" etc.—then they are also committed, again however unwittingly (although, again, most of them are quite happy to be), to applying univocal language to divine activity: God "acts" and "functions as a cause" in a univocal way to how humans act and function as causes. As Langdon Gilkey writes about biblical language: "When God was said to have 'acted', it was believed that he [sic] had performed an observable act in space and time."[1] If God is good in the same way that creatures (humans) are good, just to a far greater degree, then God is a cause in the same way that creatures are causes, just far less limited in the range of "things", "events", or "states of affairs" that God can cause.

At the risk of setting up a straw man to pull down, Joanna Leidenhag is perhaps illustrative of this approach when she says that "there is a divine creator who is an immaterial mind, who desires to create other immaterial minds for its own glory and delights in empowering this creation with its own causal powers", a position that she claims "the Judaeo-Christian tradition broadly affirms".[2] It is clear that Leidenhag treats God univocally with creatures: both are immaterial minds. Put

---

[1] Langdon Gilkey, "Cosmology, Ontology, and the Travail of Biblical Language", in Owen Thomas (ed.), *God's Activity in the World: The Contemporary Problem* (Chico, CA: Scholars Press, 1983), p. 32.

[2] Joanna Leidenhag, "God, Consciousness, and Conjunctive Explanations", *Conjunctive Explanations in Religion and Science*, forthcoming.

differently, God is a person who creates other persons. God is seen as something of a "cosmic parent" who, without the need for the "messiness" of human procreation, can "give birth" to the universe. Perhaps better, God is like a "cosmic builder" who, unconstrained by the absence of any materials with which to build something, can nevertheless construct the world completely. God constructs other persons (and other matter), not from previously existing "clay" or "dirt" but from "nothing". In this way the "nothing" of *creatio ex nihilo* becomes a material cause; nothing is the material from which God constructs, forms, or builds the universe. For the theistic personalists, God creates in precisely and exactly the same way that humans create, with the only exceptions that (a) creatures are more limited and constrained in what they can create and (b) they require previously existing materials. For the "theistic personalist", the only difference between God and a demiurge is that the latter only has the power to mould pre-existing matter, whereas the former can mould from nothing. God and the demiurge (and creatures) are not essentially different; it is only the relative range of powers that they have and the limits placed on those powers that differ. A demiurge might be limited to needing pre-existing matter to mould, but the content of the act of creation is the same for both the demiurge and God.

Philip Hefner is a perfect example of this mistake. He calls humans "created co-creators" and argues that humans contribute to and continue the creative work of God. He writes that "human beings are God's created co-creators whose purpose is to be the agency, acting in freedom, to birth the future that is most wholesome for the nature that has birthed us",[3] and, thus, "the conditioning matrix that has produced the human-being—the evolutionary process—is God's process of bringing into being a creature who represents the creation's zone of a new stage of freedom".[4] For Hefner, God is being treated univocally with creatures, or, at the very least, his argument strongly leans towards univocality. If creatures can genuinely create *for* God, then the act of creation is being used identically to describe both. If creatures can continue the creative work of God, then

---

[3]   Philip Hefner, *The Human Factor* (Minneapolis, MN: Augsburg Fortress, 1993), p. 27.

[4]   Hefner, *The Human Factor*, p. 32.

God creates in precisely the same way that creatures create; God becomes nothing more than a less-limited version of a human creator.[5] As Philip Clayton criticizes, theologians who conceive divine activity in this way are not "radical enough", and "have often continued to conceive of God as a being who stands alongside the world, which becomes a 'handiwork' he has crafted".[6]

If "theistic personalists" (and others, such as Arthur Peacocke[7]) are obliged by their particular conception of God into thinking about creation in a certain way that is univocal with human activity, then it might also be possible to show that this particular way of thinking about how God acts/creates is also shaped and influenced through conversation with science. Quite clearly, those New Atheists and Biblical Fundamentalists who vehemently argue that one cannot hold a literal biblical account of creation and science together are treating God and creatures as univocal. If science is seen as in competition with religion, so that only one or the other is correct, then quite clearly they are more or less understanding what God does as univocal with what creatures do. For the New Atheists

---

5   Austin Farrer, who argues that theology should be concerned with the "effects" of divine activity, rather than with "causes" (Austin Farrer, *Faith and Speculation* (Edinburgh: T&T Clark, 1988), p. 65), so that history and science "treats of the things God does; but not of his doing them" (p. 95) is another who would fit into this category. This leads Farrer to claim that "Christians attribute many particular actions and many particular purposes to the divine will" and so concludes that "if God acts in the world, he [sic] acts particularly" (p. 61). If God "acts particularly", then Farrer contrasts this with what he calls the "springing point of causes", and so concludes that "God's agency does not strike us in the springing point of causes but in the finished effect" (p. 63).

6   Phillip Clayton, *God and Contemporary Science* (Edinburgh: Edinburgh University Press, 1997), p. 86.

7   E.g., see Arthur Peacocke, "Articulating God's Presence in and to the World Unveiled by the Sciences", in Philip Clayton and Arthur Peacocke (eds), *In Whom We Live and Move and Have Our Being: Panentheistic Reflections on God's Presence in a Scientific World* (Grand Rapids, MI: William B. Eerdmans, 2004), pp. 137–54.

and the Biblical Fundamentalists, what it means for God to create is identical to what it means for the Big Bang and evolution to create and so they cannot both be correct.

Therefore, when theologians claim that the "conflict thesis" is incorrect, that religion and science are not in competition with one another and, moreover, can be complementary, one might think that theologians are on the right track, and are rejecting a univocal approach. However, this is not necessarily the case. Philip Hefner has already been used to show that those who engage with science constructively are not immune from treating God and creatures univocally. In fact, quite the opposite. Hefner is not conceiving of divine creation and the Big Bang/evolution any differently than are the New Atheists or Biblical Fundamentalists, he just disagrees that they are in competition. Albeit rather crudely put, Hefner (and others like him) differ from the New Atheists and Biblical Fundamentalists in positing that the Big Bang and evolution are caused by God, rather than being in opposition to the work that God does.

Other commentators have also noticed this tendency to a diminished/univocal sense of creation among those who profess to see religion and science as mutually complementary. The reason for this tendency, they argue, is that the scientific revolution led thinkers to reduce the various ways in which medieval and scholastic philosophers had understood "efficient cause" into one simple sense—the "mechanical cause". In other words, after the scientific revolution, "cause" was diminished to meaning only a "billiard-ball-type cause" or it was not a "cause". Thus, as Michael Dodds notes, "When causality was reduced in modern science to the force that moves the atoms, it seemed to many theologians that, if God were to act in the world, he [sic] would have to act as a force. He would have to move some atoms around."[8] After the scientific revolution, God

---

[8]   Michael Dodds, "Science, Causality, and God: Divine Action and Thomas Aquinas", *Angelicum* 91:1 (2014), p. 22; see also David Bentley Hart, *The Experience of God: Being, Consciousness, Bliss* (London: Yale University Press, 2013), pp. 55–7, W. Norris Clarke, *The Philosophical Approach to God: A New Thomistic Perspective* (New York, NY: Fordham University Press, 2007), p. 63; Edward Feser, *Scholastic Metaphysics: A Contemporary Introduction* (Heusenstamm: editiones scholasticae, 2014), p. 97.

had to be reduced to a "pusher of atoms" because that was the only way that God could function as a "cause" in the new scientific paradigm. Thus, if theologians want to be seen as complementing science, as facilitating a conversation and mutual influence between science and religion, God has to be brought into the paradigm of the scientific revolution, and so be reduced to a mere "pusher of atoms". It is not too hard to see why it was exactly this philosophical environment that saw thinkers postulate a facile deism in which God was reduced to nothing more than pushing the *first* atom or lighting the blue touch paper. God was no longer needed to push other atoms; God was only needed to get the process of atom-pushing going. Once the philosophical paradigm in which you do theology is reduced to such an extent, it is no wonder that theologians like Hefner cannot conceive of God being creator in any way other than as a "co-creator".

In other words, precisely because science, and the philosophical framework in which the modern scientific revolution occurred, drastically reduces the sense in which causality is understood, so the assumption that science and religion are compatible seems to oblige that God is subsumed within this reduced sense of causality. For theologians who pride themselves on conversation with science, this leads to the claim that the act of creation is reduced to and identified with the processes of nature. That is, when theologians (such as John Haught and John Polkinghorne) suppose that evolution helps to elucidate what is meant by creation, they conceive of creation as concerned with the material construction of the world. Far from elucidating what theologians mean by creation, the scientific paradigm is doing nothing but distorting and impoverishing the very rich and nuanced theologies of creation that the medieval and scholastic theologians passed on.

In this way, the conclusion reached in the previous chapter is pertinent. If God is truly beyond the distinction between "being" and "non-being", and between "person" and "non-person", so that God transcends the distinction between "being-itself" and "*id quod est*", then the suggestion that both theology and science can coherently discuss God is to bring God down to the level of creatures. The previous chapter, therefore, adds another dimension to the discussion in the introduction; the "engagement thesis" makes the same mistakes as the "opposition thesis".

The "separation thesis" remains the only option that takes seriously the transcendence of God.

This does not reject science as being incorrect. Far from it. The introduction to this book did nothing if it did not claim that science should be seen as an authority to be taken seriously, without seeking to censor what science says because of a need to include God in one's worldview. Rather, as the introduction concluded, NOMA should be taken as the correct way to understand science's relationship with religion. If creation cannot be understood as complementing what science says about the Big Bang and evolution—because doing so leads to nothing more than the diminished/univocal God of theistic personalism—then this chapter will show that there is a much larger theological tradition that explicitly understands creation as being entirely separate from this, having nothing whatsoever to do with the beginning of the universe and its subsequent history. Creation (and, indeed, all divine activity) is not an "act" that God "does" (after all, God is not "the kind of reality who can *literally do* anything at all"[9]) but is a relationship that creatures have with God. This chapter is nothing more than an exposition of how it can be the case that "God's creative action *just is* creation's dependence on God for its existence".[10]

Creation and essentially ordered series

While the popular conception of creation assumes that it is an *event*—something that God does—traditional theologians understand it as a *relationship*.

In order to see what this means, it is necessary first to point to a common distinction for scholastic theology. In his essay "Notes for the

---

[9]   Frank Kirkpatrick, *The Mystery and Agency of God: Divine Being and Action in the World* (Minneapolis, MN: Fortress Press, 2014), p. 1; "The Parmenidean 'being' neither sees, nor hears, nor thinks, nor acts" (John Passmore, *The Perfectibility of Man* (London: Duckworth, 1970), p. 33).

[10]   John Bishop and Ken Perszyk, "The Divine Attributes and Non-personal Conceptions of God", *Topoi* 36 (2017), p. 614 (italics in original).

History of Efficient Causality", noted Thomist scholar Étienne Gilson argues that scholastic theologians and philosophers were careful to distinguish between a "cause of being" and a "cause of motion". Crucially, these two types of "causes" produced two different types of "effects". Gilson continues that so many of the most important scholastic theologians and philosophers distinguished sharply between "two types of causality corresponding to two different types of effect produced": (a) the effect which is "a change properly speaking, that is to say, a change of state" and (b) "the [effect] whose result is the very being of the effect produced".[11] Thomas Aquinas also gave expression to such a distinction when he wrote that "*creatio non est mutatio*"[12] (or, "*creatio non est [generatio]*"[13]). Thus, *creatio* is concerned with being and *mutatio* (*generatio*) is concerned with motion, that is, with a change in state.

The crucial question then becomes "whether the cause that makes ['things'] move is the same as that which makes ['things'] exist",[14] or whether, instead, "perhaps two radically different types of causality are forced into one and the same species".[15] Gilson answers that "the motor cause belongs to the order of the physical . . . while the cause productive of being belongs to metaphysics and perhaps even to theology".[16] Others also recognize this clear delineation. David Bentley Hart, for example, sharply distinguishes between the four Aristotelian causes and "yet another kind of causality . . . exorbitantly different from them . . . [that] we might call 'ontological' cause".[17] Mariusz Tabaczek also writes, "While science deals with changes and their causes, a theological account of creation deals with the metaphysical dependence of all creatures on

---

[11]   Étienne Gilson, *Medieval Essays* (Eugene, OR: Cascade Books, 2011), p. 156.

[12]   *ST* 1, 45, 2.

[13]   "Thomas conceived of the Aristotelian *generatio* as *mutatio* (change) that could not be identified with *creatio*" (Andrzej Maryniarczyk, "Philosophical Creationism: Thomas Aquinas' Metaphysics of *Creatio ex Nihilo*", *Studia Gilsoniana* 5:1 (2016), p. 238).

[14]   Gilson, *Medieval Essays*, p. 165.

[15]   Gilson, *Medieval Essays*, p. 160.

[16]   Gilson, *Medieval Essays*, p. 160.

[17]   Hart, *The Experience of God*, p. 55.

God at every moment of their existence".[18] Already, the discussion on the relationship between science and religion—and the support for NOMA—in the introduction is central here.

In this way, it is possible to distinguish between "change"/ "cause of motion"—which is the description of causality in the universe, what David Bentley Hart describes as "transitions of energy, movements of mass, [and/or] acts of generation or destruction"[19]—and "creation"/ "cause of being"—which is concerned with the ontological dependency of the universe on God. Thus, if the latter is exclusively the prerogative of God—creatures cannot create—then the former is the prerogative of creatures—only creatures can change and cause change in others. The analogy of being is important here. If God cannot be a "being", or a "person", or "temporal", because to do so would set up "being", "personhood", or "time" as a third category that existed alongside both creatures and God which is more ontologically primary than both, then neither can "causality" be a category that describes—and so "contains"— both created/natural and divine activity. Andrew Davison is clear on this. He writes that "there is no prior category of causation in which God and creatures both share".[20] If "being" is not a "third thing" alongside God and creatures and in which God and creatures both participate, then neither is "causality". Just as much as there is no univocality of *being*, so there is no univocality of *causality*. Paraphrasing Gregory Palamas, if God cannot be "nature" "if every other thing is nature", and God cannot be "*a*" being "if all other things are beings",[21] then God cannot "act" if all other

---

[18]   Mariusz Tabaczek, "Thomistic Response to the Theory of Evolution: Aquinas on Natural Selection and the Perfection of the Universe", *Theology and Science* 13:3 (2015), p. 332.

[19]   Hart, *The Experience of God*, p. 103; remember that "Thomas [Aquinas] conceived of the Aristotelian *generatio* as *mutatio* (change) that could not be identified with *creatio*" (Maryniarczyk, "Philosophical Creationism", p. 238) so the generation and destruction of anything is a change, not a creation.

[20]   Davison, Andrew, *Participation in God* (Cambridge: Cambridge University Press, 2019), p. 44.

[21]   Gregory Palamas (tr. Robert Sinkewicz), *One Hundred and Fifty Chapters* (Toronto: Pontifical Institute of Mediaeval Studies, 1988), p. 78.

things "act". Or, more specifically, God cannot act as a "cause of motion" if all other things act as a "cause of motion". As Andrzej Maryniarczyk evidences, "Thomas shows that every agent acts in a way corresponding to how it actually exists and by what it actually exists" so that there is a "suitability of action to the agent".[22] It is not suitable for creatures to be a "cause of being", and it is not suitable for God to be a "cause of motion".

Furthermore, if the two distinct types of "cause" are distinguished because they correspond to two distinct types of "effect", then these two "causes" must cause two entirely different "effects". That is, if the "effects" of the "cause of motion" are "events"—specific, discrete, identifiable "things" that happen in space and time—then the "effect" of the "cause of being" must be entirely and completely different. As many recognize, the effect of the cause of being is more like a relationship. David Bentley Hart writes:

> The question of creation has never simply concerned some event that may have happened "back then", at the beginning of time, or some change between distinct physical states . . . but has always concerned the *eternal relation* between logical possibility and logical necessity, the contingent and the absolute, the conditioned and the unconditioned.[23]

Paul Tillich writes, "The formula *creatio ex nihilo* is not the title of a story . . . [but] is the classical formula which expresses the *relation* between God and the world."[24] William Stoeger writes that "creation is not a temporal event, but a relationship—a relationship of ultimate dependence. Thus 'cause' as applied to God should be conceived not as a physical force or an interaction, as it is in physics, but rather in terms of a relationship".[25]

---

22 Maryniarczyk, "Philosophical Creationism", p. 254.

23 Hart, *The Experience of God*, p. 304 (italics added).

24 Paul Tillich, *Systematic Theology Vol. 1* (Chicago, IL: The University of Chicago Press, 1957), p. 254 (italics added).

25 William Stoeger, "God, Physics, and the Big Bang", in Peter Harrison (ed.), *The Cambridge Companion to Science and Religion* (Cambridge: Cambridge University Press, 2010), p. 181.

Stephen Baldner and William Carroll write that, for Aquinas, creation is "an ontological relationship—a relationship in the order of being—with no reference to temporality",[26] and that "creation is the investigation of the dependence of all that is on God. In the language of metaphysics, creation is a dependence in the order of being".[27] It is important here that Balder and Carroll refer to the "order of being". Creation is not something that concerns "motion", but is something that concerns "being".

Thomas Aquinas is himself even more explicit. He writes that "God by creation produces things *without movement*. Now when movement is removed from action and passion, only *relation* remains ... Hence creation in the creature is only a *certain relation* to the Creator as to the *principle of its being*".[28] Thomas Aquinas also calls this "certain relation" "participation". That is, when *creatio* is described as "relationship", this does not mean a sort of mutual, reciprocal social relationship, but the participation of one in the other. Likewise, by participation is not meant something like "taking part" in God's act of creation in the sense that Philip Hefner might have meant it.[29] Thus, participation does not mean that creatures *share* God's being, which Holmes Rolston III claims "has the Old English and Germanic root *sker*, to cut into parts"[30] and would mean that God and creatures are in a "zero-sum" game. Rather, participation is the derivation of being from God, in the sense of an "unequal relationship between what is essential and what is derivative" so that God has being "essentially, [and] we have it derivatively and by

---

[26]   Steven Baldner and William Carroll (tr.), *Aquinas on Creation* (Toronto: Pontifical Institute of Mediaeval Studies, 1997), p. 16.

[27]   Baldner and Carrol, *Aquinas on Creation*, p. 4.

[28]   *ST* i, 45, iii (italics added).

[29]   See also Charles Birch, "Participatory Evolution: The Drive of Creation", *Journal of the American Academy of Religion* 40:2 (1972), pp. 147–63; Nicola Hoggard Creegan, "A Christian Theology of Evolution and Participation", *Zygon: Journal of Religion and Science* 42:2 (2007), pp. 499–518.

[30]   Holmes Rolston III, "*Kenosis* and Nature", in John Polkinghorne (ed.), *The Work of Love: Creation as Kenosis* (Cambridge, MA: William B. Eerdmans, 2001), p. 48.

participation".[31] In other words, creatures "do not have an existence of our own apart from our participation in God".[32]

It is undeniable that this sense of "participation" is one of the central elements of Thomas Aquinas' theology. Gavin Kerr writes that "on the basis of a Thomistic metaphysics, the creator–creature relationship is one best thought of in terms of participation".[33] In fact, it is accurate to suggest that Thomas Aquinas does not have a doctrine of creation that is not participation. Thus, in *Summa Contra Gentiles*, Aquinas writes that God "is the cause of all that is by participation, as fire is the cause of all things fiery, as such", so that, while God is "pure being", "every other being is being by participation, because there can only be one being that is its own existence. God therefore is *cause of being* to all other beings",[34] which are "a sort of participation by likeness of His being".[35] In *Summa Theologiae*, Aquinas continues this idea. He writes:

> Therefore all beings apart from God are not their own being, but are beings by participation. Therefore it must be that all things which are diversified by the diverse participation of being, so as to be more or less perfect, are caused by one First Being, Who possesses being most perfectly.[36]

Participation is what it means to be a creature. To be created is to participate in God.

There are two important implications of this claim that if the "effects" of the "cause of motion" are "events" then the "effect" of the "cause of being" is "participation". First, although Thomas Aquinas did

---

[31] Daniel Keating, *Deification and Grace* (Naples, FL: Sapientia Press, 2007), p. 99.

[32] Keating, *Deification and Grace*, p. 97.

[33] Gavin Kerr, "A Thomistic Metaphysics of Creation", *Religious Studies* 48 (2012), p. 337, pp. 349–51.

[34] Thomas Aquinas, *Summa Contra Gentiles* (London: Burns & Oates, 2005); ii, 15, iv (italics added).

[35] *SCG*; i, 75, iii.

[36] *ST* i, 44, i.

not explicitly acknowledge it as such, "imitation" can also be used as a synonym for "participation". Torstein Theodor Tollefsen writes that "the logic [of participation and imitation] is the same" so that imitation of Christ is "just another way to express the central idea of participation. To imitate God is to participate in God".[37] Analogy of being fits here as well, as outlined in the previous chapter, and so "analogy, imitation, and participation thus form a continuum rather than express radically different kinds of relationship".[38] Thus, participation points to the absence of a real relation: creatures are like God, but God is nothing like creatures; or, creatures imitate God, but God does not imitate creatures.

Second, and crucially, to say that creation is a relationship means exactly that the "act" of creation *is* that relationship; God does not create *in order to have* a relationship—a relationship that can be frustrated and then fulfilled or perfected in Christ. That is, God does not create "in order to communicate *self* and that creation exists in order to be the recipient of God's free gift of self",[39] as if "creation" and "relationship" are temporally distinct, with the former facilitating the latter. Rather, quite simply, "God's creative action *just is* creation's dependence on God for its existence".[40] The relationship that is participation *just is* creation; God does not create so that creatures can receive relationship and participate in God. It is for this reason that Andrew Davison has criticized the language of "creation as a gift". He notes that while it is quite easy to use "receive" in the present tense, so that the "creature *receives* its being from God", this sense can "easily fall into the past" and so "shift" to "the creature *received* its being from God", which becomes the meaning of "something that happened

[37] Torstein Theodor Tollefsen, *Activity and Participation in Late Antique and Early Christian Thought* (Oxford: Oxford University Press, 2012), p. 163.

[38] Norman Russell, *The Doctrine of Deification in the Greek Patristic Tradition* (Oxford: Oxford University Press, 2004), p. 2; Lewis Ayres, *Nicaea and its Legacy: An Approach to Fourth-Century Trinitarian Theology* (Oxford, Oxford University Press, 2004), pp. 321ff.

[39] Harvey Egan, quoted in Denis Edwards, *Deep Incarnation: God's Redemptive Suffering with Creatures* (Maryknoll, NY: Orbis Books, 2019), p. 91.

[40] Bishop and Perszyk, "The Divine Attributes and Non-personal Conceptions of God", p. 614.

once, in the past". Yet, he continues, "that shift is less endemic to the language of participation" and so "the verb 'to participate' lives happily in the present continuous".[41] "Being" is not something that creatures are "given"; it is something for which they require participation.

Participation and essentially ordered series

The distinction between "gift"—which describes something that is given to creatures in the past and after which creatures continue to possess independently of God—and "participation"—for which there is a constant dependence and never an independence—is an extremely important distinction to make and lies at the very heart of the distinction between "cause of motion"/"change" and "cause of being"/"creation". The giving of gifts is an event; participation is a relationship. One is appropriate for creatures; the other is appropriate for God. One is described by science, the "movement of atoms", and history; the other is described by theology and metaphysics. That distinction is further underpinned by—following Palamas—maintaining that if one is activity and causality, then the other is not.

However, there is a further distinction that can accurately describe the difference between these two types of causality and two types of effect produced that is often absent from theological discussions on creation: the distinction between an accidentally ordered series and an essentially ordered series, or, between causes *per accidens* and causes *per se*. In *Ordinatio*, John Duns Scotus gives three distinctions between essentially ordered and accidentally ordered causes:

a. accidentally ordered causes temporally precede their effects, whereas essentially ordered causes are temporally simultaneous with their effects;

b. accidentally ordered causes are ontologically identical to their effects, whereas essentially ordered causes are ontologically superior (or ontologically prior) to their effects; and

---

41   Davison, *Participation in God*, p. 35.

c. accidentally ordered effects are independent of their causes, whereas essentially ordered effects are entirely dependent upon their causes.[42]

The classic examples of these two distinct causes are, on the one hand, the relationship between mother and daughter and, on the other hand, the relationship between flame and oxygen. In the first example, the mother is related to her daughter in an accidentally ordered series. The mother must temporally precede the daughter and, crucially, the daughter's existence is subsequently independent of the mother; that is, she can continue to exist and be a cause herself even after her mother dies. As a result, the mother and daughter are ontologically equal; one is not ontologically "better" or "more perfect" or "more necessary" than the other. A builder constructing a house is a similar example: the builder temporally precedes the house that they build, which can continue to exist (and function as a house) independently of the builder. (It is pertinent that these are also the examples used in the introduction to this chapter to describe theistic personalists' univocal sense of how God creates.)

The classic example of essentially ordered causes is the relationship between the flame of a candle and the oxygen on which it depends. The oxygen does not temporally precede the flame as a cause but is simultaneous with it. When the oxygen starts being a cause, the flame is produced, and when the oxygen stops being a cause, the flame is extinguished immediately. The flame is entirely dependent on the oxygen for its existence. Without oxygen, the flame cannot exist. Thomas Aquinas' example of the sun and light is also an example of essentially ordered causality. The sun is the cause *per se* of the light; without the sun, the light would cease to exist immediately. One could also point to the relationship between a hand and a stick or pen; without the hand, the stick or pen could not function as a cause. Peter Geach uses the

---

[42]   John Duns Scotus, *Ordinatio*, in Allan Wolter (tr.), *Philosophical Writings* (Edinburgh: Thomas Nelson and Sons, 1962), I, d2, q1; see also John Duns Scotus (tr. Evan Roche), *De Primo Principio* (St. Bonaventure, NY: The Franciscan Institute, 1949), c.3, 2.

image of a musician. A musician does not make music out of "pre-existing sounds, and the music stops if he stops making it". That is, the sound is only sustained so long as the musician is acting as a cause.[43] (Although the sounds have a beginning and end that is caused by the musician, nevertheless, the point is well made.)

One might characterize them as the difference between, on the one hand, a series of spatiotemporal events related to one another like pearls strung together on a spatiotemporal string tied together by mechanical "billiard-ball-type" causality and, on the other, a series of hierarchical relations in which the being, existence, and power of one is entirely dependent on the other, tied together through participation/imitation. Thus, whereas an accidentally ordered series describes a series of "events" or "acts", that are related through spatiotemporal mechanical causality, an essentially ordered series is a series of hierarchical relationships or participations.

Crucially, there is a correlation between "cause of being" and cause *per se* on the one hand, and between "cause of motion" and cause *per accidens* on the other. David Bentley Hart, for example, explicitly identifies "causes *per accidens*" (or "accidentally ordered" series) with "transitions of energy, movements of mass, acts of generation or destruction"[44] and "cause *per se*" (or "essentially ordered" series) with "donation of being", which follows that scholastic distinction, already acknowledged above, that *mutatio*—i.e., the efficient cause of motion, that which is "a change of state"—"belongs to the order of the physical", and *creatio*—i.e., the efficient cause of being, that "whose result is the very being"—is concerned with "metaphysics" or "theology".[45] Celia Byrne writes that for Ibn Sina (Avicenna), the "cause of existence"—efficient cause of being—is essentially ordered, while "cause of coming to be"—efficient cause of

---

[43]   G. E. M. Anscombe and Peter Geach, *Three Philosophers* (Ithaca, NY: Cornell University Press, 1976), p. 110; see also Frederick Bauerschmidt, *Thomas Aquinas: Faith, Reason, and Following Christ* (Oxford: Oxford University Press, 2013), p. 112.

[44]   Hart, *The Experience of God*, p. 103.

[45]   Gilson, *Medieval Essays*, p. 160.

origination/motion—is accidentally ordered.[46] In this way, causes *per accidens* are described by history and science, and are "more or less, what is usually meant by 'cause' in contemporary philosophy".[47] On the other hand, causes *per se* are described by metaphysics.

Such a sharp distinction can be even further sharpened by the fact that some philosophers doubt whether there can actually be *any genuine* essentially ordered causes in nature.[48] Even though the relationships between flame/oxygen, light/sun, and hand/pen are used to illustrate what is meant by essentially ordered causes, there is a sense in which the oxygen, the sun, and the hand must *temporally precede* the flame, the light, and the pen, even if it is only a negligible temporal priority. Given the modern scientific paradigm, one might quite correctly maintain that the flame is kept alight, not because the oxygen is temporally simultaneous with it, but because the oxygen is transferring energy through a billiard-ball-like "movement of atoms". In this sense—drawing on Holmes Rolston III's example of "share"—strictly speaking, the flame "shares" the oxygen so that there is a zero-sum relationship—the longer the flame lasts, the more oxygen it "shares" and so the less oxygen there is. In other words, even those examples which are so often used to describe an essentially ordered cause are actually concerned with "transitions of energy, movements of mass, [and/or] acts of generation or destruction"[49] and so are more accurately examples of accidentally ordered series.

---

[46] Celia Byrne, "The Role of Essentially Ordered Causal Series in Avicenna's Proof for the Necessary Existent in the Metaphysics of the Salvation", *History of Philosophy Quarterly* 36:2 (2019), p. 135, n. 17; see also Mariusz Tabaczek, "What Do God and Creatures Really Do in an Evolutionary Change? Causal Analysis of Biological Transformism from the Thomistic Perspective", *American Catholic Philosophical Quarterly* 93:3 (2019), pp. 14–15.

[47] Feser, *Scholastic Metaphysics*, p. 97.

[48] See Timothy O'Connor, "Scotus on the Existence of a First Efficient Cause", *International Journal for Philosophy of Religion* 33:1 (1993), pp. 22–3; see also Juan Carlos Flores, "Accidental and Essential Causality in John Duns Scotus' Treatise 'On the First Principle'", *Recherches de théologie et philosophie médiévales* 67:1 (2000), pp. 96–113.

[49] Hart, *The Experience of God*, p. 103.

For Richard Swinburne, this observation that even the examples that describe essentially ordered causes turn out to be accidentally ordered means that the distinction itself is false; he therefore dismisses the very idea of essentially ordered causes as logically or philosophically absurd on the basis that there can be no such thing as temporally simultaneous cause and effect.[50] For Swinburne, however minuscule the interval between cause and effect, the cause *must* temporally precede the effect. It is pertinent that Swinburne denies divine atemporality,[51] and he is no doubt influenced by this rejection into also rejecting the notion that there could be simultaneous causality between God and the universe. However, while Swinburne might be correct that there are no genuine essentially ordered causes *in nature*, this need not necessarily lead to the conclusion that the idea of essentially ordered causality itself is philosophically incoherent; it may be the case that the failure to find evidence of essentially ordered causality in nature could be read as support for the absolute, sharp distinction that creation is entirely distinct from created/natural causality. Thus, it would seem, so sharp and absolute is the distinction between these two types of causality and two types of effect, that a suitable illustration of an essentially ordered series can only be the participation of creatures in God that is creation. Accidentally ordered causes are appropriate to created causes and essentially ordered causes are appropriate to God, and "there is no prior category of causation in which both ... share."[52]

Accidentally ordered, essentially ordered, and instrumental causes
The failure to find any genuine essentially ordered causes in nature leads to a further distinction that is important to recognize at this point: the

---

[50] Richard Swinburne, "Causation, Time, and God's Omniscience", *Topoi* 36 (2017), pp. 677–8; see also William Lane Craig, "Creation and Conservation Once More", *Religious Studies* 34:2 (1998), pp. 177–88.

[51] See Richard Swinburne, *The Coherence of Theism* (Oxford: Clarendon Press, 1993), pp. 234ff.; William Lane Craig, "Divine Timelessness and Personhood", *International Journal for Philosophy of Religion* 43:2 (1998), pp. 109–24.

[52] Davison, *Participation in God*, p. 44.

relevance of what could be termed "instrumental" causes, which seem to function as something in between essentially ordered and accidentally ordered causes. To use the example of the hand, stick, and stone, the hand does not act as a "cause of being" on the stick, which then acts as a "cause of motion" on the stone. Rather, the stick is used as an instrument for the hand to act as a "cause of motion" on the stone. The intention is not to give the stick the power to act as a "cause of motion" but to use the stick to achieve the hand's own ends.

One must be cautious here. Distinguishing between "secondary causes" and "instrumental causes", Tabaczek writes that some secondary causes "act according to their natural dispositions, while others produce effects beyond their capacities".[53] The hand does not constrain the movement of the pen as if the pen were wildly making marks indiscriminately across the page and the hand gives order to those marks. The pen is thus an "instrumental cause" because the hand causes the pen to "produce effects beyond [its] capacities". A secondary cause—one which acts as a cause of motion freely (e.g., a human)—is different from an instrumental cause—one which is only used as an instrument in an accidentally ordered series. The first is one who receives *being* from the primary cause; the second is one who receives *motion* from *another* secondary cause.

In a discussion of Duns Scotus' theology of causation, divine agency and primary causation, Richard Cross writes that "God is the *primary* cause; the created causes that act concurrently with God are *secondary* causes" and the relationship between them, as has already been established, is as "between the first member of an E-series and any subsequent member", that is, an essentially ordered series.[54] Scotus draws a further distinction between "secondary causes"—which "have intrinsic causal powers"—and "instrumental causes"—which "do not have causal powers; or, if they do, these powers are caused by a principal agent, and endure only for as long as the principal agent uses its instrument".[55] Cross continues that, for Scotus:

[53]   Tabaczek, "What Do God and Creatures Really Do in an Evolutionary Change?", p. 6.

[54]   Richard Cross, *Duns Scotus* (Oxford: Oxford University Press, 1999), p. 56.

[55]   Cross, *Duns Scotus*, p. 56; see John Duns Scotus, *Ordinatio* 4.1.1., nn. 26–7.

[A] secondary cause is activated by the activation of its causal powers. That its causal powers function when they do is presumably the result of the causal activity of the primary cause. But a secondary cause—unlike an instrument—is a cause in the sense that the effect caused by its causal powers is not caused by the higher cause.[56]

While both "secondary causes" and "instrumental causes" are essentially ordered to the "primary cause" (God), an "instrumental cause" differs from a "secondary cause" in that its motion is exercised and constrained by the intention of the "primary cause"—like a hand and a pen. A "secondary cause" can only function as a cause because it participates in the causal power of the "primary cause", but whether and in what way that causal power is exercised is not constrained in any way by the "primary cause". Yet, an "instrumental cause" can only function as a cause because it is moved to do so by another cause. For example, the pen has the power to write because it participates in the power of the hand, *which also* forces and constrains it to write something specific, but the person writing, while they have the power to cause the pen to write because they, in turn, participate in the power of God, is not being forced and constrained to write by God. One might put it differently: a "secondary cause" is only in an essentially ordered series to the "primary cause", but an "instrumental cause" is in both an essentially ordered series *and* an accidentally ordered series. This does not mean that a "secondary cause" does not have a prior accidental cause—a person still has a parent who gives birth to them—but that prior accidental cause is not constrained by God.[57]

---

[56]   Cross, *Duns Scotus*, p. 56.

[57]   Perhaps a good example of the "instrumental cause" is the fact that Thomas Aquinas describes Christ's human nature as an "instrument" of God. Aaron Riches writes that "the [Thomist] language of *instrumentum divinitatis* carefully signifies the absolute *unio* of operation of divinity and humanity in the incarnate son by stipulating that the integral human nature only 'acts' insofar as it acts as 'one' with the divine logos" (Aaron Riches, *Ecce Homo* (Grand Rapids, MI: William B. Eerdmans, 2016), p. 182) so that "[Christ's] divine operation uses his human operation, and his human operation

Perhaps this only adds further support to O'Connor and Swinburne's claims that there are no *genuine* essentially ordered causes in nature. Even those that appear to be causes *per se* are not truly such. The fact that the relationship between flame and oxygen can so easily be recast as that between one giving energy to the other in an accidentally ordered series only serves to evidence that perhaps the idea of "instrumental causation" is muddying what is a simple distinction. Likewise, the example of the hand and the stick or pen can quite easily be recast in terms of one "using"

---

participates in the power of the divine operation" (Riches, *Ecce Homo*, p. 184; see *ST* 3, 19, 1). Richard Cross advises caution and so suggests that one must take care with these issues. He acknowledges that Thomas Aquinas held that Christ's human nature was an "instrument" of God (Richard Cross, *The Metaphysics of the Incarnation* (Oxford: Oxford University Press, 2002), p. 220), but qualifies this, writing that "on Aquinas's usual account of instrumental causality, instruments do not have intrinsic causal powers at all: their causal activity is caused in them in virtue of the causal powers of the primary agent" (p. 221). Tabaczek and Cross have been quoted making the same comments above (although, interestingly—given that Scotus is used to support this definition of instrumental cause—Cross notes that Scotus does think that Christ's human nature is an instrument (pp. 221–2)). Thus, here Cross continues that "perhaps Aquinas is trying to spell out some sort of causal co-operation according to which the human nature never acts in any sense independently of the divine nature" (p. 221). Yet, regardless of the fact that the use of the language of "instrument" might need care and qualification, "the less we think of the human nature as an instrument, the harder it will be for Aquinas to explain how Christ's human actions are actions of the Word" (p. 221). Certainly, the human nature has causal powers in the same way that all humans have causal powers—through participation in God—but not only is Christ's human nature causally potent through participation, the particular things that Christ does are also constrained by God. Thus, one can see the difference between Christ and other humans as illustrating the difference between secondary and instrumental causes: all humans are secondary causes—they participate in God's causal power but are not constrained by God—whereas Jesus is an instrumental cause—he participates in God's causal power *and* is constrained by God.

the other to extend an accidentally ordered series: the hand is not giving the stick the power to act as a cause, but is moving the stone. Clearly, both of these examples are concerned with "motion", not "being". Here, then, is the crux of the issue. As useful as the distinction between accidentally ordered and essentially ordered causes is for distinguishing between *mutatio* and *creatio*, the real distinction is between the latter, not the former. If some of the illustrations tend to blur the distinction between accidentally ordered and essentially ordered series, they absolutely do not blur the distinction between *mutatio* and *creatio*. Whatever else might be said, the oxygen does not *create* the flame, neither does the hand *create* the pen.

That is, drawing on Gilson's question of "whether the cause that makes ['things'] move is the same as that which makes ['things'] exist",[58] or whether one is making the mistake of "forcing two radically different types of causality into one and the same species",[59] the essentially ordered "cause of being" *cannot constrain* the "motion" of that to which it gives 'being'. An "instrumental cause" might be essentially ordered but it is concerned with "motion", not "being", and so it is described by science, not theology. Causes of "being" (*creatio*) cannot constrain how or whether things "move" or change (*mutatio*). To say that the cause of *being* can constrain how or whether things move is to do exactly what those scholastic theologians warned against: it is to confuse two entirely different types of cause.

Simon Kittle appears to agree with this claim when he criticizes proponents of a "primary/secondary causality" approach for making a "special pleading". By this, Kittle means that proponents of a "primary/secondary causality" approach claim on the one hand that certain implications of that primary/secondary distinction are denied—e.g., that God can be considered a "cause among other causes"—but other implications are affirmed—e.g., that God can exert "control" over the universe and guide and influence other causes—without any seeming

---

[58]   Gilson, *Medieval Essays*, p. 165.

[59]   Gilson, *Medieval Essays*, p. 160.

consistency and therefore leading to a contradiction.[60] This, Kittle concludes, leaves two options. One could affirm something like the following: that (using the example of a storm) "God will be intimately involved in that storm inasmuch as God's primary causation will be upholding all the water molecules, the forces of the wind, and so on. But God would not have control over *whether or not* the storm occurs".[61] (That is, God is the "cause of being" of everything, but has no control of whether anything acts as a "cause of motion" or how it acts as a "cause of motion".) Or, one could claim that God must be considered a "cause among other causes" in some way. Kittle takes the second option (and is likewise taken by "theistic personalists"); this book takes the first option.

Richard Grigg also criticizes what Kittle has called the "primary/secondary causality" approach. He writes that:

> If the assertion that God acts through secondary causes is to be more than merely a poetic flourish, if it is meant to suggest that there really is a God who makes things happen in the physical universe that would not have happened without divine action, then God must add something to or change the direction of the natural, or secondary, causal processes of the world.[62]

Sarah Lane Ritchie makes the same observations. She writes that "if God . . . has specific purposes to be enacted in the natural world, then at some point the divine will must meet physical processes",[63] and so "at some point, the transcendent, immaterial God would have to actually

---

[60]   Simon Kittle, "God is (Probably) a Cause among Causes: Why the Primary/Secondary Cause Distinction Doesn't Help in Developing Noninterventionist Accounts of Special Divine Action", *Theology and Science* 20:2 (2022), pp. 255–6.

[61]   Kittle, "God is (Probably) a Cause among Causes", p. 258.

[62]   Richard Grigg, "Religion, Science, and Evolution: Paul Tillich's Fourth Way", *Zygon: Journal of Religion and Science* 38 (2003), p. 944.

[63]   Sarah Lane Ritchie, "Dancing around the Causal Joint: Challenging the Theological Turn in Divine Action Theories", *Zygon: Journal of Religion and Science* 52:2 (2017), p. 370.

interact with the brute, physical mechanisms explicated by contemporary science".[64] In other words, it is all very well to maintain that God is concerned with "being" and creatures concerned with "motion", and that the latter participates in the former for its ability to function as a "cause", but as soon as one claims that God can influence the latter *precisely because* it participates in God, then problems occur.

Whatever might be the case here, whatever the correct definition of "instrumental causes" is, whether there are any genuine examples of true causes *per se* in nature, the important thing to note is that there is a correlation, one the one hand, between cause *per se*, *creatio*, and cause of being, and, on the other hand, between cause *per accidens*, *mutatio/generatio*, and cause of motion. *Creatio* gives *mutatio* being and the power to be *mutatio*, but it cannot constrain the particular movement of that *mutatio*. As Rowan Williams puts it, "What infinite agency causes simply is the system of secondary causality";[65] God does not then act as another cause within that system of secondary causality. That is, an essentially ordered series holds an accidentally ordered series in being, but it does not constrain how an accidentally ordered series moves, because "being" and "motion" are entirely mutually exclusive.

Creation, essentially ordered series, and time

Atemporality is incredibly important for further distinguishing these two causes and the effects they produce. Indeed, the classic definitions of accidentally ordered and essentially ordered series include references to time.

Before a consideration of the (a)temporal implications of distinguishing so sharply and absolutely between "cause of being" and "cause of motion", a few comments are necessary to illustrate that philosophers have found the notion of an atemporal agent incoherent. Thaddeus Metz, for example, writes that an atemporal being "appears unable to engage in goal-directed activity. Specifically, the problem is that activities are events, and events seem fundamentally to involve change

---

[64]   Ritchie, "Dancing around the Causal Joint", p. 377.

[65]   Rowan Williams, *Christ the Heart of Creation* (London: Bloomsbury Continuum, 2018), p. 5.

and time".[66] Arjan Markus agrees that a "timeless being would allegedly be unable to act", because "act has a beginning and an end, and thus it has both temporal location and duration and, therefore, temporal extension . . . temporal order and succession".[67] Nelson Pike, too, argues that a "timeless individual could not produce, create, or bring about an object, circumstance or state of affairs",[68] for an identical reason: it would temporally locate God. If God is atemporal then God cannot be an agent. Lucas and Plantinga were noted in the last chapter making the same observations, and moved from this to argue that God cannot be atemporal. Others agree. However, if, as was put forward in the previous chapter, the opposite conclusion is reached—that this means that God cannot *act*—then how is this to be understood? The answer is that while God certainly causes those events to "be", God cannot be responsible for the motion and/or change that those events go through. As Ignacio Silva writes, "God causes changes to be the changes that they are, but such divine causing is not itself a change."[69] *Creatio* is not an "act"/"event"; *creatio* is a hierarchical, ontological relationship called participation that "grounds" those changes in "being".

To put this into the language of accidentally ordered and essentially ordered series, if God is genuinely atemporal, then God cannot possibly act as a cause *per accidens* or cannot initiate an accidentally ordered series. Causes *per accidens* are necessarily temporal. They are concerned with temporal priority and temporal succession; they necessarily have beginnings and endings—times before they are causing and times after

66 Thaddeus Metz, "Could God's Purpose Be the Source of Life's Meaning?", *Religious Studies* 36:3 (2000), p. 309; see also William Lane Craig, "Timelessness, Creation, and God's Real Relation to the World", *Laval théologique et philosophique* 56:1 (2000), pp. 93–112.

67 Arjan Markus, "Divine Timelessness", *Sophia* 43:2 (2004), p. 31.

68 Nelson Pike, *God and Timelessness* (New York: Schocken Books, 1970), p. 110; see also Delmas Lewis, "Timelessness and Divine Agency", *International Journal for Philosophy of Religion* 21:3 (1987), pp. 151–4.

69 Ignacio Silva, "Thomas Aquinas and William E. Carroll on *Creatio ex Nihilo*: A Response to Joseph Hannon's 'Theological Objections to a Metaphysicalist Interpretation of Creation'", *Theology and Science* 19:2 (2021), p. 98.

they are causing (although an accidental *series* may not have a beginning and an end, each cause *in* the series does). Causes *per se*, on the other hand, are not *necessarily* temporal. They are concerned with ontological primacy and ontological hierarchical relations. Given the discussion above about whether there are any genuine causes *per se* in nature, it may be possible for causes *per se* to be temporal (i.e., hand and stick). What is important here is not that there are no genuine causes *per se* in nature (although it certainly appears that there are not), but that God cannot act as a cause *per accidens*; God can *only* "act" as a cause *per se*. If there are no causes *per se* in nature, then this only reinforces and further cements the strong ontological distinction between *creatio*—cause of being—and *mutatio*—cause of motion—that this chapter has keenly argued. Therefore, if God is genuinely atemporal, then God's "act" cannot be before or after anything, and so cannot be accidentally related to the universe, and must be essentially ordered; that is, it is not an "act" at all, it is a relationship.

Importantly, this does not mean that God is "omnitemporal". That is, to say that God is temporally simultaneous with the universe does not mean that God has infinite duration that is temporally simultaneous to the whole temporal duration of the universe. In this scenario, time (the universe) and eternity (God) would be like "two infinite, parallel horizontal lines, one representing time, the other eternity. On the temporal line the present is an ever-moving point of light, but the eternal line is all light, all present", so that "God is copresent with the whole of time by His [sic] life's being stretched out alongside it".[70] Rather, it means that God is "atemporal", which means that, as Wolfgang Smith writes, "'The instantaneous and imperceptible moment of creation', to use St. Basil's phrase, is 'equidistant' . . . to all times, even as the center of a circle is equidistant to all points on the circumference."[71] Or, as Anselm held, "Just as the present time contains all place and whatever exists in any

70 Katherin Rogers, "Eternity Has No Duration", *Religious Studies* 30:1 (1994), pp. 1–2, quoting Brian Leftow, *Time and Eternity* (Ithaca, NY: Cornell University Press, 1991), p. 117.

71 Wolfgang Smith, *Teilhardism and the New Religion* (Rockford, IL: Tan Books and Publishers inc., 1988), p. 72; see also Katherin Rogers, "Anselm on Eternity as the Fifth Dimension", *The Saint Anselm Journal* 3:2 (2006), p. 7.

place: in the same way all time and what exists in any time is enclosed in the eternal present."[72] In other words, all temporal points are present in one eternal "moment", just as all spatial points are present in one temporal moment.[73] Katherin Rogers calls this "five-dimensionalism", by which she means that if all three spatial dimensions are simultaneously present in the fourth temporal dimension, then all four spatiotemporal dimensions are simultaneously present in the fifth eternal dimension.[74]

The absence of a real relation is crucial for understanding this distinction. If God were "omnitemporal" then God would be present to all times; however, if God is atemporal then all times would be present to God. The correct image for this scenario is that of the centre of a circle to its circumference. God—who is atemporal—is "temporally" simultaneous to all spatiotemporal points as the centre of a circle is simultaneous with its circumference. All creatures participate in God—who is the ground of their being—as the circumference participates in the centre of a circle. In fact, it might not be too outlandish to suggest that the image of eternity as "an ever-moving point of light" is a suitable image of an accidentally ordered series—a sort of infinitely long string of pearls—and the image of eternity as the centre of a circle is a suitable image for an essentially ordered series—a sort of relationship. It is not altogether irrelevant that the first image of eternity is about "motion"—i.e., it explicitly likens eternity to "ever-moving"—which makes it more reasonable to suggest that the circle image could be about "being".

Thus, there are two important reasons why there should be such a razor-sharp, mutually exclusive distinction between accidentally ordered and essentially ordered causality: (a) an atemporal God cannot be an example of the former, and (b) there can be no examples of the latter in nature.

---

72 Anselm, quoted in Rogers, "Eternity has no Duration", p. 15.

73 See also Anselm, *Collected Works* (Oxford: Oxford University Press, 1998), *Monologion* 21.

74 Rogers, "Anselm on Eternity as the Fifth Dimension", p. 7.

God cannot be a cause

If God is a "person", then God is accidentally ordered to the universe, and so stands alongside it in a "subject/object relation", and so cannot be essentially ordered to it as *creatio*. Likewise, if God is the "ground of being", then God is like the centre of a circle to its circumference, essentially ordered to all creatures as their cause of being, and so God cannot be accidentally ordered to it as *mutatio*. Ian McFarland makes the same point differently. He writes that "for God to be present to a creature as that which the creature might encounter, it would be necessary for God also to be other, one item in the world rather than the one who sustains the world, and thus cease to be God . . . In this way, the diversity of creatures suggests that God's radical, sustaining presence *in* the world as Creator precludes God's objective presence *to* creatures as the one who can be known and loved."[75] McFarland uses different language here, but the point is the same: creatures cannot be the object of an act that God "does", or this makes God what God is not.

If creation is a cause *per accidens*, then the universe becomes the object of an act of which God is the subject, and so it becomes univocal with how humans create. If creation is a cause *per se*, then creation is a participation. In other words, creation is not something that God "does"—because "'doing' (acting) is not possible for the kind of reality that God, in God's deepest and most cognitively inaccessible being, essentially *is*"[76]—rather, "God's creative action *just is* creation's dependence on God for its existence",[77] that is, it is participation. Or, as Frederick Bauerschmidt writes, creation "tells us something about creatures . . . but it does not tell us something about God".[78] Creation tells us about creatures' participation in God, not about God "doing" something.

---

[75] Ian McFarland, *The Word Made Flesh: A Theology of the Incarnation* (Louisville, KY: Westminster John Knox Press, 2019), p. 60.

[76] Kirkpatrick, *The Mystery and Agency of God*, p. 1.

[77] Bishop and Perszyk, "The Divine Attributes and Non-personal Conceptions of God", p. 614.

[78] Bauerschmidt, *Thomas Aquinas: Faith, Reason, and Following Christ*, p. 115.

Of course, one might complain that this chapter has presented the situation too simply, that this chapter has contrasted "participation" with "mechanical cause" as if these were the only two options, when the situation is far more complex. Helen Oppenheimer, for example, asks, "Can [God], as it were, push His [sic] creatures about, and if He can, will He?" Crucially, she then asks, "Is His action confined to personal influence upon personal beings, or does He act as a kind of physical cause upon the material creation?"[79] Thus, someone like Philip Clayton might point to a contrast between "energy" and "information", and so argue that "since God's direction involves an 'input of information' rather than energy transfers, the old dilemma of how God as non-physical being could bring about physical effects disappears".[80] Someone who agrees with Clayton might question whether this chapter's insistence that God either acts as "mechanical cause" or God cannot influence the world at all is deficient. However, it is not clear whether it is possible to have "personal influence" that is not a "mechanical cause".[81] Nevertheless, even if God

---

[79]   Helen Oppenheimer, *Incarnation and Immanence* (London: Hodder and Stoughton, 1973), p. 49.

[80]   Clayton, *God and Contemporary Science*, p. 226.

[81]   Although, some would question whether it is possible to have an introduction of information that is not accompanied by an introduction of energy. Thus, Nancey Murphy writes that "while information flow is not the same as flow of matter or energy, 'in actual systems no information flows without some exchange of energy and/or matter'. So the proposal that God arranges patterns in the world that convey information to humankind is open to the question of how God causes one pattern of events to obtain rather than another" (Nancey Murphy, "Emergence, Downward Causation, and Divine Action", in Robert Russell, Nancey Murphy and William Stoeger (eds), *Scientific Perspectives on Divine Action: Twenty Years of Challenge and Progress* (Vatican City: Vatican Observatory Foundation, 2008), p. 129). Likewise, Gerard Verschuuren notes that "information is information, neither energy nor matter . . . but it does need matter for its embodiment as well as energy for its communication. There is no information without a carrier; without a signal there could be no message" (Gerard Verschuuren, *Aquinas and Modern Science* (Kettering, OH: Angelico Press, 2016), p. 139). It is not clear that one can make such a

did only introduce information or "personal influence" and not energy or "move atoms about", this would *still* be an accidentally ordered series because God would still temporally precede the information or "personal influence" and there would still be an "after" that is independent of the "giving" of information. In other words, the "personal influence" would still be the intentional acts of "*an*" individual being, not the dependence on the "ground of being"; that influence would manifest as "events", not a relationship. Thus, there is still an acceptance that God is a "person" who is in a personal relationship with the universe. In other words, whether or not God acts through "mechanical" or "personal" influence, one is still thinking of God as a person; one who acts through multiple "events" strung together like pearls on a string that build on one another. Yet, if God is not a person, then neither of these ideas of divine activity are appropriate. Oppenheimer and Clayton might have a problem with the language used, but they are still thinking of God as a person who does things—who causes things in a "mechanical" way, whether through energy or information—rather than that in which all creatures participate.

Other examples

This chapter has so far relied on scholastic categories to explain that God cannot "act" at all if God is not a person. Yet others make precisely the same distinction using different language. For example, Caleb Cohoe (admittedly still situated within the scholastic tradition) describes precisely this distinction, but differentiates between what he calls "horizontal" and "vertical" causality.[82] The fact that he uses "spatial"

---

distinction; if God interacts with the world *at all*, whether through "moving atoms about" or "personal influence", then God has to introduce energy in some way. God cannot influence personally without moving some atoms.

[82] Caleb Cohoe, "There Must Be a First: Why Thomas Aquinas Rejects Infinite, Essentially Ordered, Causal Series", *British Journal for the History of Philosophy* 21:5 (2013), p. 841; See also Andrew Davison, "Looking Back Towards the Origin: Scientific Cosmology as Creation *ex nihilo* Considered 'From the Inside'", in Gary A. Anderson and Markus Bockmuehl (eds), *Creation Ex Nihilo: Origins, Development, Contemporary Challenges* (Notre Dame, IN: University of Notre Dame Press, 2018), pp. 371ff.; Philip Sherrard,

language does not mean that he is making a spatial argument. He means nothing more than that divine activity is not part of the historico-scientific nexus of billiard-ball-like "mechanical" causality of the universe, but is that which "upholds" or "grounds" that nexus. That is, divine activity runs "perpendicular" to creaturely activity, not "parallel" to it. Philip Sherrard, too, writes that "to speak of what is 'prior' to creation is not, therefore, to refer to a time that precedes creation ... It is to refer to the ontological and pre-ontological realms of the divine that stand, in a vertical hierarchy, prior to the realm of creation".[83] As already implied, perhaps "primary", which has fewer temporal connotations, is better than "prior", but the point is well made. Torstein Tollefsen, again, referring to Pseudo-Dionysius, writes that "all causes ... are ... vertically dependent on God as the final ... efficient ... and paradigmatic ... principle or source".[84]

Sergei Bulgakov is another who describes this same distinction, rejecting the idea that God can be a "cause" at all, albeit explicitly criticizing Thomas Aquinas. Bulgakov criticizes the theology of Thomas Aquinas precisely because he sees it as characterizing the relationship between God and the world as "cause". In *The Bride of the Lamb*, he criticizes Thomas Aquinas for making God the "first cause", which Bulgakov claims reduces God to a part of the world,[85] makes God subject to the conservation of energy,[86] and so makes creation something that happens at the beginning of time. Contrasting "creation" with "cause"—characterizing the latter as an "intramundane category, which

Christianity: Lineaments of a Sacred Tradition (Edinburgh: T&T Clark, 1998), p. 239; Tollefsen. *Activity and Participation in Late Antique and Early Christian Thought*, p. 113.

[83] Sherrard, *Christianity: Lineaments of a Sacred Tradition*, p. 239; See also Davison, "Looking Back Towards the Origin", pp. 371ff.

[84] Tollefsen, *Activity and Participation in Late Antique and Early Christian Thought*, p. 113.

[85] Sergei Bulgakov, *The Bride of the Lamb* (Grand Rapids, MI: William B. Eerdmans, 2002), p. 35.

[86] Bulgakov, *The Bride of the Lamb*, p. 36.

presupposes the presence of the world's being"[87]—Bulgakov writes that "God the creator is above and outside the causality that exists in the world itself. In *this* sense, God is not the cause of the world but its creator, just as the world is not the *effect* of divine causality but God's creation".[88] Bulgakov criticizes Thomas Aquinas for positing God as a cause of the world, rather than its creator.[89]

However, while Bulgakov's theology of creation is absolutely correct, and agrees completely with what has been outlined here, his characterization of Thomas Aquinas is incorrect.[90] That is, what Aquinas means when he writes that "God by creation produces things without movement"[91] is more or less what Bulgakov means. While Tillich and Bulgakov do not utilize the language of participation, it is clear that they are motivated by the same concerns that led Aquinas to talk of participation. Whereas Aquinas is happy to use the word "cause", only insofar as that is qualified as analogous, Bulgakov is far more cautious; if creatures are causes, then God is not.

To return to the previous illustrative examples, the flame and oxygen is an illustrative example of an essentially ordered series (to the extent that there can be *genuine* examples of this in nature) because the flame depends on the oxygen at all times for its continuing existence. We might say, then, that oxygen is not the *cause* of the flame—because it does not explain its origin (the flame is *caused* by a spark or something similar)— but is the *creation* of the flame—that is, the flame continually depends on the oxygen for its being (of course, God is ultimately the *creation* of the

---

[87] Bulgakov, *The Bride of the Lamb*, p. 62; Paul Tillich also makes a similar distinction (Tillich, *Systematic Theology Vol. 1*, pp. 196–8. See also Grigg, "Religion, Science, and Evolution", p. 948); see also Stoeger, "God, Physics, and the Big Bang", p. 181.

[88] Bulgakov, *The Bride of the Lamb*, p. 37 (italics in original).

[89] Tillich, *Systematic Theology Vol. 1*, pp. 196–8 (see also Grigg, "Religion, Science, and Evolution", p. 948).

[90] Although, for Aristotle, "God fills the role of cause . . . [and] is not the maker of the cosmos" (Tollefsen, *Activity and Participation in Late Antique and Early Christian Thought*, p. 24).

[91] *ST* i, 45, iii.

flame, but the example is useful to illustrate this difference between *cause* and *creation*). This is contrasted with the example of the hand and the pen—which was argued above as more appropriate as an illustration of an "instrumental cause"—because as well as the hand being the *creation* of the pen's movement—i.e., that on which the pen continues to depend for its movement—the hand is *also* the *cause* of the pen's movement—i.e., the hand explains why the pen begins to move in the first place.

Importantly, one could infer from Bulgakov's dismissal of "causation" as an "intramundane category, which presupposes the presence of the world's being", that "creation" must be an *inter*mundane category. This suggests that "essentially ordered", "vertical", and "intermundane" are all more or less synonyms that describe the divine cause of being, which are directly contrasted with their opposites—"accidentally ordered", "horizontal", and "intramundane"—that describe the natural cause of motion. The former is the exclusive domain of metaphysics/theology; the latter is the exclusive domain of science and history.[92]

---

92   The language of "*inter*mundane" seems to point to dualism. There is one sense in which the theist must be a dualist, otherwise there is no getting around the spectre of the univocality of being, that God and creature are "made from the same stuff" (to put it rather crudely). However, this does not mean an interactionist dualism (which conservation of energy seems to finally and conclusively reject). As Gregory Dawes writes, a "methodological naturalist will insist that we must proceed as if there were no supernatural agents, while an ontological naturalist will insist that there are no such agents" (Gregory Dawes, *Theism and Explanation* (New York, NY: Routledge, 2014), p. 3). Thus, "Even if the existence of God is not necessary to complete a philosophy of nature . . . God may in fact happen to exist. Not everything that is true needs to be true in order to preserve the world's intelligibility" (Lawrence Vogel, "Introduction", in Hans Jonas, *Mortality and Morality: A Search for God after Auschwitz* (Evanston, IL: Northwestern University Press, 1996), p. 21). Or, perhaps more accurately, as John Bishop and Ken Perszyk argue, there is not a "natural realm" and a "supernatural realm", but, rather, they affirm monism of which God is not a part. Drawing on apophaticism, the point here is not to *affirm* that there is a supernatural realm in which God dwells, but to *deny* that God is part of the "natural" realm (Bishop and

Whatever language one uses, there is this distinction. If God is atemporal then God cannot act as cause in any way univocally with creatures. Not only does God act as cause entirely differently, but the effect of that cause is entirely different as well. If God is atemporal, then divine causality must not be an act at all, but a relationship. That is, it must be a cause *per se*, a cause of being, *creatio*, vertical, intermundane. God can *only* act as an essentially ordered cause. Or, God creates by being that in which all creatures participate: "God's creative action *just is* creation's dependence on God for its existence."[93] Thus, only God creates (essentially ordered cause of being/*creatio*/participation) and only creatures cause change (accidentally ordered cause of motion/ *mutatio*/act).[94]

Perszyk, "The Divine Attributes and Non-personal Conceptions of God", p. 615). This is more or less what is being argued here: the existence of God is not necessary to explain why anything *in particular* happens; God is only needed to explain why anything happens *at all*; God is only needed to explain why there is something rather than nothing.

[93] Bishop and Perszyk, "The Divine Attributes and Non-personal Conceptions of God", p. 614.

[94] Although Athanasius was by no means an Aristotelian, it is precisely this causal distinction that lay at the heart of the logic he presented in *De Incarnatione*. For Athanasius (although not using the language of "cause of being" and "cause of motion"), only God could create, and so Jesus had to be God if Jesus were to re-create. He writes that "it may be duly perceived that the renewal of creation has been the work of the selfsame word that made it at the beginning. For it will appear not inconsonant for the Father to have wrought its salvation in him by whose means he made it". (Athanasius, "On the Incarnation", in Edward Hardy (tr.), *Christology of the Later Fathers* (London: Westminster John Knox Press, 1954), p. 56). Thus, he continues, "what was required for such grace and such recall, but the word of God, which had also at the beginning made everything out of naught . . . for being the word of the Father, and above all, he alone of natural fitness was both able to re-create everything, and worthy to suffer on behalf of all and to be ambassador for all with the Father". (Athanasius, "On the Incarnation", p. 62). It is crucial to Athanasius' logic that "creation" is something entirely

Creation and origins

If "cause of being" and "cause of motion" are sharply distinguished, and if that distinction corresponds to the difference between an essentially ordered series and an accidentally ordered series—where the first is about metaphysics and participation and the second about history, science, and discrete events—then *creatio* is the former and has nothing to do with the latter. Thus, when theologians—such as Thomas Aquinas and Duns Scotus—wanted to offer (cosmological) proofs for the existence of God, they did so in relation to cause *per se*. When Thomas Aquinas famously remarked that there must be a God because there must be a first cause, he absolutely did not mean that there must be a *beginning*, a temporally first moment "before" which God must have done something. He meant that there must be a *primary* cause, a cause on which everything depends for its ability to act accidentally as a cause, that itself does not depend on anything further. Thus, creation is *ex nihilo*, not *post nihilum*, which means that "nothing" is not the "material" out of which God creates, but instead refers to an ontological dependency. As Frederick Bauerschmidt puts it, the "nothing" of *ex nihilo* is not a sort of "passive potentiality", which he defines as "the capacity to receive a form".[95] That is, "nothing" is not an object on which God can act. Others might call this "passive potentiality" an "*obediential potency*", and use the example of a block of marble, which contains the potential to receive the form of a statue.[96] That is, the nothing from which God creates is not a temporally precedent

---

distinct from, and so impossible to be accomplished through, "normal" creaturely causation. Thus, if "divine" creation was univocal with creaturely (human) creation, then Jesus did not need to be God; he could just have been a "special" human. If Jesus creates, then that must mean that Jesus is "a" "cause of being" (or more accurately, as will be expounded in Chapter 4, "the" cause of being).

[95]   Bauerschmidt, *Thomas Aquinas: Faith, Reason, and Following Christ*, p. 109.

[96]   See Andrew Dean Swafford, *Nature and Grace: A New Approach to Thomistic Ressourcement* (Cambridge: James Clarke & Co., 2015), p. 15 and Lawrence Feingold, *The Natural Desire to See God According to St. Thomas Aquinas and his Interpreters* (Naples, FL: Sapientia Press, 2010), p. 149.

"nothing" which contains the "potential" to receive the form of a universe; "nothing" is that which signifies that, without participation in God, there would be no being. "Nothing" is an ontological nothing, not a material nothing. Thus, creation is the hierarchical/vertical dependence of each creature on God (i.e., *creatio ex nihilo*), not an event that can be located at the beginning of time (i.e., *creatio post nihilum*).

Islamic scholar Ibn Sina (Avicenna), who was a major influence on both Thomas Aquinas and Duns Scotus,[97] maintained that "while causes of existence must be essentially ordered and finite, causes of coming to be are accidentally ordered and must be infinite."[98] That is, while an essentially ordered series *must* be terminated by a primary cause, an accidentally ordered series *must* have *no* termination. The suggestion that accidentally ordered "causes of coming to be" *must* be infinite is odd and sounds strange to ears accustomed to thinking that there definitely is a beginning to the world in the Big Bang. Therefore, it is better to say that whereas an essentially ordered series *must* be finite and so *must* terminate in a primary cause that is not dependent on anything more primary, an accidentally ordered series *may* be infinite, and so it is *possible* for an accidentally ordered series to extend infinitely into the past and have no beginning.

Thus, both Thomas Aquinas and Duns Scotus were perfectly happy to accept that it was entirely possible for the world to be eternal, that is, for the world to have infinite temporal duration. In the *Summa Theologiae*, for example, when discussing whether it is an article of faith that the world began, Thomas Aquinas writes that "it is not impossible for a man [sic] to be generated by man to infinity."[99] Of course, Thomas Aquinas was adamant that Scripture showed quite clearly that there *was* a beginning

---

[97] E.g. R. E. Houser, "Avicenna, '*Aliqui*', and Thomas Aquinas' Doctrine of Creation", *Recherches de théologie et philosophie médiévales* 80:1 (2013), pp. 17–55.

[98] Byrne, "The Role of Essentially Ordered Causal Series in Avicenna's Proof for the Necessary Existent in the Metaphysics of the Salvation", p. 135, n. 17; see also Parviz Morewedge, *The Metaphysics of Avicenna* (London: Routledge, 1973), pp. 201–11.

[99] *ST* 1, 46, ii.

to the world, and that there *actually is not* an infinite generation of humanity, nevertheless he maintained that there was nothing illogical with the idea that it was possible for human to beget human into infinity.

The fact that there *could* have been a world with no beginning might seem to be a moot point, but it is an incredibly important affirmation that reveals exactly how one should understand Thomas Aquinas' doctrine of creation. When he constructed his famous *Quinque Viae*, he absolutely did not mean that it was possible to deduce the existence of God from the fact that the world had a beginning. One does not move backwards through time to a point where one can only explain the existence of something through a further antecedent, supernatural, cause. Rather, one moves "upward" through the ontological hierarchy to a point where one encounters the existence of something that is the source of its own being, which depends on nothing else and which does not participate but is participated. This second way of understanding it is the *ex nihilo* to which theologians refer.

To put this differently, if there is a difference between "cause" and "creation", or between "cause of motion" and "cause of being", then there is a comparable difference between "origin"/"beginning" and "creation". An "origin" or "beginning" is the first cause *per accidens*, the first in an accidentally ordered temporal series; "creation" is the essentially ordered, hierarchical, ontological dependence of one thing on a more ontologically prior other. "Origins" are about "motion"; "creation" is about "being". To return to a quotation from Étienne Gilson:

> Albert the Great emphatically stressed the distinction of two types of causality corresponding to two different types of effects produced. The first is a change properly speaking, that is to say, a change of state. Every change of this kind is the effect of a movement, whether we are dealing with the production of a new quality in an already existing substance, or of that of a new substance starting from already existing matter, the instrument of production is a moment, and the cause is the point of departure or the point of origin of this movement. That kind of production

must be distinguished from the one whose result is the very being of the effect produced.[100]

This quotation is pregnant with crucial points. First, the "first" is described by the efficient cause of motion—it is "the effect of a movement"—and can be further divided into a change in or a new quality *"in an already existing substance"*—i.e., *mutatio*—and a new substance that comes from an already existing matter—i.e., *generatio* (which is just a species of *mutatio*[101]). Second, the "first" is explicitly referred to as "the point of *origin* of this movement". The implication is clear: the origin of anything, the origin of an activity, the origin of a creature, or the origin of the universe is itself a change or generation. If the origin of the universe is itself a change, then God does not cause it.

Gavin Kerr also explicitly distinguishes between "beginnings" (or "origins") and "creation". Kerr writes that "the question of a thing's beginning and the question of a thing's creation are two formally distinct types of question", so that, whereas "the beginning of a thing signifies the time at which it came into existence ... the creation of a thing signifies the mode of its coming into existence".[102] Certainly, "often, the beginning of a thing's existence coincides with its creation, but the two are not necessarily synonymous". Thus, "one cannot have [a beginning] without [a creation], but one can indeed have [a creation] without [a beginning]".[103]

It is important to take this claim to its logical conclusion. If it is entirely *possible* for the universe to have infinite temporal duration and still be created, then *whether* there is a beginning or not is, quite literally, entirely accidental; it is entirely theologically irrelevant. That is, if there is a beginning, it is not "caused" by God. Of course, God is still responsible for a beginning, in the same way that God is responsible for everything as that in which all things participate, but this does not mean that God is the cause *per accidens* of that beginning. As William Stoeger warns, "Even

---

[100] Gilson, *Medieval Essays*, p. 156.

[101] Maryniarczyk, "Philosophical Creationism", p. 238 (italics in original).

[102] Kerr, "A Thomistic Metaphysics of Creation", p. 340.

[103] Kerr, "A Thomistic Metaphysics of Creation", p. 340.

establishing a rough parallel, or consonance, between 'the beginning of time' in the Big Bang and 'the beginning of time' in the doctrine of creation ... is very questionable."[104] Rather, as Andrew Davison writes, creation is not "some putative first moment in the past" but is "primarily about derivation of all things from God".[105]

Importantly, acknowledging that creation is not "some putative first moment in the past" is not meant as support for a doctrine of *creatio continua*, in which the apparently offensive word is "past", and so *creatio* is still ongoing. *Creatio continua* still conceives of creation as an accidentally ordered series; it just doesn't agree that it is reduced to one instance in the past, but is rather composed of a number of continuing instances, all accidentally ordered to one another. Rather, acknowledging that creation is not "some putative first moment in the past" is meant as support for the idea of participation; creation is a relation, not a physical construction. Creation means relationship with God, not spatiotemporal origins.[106]

Failure to grasp this distinction between "origins" and "creation" is a major source of theological misunderstanding. Reading Thomas

---

[104] William Stoeger, "Contemporary cosmology and its implications for the science–religion dialogue" in Robert J. Russell, William Stoeger and George Coyne (eds), *Physics, Philosophy, and Theology: A Common Quest for Understanding* (Vatican City: Vatican Observatory, 1988), p. 240.

[105] Davison, *Participation in God*, p. 26.

[106] Of course, one might complain that Genesis emphatically does tell us that God "created the heavens and the earth" *in the beginning*, but if one is willing to accept the validity of science and evolution then one is already committed to at least some allegorization of the Genesis narrative. If one is prepared to accept that the dating of the world in Genesis or the absence of evolution in Genesis is allegorical, then why not "in the beginning" as well? (Of course, Genesis' reference to a beginning is accepted as sufficient proof by Thomas Aquinas et al. that there is a beginning (i.e., that infinite temporal duration is only a possibility but not a reality), but acceptance of a beginning does not mean that God creates *in* the beginning; there is a beginning, but God creates *from* eternity. That is, Genesis is allegorical not in postulating a beginning to the universe, but in postulating that God is temporal and that the "act" of creation can be temporally located.)

Aquinas and assuming that the "cosmological proof" meant that one must temporally recede backwards to a Big Bang moment is exactly what one would expect from a scientist, or one (such as Hefner, Haught, and Polkinghorne) who is working within a scientific paradigm. As Michael Dodds recognizes, if you work within the paradigm of modern science, with its narrow sense of what a "cause" is, then you need to have God "move some atoms", and so it is obvious that a scientist reading Thomas Aquinas would assume this is what he meant: a regression back to an initial/original state without movement into which movement is introduced. David Bentley Hart makes exactly this observation of Richard Dawkins' *The God Delusion*. Hart chastises Dawkins for "not knowing the scholastic distinction between primary and secondary causality", and so for assuming that "Thomas's talk of a 'first cause' referred to the initial temporal causal agency in a continuous temporal series of discrete causes". This means that Dawkins "thought that Thomas's logic requires the universe to have had a temporal beginning, which Thomas explicitly and repeatedly made clear is not the case". Dawkins thought, Hart continues, that "Thomas's proof from universal 'motion' concerned only physical movement in space, 'local motion', rather than the ontological movement from potency to act".[107] That is, Dawkins did *exactly* what Dodds cautioned against: Dawkins assumed that because science has reduced all causality to "mechanical" cause so all theological talk of "cause" means is that God has to move some atoms.

Richard Dawkins is not alone in making this mistake. As Hefner, Haught, and Polkinghorne evidence, theologians make this mistake too.[108] Ted Peters is another. He writes that "the theological idea of creation out

---

[107] Hart, *The Experience of God*, pp. 21-2.

[108] See Mark William Worthing, *God, Creation, and Contemporary Physics* (Minneapolis, MN: Fortress Press, 1996), pp. 104-5; see also Michael Chaberek, *Catholicism and Evolution: A History from Darwin to Pope Francis* (Kettering, OH: Angelico Press, 2015), p. 297; Ted Peters, "On Creating the Cosmos", in Robert J. Russell, William Stoeger and George Coyne (eds), *Physics, Philosophy, and Theology: A Common Quest for Understanding* (Vatican City: Vatican Observatory, 1988), p. 274; Paul Davies, "Introduction", in Werner Heisenberg, *Physics and Philosophy* (London: Penguin, 1989), p. ix.

of nothing—especially in the form of a temporal beginning—is just as consonant with contemporary science as is continuing creation".[109] Even some Thomists appear to make this error. Polish Dominican theologian Michael Chaberek also writes that "creation *ex nihilo* is recognized by science as the 'Big Bang', a theory positing a temporal beginning of the universe".[110] Even Mariusz Tabaczek, a fellow Polish Dominican (who normally seems to present an accurate account of Aquinas' theology), discusses "entities that came into being *ex nihilo* at the beginning of creation",[111] and so "restricts" creation to "the most basic physical matter of the elements",[112] implying, at least, that he is also confusing *ex nihilo* with *post nihilum* and so treating *creatio* as a temporal category, rather than an ontological one.[113] Theologians, it seems, are not immune to reading Thomas Aquinas and other scholastic theologians and assuming that they were referring to the beginning of the universe rather than the creation of the universe. As Dodds evidences, the scientific revolution has so pervaded the popular understanding of words like "cause" that even theologians are not immune to the mistakes in interpretation.

Mark William Worthing is yet another. He correctly acknowledges that Thomist theology allows the possibility of "maintain[ing] a rational belief in *creatio ex nihilo* without accepting a *creatio originans* as its logical and necessary corollary" and so deems it prudent to discuss them separately.[114] Yet, he undermines this observation by writing that the discovery of a physical nothing that either "precedes" the Big Bang or is that from which the Big Bang emerges "would cut both ways for theology". On the one hand, it would "certainly add fodder to the

---

[109] Peters, "On Creating the Cosmos", p. 274.

[110] Chaberek, *Catholicism and Evolution*, p. 298.

[111] Tabaczek, "What Do God and Creatures Really Do in an Evolutionary Change?", p. 17.

[112] Tabaczek, "What Do God and Creatures Really Do in an Evolutionary Change?", p. 37.

[113] See also Paul Copan and William Lane Craig, *Creation out of Nothing: A Biblical, Philosophical, and Scientific Exploration* (Grand Rapids, MI: Baker Academic, 2004), pp. 219–48; Davies, "Introduction", p. ix.

[114] Worthing, *God, Creation, and Contemporary Physics*, p. 79.

popularized apologies for theistic belief", yet, on the other hand, "a purely scientific model of an *ex nihilo* origin of the universe would ... seem to make the Creator redundant",[115] which seems to undermine the fact that *creatio ex nihilo* has nothing to do with a *creatio originans*.

This confusion that the discovery of a beginning to the universe means that there cannot be a creator is reminiscent of other scientists' mistakes (albeit the other way round). Stephen Hawking, for example, accurately recognizes that the real question is, "What is it that breathes fire into the equations and makes a universe for them to describe?"[116] However he seems to assume (perhaps unwittingly) that whatever it is that breathes fire into the equations, it is synonymous with a beginning, so that "so long as the universe had a beginning, we could suppose it had a creator. But if the universe is really completely self-contained ... what place, then, for a creator?"[117] The German atheist philosopher Adolf Grünbaum, who draws on Hawking's theory of a temporal boundary without a beginning, makes the same mistake. Even though he seems to recognize correctly that the question "does the physical universe have a temporal *origin*, and—if so—what does physical cosmology tell us about it?" is different to "[w]as there a *creation* of the universe, and—if so—what light can science throw on it, if any?"[118] However, he then incorrectly moves to suppose that since the answer to the former can be exhaustively explained by science, so the latter is a "pseudo-problem".[119] Another atheist cosmologist, Sir Fred Hoyle, also demonstrates this mistake. When Hoyle refused to accept the theory of the Big Bang in favour of a temporally infinite, steady-state universe, it was precisely because he made the same confusion. He assumed that a beginning requires a creator and so refused to accept there could be a beginning to the universe. The fact that he was so ideologically opposed to the idea that there was a God who created

---

[115] Worthing, *God, Creation, and Contemporary Physics*, pp. 104–5.

[116] Stephen Hawking, *A Brief History of Time* (London: Transworld Publishers, 1988), p. 174.

[117] Hawking, *A Brief History of Time*, pp. 140–1.

[118] Adolf Grünbaum, "The Pseudo-Problem of Creation in Physical Cosmology", *Philosophy of Science* 56:3 (1989), p. 373.

[119] Grünbaum, "The Pseudo-Problem of Creation in Physical Cosmology", p. 373.

the universe meant that he simply could not accept that the universe had a beginning.[120] Perhaps if Hawking, Grünbaum, and Hoyle were more versed in Thomas Aquinas, they would have understood that there is no contradiction in claiming that the world can be created *and* eternal.[121]

Creation and the Big Bang

If "origin" and "creation" are entirely separate, so that the fact that the universe has a beginning makes absolutely no claim about whether or not there is a creator, how should the theologian understand the Big Bang and the beginning of the universe (assuming, of course, that there is one)? Perhaps more pertinently, if God does not *cause* the beginning of the universe, then (again, assuming that there is one) what does?

The answer to the first question has already been suggested: NOMA. Science can exhaustingly explain the *origin* of the universe, but it is absolutely impotent when it comes to explaining the *creation* of the universe. Similarly, one might say that the theologian is entirely out of their depth when it comes to explaining the origin of the universe. They might want to appeal to Genesis to claim at least that it has one, but it must be science that explains it. That theologians have increasingly allegorized the Genesis narrative in favour of modern science shows quite clearly that this is the case.

If science explains the universe's origin, then this means that just because the Big Bang is the first in an accidentally ordered series does not mean that it is not itself part of that series.[122] Likewise, just because the Big Bang is the *first* change does not lessen the fact that it *is* a change. If the Big Bang is a change—even if it is the first change—then it has nothing

---

[120] Joshua M. Moritz, "Rendering unto Science and God: Is NOMA Enough?", *Theology and Science* 7 (2009), p. 372.

[121] Thomas Aquinas, *De Aeternitate Mundi*, in Thomas Gilby (tr.) *Philosophical Texts* (Durham, NC: The Labyrinth Press, 1982), pp. 142–7; See also Gilson, *Medieval Essays*, p. 170; Timothy B. Noone, "The Originality of St. Thomas's Position on the Philosophers and Creation", *The Thomist: A Speculative Quarterly Review* 60:2 (1996), pp. 275–300.

[122] Richard Cross, *Duns Scotus on God* (Aldershot: Ashgate Publishing, 2005), p. 23; Verschuuren, *Aquinas and Modern Science*, p. 104.

to do with creation. David Bentley Hart explicitly affirms this. When describing causes *per accidens* as "transitions of energy, movements of mass, acts of generation or destruction",[123] he explicitly offers the Big Bang as an example of what he means by this.[124] The Big Bang is the *origin* of the universe; it is the beginning of the universe; it is the "cause of coming to be", as Celia Byrne calls it,[125] and so is accidentally ordered to the rest of cosmic history. The Big Bang is *part* of the causal nexus and its origin/ beginning. It is the first cause *per accidens*, but this does not make it any more than a cause *per accidens*.

In this way, the answer to the second question is suggested. If the Big Bang is the first in an accidentally ordered series and so is not caused by God, then it is caused by whatever science tells us it is caused by. Most probably, given current thinking, the universe spontaneously self-originates.

To put it as bluntly as possible, how would an atheist cosmologist explain the existence of the universe? If one is committed to NOMA, then the fact that this cosmologist is an atheist should make no difference; whatever they claim about the "origin" of the universe should still be precisely the same as what the religious cosmologist thinks about the existence of the universe. In other words, the theologian committed to NOMA can point to what has already been said about *creation* as a relationship/participation and still agree with the atheist about the *origin* of the universe. That atheist cosmologist might say (with Fred Hoyle) that the universe is eternal (i.e., that it has infinite temporal duration and has no beginning). They might say (with Stephen Hawking) that the universe is temporally finite but with no temporal boundary. They might say that "because there is a law like gravity, the universe can and will create itself from nothing" so that "spontaneous creation is the reason there is something rather than nothing, why the universe exists, why we exist",[126] or that the universe "'switch[es] on', or pop[s] into existence,

---

123 Hart, *The Experience of God*, p. 104.

124 Hart, *The Experience of God*, p. 104.

125 Byrne, "The Role of Essentially Ordered Causal Series in Avicenna's Proof for the Necessary Existent in the Metaphysics of the Salvation", p. 135, n. 17.

126 Stephen Hawking, *The Grand Design* (London: Bantam Press, 2010), p. 180.

without the need for prior causation, entirely in accordance with the laws of quantum physics",[127] and that it is able to do this because "nothing . . . is unstable".[128] (Of course, the use of the word "create" in these quotations is not the theological "create" that this chapter uses.)

The point is that none of these are of any consequence for the theologian, not because, as an immaterial, spiritual person, God can act on the world (as an accidentally ordered cause) in ways that do not conflict with natural "causes"—like a cosmic builder—or that God, because so unlimited, can do things without violating the conservation of energy. These ways still conceive of God as univocal with creatures and so in competition with them as an explanation. Rather, none of these are of any consequence for the theologian because creation is entirely distinct from origins. Whatever the scientist says about *origins* is entirely compatible with what the theologian says about *creation*, because the two are entirely different explanations of two entirely different ideas that have nothing whatsoever to do with one another.

Thus, theologians should not offer God as a *competing* cause for the *origin* of the universe (as if only God *or* whatever-that-cause-is can be correct)—i.e., the "opposition" thesis—but neither should theologians offer God as a *complementary* cause (as if God *and* whatever-that-cause-is work together to cause the universe)[129]—i.e., the "engagement" thesis. In

---

[127]   Paul Davies, "The Day Time Began", in Jeremy Webb (ed.), *Nothing* (London: Profile Books, 2013), p. 50.

[128]   Lawrence Krauss, *A Universe from Nothing* (London: Simon & Schuster, 2012), p. 170.

[129]   As Austin Farrer—who argues that "if God acts in the world, he acts particularly" (Farrer, *Faith and Speculation*, p. 61) so that "God's agency does not strike us in the springing point of causes but in the finished effect" (p. 63)—might think. Farrer calls this "double causality", that God is another cause alongside others. For Farrer, for example, God does not move the Assyrians to invade Israel, but the effect of Israel being invaded is as much a result of divine activity as it is caused by the Assyrians (p. 63). Thus, for Farrer, this is not to say that God causes the Big Bang *in addition to* or *in conjunction with another* physical/natural/material cause, but that the Big Bang is the effect of God.

different ways, both view divine activity as univocal with creatures: the first thinks that divine causes and created causes are the same; the second thinks divine causes are entirely different from created causes but can produce the same *effect*. That is, neither conforms to that for which this chapter has argued: that divine and created "activity" are "two types of *causality* corresponding to two different types of *effect* produced".[130]

"God creates a universe in which things have their own causal agency, their own self-sufficiency",[131] and so *creation* gives the universe the causal power to act as a cause itself, including being the cause of its own beginning. This might seem contradictory, as it seems to argue that, if the universe is the cause of its own beginning, there can be nothing that receives the power to then originate itself. However, such a contradiction is only a contradiction if one fails to recognize what *creation* actually means, and continues to conceive of it as an accidentally ordered origin. As Thomas Aquinas writes, "By bestowing *esse*, God produces also that which receives the *esse*, and thus there is no need for him to operate out of something that was already in existence".[132] In other words, there does not need to be something that temporally precedes God's bestowing of being that receives that being; the bestowal of being is the creation of that which also receives it. This same point was made above: God does not create *in order to have* relationship or participate; the relationship/ participation *is* the creation.

Importantly, this means that the question (often posed by atheists thinking they have trapped the theologian in a contradiction) that if God creates the world, then "who made God?"[133] is an entirely misunderstood question. If God is a "person" who "does things" and is the agent of discrete, particular, accidentally ordered events, one of

[130] Gilson, *Medieval Essays*, p. 156.

[131] Verschuuren, *Aquinas and Modern Science*, p. 104.

[132] Thomas Aquinas, quoted in Cornelio Fabro, "The Intensive Hermeneutics of Thomistic Philosophy: The Notion of Participation", *The Review of Metaphysics* 27:3 (1974), p. 473.

[133] Dawkins, *The God Delusion* (London: Black Swan, 2006), p. 136.

which is the origin of the universe, then the question "who made God?" becomes valid. Thomas Aquinas' recognition that it was philosophically possible (even if historically inaccurate) to suppose that there could be an infinite regression means that he would agree that if God causes the origin of the universe, then it is at least philosophically coherent to ask "who made God?" even if, in practice, the question does not quite make sense. However, if God is the *creator* of the universe, so the first in a finite ontological hierarchy of participation, and has nothing to do with the origin of the universe, then Dawkins' question becomes incoherent. God is the creator of the universe; God is that in which all things participate as the ground of being; God has nothing to do with the origin of the universe.

Creation, origins, and simplicity

As a result of the diminishing and impoverishing understanding of "causality" caused by the philosophical reactions to the scientific revolution, so scientists and even some theologians are prone to the mistake of thinking that if God is the creator, then God has to be responsible for the first "movement of atoms" at the origin/beginning of the universe. However, even theologians who are quite happy to see *creatio* as relationship and participation are prone to another mistake: even those who accept that creation is a hierarchical relationship rather than an "event" still make the mistake of assuming that, because of this hierarchical relationship, God can, and does, constrain and guide (or lure) the specific way that the universe moves. In other words, they think that because the world participates in God for its being, so God can constrain that world into particular manifestations or a certain state of affairs (e.g., the evolutionary emergence of humanity). In other words, they argue not just that God desires a creation, but that God desires a creation in which specific things happen to specific creatures in specific ways.[134]

It has already been argued that "God's radical, sustaining presence *in* the world as Creator precludes God's objective presence *to* creatures

---

[134] Davison, *Participation in God*, p. 231.

as the one who can be known and loved".[135] That is, God's being the "cause of being" prohibits God from being a "cause of motion". However, the doctrine of divine simplicity—which, it should be remembered, is nothing more than a vehicle for the absence of a real relation—can help to further nuance this idea that if God is that in which all things participate and that on which all things depend, then God cannot constrain the universe to move in certain ways to realize certain states of affairs. Divine simplicity has already been considered in the previous chapter. What is important about claims for divine simplicity is that they must apply to divine activity in the same way that they apply to divine "nature". That is, if God is simple, then God's activity must also be simple. For example, Thomas Aquinas writes that "if [God's activity is considered] on the part of the doer, there is only one activity in God . . . but considered on the side of what is done, there are indeed different activities".[136] In relation to the theology of Bonaventure, Junius Johnson writes that "since the divine essence is simple, it is simple also in its actions, which means that in one act it created matter and space, humans and angels, donkeys and cats. The divine creativity is an act that is one in itself, but many in its effects; one in its source, many in its relations to things".[137] Joshua Benson also writes of Bonaventure that "the objects that the divine truth expresses are many (either in actuality or possibility) and thus the things of the world are diverse. However, the expression or act by which these diverse objects are brought into reality is one".[138] To call divine activity

---

[135] McFarland, *The Word Made Flesh*, p. 60 (italics in original).

[136] Thomas Aquinas, *Selected Writings* (London: Penguin, 1998), *Disputed Questions on the Power of God 7*; see also William Stoeger, "Conceiving Divine Action in a Dynamic Universe", in Robert Russell, Nancey Murphy and William Stoeger (eds), *Scientific Perspectives on Divine Action: Twenty Years of Challenge and Progress* (Vatican City: Vatican Observatory Foundation, 2008), p. 231.

[137] Junius Johnson, "The One and the Many in Bonaventure Exemplarity Explained", *Religions* 7:144 (2016), p. 12; see also Katherin Rogers, *Perfect Being Theology* (Edinburgh: Edinburgh University Press, 2000), p. 27.

[138] Joshua C. Benson, "Structure and Meaning in St. Bonaventure's '*Quaestiones Disputatae de Scientia Christi*'", *Franciscan Studies* 62 (2004), p. 74.

simple means that there is an absence of a real relation between what God "does" and what is "done".[139] To use the language of Stump and Kretzmann, simplicity means that the "effect" of God's act is *extrinsic* to the "cause". There might be one divine act—as there necessarily must be if God is atemporal and simple—but there are multiple, various, and diverse effects that this single act causes.

In this way, Philip McCosker may well be correct to claim that grace is "uniform". Drawing on Thomas Aquinas' mountain analogy, McCosker writes that "the distinctions between different kinds of grace" are not between "different kinds of stuff . . . which do this or that", but, "rather Thomas' distinctions are ways of highlighting the way God's constant gracious action appears to us in different contexts".[140] So that as "light appears differently as it illuminates different objects",[141] so "viewed from God's point of view the bestowal of grace is uniform, but viewed from the human perspective, with varying degrees of preparation and cooperation, the effects of grace differ".[142] McCosker also compares grace to electricity, which powers various and diverse things (i.e., one cause but many distinct, extrinsic effects).[143] For God, that one act is entirely and absolutely the same—it is uniform and "isotropic"; for creatures that grace appears entirely different in entirely different situations and has entirely different "effects", because the "effects" of grace are extrinsic to that grace.

Importantly, this does not mean that God is "doing" something at each and every spatiotemporal moment; it does not mean that God does one "thing" many "times". If atemporality means that all spatiotemporal points are present to God rather than God being present at all spatiotemporal

---

139 Of course, this chapter has already argued that, strictly speaking, God does not "do" anything and has no "activity", but that language will still be used to talk about God's creating.

140 Philip McCosker, "Grace", in Philip McCosker and Denys Turner (eds), *The Cambridge Companion to The Summa Theologiae* (Cambridge: Cambridge University Press, 2016), p. 210.

141 McCosker, "Grace", p. 210.

142 McCosker, "Grace", p. 216.

143 McCosker, "Grace", p. 208.

points, then it "does not follow from the world's dependence on God *at all times*" that "God's creative activity [should] therefore be understood to be performed *at all times*".[144] God does not do something at every spatiotemporal point, but every spatiotemporal point is an *extrinsic* effect of the one divine cause.

The pillar analogy is crucial to understanding this idea. Aquinas writes that "'on the right' is not applied to a column, unless it stands as regards an animal on the right side; which relation is not really in the column, but in the animal . . . [so] . . . a column is on the right of an animal, without change in itself, but by change in the animal".[145] If the column moves to being "on the left", then that change is in the animal, not in the column itself. The column does not move itself, but different things are said about it depending on the animal's relation to the column. Likewise for divine grace. There is only one (simple) grace, which God bestows "once" from eternity, but that grace can have various diverse and multiple effects due to the relation of that effect to grace. Anselm's example of God being merciful without actually being merciful is another perfect illustration.[146] Mercy is an extrinsic effect of the one divine grace; God is not actually merciful, but the recipient of grace experiences that grace as mercy depending on the relation of the recipient to God.

Further, if simplicity of activity can mean "unity"—there is only one divine "act"—and it can also mean "uniformity"—it is objectively the same for God, differentiated only by those that receive it and not in and of itself—then it can also mean "basic". Thomas Tracy writes that "the regress 'down' an instrumental series must come to an end at some point,

---

[144] Robin Attfield, *Creation, Evolution and Meaning* (Aldershot: Ashgate Publishing, 2006), p. 77 (italics added); that is, the "move" from creation to conservation is not a repetition of the *creatio ex nihilo*, or a different divine act, but a change in the *extrinsic* relation of the creature to God's eternal single act; creation and conservation are different ways of the creature relating to God's act, not a different way for God to act (see Matthew R. McWhorter, "Aquinas on God's Relation to the World", *New Blackfriars* 94:1049 (2013), pp. 3–19.

[145] *ST* 1, 13, 7.

[146] Anselm, *Proslogion* 8.

however, and it can do so only in an action that an agent undertakes without having to perform an intentionally prior action as a means to this end. Such an action is 'basic.'[147] That is, to call God's activity simple, does not mean that God does one thing that looks the same for all creatures, but that one thing is itself composed of other activity. Maurice Wiles, for example, argues that "we can make best sense of this whole complex of experience and of ideas if we think of the whole continuing creation of the world as God's one act",[148] however, he clarifies that this *one* act, "like many human acts, is complex".[149] Thus, while he is clear that "we should see the gradual emergence of our world as a *single* divine act", what he means by this is not that it is literally one single act, but that "it is a purposeful occurrence, whose disparate features are held together by a unity of intention"[150]. This is not how divine activity should be understood. If God's activity is "one" and "uniform" then it is also "basic".

Affirming that divine activity is "one", "uniform", and "basic" leads to an important implication that is often overlooked by theologians: if God's activity is "one", "uniform", and "basic", then this must correspond to God's will being "one", "uniform", and "basic". In other words, to call divine activity simple does not mean that God has complex intentions for that single activity. If God did have complex intentions or "plans" for creation, then this seems to contradict divine simplicity. Thaddeus Metz, for example, asks, "How could there be an absolutely simple being which has multiple ends, one for humans and one for animals?" So, "Even if human and animal purposes are components of a single plan for the universe, the fact of there being components would imply a lack of simplicity."[151] If there is a uniformity and basic-ness of grace,

---

147   Thomas Tracy, "Divine Action, Created Causes, and Human Freedom", in Thomas Tracy, *The God Who Acts* (University Park, PA: The Pennsylvania State University Press, 1994), p. 81.

148   Maurice Wiles, *God's Action in the World*, (London: SCM Press, 1986), p. 93.

149   Wiles, *God's Action in The World*, p. 93.

150   Wiles, *God's Action in The World*, p. 54 (italics added).

151   Metz, "Could God's Purpose Be the Source of Life's Meaning?", p. 310; see also Robert Burns, "The Divine Simplicity in St. Thomas", *Religious Studies* 25:3 (1989), p. 290.

then this must correspond to a uniformity and basic-ness of will. God cannot have different intentions for different creatures. If God cannot have different intentions for different creatures, then God cannot have different intentions for different spatiotemporal points in each individual creature's life. God, at all times and at all places, desires exactly the same basic "thing".

Yet, this does not mean that God wills *for* simplicity, only that God's will *is* simple. Clearly the world is a diverse and complex place and diverse and complex things happen to the diverse and complex creatures that populate it. That is because that diversity and complexity are extrinsic to the grace on which that universe depends. There is an absence of a real relation between the grace that is responsible for everything existing and happening and that which exists and happens. To once again appeal to the pillar analogy, grace remains exactly the same and is uniform and basic to all spatiotemporal points, but those diverse spatiotemporal points will relate to that grace differently. Thus, the absence of a real relation is the answer to the question of how a single, simple, and uniform "act" and "will" can create multiplicity and diversity. The simplicity of divine will does not mean that there is not genuine multiplicity and diversity in the world. That God has a simple will does not mean that the multiplicity and diversity are *against* the will of God. It just means that the simple will of God is manifested in various and diverse ways.

Yet, importantly, if the absence of a real relation does not mean that the simplicity of the divine will leads to a simple and uniform creation, then a diverse and complex creation does not lead to a diverse and complex will. That is, that there are various and diverse ways in which the divine will is manifested does not mean that any of those diverse ways are themselves part of the divine will. In other words, God cannot "use" the fact that there is an absence of a real relation in order to determine that the single, simple act *will have* diverse and complex effects, and certainly not in order to determine *precisely which* particular diverse and complex effects actually obtain. If God were to prefer specific particular effects of the simple divine will, then that will would not be simple to begin with. Likewise, if God did prefer some specific particular effects over others, then this would destroy the absence of a real relation; God would in fact be really related differently to some spatiotemporal points than others.

If the effect and the difference and multiplicity of effects are genuinely extrinsic to God, then this cannot be something that God utilizes in order to achieve specific ends. If God constrains how and which extrinsic effects of the single, simple, atemporal, immutable "cause" obtain, occur, or are realized, then this seems to imply that God *does* have a real relation with the world, and objectively prefers specific effects and states of affairs to others. In other words, God cannot constrain or determine *how* that single divine act is going to be manifested, or what effect it will have. If God constrains that the single divine act has this particular effect for John and that particular effect for Paul, then God's will changes from John to Paul, so is not uniform or simple. If God desires for John to "do this" and for Peter to "do that", or for "this" to happen to John and for "that" to happen to Peter, then, regardless of whether God simply does one thing to bring that diverse state of affairs about, there is a real difference between how God relates to both John and Peter.

Thus, if God is genuinely immutable and simple, God has only a basic will to create and has absolutely no preference for how that creation goes (i.e., the will is uniform). As Paul Tillich writes, "from the point of view of the creator, the purpose of creation is the exercise of his creativity, which has no purpose beyond itself because the divine life is essentially creative", so that "God's purpose is to have a communion of love with the world"[152] (although this neither makes the world necessary, nor God incomplete without it). Any other desire or want, any desire for a specific and particular state of affairs, contradicts the absence of a real relation because it would mean that God is really related differently to (i.e., God prefers) different states of affairs.

If God is simple, and has a simple will, then God cannot be thought of as *designing* the world. In *The God Delusion*, Richard Dawkins, criticizing Richard Swinburne, argues that any God capable of *designing* the universe must necessarily be complex. Dawkins writes:

> Any God capable of designing a universe, carefully and
> foresightfully tuned to lead to our evolution, must be a supremely
> complex and improbable entity who needs an even bigger

---

[152] Tillich, *Systematic Theology Vol. 1*, pp. 263–4.

explanation than the one he is supposed to provide . . . but how can Swinburne possibly maintain that this hypothesis of God simultaneously keeping a gazillion fingers on wayward electrons is a *simple* hypothesis? . . . a God capable of continuously monitoring and controlling the individual status of every particle in the universe *cannot* be simple . . . worse, other corners of God's giant consciousness are preoccupied with the doings and emotions and prayers of every single human being.[153]

In the last chapter it was suggested that by criticizing Swinburne, Dawkins unwittingly does more to support the position taken by "traditional theists" than he would care to acknowledge. The same is true here. By criticizing the "theistic personalist" sense in which God is simple but designs the universe, Dawkins is doing nothing more than unwittingly supporting what has been outlined here: the idea of a designing God cannot be reconciled with a simple God. Conor Cunningham also notes that orthodox Christianity has always distinguished between a creator God and a designer God, warning that "a designer deity would elicit atheism from a Christian, for any such deity would only be a big version of us".[154] Thus, Robert Burns warns that one must choose between "an absolutely simple being and a creative intelligence".[155] If God designed the world, then God would have specific intentions for specific spatiotemporal points. God creates, which means that the universe depends upon and participates in God; it does not mean that God does something at a specific point and then constrains the history of the universe in order for specific events to happen.

---

153 Dawkins, *The God Delusion*, pp. 176–8 (italics in original); see also p. 136 and p. 183.

154 Conor Cunningham, *Darwin's Pious Idea* (Grand Rapids, MI: William B. Eerdmans, 2010), p. 151; again, then, simplicity (like atemporality) is necessary to guard against the univocality of being, and to prevent God from being nothing more than a "super-creature", or a less-limited creature.

155 See Burns, "The Divine Simplicity in St. Thomas", p. 276.

Creation, origins and emanation

Of course, affirming that divine *activity* is "one", "uniform", and "basic" must be taken with a pinch of salt. Strictly speaking, there is no divine "activity", but these adjectives must describe the relationship that creatures have with God. Understanding the fact that God does not "do" anything but that creatures have a relation with God has led to theologians using the image of the sun to describe divine activity. That is, if divine grace is entirely one, uniform, and basic at every spatiotemporal point, is not the "cause" of anything, is essentially ordered to the universe, and is in no way identifiable with the origin of the universe, then this grace *emanates* from God.

Pseudo-Dionysius writes that the sun "exercises no rational process, no act of choice, and yet by the very fact of its existence it gives light to whatever is able to partake of its light, in its own way". It is the same with God, who "existing far above the sun, an archetype far superior to its dull image, [God] sends the rays of its undivided goodness to everything with the capacity, such as this may be, to receive it". Crucially, Pseudo-Dionysius continues that "these rays are responsible for all intelligible and intelligent beings, for every power and every activity".[156] Torstein Theodor Tollefsen also uses the imagery of light, writing that divine activity is "like a field of energy, [or] a radiance of light constantly accompanying the divine being", which is an "eternal movement of the Holy Trinity . . . *in accordance with the one divine will*".[157] John of Damascus also writes that "the divine irradiation and operation is one, simple, and undivided; and that, while it is apparently diversely manifested in divisible things, dispensing to all of them the components of their proper nature, it remains simple".[158] The simple "irradiation" of grace is the single divine act of the simple divine will; what it "illuminates" and how that thing is "illuminated" are extrinsic to it.

---

[156] Pseudo-Dionysius, *The Divine Names* 4.1

[157] Tollefsen, *Activity and Participation in Late Antique and Early Christian Thought*, pp. 131–2 (italics added).

[158] John of Damascus, *An Exact Exposition of the Orthodox Faith* (New Delhi: Isha Books, 2013), p. 38.

Two comments are necessary. The first is that there is a connection with what was concluded above in terms of the relationship of creation with the Big Bang, that is, there does not need to be a "patient" that temporally precedes the irradiation to receive it. To quote again Thomas Aquinas, "By bestowing *esse*, God produces also that which receives the *esse*, and thus there is no need for him to operate out of something that was already in existence".[159] The relationship—i.e., the participation of creatures in the divine eternal radiation of grace—*is* the act of creation; God does not create creatures who can *then* receive that radiation, but the radiation is the creation. Second, and following from this first point, precisely because the divine emanation is eternal and the universe is not, and because there is an absence of a real relation, so even the very fact that the universe *exists at all* is entirely extrinsic to God. William Lane Craig (who is critical of this aspect of Thomas Aquinas' thought), explains that the absence of a real relation means that:

> in every world God exists in every respect the same. Even in worlds in which He does not create, His act of being, by which creation is produced, is no different in these otherwise empty worlds than in worlds chock-full of contingent beings of every order. The only difference is that in worlds in which God creates there is, from God's perspective, that *relatio rationis* to finite things.[160]

That is, God does not relate to "empty worlds" and "chock-full worlds" any differently; if God did, then there would not be an absence of a real relation. The only difference between "empty worlds" and "chock-full worlds" is that there is a different relation between the latter with God. The difference between universe or no-universe is not a difference *for* God. Thus, "God is no different whether He [sic] creates or does not create and that the difference between these two alternatives lies wholly

---

[159] Thomas Aquinas, quoted in Fabro, "The Intensive Hermeneutics of Thomistic Philosophy", p. 473.

[160] Craig, "Timelessness, Creation, and God's Real Relation to the World", p. 109.

in the created being".[161] The only difference between a world in which God does create and a world in which God does not is that in a world in which God does create there are creatures that have a mixed relation to God; God does nothing different or is not different.

For Thomas Aquinas, this was because there could be no potentiality in God—God is "*actus purus*".[162] The change from no universe to universe is a change, not creation. That is, the move from no universe to universe does not represent a move from potentiality to actuality *for* God. God is immutable, so whether there is a universe or no universe represents no change *for* God; God is the same whether there is a universe or not.[163]

The use of such terms as "*emanatio*" might be problematic to modern sensibilities (who normally object to it on the basis that it denies God's *free choice* to create),[164] but they are used to show that creation is not an "event", but a relationship; they are used to show that creation is *participatio*. God's "act" is eternal, it has no start, and it does not change. It is the same whether and to what extent anything participates in it, so it is simple. Precisely because God is immutable, so any difference in whether or to what extent things participate in grace must be extrinsic to God. God creates, but whether there actually is a universe and what happens to that universe is due to a change that happens in the universe and so is extrinsic to, and undetermined by, God.

---

[161] Craig, "Timelessness, Creation, and God's Real Relation to the World", p. 109.

[162] This same idea—i.e., the sun analogy by which the divine "activity" is seen as emanation—can be put differently. Thomas Aquinas also referred to this idea as God as *actus purus*, by which he meant that God is "pure actuality" and has no potential. If God is "pure actuality" and so there is no potential in God, then the universe moving (or changing) from potential to actual cannot be real for God. Even the very creation of the universe—i.e., the fact that the universe actually obtains—does not change God in any way.

[163] McWhorter, "Aquinas on God's Relation to the World"; see also Kerr, "A Thomistic Metaphysics of Creation", pp. 345–7.

[164] See pp.353ff. for further discussion of this apparent denial of God's free choice.

Creation and conservation

Richard Cross distinguishes between creation as an event and creation as emanation by delineating them as creation in a "strong sense" and creation in a "weak sense". The "strong sense" of creation is defined as "the view that God's activity is at some time causally sufficient for the existence of everything else at that time" and is characterized as "conservation is reducible to creation". The "weak sense" of creation is defined as "the view that God's activity is never more than causally necessary for the existence of things" and is characterized as "creation is reducible to conservation".[165] For those who accept the "strong sense" of creation, all conservation is just "repeated" or "continuing" creation. Philip Quinn would be a good example of this. He writes that "divine conservation just is continuous creation".[166] This means that "if God's bringing about of contingent existence is all the creation there is . . . and divine creation just is creation *ex nihilo* . . . then all creation is creation *ex nihilo*".[167] Thus, Quinn writes that the difference between creation and conservation is that creation is a "case in which divine volition brings about the existence of a creature at a time and that instance of time is one prior to which there is no other at which that creature existed", whereas conservation is an identical case yet "that instant of time is one prior to which there are others at which that creature existed".[168]

However, as Quinn himself recognizes, this can lead to occasionalism. William Lane Craig criticizes Quinn, suggesting that if every single millisecond is a *creatio ex nihilo*, then there is nothing to connect the successive moments of time, which provokes the question, "If at every *t* God creates *ex nihilo*, is it really *x* which exists at successive instants rather than a series of simulacra?",[169] and if it is just a series of simulacra, then

[165]   Richard Cross, "The Eternity of the World and the Distinction between Creation and Conservation", *Religious Studies* 42:4 (2006), pp. 405–7.

[166]   Philip Quinn, "Divine Conservation, Secondary Causes, and Occasionalism", in Thomas Morris (ed.), *Divine and Human Action: Essays in the Metaphysics of Theism* (Ithaca, NY: Cornell University Press, 1988), p. 54.

[167]   Quinn, "Divine Conservation, Secondary Causes, and Occasionalism", p. 71.

[168]   Quinn, "Divine Conservation, Secondary Causes, and Occasionalism", p. 54.

[169]   Craig, "Creation and Conservation Once More", p. 184.

it is reasonable to suggest they do not have genuine causal power. That is, the accidentally ordered series of cause and effect that all creatures experience in the world is an illusion because, for Quinn, at every single spatiotemporal point the entire universe is being created again *ex nihilo*.

However, there is another reason why this "strong sense" of creation should be criticized: it assumes that creation is the origin of the universe. The "strong sense" of creation assumes that God does something at a particular point and *then* conserves it. To put this differently, this "strong sense" of creation seems to assume that God is "omnitemporal": that God is present at all spatiotemporal points and is doing something at each of those points in order to create and then conserve the world. All Quinn claims is that God is doing the same thing at each of those spatiotemporal points; but God must be present and doing something at each spatiotemporal point, even if that "thing" is the same "thing". The "strong sense" of creation, therefore, assumes that God's life is stretched out alongside the life of the universe. Yet, as already quoted from Robin Attfield, that the world depends on God at every moment does not mean that God does something at every moment.[170] Creation does not mean that God is doing something at each spatiotemporal point, but that each spatiotemporal point is dependent on God and participates in God. Each spatiotemporal point is related to God as the circumference of a circle to its centre. The "weak sense" of creation—that all creation is conservation—has precisely this meaning. In the "weak sense" of creation, God does not do anything—least of all "in the beginning"—but creation is the relation that creatures have to God, who depend entirely on God. Claiming that all creation is conservation is simply another way of affirming that creation is completely different from origins, and is thus essentially ordered to the universe, not accidentally ordered.[171]

---

[170]   Attfield, *Creation, Evolution and Meaning*, p. 77.

[171]   This also points to why *creatio continua* must be incorrect. Creation is not limited to "some putative first moment", but neither does it continue throughout the temporal duration of the universe; both ideas conceive of God as "omnitemporal". If God is atemporal—so that all spatiotemporal moments are present to God, rather than God being present to all spatiotemporal moments—then God sustains the world at every moment because every

The "strong sense" of creation seems to confuse "creation" and "origins", and has God doing something at each spatiotemporal point; the "weak sense" of creation separates "creation" from "origins", and has each spatiotemporal point participating in God. Thus, if Plantinga completely missed the point about simplicity because he failed to acknowledge that it means absolutely nothing about simplicity but is actually a vehicle for the absence of a real relation, then those such as Quinn and Craig completely miss the point about creation and conservation because they fail to acknowledge that identifying creation and conservation means absolutely nothing about the content of those activities but is actually a vehicle for the absence of a real relation. In other words, for the "weak sense" of creation, the distinction between creation and conservation is extrinsic to God. As above, this does not mean that God is causally impotent or that something else must be causally responsible for the Big Bang. It just means that "creation" is not something that is concerned with the origin of the universe. If that is the case, then this cannot be separate from "conservation". It is not that the theologian is involved in a theological sleight-of-hand that forces together and confuses two logically distinct activities; it is that the distinction between them is extrinsic to God.

Theism or deism?

What this chapter has done is to argue that, if one subscribes to an atemporal and simple God then, as many commentators recognize, one is obliged to argue that there is only one single divine act. God's act cannot be temporally or typally divided in any way whatsoever. If God's act were temporally divided—i.e., God did one or many "things" many times— then God would be subject to time. If God's act were typally divided—i.e., God did many different "things" either once or many times—then God would be complex and have a complex range of intentions for different creatures at different spatiotemporal points. Yet, Thomas Aquinas was

---

moment participates in God, not because God "continues" to "do" something at every moment.

absolutely clear that "God's activity can be considered either on the part of the doer or of the done" and, if it is considered "on the part of the doer, there is only one activity in God . . . but considered on the side of what is done, there are indeed different activities".[172] Moreover, if Lucas, Plantinga, Metz, Marcus, etc., are correct that an atemporal and simple God would be unable to act, then the simple and eternal divine "act" is not really an "act" at all; it is an eternal emanation of grace that is essentially ordered to all spatiotemporal points and all creatures, who depend on it for their being through participation/imitation. Such is the content of the doctrine of the absence of a real relation and God as "pure actuality". It is not that God does things; it is that creatures depend on God for their very being.

It should also be evident that the distinction between creation as accidentally ordered act/origin and creation as essentially ordered emanation/participation is perfectly capable of being mapped onto the distinction made in the previous chapter. Those who subscribe to "theistic personalism" are obliged to argue for the former and those who subscribe to "traditional theism" are obliged to argue for the latter. Crucially, then, if the latter is more amenable to deism, then the fact that this leads to the suggestion that there is only one divine "act" seems to further substantiate the conclusion that deism is supported by what has been argued for here. Yet, those theologians mentioned here in support of it—specifically Thomas Aquinas—emphatically did not argue for deism. Thus, a few comments are necessary to explain how a theology that is explicitly theistic can be marshalled in support of deism.

The theology that is presented here has drawn heavily on Thomas Aquinas, but it is not entirely faithful to Aquinas' position. That is, in as much as it might be a valid application of Thomas' theology, it is not exactly what he *actually* thought. He certainly did see creation as being a relation that creatures had with God, and he certainly did see creation as an emanation that does not change God whether or not a universe actually exists. However, Thomas also certainly thought that God could realize specific things in the universe, either as working

---

[172] Aquinas, *Disputed Questions on the Power of God* 7; see also McCosker, "Grace", pp. 208–16.

through secondary causes or immediately through miracles.[173] After all, if Eleonore Stump argued that Thomas Aquinas thought that God was both the "ground of being" *and* "*a* being", then it is unsurprising that Thomas Aquinas thought that God could act as both a "cause of being" *and* a "cause of motion". While this book has sought to draw a sharp distinction between "God as person"—who does things as a cause *per accidens*—and "God as ground of being"—who is depended upon (participated in) as a cause *per se*—Thomas Aquinas saw them as being compatible.

How or why might this be the case? Étienne Gilson writes that Thomas Aquinas "intentionally buried" the distinction between "cause of being" and "cause of motion" in favour of "a quite general notion of efficient cause".[174] Whereas Thomas' teacher, Albert the Great, and other scholastic writers were keen to distinguish them, Thomas Aquinas was quite happy to see them as being more or less the same (perhaps Swinburne was correct after all, and Thomas leant towards univocality of being). It is no surprise, then, to learn that commentators such as Richard Dawkins confused Thomas' meaning when reading his *Quinque Viae* after the scientific revolution had impoverished the meaning of "cause". Thomas certainly understood two different types of cause, but he was content to keep them together under the heading of "efficient cause".

It is no coincidence that, as outlined here, Thomas Aquinas was adamant that God acted both as the "ground of being" and as a distinct individual who could bring about specific events or states of affairs because, as outlined in the previous chapter, Thomas Aquinas thought that God was both "*a*" being and the "ground of being". However, while Stump might be correct that this is what Thomas thought, this chapter has sided with Tillich (and Kittle, Grigg, and Ritchie) in suggesting that perhaps Thomas made a mistake in so thinking. Tillich was adamant that Thomas had failed to follow the logic of his own position.[175] This chapter agrees with that assessment. What is being offered here, then, is a Thomism seen through the lens of Tillich or a Tillichism described in scholastic language. Thus, God as "ground of being" prevents God

---

[173] *ST* 1, 105, 6.

[174] Gilson, *Medieval Essays*, p. 156.

[175] Tillich, *Systematic Theology Vol. 1*, p. 205, p. 236.

from being accidentally ordered to the universe and everything that goes with it. Miracles are only possible if divine activity is univocal with creaturely activity, in that it supposes that what God does is the same as creatures (i.e., cause an observable change in the observable universe) but just infinitely greater. Yet, if the sharp distinction between accidentally ordered and essentially ordered causation accurately maps onto the distinction between cause of being and cause of motion and *creatio* and *mutatio*, then God being a cause of motion would necessarily temporally locate God. Such a sharp distinction must be maintained: contra Thomas, God cannot constrain whether and how the universe moves, and neither can God manipulate the absence of a real relation to ensure that God's simple will is manifested in specific ways at specific spatiotemporal points to specific creatures. This conclusion looks very much like deism: God creates but cannot be thought of as "subsequently" influencing the universe in any way.

Moreover, the fact that Thomas Aquinas thought that God *could* influence the world in specific ways to bring about specific states of affairs entirely through constraining the way that secondary causes "move" means that he is open to the charge of occasionalism, i.e., that creatures only have the appearance of causality; they do not actually possess any causal power. If God is the source of every accidentally ordered cause of motion then this significantly weakens the claim that secondary causes— such as humans—retain any genuine freedom or causal power. It is easy to see how such comments made by Thomas Aquinas as claiming that secondary causes are "the executors of His [i.e., God's] order",[176] or that "all agents act in virtue of God himself: and therefore He [sic] is the cause of action in every creature",[177] and so "God is more especially the cause of every action than are the secondary agent causes"[178] have led critics to question whether Thomas was (however unwittingly) an exponent of occasionalism.[179] Ignacio Silva gives expression to these questions,

---

[176] *ST* I, q. 22, a. 3, ad 2.

[177] *ST* I, q. 105, a. 5.

[178] *SCG* III, 67, no. 5.

[179] If God influences the outcome of events in the world, then, so some commentators argue, creatures do not have genuine causal freedom.

writing that "emphasizing God's action as primary cause runs the risk of falling into a form of occasionalism, where it is only God who causes events in nature"[180] and that if the doctrine of primary and secondary causality is understood as "God's being one of the efficient causes affecting every event" then this "comes close to occasionalism or to denying God's divinity".[181] Kittle, Grigg, and Ritchie have already been quoted criticizing this aspect of Thomas' thought. If one wishes to retain Aquinas' general scheme, but without leaving oneself open to the charge of occasionalism, then one has to do what Thomas did not: i.e., sharply and explicitly distinguish between "cause of being" and "cause of motion", and maintain that God's primacy as the former does not imply that God can influence the latter. That is, Thomas' system only leads to occasionalism if "cause of being" and "cause of motion" are "forced together [into] one and same species",[182] so that "the cause that makes ['things'] move is the same as that which makes ['things'] exist".[183]

The example of French Dominican theologian Durandus of Saint-Pourçain is illustrative here. Durandus found the inference that Thomism led to occasionalism problematic and so reacted against this element of

---

Creatures only have the illusion of freedom. God is like a cosmic magician, who tells us we can freely choose whichever card we wish when really God is forcing a card upon us. No doubt, as already noted above, some will say that God's influence and creaturely activity are not in competition with one another, so God can influence the world and creatures have genuine freedom. However, this is the point of the chapter's sharp distinction between "being" and "motion". If God is concerned with "motion", then there is no possible way that God's influence *cannot* be in competition with creaturely activity, which is also "motion". Once the divine influence is reduced to "moving some atoms" (i.e., "motion"), then it does not matter *how* God brings about this motion—either directly or through secondary causes—there is no way that it *cannot* be in competition with created activity.

[180] Ignacio Silva, "Divine Action and Thomism: Why Thomas Aquinas's Thought is Attractive Today", *Acta Philosophica* 25:1 (2016), p. 79.

[181] Silva, "Divine Action and Thomism", p. 80.

[182] Gilson, *Medieval Essays*, p. 160.

[183] Gilson, *Medieval Essays*, p. 165.

Thomist theology. Durandus argued that God creates and conserves the world, but he disagreed with the Thomist position that every natural act was properly the work of God, being ascribed to both the natural agent *and* God, which he saw as being indistinguishable from occasionalism. Instead, Durandus argued, a natural act was properly the work of the natural agent, thereby "restricting" the work of God to just creation and conservation. Durandus was no deist—deism emerged with the scientific revolution a few hundred years later—but his criticisms of Thomas can certainly be seen as comparable with deism. It is certainly Thomism, but Thomism that sharply distinguishes between "cause of being" and "cause of motion" and so prohibits God from being concerned with "motion" entirely.

However, the problem with Durandus' position is that he saw the natural agent as being the *source* of their own causality, and denied that they participate in, and thus depend upon, God for their being able to act as cause.[184] For Durandus, if participation in God's causal power led to occasionalism, then, while creatures participated in God for their being, they did not participate in God for their causal power. Durandus must not be correct here. To suppose that the individual agent is the source of their own power to act is to elevate them to being independent of God. Surely, Thomas must be correct in the sense that the creature cannot have the power to act as a cause independently of their ontological dependence on God.[185] Yet, surely, Durandus must be correct that one cannot sustain a theological position in which God becomes not only the source of one's causal power, but also constrains how and whether that causal power is used. For Durandus, God is removed as the cause *per se* of each creature; for Thomas, all creatures become a sort of instrumental cause, no different from the stick that is moved by the hand. One does not wish to go as far as Durandus in claiming that the creature is the source of their own motion, but neither does one want to completely endorse Thomas' claim that God can constrain the movement of creatures.

---

[184] See Alfred Freddoso, "Introduction", in Alfred Freddoso (ed.), *On Creation, Conservation, and Concurrence* (South Bend, IN: St. Augustine Press, 2002), pp. lxxxvi–xcvii.

[185] See also Pseudo-Dionysius, *The Divine Names* 8.2.

Here, then, is where Duns Scotus' contribution might offer something of a middle position. For Scotus, there are three "types" of divine activity: (a) direct intervention, otherwise known as miracles (primary cause without secondary cause) or what Scotus termed "omnipotence";[186] (b) indirect intervention, otherwise known as instrumental cause (primary cause constraining the motion of the secondary cause); and (c) indirect "conservation" (primary cause as the source of the secondary cause's motion, but in no way constraining it).[187] Scotus and Aquinas accepted all three (although it is possible, given what has already been argued, that Thomas blurred the second two). Most modern theists would reject the first (or, if they are going to permit "miracles", reinterpret them to make them amenable to a world in which scientific investigation does not prohibit them), but accept the second two. Durandus and deists would reject both the first and second and accept something like the third. This book argues that, as modern theists mostly agree, science has made the first type untenable. It also suggests that a correct understanding of God as "ground of being"—which prohibits God from acting as a cause of motion at all (and seen through the lens of NOMA)—also makes the first type untenable. However, as this chapter has argued, that correct understanding of God as "ground of being"—when seen through the lens of the distinction between "cause of being" and "cause of motion"—also makes the second type untenable. Therefore, the third type is the only possible way of conceiving divine activity. Assuming that one accepts the notion that God cannot be an individual, discrete, personal being, then deism is the only available option.

Perhaps what we are dealing with here is fine margins, academic quibbles over minute details, but the language used is important; to call it deism emphasizes that God does not influence the accidental history of the world; to call it theism emphasizes that God is involved, even if that involvement is as "sustainer" rather than as in occasionalism. The difference between the theist and the deist is quite nuanced. Deism—at least in this Thomist paradigm—does not mean that the world is "an

---

[186] Cross, *Duns Scotus*, p. 57.

[187] See Mariusz Tabaczek, "What Do God and Creatures Really Do in an Evolutionary Change?", p. 32, fig. 4.

autonomous 'self-sufficient "world" that runs on its own steam'"[188] independent of God. This would be the deism of the theistic personalists, for whom God is like a "cosmic parent"—i.e., the first in an accidentally ordered series who, after originating the world, plays no further part. Deism in this Thomist sense denies occasionalism, but also denies (which Durandus argued) that the creature has the power to function as a "cause of motion" independently of God. Thus, this chapter has argued that God is the cause *per se* of the creature's being and causal power, but this in no way permits God to constrain *how* and *whether* the creature acts as a cause *per accidens*. Or, as Ignacio Silva writes, "God causes changes to be the changes that they are, but such divine causing is not itself a change."[189] Or, as Frederick Bauerschmidt writes, "'God' is the answer not to the question of why this or that thing occurs, but the question of why *anything* occurs."[190] In the language of Bulgakov, one might say the same thing differently: God "creates" those changes but God does not "cause" those changes. As Craig Boyd and Aaron Cobb write, "Although human agents draw their being and causal efficacy from God, it need not follow that their every act is immediately caused by God's concurrent activity."[191]

In this way, Koperski is wrong to suggest that "what distinguishes theism from deism" is the Thomist principle "that God is continuously involved with natural events in some way or other".[192] He claims that if one "remove[s] the clause about sustaining" then "one is left with deism,

---

[188] Jeffrey Koperski, *Divine Action, Determinism, and the Laws of Nature* (Abingdon: Routledge, 2020), p. 23, quoting James K. A. Smith, *Thinking in Tongues: Pentecostal Contributions to Christian Philosophy* (Grand Rapids, MI: Eerdmans, 2010), p. 97.

[189] Ignacio Silva, "Thomas Aquinas and William E. Carroll on *Creatio ex Nihilo*", p. 98.

[190] Bauerschmidt, *Thomas Aquinas: Faith, Reason, and Following Christ*, p. 97.

[191] Craig Boyd and Aaron Cobb, "The Causality Distinction, Kenosis, and a Middle Way: Aquinas and Polkinghorne on Divine Action", *Theology and Science* 7:4 (2009), p. 403; see also Ignacio Silva, "Revisiting Aquinas on Providence and Rising to the Challenge of Divine Action in Nature", *The Journal of Religion* 94:3 (2014), pp. 280–1.

[192] Koperski, *Divine Action, Determinism, and the Laws of Nature*, p. 17.

which few are willing to embrace".[193] Stephen Pope makes the same mistake, and contrasts "theistic evolutionists [who] regard the Creator as continually sustaining the ongoing operation of the natural world" with deism.[194] Yet, when deism is recast in a Thomist paradigm, the opposite of deism is not theism but occasionalism. Deism becomes not a question about how involved God is in the universe as another "being" or how minutely God micro-manages the history of that universe, but in what sense, or to what extent, the hierarchical/vertical ontological "structure" of existence impinges upon the historical/horizontal spatiotemporal motion of existence. That is, in this paradigm, deism does not claim that God is "absent" or "uninterested" in the universe, but that God is only "present" or "interested" in the world as that to which all creatures are essentially ordered and as that on which all creatures depend. "God may be irrelevant to the physical universe,"[195] not because God is uninterested, but because God is concerned with "being". It is not a question of how often God gets involved in, interacts with, or influences the world, but how deeply participation constrains the freedom of creatures to act as causes of motion. God, for the deist, has everything to do with being (*creatio*) and nothing to do with motion (*mutatio*).[196] Koperski and Pope

---

[193] Koperski, *Divine Action, Determinism, and the Laws of Nature*, p. 3.

[194] Stephen J. Pope, "Does Evolution Have a Purpose? The Theological Significance of William Stoeger's Account of 'Nested Directionality'", *Theological Studies* 78:2 (2017), p. 464.

[195] Grigg, "Religion, Science, and Evolution", p. 953.

[196] The reader might find the suggestion of this chapter that God is concerned solely with "being" and has nothing to do with "motion" odd, considering that "motion" is the first of Thomas' *Quinque Viae*. The first of Aquinas' "five ways" is that "motion" must lead back to an "unmoved mover", which is God. He writes that "it is certain, and evident to our senses, that in the world some things are in motion. Now whatever is in motion is put in motion by another, for nothing can be in motion except it is in potentiality to that towards which it is in motion; whereas a thing moves inasmuch as it is in act. For motion is nothing else than the reduction of something from potentiality to actuality. But nothing can be reduced from potentiality to actuality, except by something in a state of actuality (*ST* 1, 2, 3)." It seems strange to then claim

come dangerously close to confusing Thomism with occasionalism; they assume that there is no way for creatures to participate in God at every moment without that participation meaning that "God is more especially the cause of every action than are the secondary agent causes".[197] Rather, this book argues that the sharp distinction between "cause of being" and "cause of motion"—which is common to the scholastic theologians, even if Thomas blurred it—means not just that it is possible for creatures to participate in God for being without God constraining their changing/ motion, but that it is necessary for participation not to lead to a constraint on movement.

Therefore, what is being argued for here is not the "traditional" deism of Newton (and others). They reduce God to being the origin of the world. Rather, the deism argued for here "restricts" God to being the "vertical", "intermundane", "hierarchical" "cause of being" in which all creatures participate and on which all creatures depend. The "traditional" deist, who reduces God to origins and denies that God acts subsequently or further to being responsible for the origin of the universe, is the deist of

---

that God is not concerned with motion. However, as Frederick Bauerschmidt observes, "Thomas does not mean simply 'local motion', movement from point A to point B" (Bauerschmidt, *Thomas Aquinas: Faith, Reason, and Following Christ*, p. 100). David Bentley Hart has been quoted above saying much the same thing against Richard Dawkins (see Hart, *The Experience of God*, p. 22). As Clarke and Dodds cautioned (Dodds, "Science, Causality, and God: Divine Action and Thomas Aquinas", p. 22; see also Hart, *The Experience of God*, pp. 55-7; Clarke, *The Philosophical Approach to God*, p. 63; Feser, *Scholastic Metaphysics*, p. 97), it is the scientific revolution, and particularly Isaac Newton's theory of motion, that has perhaps caused this confusion. When all causality is reduced to a sort of "mechanical cause", then "motion" only takes on one meaning, and Thomas Aquinas' first "way" seems to mean "motion" as in a temporally extended "billiard-ball-esque" type of motion—which is a change—and which is not what Thomas meant. As above, God gives changes—motion—the being to be a change, but God does not constrain or determine those changes. In the language of Sergei Bulgakov, God "creates" those motions, but God does not "cause" motion.

[197]   *SCG* III, 67, no. 5.

"theistic personalism". The universe becomes the object of an act of which God is the subject. Or, in scholastic language, God is accidentally ordered to the universe. Both the "traditional deist" and Thomas Aquinas think that "if [God's activity is considered] on the part of the doer, there is only one activity in God";[198] however, for Thomas Aquinas, that "one activity" is the "*actus purus*" or divine emanation, whereas for the "traditional deist" that "one activity" is confined to origins and so leaves unactualized much potential divine activity subsequent to the Big Bang.

Pantheism or atheism?

For some, deism is closer to atheism than theism. Paul Tillich has already been quoted as arguing that the theist, if they are to correctly understand God as "ground of being", must be an atheist.[199] St. George Mivart was also quoted in support of that claim. Maurice Wiles also remarks that deism is "widely regarded as no different from atheism",[200] perhaps referring to those early adherents who used deism to mask their atheism. In this direction, it is important to note that *analogia entis* "intend[s] to provide a middle way between univocality and equivocality—or between anthropomorphism and agnosticism".[201] The theologian does not seriously want to argue for atheism or agnosticism, but neither does the theologian want to ascribe to a facile and infantile anthropomorphic "theistic personalism" that sees God as *another* being or *another* subject who constructs and then acts *upon* the universe. To claim that the theologian must be an atheist should be seen as nothing more than a complete refutation of any anthropomorphic theology. That is, to affirm atheism is not to claim that the universe is independent of a God that does not exist, but to affirm that God is not another discrete, individual, personal being.

---

[198]   Thomas Aquinas, *Disputed Questions on the Power of God* 7.

[199]   Tillich, *Systematic Theology Vol. 1*, p. 237.

[200]   Wiles, *God's Action in the World*, p. 2.

[201]   Schubert Ogden, "What Sense Does it Make to Say, 'God Acts in History'?", in Owen Thomas (ed.), *God's Activity in the World: The Contemporary Problem* (Chico, CA: Scholars Press, 1983), p. 86; see also Erich Przywara, *Analogia Entis* (Grand Rapids, MI: William B. Eerdmans, 2014), pp. 203–6.

However, interestingly, while some see deism and atheism as more or less the same, some move in the other direction, and see deism as having more in common with pantheism. John Polkinghorne, for example, writes that "the mystic's God, who is simply the sustaining ground of all being, is not far from the deist's God, whose action is the single creatory fiat by which the world's process is sustained", arguing that where one is an immanent detached deity the other is a transcendent detached deity, and "neither is the personally purposive God of the Judeo-Christian tradition".[202] Paul Tillich also acknowledges what many have noticed: that there is essentially no difference between the pantheist and the deist.[203] Again, perhaps these observations are helpful in order to emphasize, not that the Christian should be a pantheist, but that, contra Polkinghorne, the idea of a personally purposive God is something of a facile and infantile anthropomorphism.

Ultimately, then, it does not matter whether what is being argued for here is described as theism, deism, atheism, or pantheism. Each designation has something important to contribute to the theology presented in this chapter. What is important is re-framing the problem from a discussion about whether God is reduced or limited to origins—and so, in competition with scientific explanations, making God the "God of the gaps", and legitimizing Hawking's claim that once cosmologists dismiss a beginning to the universe then the need for a creator vanishes—to a discussion about the extent to which creatures' causal power is constrained by God through participation/imitation.

Conclusion

It is no surprise that deism emerged when it did. With the scientific revolution came both (a) the idea that all causality is reduced to something like a "mechanistic force", and (b) the appreciation that no divine agent is required at all to explain anything that happens in the universe. If thinkers after the scientific revolution were working with this

---

[202] John Polkinghorne, *Science and Providence* (London: SPCK, 1989), p. 36.
[203] Tillich, *Systematic Theology Vol. 1*, p. 262.

"reduced" sense of causality as "mechanistic force", then it is no surprise that traditional deists came to reduce God to nothing more than an "originator".

For this "original" or "traditional" view of deism, writes David Bentley Hart, God "was not the fullness of being, of whom the world was a wholly dependent manifestation, but was merely part of a larger reality that included both himself and his handiwork".[204] By viewing God as "originator", the deists brought God *within* the universe and (however unwittingly) made God something within the universe and part of it. These deists were still "theistic personalists", they just disagreed with other "theistic personalists" about whether God did anything further after originating the world. They were still apologizing for a God that Plantinga et al. would also accept: an individual person/subject/agent, who does something at a specific time.

However, once divine activity is recast to be about participation in God rather than as the cause of discrete acts, then deism once again becomes attractive as a way of guarding against occasionalism. In this vein, the deist is not someone who reduces or limits God to the beginning of the universe or who limits God to being nothing more than a preface to the question of the origins of the universe. The deist can maintain "God's involvement in every action as primary cause",[205] as does Thomas Aquinas, but the deist disagrees with the theist about the causal efficacy of such "involvement". By this is meant that one can maintain that creatures participate in God for their ability to act as a cause, to have being, to have power, to be intelligible etc., without it needing to imply that God can—or, indeed, does—constrain *how* and *whether* those creatures so act.

---

[204] Hart, *The Experience of God*, pp. 61–2.

[205] Silva, "Divine Action and Thomism", p. 68.

3

Creation II: Providence, Omnipotence, and Theodicy

Creation is just one aspect of questions relating to divine activity. Providence, omnipotence, and theodicy complement the question of creation. That is, what is said about creation has implications for providence, omnipotence, and theodicy. In fact, it might very well be said that creation is a particular "instance" or "example" of omnipotence, with providence being further or subsequent "instances" or "examples" of the very same omnipotence.

However, that being said, put in its very simplest terms, the deist is one who says that creation *does* in fact exhaust questions relating to divine activity. At the very least, if the deist accepts that God is both omnipotent and providential, then they maintain that God does not exercise those characteristics, or, at the very least, that God only exercises God's omnipotence once. Nevertheless, a discussion of omnipotence and providence can help to further nuance what was said in the last chapter regarding creation. If creation is understood as a hierarchical ontological relationship, rather than an act or an event, then what do omnipotence and providence add—if anything—to how that should be understood?

This chapter will argue that if creation is about "being", then providence and omnipotence must likewise be about being. In this way, providence becomes God's bringing things to ontological fulfilment, not ensuring that a perfect arrangement of atoms or state of affairs occurs in the future. Likewise with omnipotence. Omnipotence does not (or should not) mean that God can do everything in terms of "cause of motion", but God is the "cause of being" to everything that has "being".

God cannot do anything and everything it is possible to do, but is that on which everything depends.

Providence

Perhaps understandably, the deist completely denies providence. In fact, the distinction between deism and theism could be reduced to nothing more than a difference on this very issue: the theist affirms providence, while the deist denies it. Indeed, Christopher Knight claims that it is the "spectre of deism" that has made western theologians "quasi-instinctively phobic of any suggestion of a denial of special providence".[1] If providence is meant something like how Langdon Gilkey defines it, as "the rule of God over the events that make up the course of both nature and history" or "the purpose of God unfolding itself in the development of the cosmos and of human history",[2] then it is clear that it is this sense of divine "control" over the world that the deist denies and (western) theism is so anxious to affirm.

The last chapter argued that it was possible to construct a coherent deism using Thomist categories. If all creatures participate in God for their being and causal power, this does not mean that God can then influence whether and in what way any creature has being or causal power. That is, that creatures participate in God for *being* does not mean that God can constrain the *motion* of that creature. Thomas himself did not think this. For Thomas, secondary causes were also instrumental causes that could be controlled by God, not to mention that Thomas accepted the reality of miracles—when God directly and immediately caused a particular state of affairs without the mediation of a secondary/instrumental cause. That Thomas thought that God was both the ground of being and a person

---

[1]   See Christopher C. Knight, "Divine Action and the Laws of Nature: An Orthodox Perspective on Miracles", in Daniel Buxhoeveden and Gayle Woloschak (eds), *Science and the Eastern Orthodox Church* (Abingdon: Routledge, 2016), p. 43.

[2]   Langdon Gilkey, "The Concept of Providence in Contemporary Theology", *The Journal of Religion* 43:3 (1963), p. 171.

(as Stump argues) is probably why Thomas believed that God could do so. It also meant that Thomas understood "providence" more or less as Gilkey defines it. For Thomas:

> In created things good is found not only as regards their substance, but also as regards their order towards an end and especially their last end, which . . . is the divine goodness.[3] This good of order existing in things created, is itself created by God. Since, however, God is the cause of things by His intellect, and thus it behooves that the type of every effect should pre-exist in Him . . . it is necessary that the type of the order of things towards their end should pre-exist in the divine mind: and the type of things ordered towards an end is, properly speaking, providence.[4]

In other words, Thomas says, just as God is the efficient cause of all creatures (understood, as the previous chapter outlined, as a cause *per se* of "being"), so God is the final cause of all creatures, and that means providence. Thomas Aquinas continues that nothing escapes God's providence and that such a providence is immediate.

However, Thomas' claim that such immediate providence over everything does not make necessary things unforeseen betrays his particular understanding of what providence means. That is, Thomas is here quite clear that providence pertains to the occurrence of particular events:

> The effect of divine providence is not only that things should happen somehow; but that they should happen either by necessity or by contingency. Therefore whatsoever divine providence ordains to happen infallibly and of necessity happens infallibly and of necessity; and that happens from contingency, which the plan of divine providence conceives to happen from contingency.[5]

---

[3]   See *ST* 1, 21, 4.

[4]   *ST* 1, 22, 1.

[5]   *ST* 1, 22, 4.

For Thomas, providence is about God's control of history, and how God wills that all things are ordered to their last end in divine goodness.[6]

However, one need not understand providence in this way. Irish philosopher Ernan McMullin speculates that one of the reasons why evolutionary biologists are so against the use of "teleology" as a description of biological systems stems from "widespread misunderstanding of the notion of final causality that has traditionally accompanied it".[7] McMullin continues that "confusing two of the four causes or types of explanation listed by Aristotle, the critics [of teleology] suppose that postulating a 'final' cause implies a sort of backward efficient causality, somehow causing, in an agency sense of that term, a process already in the past".[8] Yet, this is not how Aristotle would have understood it. Rather, "citing the goal of a living activity is one way (Aristotle would add: the best way) to understand that activity but in no way ought this to be taken as endorsing a counter-intuitive sort of backward-in-time efficient causal action".[9] In other words, the final cause should not be seen as concerned with the future any more than efficient cause should be seen as concerned with the past. Or, better, neither are necessarily concerned with the motion of the universe and its realizing certain states of affairs that God prefers. The question of what this might mean for the deist will be explored in Chapter 6, but here it is enough to notice that if creation is not about origins, then providence is not about the movement of that universe towards a specific state of affairs.

Paul Tillich, who has already been quoted as claiming that "from the point of view of the creator, the purpose of creation is the exercise of his creativity, which has no purpose beyond itself because the divine life is essentially creative", so that "God's purpose is to have a communion

---

6   See also *ST* 1, 19.

7   Ernan McMullin, "Could Natural Selection Be Purposive?", in Joseph Seckbach and Richard Gordon (eds), *Divine Action and Natural Selection* (Singapore: World Scientific, 2008), p. 118.

8   McMullin, "Could Natural Selection Be Purposive?", p. 118.

9   McMullin, "Could Natural Selection Be Purposive?", p. 119.

of love with the world",[10] interprets providence similarly. While Tillich allowed for what he called "directing creation"[11]—which he distinguishes from "originating" and "sustaining" creation—he did not understand that as demanding providence as Gilkey defined it. Certainly, Tillich still defines providence as the "certainty that history . . . contributes to the ultimate fulfilment of creaturely existence". Indeed, one would find it quite difficult to argue that history does *not* contribute to the ultimate fulfilment of creaturely existence (if creatures are historical beings, who cannot exist without a particular spatial and temporal context, then history must form part of the fulfilment of creatures); yet, Tillich clarifies, "this fulfilment does not lie in an eventual time-and-space future".[12] In other words, just because creatures are historical beings—and so history must form part of the identity of "what" a creature is—it does not mean that the fulfilment of those creatures is identified as a future point whereby perfection is reached and/or obtained. If creation is "the exercise of creativity", then providence is "the fulfilment of that creativity", but neither are temporal categories: *creatio ex nihilo* is not "the title of a story" that begins in creation and ends in fulfilment but is "the classical formula which expresses the *relation* between God and the world".[13] To put it rather crudely, providence, like creation, must be "vertical" (i.e., *inter*mundane, ontological) rather than "horizontal" (i.e., *intra*mundane, historical).

When Thomas' definition of providence is seen through the lens of Tillich, then the end to which God orders creation becomes not God's control over the motion of atoms (which scenario pictures God as creating in much the same way that humans do, except that the material from which God constructs the world is "nothing", whereas humans are limited to constructing from other matter), but the ontological fulfilment of atoms. Again, what this "fulfilment" means will be left to Chapter 6,

10   Paul Tillich, *Systematic Theology Vol. 1* (Chicago, IL: The University of Chicago Press, 1957), pp. 263–4.

11   Tillich, *Systematic Theology Vol.1*, p. 264.

12   Tillich, *Systematic Theology Vol.1*, p. 267.

13   Tillich, *Systematic Theology Vol. 1*, p. 254 (italics added).

but here it is important to explore what it means for the path of history if providence is a "vertical" category.

Creation and evolution

Evolution is arguably the most important and obvious example of providence for contemporary theologians (at least among those who accept the validity of evolution and providence). This does not mean that deists do not, or cannot, accept evolution if they do not accept providence. The (traditional) deist might still argue that evolution is "how" God creates. The only difference between a theist and a deist in this respect is that the theist would be happy to affirm God's continuing guidance of evolution, whereas the deist would be restricted to seeing God set up the conditions of evolution (like winding a clock), who then "lights the blue touch paper" and does nothing more. However, if providence is reinterpreted as being the "fulfilment" of participation in God, then evolution cannot be seen as an expression of that providence. Likewise, if evolution is seen by those who accept the validity of evolution as the way that God creates, then this cannot be the case if creation is understood as participation. Thus, just as the previous chapter needed to address the question of how the theologian should understand the Big Bang and the beginning of the universe if neither are theologically relevant, so there is also the question of how the theologian should understand evolution if it is no longer an example of providence.

It is, of course, entirely coincidental that Charles Darwin chose to call his treatise *On the Origin of Species*, and yet, in light of what has already been claimed about the distinction between "creation" and "origins", it is highly appropriate. Evolution is about the "origin" of certain creatures, *not* their "creation". While an entire book could be devoted to a whole host of theologians who argue keenly and intelligently that God "uses" evolution to create, so that evolution becomes a more scientifically sophisticated replacement for the Genesis narrative, it is clear that, if creation is about the donation of *being*, it can have nothing to do with the process of biological *change*.

The Dutch Calvinist theologian Anthony Hoekema—while neither writing about theological interpretations of evolution nor working within the Thomist paradigm used in this book to distinguish clearly between "origin" and "creation"—makes an observation that is illustrative of this distinction. Writing about Genesis 5:3, he notes that the author(s) of Genesis do not say that "Adam's son Seth was made in the image and likeness of God", but rather say that "Adam became the father of a son in his likeness, after his image" and because "Adam was still the image-bearer of God, as we saw, we may infer that Seth, his son, was also an image-bearer of God".[14] Here, while God is not the "origin" of Seth, God absolutely is the "creator" of Seth in the sense that Seth is "made in God's image", which could be seen as a synonym for "participation" or "dependent on God". Adam can still be responsible for the origin of Seth as the cause of motion of Seth (or, as Gilson puts it, "the production of ... a new substance starting from already existing matter"[15]) without compromising or competing with God being responsible for the creation of Seth as the cause of being of Seth. Adam's being the "cause" of Seth does not mean that Seth does not participate in and depend on God.

Alfred Freddoso, writing about the theology of Francisco Suárez, makes a similar observation. He writes that "it seems reasonable to claim that one and the same effect is from God insofar as it is something rather than nothing and from its secondary causes insofar as it is an effect of a certain species". Using the example of an armadillo, Freddoso continues that "a newly conceived armadillo is from God insofar as it is something rather than nothing and from its parents insofar as it is an animal of the species *armadillo* rather than some other sort of effect".[16] Thus, there is a distinction between the "creation" of the armadillo—which "*just is* creation's dependence on God for its existence"[17]—and the "origin" of the armadillo—which is its being born from another armadillo. It is remarkable that a twentieth-century Calvinist can have

---

[14]   Anthony Hoekema, *Created in God's Image* (Grand Rapids, MI: William B. Eerdmans, 1994), p. 15; see also Genesis 5:1-3.

[15]   Étienne Gilson, *Medieval Essays* (Eugene, OR: Cascade Books, 2011), p. 156.

[16]   Alfred Freddoso, "Introduction", in Alfred Freddoso (ed.), *On Creation, Conservation, and Concurrence* (South Bend, IN: St. Augustine Press, 2002), p. lxxxviii.

[17]   John Bishop and Ken Perszyk, "The Divine Attributes and Non-personal Conceptions of God", *Topoi* 36 (2017), p. 614 (italics in original).

such a strikingly similar perspective to that of a seventeenth-century Jesuit but, nevertheless, they seem to be making an identical distinction, a distinction between "creation" and "origin".

That distinction could be described slightly differently as between "*that* something is" and "*what* something is", which directly and exactly corresponds to the distinction between the essentially ordered cause of being (*creatio*) and the accidentally ordered cause of motion (*mutatio/ generatio*).[18] That is, the first is an appeal to an essentially ordered cause that is concerned with a theological, ontological hierarchy that ontologically transcends it, whereas the second is an appeal to an accidentally ordered cause that is concerned with the historico-scientific causal nexus that temporally precedes it. In other words, the first is concerned with participation and imitation and the second is "more or less, what is usually meant by 'cause' in contemporary philosophy".[19]

To suppose "*that* something is" and "*what* something is" is due to the same identical "cause"—as all theologians who suppose that God creates through evolution suppose—is to confuse and "force" together "two types of causality corresponding to two different types of effect produced".[20] To confuse "*that* something is" with "*what* something is" is precisely the same confusion that cosmologists and physicists (and no few theologians) make when they assume that "creation" is the same as "origins"; that is, it is to confuse "the cause that makes ['things'] move" and "that which makes ['things'] exist".[21] An armadillo (to use Freddoso's example) has its "origins" in its parents, which "causes" it to be an armadillo, but has its "creation" in God, which "creates" it. Or, as already quoted from Bauerschmidt, "'God' is the answer not to the question of why this or that thing occurs, but the question of why *anything* occurs".[22]

---

[18]   See Brian Davies, "Aquinas on What God is Not", *Revue Internationale de Philosophie* 52:204 (1998), pp. 220–1.

[19]   Edward Feser, *Scholastic Metaphysics: A Contemporary Introduction* (Heusenstamm: editiones scholasticae, 2014), p. 97.

[20]   Gilson, *Medieval Essays*, p. 156, p. 160.

[21]   Gilson, *Medieval Essays*, p. 165.

[22]   Frederick Bauerschmidt, *Thomas Aquinas: Faith, Reason, and Following Christ* (Oxford: Oxford University Press, 2013), p. 97.

Crucially, then, whereas the cause of "*what* something is" is different for each and every creature (determined with reference to its origin so that different "things" are different because they have different origins), the creation "*that* something is" is identical for all. While theologians are normally keen to emphasize the ontological superiority of humanity (quite often based on the perception that they are more conscious, more rational, and/or more free than other creatures), it is not often recognized that Patristic theologians were more ready to accept the *ontological* equality of all creatures. Thus, Andrew Louth, paraphrasing Gregory of Nazianzus, writes that "nothing is nearer or further away from God by virtue of the constitution of its being ... the most exalted archangel is, in metaphysical terms, no closer to God than a stone: God transcends all creatures infinitely".[23] "*That* something is" is identical for each and every creature; "*what* something is" is entirely different for each and every creature.

The absence of a real relation is crucial here. The Lateran formula, it was noted, defines that "between creator and creature there can be noted no similarity so great that a greater dissimilarity cannot be seen between them".[24] Indeed, in many ways, Gregory of Nazianzus could be seen as anticipating the Lateran formula in the very passage to which Louth alludes. Gregory writes:

> For though a thing be all heavenly, or above heaven, and far higher in nature and nearer to God than we, yet it is farther distant from God, and from the complete comprehension of His Nature, than it is lifted above our complex and lowly and earthward sinking composition.[25]

---

[23]   Andrew Louth, "The Cosmic Vision of Saint Maximos the Confessor", in Philip Clayton and Arthur Peacocke (eds), *In Whom We Live and Move and Have Our Being* (Grand Rapids, MI: William B. Eerdmans, 2004), p. 191; see Gregory of Nazianzus, "Oratio 28", in Philip Schaff and Henry Wace (eds), *Nicene and Post-Nicene Fathers Vol. 7* (New York, NY: The Christian Literature Company, 1894, p. 3.

[24]   *Constitutions of the Fourth Lateran Council 2.*

[25]   Gregory of Nazianzus, "Oratio 28", p. 3.

In any case, the point here is that there is a sharp and absolute difference between the question of "*what* something is" and "*that* something is". If the latter is what is meant by—and so described by—creation, then the former is what is meant by "change" and so is described by evolution. Evolution, then, has nothing to do with *creation*. This does not mean that evolution cannot be "creative", but it is only ever creative in the sense that humans (or the Big Bang) are creative—that is, creative by changing or causing others to change. Evolution can only be creative in the sense of "the production of a new quality in an already existing substance, or of that of a new substance starting from already existing matter".[26] Thus, evolution simply cannot be *how* God creates, because it can only ever describe a change in "*what* something is" not "*that* something is". Creation determines "*that* things are" (that they are something rather than nothing); evolution determines "*what* things are". Evolution, much like the Big Bang, is entirely theologically irrelevant. It is important to explicitly link this to the discussion of NOMA and the relationship between religion and science in the introduction to this book.

Others have noticed this distinction. Mariusz Tabaczek (who, as was quoted in the previous chapter, notes that "while science deals with changes and their causes, a theological account of creation deals with the metaphysical dependence of all creatures on God at every moment of their existence")[27] writes that evolutionary change should "be thought [of] as particular exemplifications of the concurrence of divine and natural causes, where the latter are regarded as secondary and instrumental agents 'moved' by the primary and principal transcendent causation of God", and continues that this change "should not be conceived as an aspect of divine creation but rather as an important part of divine providential governance and guidance of the created universe toward its end, along the path which abounds in the astonishing beauty of new types

---

26   Gilson, *Medieval Essays*, p. 156.

27   Mariusz Tabaczek, "Thomistic Response to the Theory of Evolution: Aquinas on Natural Selection and the Perfection of the Universe", *Theology and Science* 13:3 (2015), p. 332.

of inanimate and animate creatures".[28] Two observations are apparent here. First, Tabaczek is entirely correct to recognize that evolution cannot be conceived as "an aspect of divine creation" and seems to accept that creation and evolution are separate.[29] However, this does not appear to prevent him from saying that the particular course of history that evolution takes is still influenced by God. For Tabaczek, God is not *only* a cause of being, God also influences the causes of motion to move in particular ways.[30] Here, then, while Tabaczek would no doubt disagree with the comparison of his own theology with that of John Haught or John Polkinghorne (especially given that he explicitly distinguishes his own thought from theirs),[31] it is similar in that he believes that God directs the course of evolution in order to realize a specific end.

While there are serious concerns regarding the validity of the idea of a "soul"—given that so many philosophers and theologians now see those capacities that were once attributed to a soul in purely biological terms (which will be addressed below)—the way that *Humani generis* describes the distinction between body and soul is remarkably similar to the distinction expounded here. Pope Pius XII wrote:

> The Church does not forbid that, in conformity with the present state of human sciences and sacred theology, research and discussions, on the part of men experienced in both fields, take place with regard to the doctrine of evolution, in as far as it inquires into the origin of the human body as coming from pre-existent and living matter—for the Catholic faith obliges us to hold that souls are immediately created by God[32]

Although Hoekema uses the language of "being made in the image of God" rather than the "immediate creation of a soul", it is clear that the

28   Mariusz Tabaczek, "Does God Create Through Evolution? A Thomistic Perspective", *Theology and Science* 20:1 (2022), p. 47.
29   Tabaczek, "Does God Create Through Evolution?", pp. 59–60.
30   Tabaczek, "Does God Create Through Evolution?", pp. 61–2.
31   Tabaczek, "Does God Create Through Evolution?", pp. 48–50.
32   Pius XII, *Humani generis* (Vatican City, 1950), 36.

two ideas should be synonymous.[33] If that is the case, then the distinction between the claim that "souls are immediately created by God" and that of the "origin of the human body" maps onto this precisely. In this way, if the claim that "souls are immediately created by God" carries the meaning of "donates being", then Pope Pius XII is making precisely this distinction. The biological changes through which the universe goes in order to arrive at the "human body" are subject to the endeavour of human sciences and the theologian should take notice of the conclusions of that endeavour. However, when it comes to the claim that "souls are immediately created by God", this is uniquely a theological question.

If it was felicitous that Darwin chose to give his treatise on evolution *On the Origin of Species*, then it is equally felicitous that Pope Pius XII explicitly refers to the *origin* of the human body, not its *creation*. Of course, while this distinction between *origin* and *creation* might map quite helpfully onto the Catholic understanding of creation as expounded by Pope Pius XII, that mapping is not quite exact. The fact that the Catholic Church teaches that only humans have souls means that this would seem to exclude non-humans from being created. All creatures participate in God, not just those with souls, and so the "immediate creation of a soul" cannot be exactly what is meant by the distinction between "creation" and "origins". Nevertheless, it is clear that there is enough of a comparison to give authority to the understanding of creation and evolution expounded here. The Big Bang (the origin of the universe) and the subsequent evolution of the universe are changes—*generatio* and/or *mutatio*—and, as such, are entirely irrelevant to divine creation.

Evolution and participation[34]

Two questions were asked in relation to the Big Bang: (a) how should the theologian understand the Big Bang and the beginning of the

---

[33]   Not least because many theologians identify the possession of a soul as that which constitutes the image of God (see David O. Brown, *Incarnation and Neo-Darwinism: Evolution, Ontology, and Divine Activity* (Durham: Sacristy Press, 2019), pp. 58ff.).

[34]   My book, *Incarnation and Neo-Darwinism: Evolution, Ontology, and Divine Activity*, particularly Chapter 6—Participation, Imitation, and

universe (assuming, of course, that there is one); and (b) if God does not *cause* the beginning of the universe, then what does? Those same questions are pertinent in relation to evolution. The first question has already been answered: if God does not "cause" evolution then it should be thought of as answering the question of *"what* something is", rather than *"that* something is". This leaves the second question: if God does not "cause" evolutionary change, then what does? An answer to this question has two distinct (but certainly related) aspects: (i) the role of participation in accounting for change and multiplicity; and (ii) the role of divine simplicity (or, more accurately, the absence of a real relation) in accounting for diversity and multiplicity.

To turn to the role of participation first. For those who see evolution as a mechanism for how God creates, the reason why genetic mutation and natural selection occur is because either God directs which particular mutations occur and when they occur and/or because God selects which mutations survive and reproduce or determines the values against which natural selection judges which creatures survive and reproduce. Leaving aside the question of whether natural selection is alone sufficient as a mechanism to account for evolutionary change or whether subsequent mechanisms are required to complement natural selection, theologians who see evolution as the way that God creates see evolutionary change as guided in some way. However, if creation is about participation, rather than the construction of a specific state of affairs, then change cannot be explained by pointing to divine guidance. However, it can be explained by pointing to participation. This does not mean that God uses participation to bring about specific changes but means that creatures change because they participate.

W. Norris Clarke describes participation as a "condensed technical way of expressing the complexus of relations involved in any structure of dependence of a lower multiplicity on a higher source for similarity of nature".[35] Clarke identifies three elements of participation:

Neo-Darwinism (pp. 144ff.)—explains in greater detail how it is that creatures evolve *because* they participate.

[35]   W. Norris Clarke, *Explorations in Metaphysics: Being-God-Person* (Notre Dame, IN: University of Notre Dame Press, 1994), p. 93.

> (1) a source which possesses the perfection in question in a total and unrestricted manner; (2) a participant subject which possesses the same perfection in some partial or restricted way; and (3) which has received this perfection in some way from, or in dependence on, the higher source.[36]

There are questions concerning whether it is appropriate to say that God *possesses* being, or is being *itself*, but the point is well made. However, more important is participation's role in explaining or accounting for diversity. It might escape a cursory glance at Clarke's quotation that participation explains the dependence of lower *multiplicity* on a higher (presumably) *unified* source.

Therefore, to these three elements can be added a fourth: difference. Participation does not just account for the dependency of one on the other, but *precisely* because that one is dependent, so that one must be different. That is, participation is "a relation between two things that are unequal and that remain unequal and distinct".[37] There is a fundamental and essential ontological difference between God (*participatum*) and the creature (*participans*) *because* the creature depends on God for its being. However, moreover, and often missed, this also explains why there is a difference between two *participans*: because they both have "being" derivatively. Andrew Davison is clear about this connection between the difference between two *particiapans* and the difference between those *participans* and God. He writes that "these two aspects of creaturely difference (difference within creation and difference from God) are related. The difference of creation *from* its source requires the multiplicity of difference *within* creation itself".[38] This means, Davison continues, that "the inequality of creation to creator is the reason why the world is so riotously full of difference".[39] Put differently, there is *intra-*

---

[36]   Clarke, *Explorations in Metaphysics*, p. 93.

[37]   Daniel Keating, *Deification and Grace* (Naples, FL: Sapientia Press, 2007), pp. 98–9.

[38]   Andrew Davison, *Participation in God* (Cambridge: Cambridge University Press, 2019), p. 53.

[39]   Davison, *Participation in God*, p. 54.

mundane difference *precisely because* there is *inter*-mundane difference. In other words, there is difference and multiplicity in the world because it participates in God; evolution occurs because creatures participate.

Commentators have also made the same observation in relation to imitation, which is relevant here given that "the logic [of participation and imitation] is the same".[40] Imitation implies difference in the sense that imitation and identity are logical opposites; if something is *identical* to something else, then it cannot be an *imitation* of it. Elizabeth Castelli writes that between model and copy, the copy has a "derivative status"[41] and so "mimesis becomes a derivative function, in that it attempts to reproduce an unattainable origin".[42] Thus, Castelli continues that "the model is imbued with perfection and wholeness, and the copy represents an attempt to reclaim that perfection",[43] a "drive to sameness and the inability to achieve it".[44] Therefore, there is a difference between two different creatures because they both imitate God; if they were identical then they couldn't participate, so they must be different.

Moreover, if "analogy, imitation, and participation thus form a continuum rather than express radically different kinds of relationship",[45] then this same observation has been made regarding analogy. Erich Przywara writes that "the relation between the intra-creaturely analogy and the analogy between God and the creature is itself an analogy".[46]

---

[40]   Torstein Theodor Tollefsen, *Activity and Participation in Late Antique and Early Christian Thought* (Oxford: Oxford University Press, 2012), p. 163; Norman Russell, *The Doctrine of Deification in the Greek Patristic Tradition* (Oxford: Oxford University Press, 2004), p. 2; Lewis Ayres, *Nicaea and its Legacy: An Approach to Fourth-Century Trinitarian Theology* (Oxford: Oxford University Press, 2004), pp. 321ff.

[41]   Elizabeth Castelli, *Imitating Paul: A Discourse of Power* (Louisville, KY: Westminster John Knox Press, 1991), p. 69.

[42]   Castelli, *Imitating Paul*, p. 86.

[43]   Castelli, *Imitating Paul*, p. 75.

[44]   Castelli, *Imitating Paul*, p. 75.

[45]   Russell, *The Doctrine of Deification in the Greek Patristic Tradition*, p. 2.

[46]   Erich Przywara, *Analogia Entis* (Grand Rapids, MI: William B. Eerdmans, 2014), p. 219 (italics removed).

Przywara here is referring to the analogy between existence and essence in creatures, not difference between creatures,[47] but there is a similar tension that can be extrapolated. As Niels Nielsen evidences, "*analogia entis* is descriptive not only of an analogy relationship (between being and becoming) in the world, but an analogy between the realm of this worldly existence in tension between being and becoming and the realm of Being as such in its fullness and purity".[48] There is diversity in this world *because* there is an analogy between God and creatures.

Thus, creatures are subject to change, difference, diversity, and multiplicity precisely because they participate in and/or imitate God. To put this differently, "creatures are difform, imperfect imitations of the divine essence" and there is a "plurality of the ways in which God can be imitated",[49] or, "all created natures are just ways of imperfectly imitating God",[50] and those imitations mutate because they are imperfect.

Evolution and simplicity
There is difference, diversity, and multiplicity in the world because it participates in God. One creature changes into another through evolution because both of those creatures are imitations of God. However, that change is entirely *extrinsic* to God. This leads to the suggestion that, while there might be two different types of difference—the difference between God and the creature and the difference between two different creatures—this does not mean that those types of difference are the same "sort" of difference: one is ontological difference and the other is biological difference. Moreover, importantly, one is absolute difference

---

[47]   See Aaron Pidel, "Erich Przywara on Nature–Grace Extrinsicism: A Parallax View", *Modern Theology* 37:4 (2021), pp. 869–70.

[48]   Niels C. Nielsen Jr., "Przywara's Philosophy of the 'Analogia Entis'", *The Review of Metaphysics* 5:4 (1952), p. 605.

[49]   Mark Jordan, "The Intelligibility of the World and the Divine Ideas in Aquinas", *The Review of Metaphysics* 38:1 (1984), pp. 20–1.

[50]   Marilyn McCord Adams, *What Sort of Nature? Medieval Philosophy and the Systematics of Christology* (Milwaukee, WI: Marquette University Press, 1999), p. 29.

and the other is gradated difference: one is either created or not, but one can be a different creature in a (potentially) infinite number of ways.

Thus, to say that God causes each and every creature in the one single divine act is to say that each and every creature depends on God for its being in exactly the same way: participation/imitation. "*That* something is" only has two possible answers: it either "is" or "is not". Importantly, this means that one creature cannot "*be*" any more or any less than any other creature. More importantly still, one creature cannot "*be*" any more or less than any other creature *because* of "*what* it is". Both humans and mice participate in God, but neither can participate in God "more" than the other because of the "sort" of creature that it is. This is demanded by the absence of a real relation: there can be multiplicity and diversity from a single divine act, but precisely because there is a single divine act so God cannot relate to that multiplicity differently. That humans and mice have different "origins" does not make a difference to their being "created".[51]

---

[51] The reader might argue, of course, that there are instances where "being" is not absolute, where "being" is gradated, and it is precisely "*what* something is" that determines "*that* something is" more and/or to a greater extent, namely, God. God, as the creator, must "be" to a greater extent than creatures because God has "being" necessarily and fully, whereas creatures only participate in being, and so have it derivatively and less fully. However, this is an incorrect understanding of participation. God does not "have being"—that would make God another individual being to whom certain things can be attributed. As Przywara has already been quoted as saying, this would make "being" a "third thing" (Przywara, *Analogia Entis*, p. 233; see also Jean-Luc Marion, *God without Being* (Chicago, IL: The University of Chicago Press, 2012), p. 209) that exists alongside both God and creatures and so both God and creatures participate in "being". In other words, this would lead to the univocality of being. God is not another "being", another individual who has "being" to a greater extent or degree; God *is* being, God is the "ground of being", which creatures participate in order to have "being". As already quoted from Pseudo-Dionysius, God "falls neither within the predicate of nonbeing nor of being" and "is beyond assertion and denial" (Pseudo-Dionysius, *The*

Certainly, "there cannot really be distinct ideas in God" so that "there is not a plurality of ideas in God at all, but only one simple essence",[52] yet this does not mean that there is not a genuine plurality of creatures. Rather, the plurality is *extrinsic* to God. Thus, "what is one and indivisible in God is conceived by us as many and distinct, but in fact the ideas are all identical with each other".[53] In exactly the same way that Thomas' pillar genuinely looks different when it is on the right of the person to when it is on the left of the person despite also being genuinely the same pillar,[54] so the human and the mouse are genuinely distinct to us, but are also genuinely identical in the sense that both are imitations of God.

Mariuz Tabaczek's distinction between "metaphysical concepts" and "biological categories" is crucial for upholding this idea. Tabaczek writes that one needs to carefully distinguish between "species" and "essence", so that "metaphysical categories of 'higher' and 'lower' should not be equated with biological concepts describing organisms as 'more complex' and 'better adapted'".[55] He makes such a distinction not necessarily to affirm that there is a difference between "biological species" and "natural kind"—indeed, elsewhere he confirms that "all representatives of a species share a 'common nature' (defined by a substantial form of a particular kind)"[56]—but to prevent the conclusion that evolutionarily successful creatures are not metaphysically equal to humanity. This, Tabaczek clarifies, means that the theologian is not obliged to argue that an ant (as an example of a creature that is clearly evolutionarily successful) is

---

Mystical Theology 5); God neither "is" nor "is not", whereas creatures either "are" or "are not".

[52] Keith Ward, *Rational Theology and the Creativity of God* (Oxford: Basil Blackwell Ltd., 1982), p. 54.

[53] Ward, *Rational Theology and the Creativity of God*, p. 54.

[54] *ST* 1, 13, 7.

[55] Mariusz Tabaczek, "An Aristotelian Account of Evolution and the Contemporary Philosophy of Biology", *Dialogo* 1:1 (2014), p. 60.

[56] Mariusz Tabaczek, "The Metaphysics of Evolution: From Aquinas's Interpretation of Augustine's Concept of *Rationes Seminales* to the Contemporary Thomistic Account of Species Transformism", *Nova et vetera* 18:3 (2020), p. 964; see also p. 967.

on the same metaphysical footing as, say, Neanderthals (as an example of an evolutionarily unsuccessful creature).[57] Although Tabaczek does not explicitly refer to Neanderthals, one would presume that he would agree that, despite their clear lack of evolutionary success, they are metaphysically superior to ants because, he argues, just because a creature is evolutionarily well-adapted does not mean that it is metaphysically superior.

However, the fact that Tabaczek still sees humanity as being more metaphysically superior to, say, ants means either that he *does* think that the possession of rational self-consciousness—which is clearly a biological concept—should translate to metaphysical superiority, or that it is the possession of something else—something non-biological— that constitutes metaphysical superiority.[58] Thus, Tabaczek still suffers from those problems that plague those who still wish to point to a soul. As Nancey Murphy writes, "Nearly all of the human capacities or faculties once attributed to the *soul* are now seen as functions of the brain," and that "human behaviour can be *exhaustively* explained by means of genetics or neurobiology".[59] That is, by pointing to the soul, all Tabaczek is doing is kicking the explanatory can down the road. Tabaczek might say that metaphysical superiority is due to the soul, but the soul is described by capacities that are now clearly purely biological

---

[57]   Biologists and evolutionary historians may want to question whether Neanderthals should rightly be considered "unsuccessful". I take it that their extinction is evidence that, as successful as they may have been, they are no longer. While I accept there may be disagreements here, the purpose in using them as an example is to contrast them with ants. Despite the fact that ants are (still) evolutionarily successful they are, for Tabaczek, not as "metaphysically" superior as Neanderthals, who are (at least now) evolutionarily unsuccessful.

[58]   Tabaczek, "The Metaphysics of Evolution", p. 971; see also *Humani generis* 36, and Christopher Haw, "The Human Soul and Evolution: A Mimetic Perspective", *New Blackfriars* 102:1097 (2021), pp. 41–74.

[59]   Nancey Murphy, "Human Nature: Historical, Scientific, and Religious Issues", in Warren Brown, Nancey Murphy and H. Newton Malony (eds), *Whatever Happened to the Soul: Scientific and Theological Portraits of Human Nature* (Minneapolis, MN: Augsburg Fortress Press, 1998), pp. 1–2, 16ff.

and exhaustively accounted for by evolution. The soul—which certainly is a "metaphysical concept"—might very well point to a metaphysical superiority, but if the possession of a soul is determined by pointing to "biological categories", then Tabaczek hasn't done anything: he is still pointing to "biological categories" as markers of "metaphysical concepts". Rather, there is nothing about humans that separates them biologically from any other creature.[60]

However, such a separation of "metaphysical category" and "biological concept" can have the opposite result to that which Tabaczek thinks. Removing the connection between metaphysics and biology does not mean that metaphysical superiority is unconnected from evolutionary success, but means that while there can be biological difference and evolutionary superiority, there cannot be any such distinction in metaphysics. That is, while Tabaczek must be correct to reject any correlation between biological capacity and metaphysical value, this cannot have the effect that he appears to intend. Biological difference (*what* something is) has no impact on or relevance to metaphysical value (*that* something is). The first, as Tabaczek recognizes, deals with "the metaphysical dependence of all creatures on God at every moment of their existence"[61] and uses the language of theology and metaphysics; the second deals with "the order of the physical"[62] and "with changes

---

[60] As Ron Cole-Turner has argued, recent biological and anthropological evidence confirms that *Homo sapiens* did not come into existence, either biologically or genetically, "with any sort of abruptness" and neither is there a comparable "cultural Big Bang" or "sudden lights-on moment" of culture (e.g. art, music, religion etc.), lending more support to the Darwinian accumulation thesis (Ron Cole-Turner, "New Perspectives on Human Origins: Three Challenges for Christian Theology", *Theology and Science* 18:4 (2020), p. 530). Perhaps more pertinent is that this leads Cole-Turner to acknowledge that the theological claim of human uniqueness "continues to lose its meaning and coherence" (p. 531; see also Lucas Mix and Joanna Masel, "Chance, Purpose, and Progress in Evolution and Christianity", *Evolution* 68:8 (2014), p. 2444).

[61] Tabaczek, "Thomistic Response to the Theory of Evolution", p. 332.

[62] Gilson, *Medieval Essays*, p. 160

and their causes", and uses the language of science and history.[63] Thus, it was argued that "*what* something is" is determined by its "origin", so that different "things" have different "origins", and what its "origin" is determines what sort of "thing" it is.

While Ruth Page is no Thomist, the theology she offers is remarkably similar to that offered here. She writes that evolution and history are not divinely designed,[64] so that creation does not involve "God setting up the initial conditions with the express design to produce complexity and human consciousness and intelligence". Instead, in creation, God "let[s] be whatever would and could emerge from that freedom, and enjoy[s] *all* responses of *all* kinds as they have occurred from the beginning of time, with their various qualities, of which intelligence is only one",[65] and so creatures are "entirely free from God's shaping or directing hand in [their] development".[66] Despite the fact that Page claims that God does not guide history and so creatures are free from God's directing hand in their development, she qualifies this by claiming that "God undoubtedly has desires for how creation goes",[67] which God realizes not through "mighty acts" but through "attraction, of drawing the attention and concern of the other without extinguishing that other's freedom".[68] This qualification ultimately places Page at odds with the theology presented in this book, which disagrees that God has a desire for how creation should go and lures creation to get there as it would contravene the absence of a real relation. Nevertheless, her claim that God "let[s] be whatever would and could emerge from that freedom, and enjoy[s] *all* responses of *all* kinds as they have occurred from the beginning of time, with their various qualities, of which intelligence is only one",[69] fits remarkably well with the exposition of divine simplicity that this book has offered.

---

[63]   Tabaczek, "Thomistic Response to the Theory of Evolution", p. 332.

[64]   Ruth Page, *The Web of Creation* (London: SCM Press, 1996), p. 8.

[65]   Page, *The Web of Creation*, p. 80.

[66]   Page, *The Web of Creation*, p. 54.

[67]   Page, *The Web of Creation*, p. 103.

[68]   Page, *The Web of Creation*, p. 60, p. 58.

[69]   Page, *The Web of Creation*, p. 80.

God does not value one creature over any other, but rather enjoys all responses of all kinds. God could hardly enjoy all responses of all kinds if God prefers one response more than others or if God placed higher metaphysical value in one response over others and manipulated the course of history to ensure that preference. Basil Hume seems to agree with this assessment. He teaches that:

> each one of us is unique, absolutely unique, and behind that uniqueness is a purpose which is ultimately God's purpose; and that purpose of God is determined by his love. That is the total explanation of his creative and redemptive work; and so his love for each is different, but differentiated only by the object of the loving—which is ourselves, each one of us. As love emanates from God it cannot in itself change—increase or diminish. It is differentiated by us—to use simple terms—by the degree of our willingness to receive it.
>
> The relationship between God and ourselves, between him and myself, is unique, and when you reflect that in him there is no change, no increase, no diminution, it follows that the totality of his love is concentrated on each one of us individually.[70]

Such a long quotation is necessary to get the full force of Hume's teaching; however, the crucial passage is clearly the claim that "the totality of [God's] love is concentrated on each one of us individually". God does not distinguish or favour any individual; it is only the individual who receives grace that places barriers before it. God loves all equally—God enjoys all responses of all kinds—it is the individual that experiences that more strongly or weakly than any other depending entirely on their openness to it.

Anna Williams can also be seen to agree with Hume, writing that "sanctifying grace cannot differ in degree because its nature is to effect the union with God, but grace may differ in degree from the perspective of the subject, who may receive more or less of it and be more or less

---

[70]   Basil Hume, *Searching for God* (York: Ampleforth Abbey Press, 2002), p. 57.

enlightened than another subject".[71] If "viewed from God's point of view the bestowal of grace is uniform",[72] then God must love all creatures equally. If the totality of God's love is concentrated on each one of us individually in its totality, then it must be equally concentrated on every single creature (at each and every spatiotemporal point), as already quoted from Thaddeus Metz: "How could there be an absolutely simple being which has multiple ends, one for humans and one for animals?"[73] The absence of a real relation, again, is crucial to understanding this tension; there is a single, simple, uniform, basic will, but a multiple experience of it, which is extrinsic to it.

Anthropocentrism
Divine simplicity leads to the conclusion that there is a distinction between "*that* something is" and "*what* something is", and that while there may be multiplicity and difference in the latter, this does not lead to difference in the former. Any suggestion that God *prefers* humanity over other creatures, and constrains the evolutionary "process" in such a way that a self-conscious, rational, human-like creature is certain to emerge, looks at the world through anthropocentric lenses. Why is it that the particular values that humanity favours should also be favoured by God? If God is nothing more than a "person" in the same way that humans are persons, then it is easy to see why that assumption is made; but if God is not to be thought of as a person, then there is no reason to think that God favours and prefers anything, let alone those particular values that humans favour and prefer.

One can compare this to the parable of the widow's mite. The rich man put great sums into the offertory and (one might assume as the Gospel

---

[71]   Anna Williams, *The Ground of Union: Deification in Aquinas and Palamas* (Oxford: Oxford University Press, 1999), p. 86.

[72]   Philip McCosker, "Grace", in Philip McCosker and Denys Turner (eds), *The Cambridge Companion to The Summa Theologiae* (Cambridge. Cambridge University Press, 2016), p. 216.

[73]   Thaddeus Metz, "Could God's Purpose Be the Source of Life's Meaning?", *Religious Studies* 36:3 (2000), p. 310; see also Robert Burns, "The Divine Simplicity in St. Thomas", *Religious Studies* 25:3 (1989), p. 290.

narrative does not say) thinks he is better than the widow, who has little to offer. The widow, Jesus tells his disciples, has put more into the offertory because she has put in all she has. Of course, this book has emphasized as much as possible that God does not prefer anything, whether the riches of the rich man or the little of the widow, but the point here is that it is anthropocentric to think that God would prefer the rich man because humanity prefers riches to poverty. In the same way, it is anthropocentric to think that the riches of humanity's self-conscious rational imitation of God are preferred to the poverty of (say) a tree's imitation. Thomas Merton writes:

> A tree gives glory to God by being a tree. For in being what God means it to be it is obeying him. It "consents" so to speak, to his love. It is expressing an idea which is in God and which is not distinct from the essence of God, and therefore a tree imitates God by being a tree.[74]

God is just as pleased with a tree being a tree as God is with a human consciously responding to Jesus. As Pseudo-Dionysius writes, "All things desire [God]: Everything with mind and reason seeks to know [God], everything sentient yearns to perceive [God], everything lacking perception has a living and instinctive longing for [God], and everything lifeless and merely existent turns, in its own fashion, for a share of [God]."[75] Humans, who have mind and reason, yearn for God through the gifts that they have; trees, which have a living and instinctive longing, yearn for God through the gifts that they have. Neither is preferred by God—since the "the totality of [God's] love is concentrated on each one of us individually"—but each one imitates God in their own way.

Consciousness might very well have allowed humanity to become evolutionarily successful, but the absence of consciousness certainly hasn't hindered trees or bacteria from being incredibly successful either. To suppose, as Teilhard de Chardin does (who is representative

---

[74] Thomas Merton, *New Seeds of Contemplation* (London: Burns & Oates, 1961), p. 30.

[75] Pseudo-Dionysius, *The Divine Names* 4.4.

of many—if not most—theologians), that "it is better, no matter what the cost, to be more conscious than less conscious" and so to make consciousness "the absolute condition of the world's existence"[76] is to have the same mindset and outlook as the rich man. To say that "it is better to be conscious than not conscious" is to say precisely the same as the rich man, who thinks that "it is better to be rich than to be poor". To think that being rich or being conscious is better than being poor or not being conscious is to think so narrowly that it misses that there are other ways of looking at the world. Jesus is condemning this way of looking at the world when he condemns the rich man.

John C. Greene makes similar claims in response to Theodosius Dobzhansky's argument that evolution creates for God. Considering why it is that evolution has changed the eohippus into the modern horse, Greene asks:

> But why should we regard the modern horse as better than Eohippus? I would think that the two creatures were equally happy and equally valuable in God's sight. "Better" in evolutionary lingo is somewhat like "better" in modern advertising—the indefinite comparative. Our product is "better." Better than what? Better for whom?[77]

Evolutionary "better" is certainly not better for the eohippus—who dies before, and so cannot in any way benefit from, any "progress" in evolution—and certainly not better for God, "the totality of [whose] love is concentrated on each one of us individually". In this way, it is possible to agree with Roger Scruton, who writes:

> If we are to consider the interests of all future creatures then it is impossible to know how we should treat the environment at all.

---

[76] Teilhard de Chardin, Pierre, *Christianity and Evolution* (London: Harvest, 1971), p. 108.

[77] John C. Greene and Michael Ruse, "On the Nature of the Evolutionary Process: The Correspondence between Theodosius Dobzhansky and John C. Greene", *Biology and Philosophy* 11 (1996), p. 460.

Suppose we spoil our existing resources, through anthropogenic
climate change, plastic pollution, deforestation and soil depletion,
so that the human species dies out. But suppose that, in doing so,
we create a new biosphere to which some future species adapts.
Members of that future species would have cause to thank us,
that we have provided the great plastic deposits which they mine
for their favourite snacks; and they would react with distaste
and horror on encountering the record of a previous world of
lush vegetation, temperate climate and gentle breezes in which
they could never have survived. Should we not take account of
these creatures and their interests? Why does the discount rate
suddenly rise to 100 per cent when we begin to contemplate their
alien interests?[78]

Of course, this is not intended as a denial of climate change or a call to
shirk the responsibilities that *all creatures* have to care for the world in
which we live, but Scruton does raise an interesting conundrum. Is not the
point of efforts to live sustainably about looking after future populations?
Yet, does not the effort to maintain rainforests etc. mean that some
creature perfectly suited to living in a world without rainforests suffers?
Why do creatures that are adapted to the world now have precedence
over creatures that might be adapted to some future state? Why should
we assume that future populations would prefer an environment that is
suited to our particular preferences?

If, as it has already been argued, there is no reason why humans are better
than any other creature (certainly not as a result of their consciousness),
then there is no reason why evolution had to "produce" them. When
there is no need to constrain evolution to follow a specific path, then the
neo-Darwinian notion of "evolution without purpose" becomes entirely
plausible for the theologian. If creation is about "ontological dependence",
then evolution can indeed be entirely meaningless and purposeless. The
meaning and purpose are in participation and imitation, not motion and
change, and so evolution.

---

[78]   Roger Scruton, *Green Philosophy* (London: Atlantic Books, 2013), pp. 192–3.

Divine indifference?

One can (and perhaps ought) to say the same thing regarding the laws of nature themselves. God does not institute or set the natural laws *at the beginning*, and then set the universe in motion. That would make God accidentally ordered to the world in the same way that God would be if God's act of creation were coincident with origin. Just as the theologian can dismiss the *"what* it is" question as being theologically (i.e., metaphysically) irrelevant, so it is theologically inconsequential what the particular laws of nature are. That is, the natural laws that govern the universe are themselves evolved.[79] Lee Smolin has suggested such a scenario in which the cosmological constants and natural laws are themselves selected for in a process similar to natural selection, in which universes reproduce themselves with various mutations in constants and laws etc.[80] While Smolin's theory has received widespread attention, it does not have the assent of the whole cosmological community (although very few scientific theories can boast universal acceptance). It is mentioned here only to add that, just as creation is not consonant with the Big Bang, nor coincident with the natural process of evolution, so God is not concerned with precisely fine-tuning the cosmological constants and/ or natural laws. That is, the very cosmological constants and natural laws themselves are not "created" by God, they are determined by their "origin". Differently, the cosmological constants and natural laws are just as much a question of *"what* something is" as are the differences that obtain between creatures. *"That"* there are natural laws, which regulate

---

[79] This question obviously assumes that the natural laws are themselves real "things" that could be discovered, rather than human inventions, which are nothing more than models of the world, rather than accurate depictions of the universe as it actually is. Thus, Yury Balashov writes that "with the progress of science, a deepening synthesis of knowledge is accompanied with the formulating of more and more general laws of science. This evolution of knowledge apparently has nothing to do with the evolution of natural laws themselves" (Yury Balashov, "On the Evolution of Natural Laws", *The British Journal for the Philosophy of Science* 43:3 (1992), p. 346).

[80] See Lee Smolin, *The Life of the Cosmos* (London: Weidenfeld & Nicolson, 1997).

the universe and allow life to happen, is because they are created; but *"what"* they are—which specific laws and constants actually obtain—is entirely accidental. God "breathes life" into those laws as cause *per se*—i.e., those constants and laws are themselves creatures that participate in God as much as corporeal, material creatures do—God does not determine which particular laws/equations/creatures actually obtain/occur.[81] God lets be and enjoys all worlds, let alone all creatures within all worlds.

One might read such comments (and those made above in relation to simplicity and anthropocentrism) and conclude that this makes God indifferent to the world. Indeed, this is precisely why theologians such as William Lane Craig have a problem with the "absence of a real relation", which he understands leads to a God who "is no different in these otherwise empty worlds than in worlds chock-full of contingent beings of every order".[82] Surely, if God is the creator, then a universe that has existence is better than one that has no existence? It is easy to understand why someone might find the suggestion that a world void of any life at all—perhaps a world in which nothing more complex than hydrogen atoms could exist, or a world in which gravity was a tad too strong so that it quickly collapsed just as soon as it had started—has equal inherent value to one which contains all the various tangled bank of diversity problematic; however, to concentrate on this aspect of the question misses the point.

In his book *Darwin and Design: Does Evolution Have a Purpose?* Michael Ruse reminds his readers of Plato. He writes that "we have forgotten our Plato: purpose occurs when *values* are at stake".[83] Assuming Plato is correct, creation—and evolution—only has any purpose when values are at stake; if there are no values at stake, then there is no purpose.

---

[81]   That biblical accounts of creation have God "breathing life into" creatures (e.g., Genesis 2:7) is not altogether irrelevant on this matter, although there is no space to explore the connection here. Creation, in this sense, is God breathing life into the laws and matter, not that which accounts for its origin.

[82]   William Lane Craig, "Timelessness, Creation, and God's Real Relation to the World", *Laval théologique et philosophique* 56:1 (2000), p. 109.

[83]   Michael Ruse, *Darwin and Design: Does Evolution Have a Purpose?* (Cambridge, MA: Harvard University Press, 2003), p. 264 (italics in original).

In other words, to say that there is no value at stake—because God values all creatures equally—suggests that the universe appears to have no purpose. When there are no values at stake, then, as Richard Dawkins might put it, "the universe we observe has precisely the properties we should expect if there is, at bottom, no design, no purpose, no evil and no good, nothing but blind, pitiless indifference".[84]

This is precisely the same problem that critics of deism cite. The deist God, to use Richard Dawkins' definition, "certainly has no specific interest in human affairs".[85] However, that "specific" is interpreted by critics of deism to mean "indifference", but if, instead, it means "greater", then we are left with a theology that is like Page's. God "certainly has no *specific* interest in human affairs", not because God is indifferent to the world, but because God "certainly has no *greater* interest in human affairs". One can say the same in response to Craig. God is not *indifferent* to whether the world is empty or chock-full of contingent beings, it is just that God has no *greater* interest in one particular world than any other. Or to put this differently, Craig looks at the "empty worlds" and thinks that if they are valued the same as worlds "choc full of contingent beings of every order", then this relegates those "choc-full worlds" to a divine indifference. However, if one looks at the problem from the opposite perspective, then this does not de-value those worlds "choc full of contingent beings of every order", but it adds value to those "empty worlds". Claiming that God values "empty worlds" just as much as those "choc full of contingent beings of every order" does not mean that God is indifferent to those "choc full of contingent beings of every order", but that God values even those that are empty.

It is important at this point to recall, and so specifically link this argument with, what was argued in the previous chapter regarding God's single, uniform, "basic" divine will. God wills for there to be a creation; God does not will for evolution to take a specific path. The point, then, is that if God has no particular values that God needs to realize, then God does not need to influence the world in any way. God does not get

---

[84] Richard Dawkins, *River Out of Eden: A Darwinian View of Life* (London: Phoenix, 1996), p. 155.

[85] Richard Dawkins, *The God Delusion* (London: Black Swan, 2006), p. 39.

involved in the world, not because God is indifferent but because God has nothing to achieve by doing so. To quote Sarah Lane Ritchie, "If God . . . has *specific purposes* to be enacted in the natural world, then at some point the divine will must meet physical processes,"[86] and so, regardless of the indeterminacy, immanence or non-intervention of divine activity, "at some point, the transcendent, immaterial God would have to actually interact with the brute, physical mechanisms explicated by contemporary science";[87] then one only needs to explain *how* God can influence and constrain physical processes *if* one assumes that God has "*specific purposes*". Yet, if God does not have any *specific purpose* then one does not need God to display any "power".

Thus, when theists such as John Polkinghorne write that a God with power but no love is a "deistic bystander, watching the play of history unfold without any influence upon its course",[88] all they do is narrowly situate God's love within the paradigm of "power" and "providence" and cannot understand that it is possible to have great love for something without that love demanding the need for "interference". To put that differently, if a God who is nothing but a "bystander" who "watch[es] the play of history unfold without any influence upon its course" is the definition of a God who has power but no love, then one is seeing influence in/on the world as a proxy for love. Yet, why does God need to influence the world in order to love it? In the words of Ruth Page, God can genuinely love the world and still "[let] be whatever would and could emerge from that freedom, and [enjoy] *all* responses of *all* kinds as they have occurred from the beginning of time".[89] To use a rather crude example, a spectator at a game of snooker can still be enthralled with and interested in the outcome of the game, without getting involved in

---

[86]   Sarah Lane Ritchie, "Dancing around the Causal Joint: Challenging the Theological Turn in Divine Action Theories", *Zygon: Journal of Religion and Science* 52:2 (2017), p. 370 (italics added).

[87]   Ritchie, "Dancing around the Causal Joint", p. 377.

[88]   John Polkinghorne, "Kenotic Creation and Divine Action", in John Polkinghorne (ed.), *The Work of Love: Creation as Kenosis* (Grand Rapids, MI: William B. Eerdmans, 2001), p. 91.

[89]   Page, *The Web of Creation*, p. 80.

or otherwise influencing the outcome of the game themselves, or even having a preference for the outcome. One can be interested in a game of snooker for no other reason than the love of the game. In the same way, it is perfectly reasonable to suggest that God can be enthralled with the universe, and genuinely interested in it, without that implying that God has to be an actor within it or that God has a preference for what happens in/to it. Divine involvement (whether intervention, influence etc.) should not be a proxy for divine interest. God can still be enthralled "*that*" a game of snooker is happening, and yet still have no *particular* desire regarding "*what*" course that game takes. Indeed, one gets the same comments from atheists working in a scientific paradigm: if God does not interact with, and so influence the course of, the history of the universe, then what is the "point" of God?

Thus, returning to Polkinghorne, his relationship between "power" and "love" assumes anthropocentrism. If one holds that God loves all creatures equally—that God neither "wishes . . . for *certain things* to happen" nor wishes "for them to happen in *certain ways*"[90]—then, following Ritchie's logic, one does not need to explain how God is "powerful".[91] If God "enjoy[s] *all* responses of *all* kinds as they have occurred from the beginning of time, with their various qualities, of which intelligence is only one",[92] then God does not need to act to bring about *specific* states of affairs. It is easy to see, then, that simply accepting that God does not have *specific* purposes to be enacted because "the totality of [God's] love is concentrated on each one of us individually"[93] need not lead to a doctrine of divine indifference.

This does not mean that God is indifferent; it means that God values creation precisely for just being creation, not because of what it could become. As previously quoted from Tillich, "From the point of view of the creator, the purpose of creation is the exercise of his creativity, which has

---

[90]   Davison, *Participation in God*, p. 231.

[91]   Of course, this book has defined divine power in a specific way to refer to "ontological cause" rather than anything else, but the point should still be clear.

[92]   Page, *The Web of Creation*, p. 80.

[93]   Hume, *Searching for God*, p. 57.

no purpose beyond itself because the divine life is essentially creative".[94] Why there is something rather than nothing is a uniquely theological question (metaphysical category) and it requires a uniquely theological answer (creation). On the other hand, why a particular something is the particular thing it is, is a uniquely scientific question (biological concept) and it requires a uniquely scientific answer (origins/evolution). Ultimately, this book subscribes to deism because it holds that God is *only* concerned with the *"that"* question and is indifferent to the *"what"* question.

Omnipotence

The idea of a providential God who guides history is too close to an anthropomorphic God who has desires and wants and acts in discrete ways to realize these desires. If God is not a God who guides the universe, then neither is God a God who can "do" anything that it is possible to do. Indeed, it has already been argued that "God cannot be the kind of reality who can *literally do* anything at all because 'doing' (acting) is not possible for the kind of reality that God, in God's deepest and most cognitively inaccessible being, essentially *is*".[95]

If this book has endorsed Paul Tillich's particular understanding of creation as "the classical formula which expresses the *relation* between God and the world",[96] the purpose of which "is the exercise of [God's] creativity, which has no purpose beyond itself",[97] and has endorsed Tillich's idea of providence as the "certainty that history . . . contributes to the ultimate fulfillment of creaturely existence" without that fulfilment "l[ying] in an eventual time-and-space future",[98] then this book also endorses Tillich's idea of omnipotence. Tillich criticizes the popular view

---

[94]   Tillich, *Systematic Theology Vol.1*, pp. 263–4.

[95]   Frank Kirkpatrick, *The Mystery and Agency of God: Divine Being and Action in the World* (Minneapolis, MN: Fortress Press, 2014), p. 1.

[96]   Tillich, *Systematic Theology Vol. 1*, p. 254 (italics added).

[97]   Tillich, *Systematic Theology Vol. 1*, pp. 263–4.

[98]   Tillich, *Systematic Theology Vol. 1*, p. 267.

of omnipotence, on the basis that it severely diminishes God. He writes that "the concept 'omnipotence' implies a highest being who is able to do whatever he wants … [which] makes God into a being alongside others"[99] and, instead, argues that "omnipotence [should] mean divine power through which God is creative in and through everything in every moment".[100] In other words, God's power does not lie in God's supreme and maximal ability to do every act possible or to bring about any and every state of affairs that God so chooses. Rather, God's power lies in God's being that in which all matter and every creature participates for their being. God's power lies in God being *the* "cause of being", not in God being *a* supreme or maximal "cause of motion".

Most philosophers would disagree with what might be called the "absolutist theory of omnipotence",[101] which holds that omnipotence means that God can do anything and everything that it is *both* logically possible to do *and* logically impossible to do, regardless of whether or not it contains a contradiction (because, as argued by Rene Descartes, what is logically impossible is only logically impossible because God has defined it as such; it could easily and coherently have been otherwise[102]). This "absolutist theory" is normally rejected in favour of the more modest notion that omnipotence means that God can do anything and everything that it is logically possible to do.[103] Thus, Nicholas Lombardo identifies that there are some things "not open to God due to a logical contradiction on the side of creation (e.g., creating a square circle)", and some things "not open to God due to a logical contradiction on the side of God's nature (e.g., damning Peter)".[104] That is, there are logical and moral

---

[99] Tillich, *Systematic Theology Vol. 1*, p. 273, see also p. 235.

[100] Tillich, *Systematic Theology Vol. 1*, p. 273.

[101] See Nick Trakakis, "The Absolutist Theory of Omnipotence", *Sophia* 136:2 (1997), pp. 55–78.

[102] Lilli Alanen, "Descartes, Duns Scotus and Ockham on Omnipotence and Possibility", *Franciscan Studies* 45 (1985), pp. 162–4; see also Trakakis, "The Absolutist Theory of Omnipotence".

[103] *ST* 1, 25, 3.

[104] Nicholas Lombardo, "What God Cannot Do: Divine Power, the Gratuity of Grace, and Henri de Lubac", *Modern Theology* 37:1 (2021), pp. 114–38.

"limits" to omnipotence. The theologian, then, has already accepted the principle that omnipotence does not mean that God can do *anything*, and already accepts that God could not do some things.

However, while it might not seem that controversial to claim that God cannot do things that are logically impossible, most theologians would also want to place further restrictions on what God can and cannot do. If God cannot do things that are logically impossible (e.g., create a square circle), then God also cannot do things that would place limitations on God. Katherin Rogers argues that "any 'ability' for which a creaturely limitation such as being corporeal or weak or caused is a prerequisite will be an 'ability' not possessed by God".[105] She gives the example of "sitting". The ability to sit, she argues, cannot be a part of what is meant by omnipotence because sitting requires a body that is subject to space, which would mean ascribing creaturely limitations to God. God cannot sit "because to sit is to assume a certain position with your body. No body, no sitting".[106] This is hardly controversial.

The theologian, then, is already involved in limiting and restricting what omnipotence means. God cannot do things that are logically impossible, but neither can God do things that are logically possible but which require God to have a body or other such creaturely limitation. However, if Richard Grigg is correct that "causality [i]s one of the categories of finite being" and so "cannot apply to God as being-itself or to God's relation to the world"[107] (of which Bulgakov has also already been quoted in support), and if philosophers are correct that a "timeless being would allegedly be unable to act" because "act[ing] has a beginning and an end, and thus it has both temporal location and duration and, therefore, temporal extension . . . temporal order and succession",[108] then it would seem that, following Rogers' logic, God cannot "act", because

---

[105] Katherin Rogers, *Perfect Being Theology* (Edinburgh: Edinburgh University Press, 2000), p. 93.

[106] Rogers, *Perfect Being Theology*, p. 97.

[107] Richard Grigg, "Religion, Science, and Evolution: Paul Tillich's Fourth Way", *Zygon: Journal of Religion and Science* 38 (2003), p. 948; see Tillich, *Systematic Theology Vol. 1*, pp. 196–8.

[108] Markus, Arjan, "Divine Timelessness", *Sophia* 43:2 (2004), pp. 30–1.

acting requires a creaturely limitation. Or, more specifically given the discussion in the previous chapter, God cannot act as a cause *per accidens*, because acting as part of an accidentally ordered series (even as the first in that series) requires a creaturely limitation. If God acts as a cause *per accidens*, then God must be *a* being or agent who exemplifies causality, rather than being "causality" itself, that in which *other* beings participate for their causal power as a cause *per se*.[109] Herbert McCabe makes much the same point, writing that God cannot "interfere" in the universe, not because God lacks the power to do so, but because God has *too much power*.[110] The essential point is the same: to assume that God can act as a "cause" is to "reduce" or "diminish" God. The theistic personalists would surely disagree—hence their rejection of divine atemporality—but if the logic followed through in this book is correct then no other conclusion is possible: God cannot act as a "cause". (Following the convention outlined in the last chapter, the designations "cause of being" and "cause *per se*" will still be used to refer to *creatio*, but this does not mean "cause" as "is usually meant by 'cause' in contemporary philosophy",[111] which is designated as "cause of motion" or "cause *per accidens*".)

This is surely what Tillich means when he writes that the superlatives— i.e., most powerful, most perfect etc.—become diminutives.[112] That is, the more one argues that God is the most powerful being, the more such

---

[109]   Anette Hagan, commenting on the theology of Friedrich Schleiermacher, writes that "any kind of co-operation [between God and creatures] would imply that something within the nature system was independent of God so that it could co-operate with God, and thus that something would have to be posited outside the relation of absolute dependence" (Anette Hagan, "Divine Sovereignty and Human Freedom: Divine Providence in the Theology of Friedrich Schleiermacher", *Testamentum Imperium* 2 (2009), p. 11). Here, there is a similar approach to Tillich. If God acted within the natural system, then this would imply that God is another being that is separate from the ground of being.

[110]   Herbert McCabe, "Creation", *New Blackfriars* 61:724 (1980), p. 412 (italics added).

[111]   Feser, *Scholastic Metaphysics*, p. 97.

[112]   Tillich, *Systematic Theology Vol. 1*, p. 235.

a designation anthropomorphizes God. Therefore, somewhat ironically, affirming that God can do anything and everything that it is logically possible (or impossible) to do actually has the effect of *diminishing* God by bringing God into the subject/object relations of the universe. Omnipotence, then, does not mean that God has an infinite range of powers that God can utilize to bring about any state of affairs in the world. Nor does it mean that God "is capable of producing any effect without the causal concurrence of secondary causes", like being "able to burn something without fire",[113] or like being able to cause a billiard ball to move without introducing new energy. Rather, omnipotence means nothing more than that God is the power of every single being, and the power through which those beings act as causes themselves.

Once again, while this borrows scholastic language, it does not follow exactly what Thomas Aquinas actually thought. Thomas writes that "the more simple a thing is the greater the number of its concomitant relations: since its power is so much the less limited and consequently its causality so much more extended".[114] David Bentley Hart likens this to the difference between an axe and a guillotine. He writes that "a broadaxe and a guillotine can both perform one very similar unpleasant task, but the former can do innumerable other things as well, not nearly as unpleasant, like cutting down a dead tree or hacking a guillotine to pieces",[115] precisely because it is more simple and less complex. This means, he continues, that "God's metaphysical simplicity [speaks] of the total absence of . . . limitations".[116]

Of course, this book is not arguing that divine simplicity does *not* mean a total absence of limitations. Rather it is arguing that a total absence of limitations does not lead to a "greater extension of causality" because "causality" itself is a limitation, or, more accurately, one requires creaturely limitations in order to function as a cause. To put this differently, this

---

[113] Richard Cross, *Duns Scotus* (Oxford: Oxford University Press, 1999), p. 57.

[114] Thomas Aquinas, *Quaestiones Disputatae de Potentia Dei* (Westminster, MD: The Newman Press, 1952), q.7 a.8.

[115] David Bentley Hart, *The Experience of God: Being, Consciousness, Bliss* (London: Yale University Press, 2013), p. 136.

[116] Hart, *The Experience of God*, p. 136.

"total absence of limitations" can only be the "total absence of limitations" in relation to "being", not "motion". In this way, one might say that God is omnipotent as "cause of being", that God "[has] the power, knowledge and wisdom to *bring into being* anything that can (without contradiction) be *brought into being*",[117] but is impotent as a "cause of motion", because motion requires temporality etc. One might say that God is omnipotent as a cause *per se*, but impotent as a cause *per accidens*. Thus, "'God' is the answer not to the question of why this or that thing occurs, but the question of why *anything* occurs".[118] Here, Bulgakov's criticisms of Thomas' language of "causality" seem to be relevant:[119] divine simplicity does not mean that God has a "greater extension of causality", but that God "*creates*" rather than "*causes*".

Omnipotence and Almighty

If God is omnipotent as a "cause of being" but impotent as a "cause of motion", then classic debates about omnipotence become somewhat irrelevant. For example, the debate about whether "God could create a stone that God could not lift" is entirely irrelevant because it misconstrues what is meant by creation. Not only that, but it assumes that God is a discrete, individual, personal being who is in a subject/object relation with the stone and who can experience the movement from stone-not-lifted to stone-lifted. Richard Swinburne is surely correct to dismiss the debate on the basis that (an immaterial) God cannot lift anything,[120] but (perhaps because of this adherence to theistic personalism) he fails to notice any further problem with the debate and so simply reframes it as, say, whether God could create anything that God could not destroy. That

---

[117] Robin Attfield, *Creation, Evolution and Meaning* (Aldershot: Ashgate Publishing, 2006), p. 24 (italics added); see also Brian Davies, *An Introduction to the Philosophy of Religion* (Oxford: Oxford University Press, 2004), pp. 183–6.

[118] Bauerschmidt, *Thomas Aquinas: Faith, Reason, and Following Christ*, p. 97.

[119] Sergei Bulgakov, *The Bride of the Lamb* (Grand Rapids, MI: William B. Eerdmans, 2002), pp. 35–7.

[120] Richard Swinburne, "Omnipotence", *American Philosophical Quarterly* 10:3 (1973), p. 233.

this shows that Swinburne is understanding "creation" as univocal with how humans create is exactly the point. For Swinburne, God is nothing more than a super-human.

Here Peter Geach makes an excellent suggestion that helps to refocus the meaning of omnipotence. The problem with omnipotence, he argues, is that theologians have distorted its original intention and have tried to prove something that it was never intended to prove. He writes that one can have no objection to the term "omnipotence" if it is used as a way to "merely express a desire to give the best honour we can to God our Maker, whose Name only is excellent and whose praise is above heaven and earth". However, the problem is when "theologians have tried to *prove* that God can do everything, or to derive conclusions from this thesis as a premise". These theologians, he suggests, have turned the signification of "Pious Intention" into one of "Philosophical Truth". The solution, Geach suggests, is that one calls God "almighty"—"God's having power *over* all things"—*not* "omnipotent"—the "ability to *do* everything" (however understood).[121] It is entirely acceptable to retain the word "omnipotent" to describe God, but if it is taken to mean that "God can do everything", then it severely distorts the intention behind using the word to begin with.

It is interesting that this book has suggested that "theistic personalists" have done *precisely* this with the ideas of "person" and "cause". Karl Rahner (and others) is clear that "theistic personalists" have taken the Patristic idea of *hypostasis* and interpreted it to mean what modern philosophers mean by "person". These "theistic personalists" assume that what modern philosophy means by "person" is exactly what the Greek Fathers had in mind when they endorsed "personal" language to describe the Trinity. Likewise, Michael Dodds (and others) is clear that modern theologians have taken the scholastic idea of "cause" and interpreted it to mean what modern philosophers after the scientific revolution mean by "cause". These "theistic personalists" assume that what modern science/philosophy means by "cause" is exactly what the Latin schoolmen had in mind when they endorsed "causal" language to describe God's relation

---

[121] Peter T. Geach, "Omnipotence", *Philosophy* 48:183 (1973), p. 7 (italics in original).

with creation. (Arguably, Bulgakov does the same thing when he criticizes Thomas Aquinas for using "causal" language of God, but then expounds a theory of divine activity that is strikingly similar to Thomas'.) Peter Geach simply makes the same observation about omnipotence.

Inevitably, some will disagree with this definition. Richard La Croix dismisses certain definitions of omnipotence that simply identify a range of acts that are taken to constitute omnipotence (as opposed to defining omnipotence as being able to do *all* acts), because "preanalytically" they do not seem to be acceptable as omnipotence.[122] Likewise, Scott Hill argues that "directly moving a red ball from the centre of the galaxy to my office seems like something an omnipotent being should be able to do",[123] thereby taking the same stance as La Croix, that omnipotence seems to suggest something has "maximal ability". Presumably, these philosophers (and others who share their view) would disagree with the definition of omnipotence presented here, as they would presumably disagree with much that has been argued in this chapter.

Nevertheless, the point of this understanding of omnipotence is that it is defined in terms of "cause of being" because all and every other definition of omnipotence requires a creaturely limitation to be applied to God. If omnipotence means that God can bring about all and every change that it is possible to bring about, then this cannot be applied to God. God is omnipotent because all creatures depend on God for their being, not because God can cause all and every motion. If "preanalytically" this does not look like omnipotence, then God is not omnipotent, as Geach argues. Invariably, those who see the denial that God can act as a "cause of motion" *at all* as placing limitations on God because God—as simple—should have far fewer limitations will find this notion that God is not omnipotent problematic. However, all that is being claimed here is that God cannot "interfere" in the universe, not because God lacks the power to do so, but because God has too much

---

[122]   Richard La Croix, "The Impossibility of Defining 'Omnipotence'", *Philosophical Studies: An International Journal for Philosophy in the Analytic Tradition* 32:2 (1977), p. 183.

[123]   Scott Hill, "Giving up Omnipotence", *Canadian Journal of Philosophy* 44:1 (2014), p. 101.

power.[124] Or, more accurately, God does not *have* any power; God is that in which all creatures participate for power.

Omniscience

It is impossible to deal with omnipotence without saying something about omniscience, not least because the "common Scholastic conviction ... [that] the principle of being and the principle of intelligibility are identical"[125] means that what God "does" and what God "knows" are exactly the same. Or, to put that differently, God's "knowing" and God's "doing" are the same "activity". As Katherin Rogers writes:

> God's power is His knowledge. He creates by thinking. Whatever is is sustained immediately by the knowledge of God. If God did not know this particular planet, cat or sub-atomic particle, and know it directly, right now, it would blink out of being.[126]

It stands to reason, therefore, that the same sorts of issues are applicable for omniscience as they are for omnipotence, especially if omnipotence means that God cannot be conscious without implying a limitation on God's part.

Thus, if omnipotence does not mean that God can do anything that is illogical, or that God can do anything that requires a creaturely limitation, then the same must be true of omniscience. That is, Paul Helm argues, "there are going to be ways of knowing facts which an individual in time will have that a timeless being cannot have, and vice versa. No appeal to omnipotence or omniscience can alter that fact".[127] In other words, as with omnipotence, as soon as one starts making claims about the difference between God and creatures, then this is going to impact the definition of omniscience that one is happy with. Thus, Helm continues,

---

[124]   McCabe, "Creation", p. 412.

[125]   Zachary Hayes, "Christology and Metaphysics in the Thought of Bonaventure", *The Journal of Religion* 58 (1978), p. S91.

[126]   Rogers, *Perfect Being Theology*, p. 75.

[127]   Murray MacBeath and Paul Helm, "Omniscience and Eternity", *Proceedings of the Aristotelian Society, Supplementary Volumes* 63 (1989), p. 79.

this conclusion [that there is some knowledge that God cannot have] ought not to be thought to have any adverse consequences for divine omniscience, since any account of the omniscience of God must be consistent with the sort of being God is. The sort of being he [sic] is—timeless or otherwise—determines the sort of omniscience that he has, and necessarily one sort of omniscience will contain features that the other sort of omniscience does not have.[128]

Paul Fiddes makes the same observation. He questions whether a truly omniscient God can have genuine knowledge of what it's like to be a refugee on Monday (cold and hungry) because to do so requires that God does not know what it is like to be relieved on Wednesday.[129] If God is immutable, then God cannot genuinely know what it is like to suffer because suffering requires that one does not have knowledge of relief. Likewise, others have questioned whether God can genuinely experience panic, fear, dread, embarrassment etc. because such experiences (regardless of whether God requires a body to feel them or not) conflict with certain other divine attributes, such as immutability.[130]

Just as omnipotence requires the rejection of any interpretation that would posit a creaturely limitation on God, so omniscience requires the rejection of any interpretation that would posit a creaturely limitation on God. Importantly, if that logically leads to the conclusion that God cannot "act" as a "cause" in any way, then this must also lead to the conclusion that God cannot "know" any "datum" in any way. If omniscience means the complete possession of every single possible datum that it is possible to have, then God has to be conceived as a discrete, individual, conscious subject that has a super-intelligence. It assumes that God is in a subject/

---

[128] MacBeath and Helm, "Omniscience and Eternity", p. 79.

[129] Paul Fiddes, *The Creative Suffering of God* (Oxford: Clarendon Press, 1988), pp. 91–2; see also Henry Simoni, "Omniscience and the Problem of Radical Particularity: Does God Know How to Ride a Bike?", *International Journal for Philosophy of Religion* 42 (1997), p. 11.

[130] David Blumenfeld, quoted in Simoni, "Omniscience and the Problem of Radical Particularity: Does God Know How to Ride a Bike?", p. 10.

object relationship with the universe, and has perfect knowledge about what the universe is, how it works, and what happens in it. Yet, if God is not "*a*" being, so cannot be the "sort" of "being" who is in a subject/object relation with the universe, and so cannot be the subject of any act, however "maximal", then God cannot be the "sort" of "being" who can have knowledge at all.

If that understanding of omnipotence criticized theistic personalists for translating a traditional category into an alien, modern language, then the same could be said of omniscience. As Pseudo-Dionysius writes, "It is not simply the case that God is so overflowing with wisdom that 'his understanding is beyond measure' but, rather, he actually transcends all reason, all intelligence, and all wisdom."[131] Thus, like omnipotence, omniscience is not a complete set of data, so that God knows every possible datum, but, rather, omniscience means that God is that in which all things are intelligible. Paul Tillich also gives expression to this interpretation of omniscience. He writes that omniscience "is not the faculty of a highest being who is supposed to know all [things]" but is that which indicates that "nothing is outside the centred unity of [God's] life; nothing is strange, dark, hidden, isolated, unapproachable",[132] and this also means that "nothing falls outside the *Logos* structure of being".[133] Here, then, is the crux of the matter: omniscience is not the possession of all possible data; it is that which makes the world intelligible because the world participates in God. Omniscience, then, has nothing whatsoever to do with "knowing", just as omnipotence has nothing whatsoever to do with "doing"; both are principles that affirm God is the source of "being", "power", and "intelligibility". Without God, no creature could be, do, know, or be known but, crucially, this does not mean that God can also do and know what those creatures do and know.[134]

---

131 Pseudo-Dionysius, *The Divine Names* 7.1.

132 Tillich, *Systematic Theology Vol.1*, pp. 277–8.

133 Tillich, *Systematic Theology Vol.1*, pp. 277–8.

134 In this way, as already hinted above, this book follows the Franciscan position in arguing that there is only one idea in God. Bonaventure, for example, holds that God cannot know by "gaz[ing]" at the world, but knows all *through* God's being the exemplary cause of all creatures. Whereas for Augustine, the focus

is on the role of divine ideas "in the *creation* of particulars, namely as a divine template that guides the creative act", for Bonaventure, the focus is on "the epistemological dimension, and specifically with the question of how God knows things" (Junius Johnson, "The One and the Many in Bonaventure Exemplarity Explained", *Religions* 7:144 (2016), p. 3). For Bonaventure, "God knows creatures not by means of their own essences as they exist in the world, but by means of the eternal ideas, identical to God's own being", so that "God knows things internally, by means of the eternal reasons that are identical with his own existence" (Joshua C. Benson, "Structure and Meaning in St. Bonaventure's *'Quaestiones Disputatae de Scientia Christi'*", *Franciscan Studies* 62 (2004), p. 74). The fact that God's knowledge is causal is relevant here. An important element of this argument is the distinction between two types of knowledge: "That which is caused by things, and that which causes things" (Johnson, "The One and the Many in Bonaventure Exemplarity Explained", p. 11). The first is caused by something "outside" and so leads to an "addition in the knowing intellect by the introduction of a likeness that comes from outside the intellect", whereas the second is the opposite and "is based upon a likeness that does not come from outside the knowing intellect, and is in fact the divine intellect, the highest light, the full truth, and pure act" (Johnson, "The One and the Many in Bonaventure Exemplarity Explained", p. 11). God, being perfect and eternal, cannot have the first "sort" of knowledge, so must have the second. Likewise, it can be inferred, creatures cannot have the second because creatures cannot create. Thomas Aquinas (in fitting with his claim, outlined above, that God is both entirely transcendent and person, and can be both that in which creatures participate and another cause in the world), held that God could have both types of knowledge (*ST* 1, 14, 6). This book takes the Franciscan approach. Thus, God has knowledge of "only one truth from which all others are deducible" (John Abbruzzese, "The Coherence of Omniscience: A Defense", *International Journal for Philosophy of Religion* 41 (1997), p. 33). That is not to say that God does any "deducing", but to emphasize that from God's atemporality and simplicity God only knows one thing, and that one thing is the Christ through which God creates all creatures and so is the exemplary cause of all creatures. Or, as Alexander of Hales held, "God does not understand infinitely many things", rather, "God's knowledge of singulars is like knowing many in virtue

What is crucial about Tillich's definition of omniscience is that it makes explicit reference to Christ. All things are intelligible because "nothing falls outside the *Logos* structure of being". It is because all things are imitations of Christ that they are intelligible. Others have said much the same thing. Robert Barron also writes that:

> Just as the Logos of the Father is the power through which all things are intelligible, so that same Word is the power through whom all things are known. Accordingly, it is in Christ and through Christ that even the simplest act of cognition takes place; 'natural' reason is thoroughly Christological . . . what we know and how we know is conditioned by what was revealed in Jesus Christ.[135]

It is not just God in which all things are intelligible; it is not even just the *Logos*; it is Jesus Christ in which all things are intelligible. The Franciscan theologian Zachary Hayes makes the same observation. He writes that "if all things are constituted in being through the Word, and if it is impossible to understand a creature except through that by which it was made . . . then in some way the Word is involved in all genuine knowledge at whatever level".[136] It is difficult, if not impossible, to overestimate the importance of the implications of this claim. If "acting"—and so creation—is identical to "knowing", and all things are intelligible insofar as they imitate Christ, then all things have "being" insofar as they imitate Christ. In the language

---

of a single universal" (Rega Wood, "Distinct Ideas and Perfect Solicitude: Alexander of Hales, Richard Rufus, and Odo Rigaldus", *Franciscan Studies* 53 (1993), p. 13). God only "knows" Christ and, so, because "God's power is God's knowledge", God only "acts" in Christ and God only knows (and creates) insofar as creatures are imitations of Christ (indeed, one can only be created insofar as one imitates Christ). It is also crucial to explicitly link this with the above discussion of God's single, uniform, "basic" will and evolution. The single divine idea is identical to the single divine will, which is Christ.

[135] See also Robert Barron, *The Priority of Christ: Towards A Postliberal Catholicism* (Grand Rapids, MI: Brazos Press, 2007), p. 148.

[136] Hayes, "Christology and Metaphysics in the Thought of Bonaventure", p. S92.

used above, "*that* something is"—that a thing is something rather than nothing—is because they imitate Christ; all "things" are "things" because they imitate Christ. *How* they imitate Christ—i.e., "*what* something is", "*what*" "sort" of imitation something is—is entirely accidental, but one can only "be" if one is an imitation of Christ.

Theodicy

The theodicy question is, undoubtedly, one of the most often-quoted reasons for having difficulty in accepting that there could be a God. How could a loving God create a world that is so full of suffering? An answer to that question necessarily draws upon how one answers the previous two questions: providence and omnipotence. So the popular argument goes, either God is unwilling to alleviate suffering (i.e., God is not providential)—in which case, God is undeserving of worship—or God is incapable of alleviating suffering (i.e., God is not omnipotent)—in which case, God is unworthy of worship. The fact that suffering exists proves that God cannot be both all-good and all-powerful.

Some quite novel answers to this problem have been given over the centuries. Some point to *kenosis*, and so suggest that God has freely given up God's ability to intervene.[137] Some suggest that the suffering that inevitably forms a part of the world is necessary to ensure that certain values are cultivated—one cannot have sacrifice without genuine suffering.[138] These, and others, point to the fact that, while suffering surely exists, it is better to have genuine freedom, which necessarily includes

---

[137] Nicola Hoggard Creegan, "A Christian Theology of Evolution and Participation, *Zygon: Journal of Religion and Science* 42:2 (2007), p. 502; see also John Polkinghorne (ed.), *The Work of Love: Creation as Kenosis* (Grand Rapids, MI: William B. Eerdmans, 2001).

[138] Christopher Southgate, *The Groaning of Creation* (Louisville, KY: Westminster John Knox Press, 2008); Christopher Southgate, "Re-reading Genesis, John and Job: A Christian Response to Darwinism", *Zygon: Journal of Religion and Science* 46:2 (2011), pp. 370–95.

the possibility of suffering, than a sort of wooden existence in which there is no real freedom.

The reader may judge for themselves the relative merits of these and other prospective responses to the problem of suffering. The free-will defence—that suffering is a necessary by-product of living in a world in which freedom and failure are genuine possibilities—certainly has merits, but it seems to involve thinking about the relationship between God and the universe as a subject/object relationship. In other words, there are certainly merits to explaining the presence of suffering as the necessary corollary to genuine freedom, but the suggestion that God *could* intervene in, or influence, the world in some way to alleviate that suffering but does not because God has freely relinquished that ability (i.e., freely relinquished omnipotence) or God refrains in order to cultivate some favourable value (i.e., as a way to providentially fulfil the universe) involves thinking about God as a "person", which this book has so far wholly rejected. To suppose that God *could* alleviate suffering is to suppose that God is not the "ground of being". To suppose that God freely relinquishes God's ability to act (*kenosis*) or simply withholds acting through choice is to suppose that God's activity is accidentally ordered; it is to suppose that God can do something discrete at a certain point in time after which the world has changed.

Moreover, these ways of thinking about God appear to violate the "absence of a real relation". To suppose that God could alleviate suffering is to suppose that God prefers certain particular ends—is really related differently to different spatiotemporal points—and acts in discrete particular ways in order to realize them. If divine activity is about ontological participation and the creature's *per se* dependence on God at all spatiotemporal points, then any suffering must, quite literally, be "accidental" to that. If God remains unchanged whether or not a universe actually obtains at all, then God also remains unchanged whether or not there is suffering in the world.

That last claim might come across as offensive to those who are experiencing genuine suffering. People come to God to find solace and respite; it is a cold person who responds to that desire for solace and respite with the claim that suffering is "theologically irrelevant". To suggest that God remains unchanged by the presence of genuine suffering seems quite forcefully to lend support to those "theistic personalists" who claim that "we admire people who can be moved by tragic events. We admire people who can become elated when good things happen. And . . . we can admire God only if he [sic], like admirable people, is suitably affected by the good and the bad which occurs in the world".[139] Likewise, Murray MacBeath suggests that a God who "cannot share in our relief that some dreadful episode is over" is unattractive,[140] and Marcel Sarot argues that a God who does not have knowledge "feelingly" is "theologically irrelevant" and so God has to be able to "undergo feelings and experiences"[141] or theism becomes incoherent. In the same way, it is easy to be sympathetic to process theologians who, in opposition to the "stoic" Thomistic God (and the conception of divine love as "pure giver"),[142] claim that "it is essential to [God's] being love that he [sic] can be changed and affected by what his own power permits to be"[143] and so "divine creating activity [is] based upon responsive[ness] to the world".[144]

It is difficult to look at the question of suffering and not find theologies that claim God is unchanged by any suffering in the world as being deficient in some way. Nevertheless, this fact follows logically from what has already been argued. If providence and omnipotence are "radically" reinterpreted to be concerned with "being" rather than "motion"—which is necessary if creation is about ontological relationship rather than origins—then this suggests that God neither guides history, nor can influence the motion/change in the world. This is not to suggest that suffering is not important, that suffering is not a very real problem, that suffering does not blight people's lives or inhibit their growth and

---

[139] Davies, *An Introduction to the Philosophy of Religion*, p. 13.

[140] MacBeath and Helm, "Omniscience and Eternity", pp. 69–70; see also Davies, *An Introduction to the Philosophy of Religion*, pp. 9–14.

[141] Marcel Sarot, "Omniscience and Experience", *International Journal for Philosophy of Religion* 30:2 (1991), p. 90.

[142] See *ST* i, q. 20, a.2.

[143] Ward, *Rational Theology and the Creativity of God*, p. 151; see also John B. Cobb and David Ray Griffin, *Process Theology: An Introductory Exposition* (London: The Westminster Press, 1976), pp. 51–2.

[144] Cobb and Griffin, *Process Theology*, pp. 51–2.

fulfilment, but it is to suggest that God cannot have anything to do with it without significantly reducing God to a super-creature.

In many ways, then, more forcefully than any question that has been addressed so far, the theodicy question indicates that what is being argued for in this book—regardless of the fact that it draws upon traditional theological themes and situates itself within the theological systems of Pseudo-Dionysius and Thomas Aquinas—is deism. The God for which this book apologizes—if that God is "unmoved" or "unchanged" by the presence of genuine suffering among the creatures that God creates—is the "impersonal God" of the deist. If the God for which this book apologizes is "unmoved" by suffering and does not intervene to alleviate that suffering because such a God would be unable to do so, then it is practically no different from atheism. Tillich and Mivart have been quoted in support of that very claim.

Conclusion

Providence, omnipotence, and theodicy have all been radically reinterpreted. That reinterpretation, it is argued, follows quite logically from what was argued in the previous chapter. Following Paul Tillich, that reinterpretation argues that Thomas Aquinas did not follow the logic of his own system and so, while it draws heavily on Thomist categories and themes, does not ultimately look very much like Thomism at all. Indeed, it looks very much like deism. As argued in the previous chapter, this is not a "traditional" deism. This is a deism that sees all creatures as participating in God at every single spatiotemporal point as the "ground of being". However, God does not act in ways to influence the specific history of the universe. Rather, God "let[s] be whatever would and could emerge from that freedom, and enjoy[s] *all* responses of *all* kinds as they have occurred from the beginning of time, with their various qualities, of which intelligence is only one".[145] This is deism, but it draws on very traditional understandings of divine nature and divine activity.

---

[145] Page, *The Web of Creation*, p. 80.

4

The Incarnation

The last two chapters illustrated that absolutely nothing about the history of the universe, from its origin in the Big Bang, through the birth, death, and evolution of everything in it, to its (probable) collapse in the Big Crunch, is part of what the theological doctrine of creation means. Creation is about *why* there is something rather than nothing; "*what*" that "something" is, is entirely and completely accidental to that theological doctrine of creation. This is comparable to a deist interpretation of Thomism, in which God is only responsible for creation (being)— "*that*" the world is—and has nothing to do with anything else, including "*what*" that particular world might be.

As Helen Oppenheimer perceptively notes, such an interpretation is permitted by the Nicene-Constantinopolitan creed, which "say[s] nothing about divine providence arranging what happens in the world".[1] Although the biblical scholar might have some reservations about deism being a legitimate interpretation of *biblical theology*, deism is certainly a legitimate interpretation of the *creed*. However, the incarnation appears to immediately frustrate any deistic longings the theologian might have. After all, the creed moves swiftly from affirming nothing more than that God creates all that is visible and invisible to the affirmation that the Son was that through whom all things were made and who came down from heaven by the Holy Spirit and became incarnate of the Virgin Mary. If the incarnation is a central part of Christian theology, then one seems to be presented with an ultimatum: one cannot be a deist and a Christian.

---

[1] Helen Oppenheimer, *Christian Faith for Handing On* (Cambridge: James Clarke & Co., 2014), p. 85.

Many scholars agree with this ultimatum. David Brown writes that the deist, "while committed to belief in God, rejects Jesus Christ and his doctrines" so that "if there is to be a proper incarnation, God the Son cannot stand aloof from the created order but must become interrelated with it".[2] Gerald O'Collins also writes that "the logic of deism excluded the possibility of any such special sub-acts of God . . . [e.g.] an incarnation".[3] Chris Isham makes a similar observation, writing that "the God of Christianity is not only 'the ground of Being'. He is also Incarnate",[4] implying, at least, that the incarnation is something subsequent and additional to God's role as "ground of being".

In this way, Helen Oppenheimer describes a sort of "two act" deism. Recognizing that the creed permits deism, but agreeing with the sentiments just quoted, she finds this problematic for the next part of the creed, and so "tags on" the incarnation. It is at once obvious what is so very wrong with deism from the Christian point of view, Oppenheimer claims: it leaves out the Gospel.[5] She calls this "incarnational deism"[6] although she claims this way "may eventually lead into a cul-de-sac".[7] However, this book does not follow Oppenheimer in arguing for a "two act" deism. First, a "two act" deism seems to contradict one of the very reasons that this book gave for supporting deism in the first place: there can only be *one* divine act. Second, Oppenheimer seems to overlook an important implication of the creed: the Christ-event is not *separate* from creation. That is, the creed might permit deism, but is also empathic that Christ is the agent of creation. If "all" God does is create, then God does this through Christ: Christ is the creator.

---

[2]   David Brown, *The Divine Trinity* (London: Duckworth, 1985), p. 14.

[3]   Gerald O'Collins, *Christology: A Biblical, Historical, and Systematic Study of Jesus* (Oxford: Oxford University Press, 1995), p. 217.

[4]   Chris Isham, "Creation of the Universe as a Quantum Process", in Robert J. Russell, William Stoeger, and George Coyne (eds), *Physics, Philosophy, and Theology* (Vatican City: Vatican Observatory, 1988), p. 405.

[5]   Helen Oppenheimer, *Incarnation and Immanence* (London: Hodder and Stoughton, 1973), p. 57.

[6]   Oppenheimer, *Christian Faith for Handing On*, p. 85.

[7]   Oppenheimer, *Incarnation and Immanence*, p. 57.

This is central to New Testament theology. Whether or not John had access to Paul's letters, it is also clear that chief among those theological developments that separate his Gospel from the other, synoptic, Gospels was a retrospective extrapolation of Christ beyond the period from his birth to death. For John, so great was the Christ event that he identified him with the God of Genesis. Some might see this development in John's Gospel as a Gnostic infiltration, a tendency of which John has been accused. However, that Paul made precisely the same move is perhaps evidence enough that the identification of Christ with the creator God is a legitimate theological move. Such a theological move is perhaps the best insight into what the New Testament authors thought Christ was doing in the incarnation and the crucifixion, that is "the doctrine of Christ's agency in creation arose first as a response to the re-creative mighty works of Jesus".[8] Paul and John clearly saw Christ as creating in the incarnation, and so it became clear to them that, if Christ was creating, then he must have been responsible for the "original" creation (if it can be so called). If Paul can write that "if anyone is in Christ, there is a new creation",[9] then Christ must be an agent of creation, and so it is only natural to then extrapolate to this the "original" creation. By the time Athanasius had appeared on the theological scene, what was implicit in John and Paul's identification of Christ's activity with the "original" creation was made explicit: Christ had to be divine. Thus, Athanasius could write that "it may be duly perceived that the renewal of creation has been the work of the selfsame Word that made it at the beginning".[10]

Chul Won Suh cautions that identifying the agent does not necessarily mean identifying the acts. He writes that "the personal identity of the author in the divine drama does not induce us to regard the two works as the same or the continuation of one another"; just because "the same

---

[8] Sean McDonough, *Christ as Creator: Origins of a New Testament Doctrine* (Oxford: Oxford University Press, 2009), p. 235.

[9] 2 Corinthians 5:17.

[10] Athanasius, "On the Incarnation", in Edward Hardy (tr.), *Christology of the Later Fathers* (London: Westminster John Knox Press, 1954), p. 56.

author works", does not mean that "one [i]s the continuation of the other".[11] However, it can certainly be implied from such an identification, even if it is not logically necessary. Moreover, following the logical moves seems to point to this very conclusion: that is, John and Paul (and Athanasius) did not identify the two acts because they saw them as being performed by the same author; rather, they were moved to identify the agents *precisely because* they identified the acts. That is, they first recognized the identity between the two acts, and so posited that they must have the same agent. Celia Deane-Drummond also evidences this identification. She writes that "there are similarities between the incarnation and the creation of the world in that both are acts of condescension".[12] The idea of "condescension", otherwise known as *kenosis*, will be considered in the next chapter; for here, it is enough to notice that creation and incarnation are seen as the same "type" of act: what God does in the incarnation is identical to what is done in creation.

Three interpretations of this fact are possible. Either (a) the incarnation is a completion of the *creatio originalis*; (b) the incarnation is a repetition of the *creatio originalis*; or (c) the incarnation *is* the *creatio originalis*. The first two interpretations have an historical precedent. The first can be represented by John Duns Scotus and Franciscan theology, although is popularly seen to be more prevalent in the eastern tradition.[13] The second can be seen in Athanasius (as already quoted) and Thomas Aquinas, who writes that "the first creation of things was made by the power of God the Father through the Word; hence the second creation ought to have been brought about through the Word".[14]

---

[11] Chul Won Suh, *The Creation-Mediatorship of Jesus Christ* (Amsterdam: Rodopi, 1982), p. 269.

[12] Celia Deane-Drummond, *Christ and Evolution* (London: SCM Press and Minneapolis, MN: Fortress Press, 2009), pp. 114–5.

[13] See Bogdan Bucur, "Foreordained from All Eternity: The Mystery of the Incarnation According to Some Early Christian and Byzantine Writers", *Dumbarton Oaks Papers 62* (2008), pp. 199–215; See also John Macquarrie, *Jesus Christ in Modern Thought* (London: SCM Press, 1990), pp. 58–9.

[14] *ST* 3, 3, 8; see Joseph Wawrykow, "Aquinas and Bonaventure on Creation", in Gary Anderson and Markus Bockmuehl (eds), *Creation ex nihilo: Origins,*

For the deist (at least, the traditional deist), neither of these interpretations are possible. Both seem to imply that God does more than one thing—the incarnation is either another act that continues the first or another act that repeats the first. Moreover, it is not just problematic for the deist. Thomas Aquinas and Bonaventure both held a strict doctrine of atemporality and simplicity, and yet both were quite clear that the incarnation was numerically and temporally distinct from *creatio originalis*. Thomas Aquinas called the incarnation a "second creation"[15] and Bonaventure writes that "just as God had created all things through the Word Not Made [sic], even so he restored all things through the Word Made Flesh [sic]".[16] Even Athanasius, who has been used as support for identifying the acts of creation and incarnation, held them to be distinct instances of acting.[17] Thus, J. W. C. Wand writes that "twice that word had spoken; once in creation, when 'God spoke and it was done'; and a second time at the incarnation, when 'the word was made flesh and tabernacled among us'".[18] Edward Oakes also writes, "God's power to create and sustain the universe in being is not the same as his power to become incarnate",[19] and Karl Rahner, too, explicitly argues that "we can understand creation and Incarnation as two moments and two phases of the *one* process of God's self-giving and self-expression", but then qualifies that claim with the comment that "it is an *intrinsically differentiated* process".[20] In other words, the incarnation and creation are *intrinsically* different *for* God, which seemingly does not conform to the absence of a real relation and divine simplicity.

Development, Contemporary Challenges (Notre Dame, IN: University of Notre Dame Press, 2018), pp. 187–8.

[15] *ST* 3, 3, 8.

[16] Bonaventure, *Breviloquium* (Paterson, NJ: At. Anthony Guild Press, 1963), IV, 1, 2.

[17] Athanasius, "On the Incarnation", pp. 168–9.

[18] J. W. C. Wand, *The Four Great Heresies* (London: Mowbray, 1961), p. 27.

[19] Edward Oakes, *A Theology of Grace in Six Controversies* (Grand Rapids, MI: William B. Eerdmans, 2016), p. 38.

[20] Karl Rahner, *The Foundations of Christian Faith: An Introduction to the Idea of Christianity* (New York, NY: Crossroad, 1978), p. 97 (italics added).

This leaves the third interpretation, that the incarnation *is* creation. While this might initially seem a somewhat strange assertion, once it is accepted that creation is a relationship, and not "some putative first moment in the past",[21] then the theologian is not looking for an "event" that can be identified as the single divine act that "gets the world started", but is rather looking for a relationship. Here, the Big Bang is no longer satisfactory as a means to locate the divine "cause" in creation. Instead, the obvious answer becomes Emmanuel, "God with us". Jesus is not just God's self-revelation of Godself to all of God's creatures; Jesus is also *constitutive of* the relationship between them.

Likewise, if God is so utterly transcendent of, and ontologically other to, creatures, then something "else" is needed to explain how it is that creatures can be related to, and participate in, God at all. Certainly that relation is a "mixed relation"—so that while creatures are really related to God, God is not really related to creatures—but if God is so utterly transcendent so as not to allow of a relation between God and creatures, then how is it that there can be a relation between creatures and God? That is, if God is so utterly ontologically other, as the first chapter argues, how can creatures have a relation with God? The answer: the incarnation.

This chapter will make a number of claims that help to expound how this can be so. First, it will be shown that when the creed and Bible talk about Christ as creator, or Christ as that through which God creates, it is reasonable to understand this as suggesting that Christ is the agent of creation. It will then be shown that Christ as mediator between God and creatures is sufficient to illustrate that, regardless of how transcendent God is, creatures can be related to God through Christ. If this is the case, then it is crucial that one understands Chalcedon correctly. That is, Christ can only function as a mediator because Christ is *both* God *and* creature *simultaneously*. Furthermore, it will be demonstrated that this hypostatic union is not an historical relation, but an ontological one. This means that "God is never in the state of not having an assumed human

---

21   Andrew Davison, *Participation in God* (Cambridge: Cambridge University Press, 2019), p. 26.

nature".[22] If that is the case, then "God is never without his [sic] Logos, the divine Wisdom, in and through whom the world is created, ordered, and sustained".[23] In other words, if creation is a relation that creatures have with God, then this relation is mediated and constituted by the hypostatic union that is the person of Jesus Christ.

Christ is the creator, not because Christ "lights the blue touch paper", but because Christ is that through which all things participate in God for their being. That is, whatever was concluded in the previous chapter does not happen outside of and/or without the incarnation. The incarnation is not an addition to God being the "ground of being"; the incarnation is *how* God is the ground of being. If "the formula *creatio ex nihilo* is not the title of a story ... [but] is the classical formula which expresses the *relation* between God and the world",[24] then "it is the *eternal relation* of God to man which is manifest in the Christ".[25]

Christ as creator

The centrality of the doctrine of Christ as creator for New Testament theology is well established, and much has been written on the subject. More is not needed here. Rather a few comments are necessary to understand *how* it is that Christ is the creator.

For Thomas Aquinas, Christ was the creator as a formal cause. In his *Commentary on John*, he writes, "For whoever makes something must preconceive it in his wisdom, which is the form and pattern of the thing made: as the form preconceived in the mind of an artisan is the pattern of the cabinet to be made." Christ, Thomas argues, is the creator in this

[22] Eleonore Stump, *The God of the Bible and the God of the Philosophers* (Milwaukee, WI: Marquette University Press, 2016), p. 100.

[23] David Bentley Hart, *The Experience of God: Being, Consciousness, Bliss* (London: Yale University Press, 2013), p. 235.

[24] Paul Tillich, *Systematic Theology Vol. 1* (Chicago, IL: The University of Chicago Press, 1957), p. 254 (italics added).

[25] Paul Tillich, *Systematic Theology Vol. 2* (London: SCM Press, 1978), p. 96 (italics added).

sense: as the "form" that is "preconceived in God's wisdom". He continues that "God makes nothing except through the conception of his intellect, which is an eternally conceived wisdom, that is, the Word of God, and the Son of God. Accordingly, it is impossible that he should make anything except through the Son".[26]

In his *Commentary on Colossians*, Aquinas repeats this assertion that God creates through Christ as a form preconceived in wisdom. He writes that "we should note that the Platonists affirmed the existence of Ideas, and said that each thing came to be by participating in an Idea, like the Idea of man, or an Idea of some other kind". However, Aquinas continues that "instead of all these we have one, that is, the Son, the Word of God. For an artisan makes an artefact by making it participate in the form he has conceived within himself, enveloping it, so to say, with external matter; for we say that the artisan makes a house through the form of the thing which he has conceived within himself."[27]

Thomas' claim here is not that Christ actually *creates*, but rather that Christ is the creator as the "plan" or "form" of creation, according to which God creates. When it is acknowledged that one can also translate the Greek word λόγος (*logos*) as "ratio" in addition to "word"—and, moreover, "this translation is even more rational than the traditional one"[28]—then this understanding appears to have some support. The important passage from the Gospel of John is then retranslated: "In the beginning, there was the ratio, and the ratio was with God and the ratio was God".[29] This appears to support Thomas' claim; Christ is the "ratio" according to which God creates.

---

[26]   Thomas Aquinas, *Commentary on John* (Albany, NY: Magi Books, Inc., 1998), 1, 77.

[27]   Thomas Aquinas, *Commentary on Colossians* (Naples, FL: Sapientia Press, 2009), 1, 4, 37; it is important that Thomas Aquinas refers to Christ as the "one" idea, supporting the comments made in the previous chapters that there is one idea in God because of divine simplicity.

[28]   Charles Seife, *Zero: The Biography of a Dangerous Idea* (London: Souvenir Press, 2000), p. 26 fn.*.

[29]   Seife, *Zero*, p. 26.

In arguing for this position, Thomas dismisses the suggestion that Christ could be the creator as an "efficient cause" or as an "instrument".[30] If Christ is the efficient cause of creation, Thomas argues, then it seems to imply that the word is the source of God's power. This serves to make the word more ontologically primary than God, and so would mean that God participates in the word, which is obviously incorrect. If, on the other hand, Christ is the instrument of creation—like the pen is the instrument of the hand's writing—then this makes Christ inferior to God. Both are incorrect interpretations of creation, so Aquinas concludes, as one makes Christ superior to God and the other makes Christ inferior to God. For Thomas, it is truly God who creates, and Christ is the pattern from which God creates.

However, this interpretation of Christ as creator does not particularly lend itself to a truly, genuinely simple God, who is not really related to creatures. That is, despite the fact that Thomas Aquinas clearly supports the notion of the absence of a real relation, particularly its use as an interpretation of divine simplicity, it seems that Aquinas does not take it into consideration when arguing for Christ as formal cause. That is, if Christ is the "formal cause" and not the "efficient cause", then this seems to imply that the difference between "efficient" cause and "formal" cause is *intrinsic* to God. Certainly, it should be possible for *creatures* to look at the simple, single, uniform divine act and distinguish "efficient" and "formal" causes, but this does not mean that these (and the "final" cause, which is often related to the work of the Spirit[31]) are not entirely and completely identical and synonymous *for God*.[32]

---

30 Aquinas, *Commentary on John*, 1, 76.

31 See Davison, *Participation in God*.

32 Indeed, Frederick Bauerschmidt writes that "though the third part of the *Summa Theologiae* and the fourth book of the *Summa Contra Gentiles* treat Christology in great detail, Thomas's Christology is not typically seen as either the center or the crowning achievement of his thought" and, drawing on Alois Grillmeier's observations, suggests that "in the concrete development of [his] system Christology ... appear[s] too late in Thomas" (Frederick Bauerschmidt, *Thomas Aquinas: Faith, Reason, and Following Christ* (Oxford: Oxford University Press, 2013), p. 179). Perhaps it would

Of course, this does not mean that the Trinitarian distinctions are not real, nor does it mean that these real distinctions violate simplicity. There are different "persons" in the Trinity, but these different persons "share" a *single* will, a *single* activity, and a *single* power. Thus, Vladimir Lossky writes that "the three, having but one nature, have but one single will, a single power, a single operation".[33] Nicholas Cabasilas writes that the Godhead "performs all things by one power, and one providence, and one creation".[34] Jaroslav Pelikan also writes that "action and will belonged, then, not to the hypostasis of the Father, Son, or Holy Spirit, but to the nature that was common to the three".[35] Certainly, there is something that the Son "does" that the other two persons do not—become incarnate (otherwise Patripassianism is unavoidable)—but this does not mean that the person of the *logos* has a will and energy that does not belong to the other two persons. Indeed, the sixth century agreement that Christ had two wills and two energies—one each for his two natures—is evidence that if the Godhead has one nature, then it must have one will and one energy.

If this single divine will and power is acknowledged, then God cannot relate to creatures here as "efficient" cause and there as "formal" cause (and in the Spirit the "final" cause). Or, to put this differently, the Son does not contribute something unique to the divine act of creation that the Father does not; the Son does not provide the "form" of the universe separate from the Father's "efficient" act of creation. In fact, so united was the "efficient" cause and "formal" cause (and "final" cause) in God that Frederick Bauerschmidt (while not noting this apparent inconsistency in Aquinas' thought), writes that "in a sense, God's efficient causality of substances is a bit like formal causality in things. The form 'chair' is a

---

be too much to say that Christology was something of an afterthought for Thomas, but the point is well made.

[33]   Vladimir Lossky, *The Mystical Theology of the Eastern Church* (Cambridge: James Clarke & Co., 1957), p. 53.

[34]   Nicholas Cabasilas, *The Life in Christ* (Crestwood, NY: St. Vladimir's Seminary Press, 1974), p. 74.

[35]   Jaroslav Pelikan, *The Christian Tradition: The Spirit of Eastern Christendom (600–1700)* (Chicago, IL: University of Chicago Press, 1977), p. 78.

cause of a chair instantaneously."[36] It does not make sense to single Christ out as "formal" cause, as distinct from the "efficient" cause.

Others offer a different interpretation. J. W. C. Wand writes that "the Apologists taught that creation is the work of the good God, the supreme being. Not that He [sic] performed it directly, by Himself, but through an intermediary, His word."[37] Gordon Fee also sees Christ's title of "Lord" as indicating that Christ is that which "mediates" divine creation. He writes that "the one who at his exaltation is granted the right to be called 'Lord', thus assuming full divine prerogatives (Philippians 2:9–11), is understood by Paul already to be present at creation as its mediating agent".[38] Similarly, Anselm of Canterbury writes that "it is quite clear that when we say that something is 'out of' something we can also say that it is 'through' that same thing, and vice versa".[39] Using the example of a carpenter, Anselm continues that "what exists 'out of' some material and 'through' a craftsman, can also be said to exist 'through' the material and 'out of' the craftsman. This is because it has its existence 'through and out of' both, that is by means of both—although the 'through and out of' the material is different to the 'through and out of' the craftsman."[40] Thus, according to Anselm, to say that the universe is created "through" Christ must have the meaning that it is created "out of" Christ. In other words, to say that God creates through Christ could have the meaning that Christ is the material "out of" which God creates, or it could have the meaning that Christ is the "author" of the work. It is obvious that Christ is not the material of creation, so it must be that Christ is the craftsman.

---

[36] Bauerschmidt, *Thomas Aquinas: Faith, Reason, and Following Christ*, p. 110; see also David O. Brown, "Creation as Participation: Essentially-Ordered Series, 'Spontaneous Creation', and the Rejection of Divine Efficient Causality", *Angelicum* 98:2 (2021), p. 292.

[37] Wand, *The Four Great Heresies*, p. 27.

[38] Gordon Fee, "St. Paul and the Incarnation: A Reassessment of the Data", in Stephen Davis, Daniel Kendall and Gerald O'Collins (eds), *The Incarnation* (Oxford: Oxford University Press, 2002), p. 68.

[39] Anselm, *Monologion* 5.

[40] Anselm, *Monologion* 5.

Moreover, "efficient" cause as applied to God is more like a relationship than an "act" that can "cause" things according to a plan or form. If creation is ontological dependence on God, if "God's creative action *just is* creation's dependence on God for its existence",[41] then Christ as creator must be seen within this paradigm of "ontological dependence". In this way, Christ is not the "formal" cause, but that which mediates that dependence: creatures participate in God *through* Christ. In other words, while Thomas Aquinas interpreted the "through" of such biblical passages as "plan", so that God creating through Christ means God creates according to the plan which is Christ, this book argues that "through" should have the meaning of "mediation". That is, "through" does not mean that Christ is the pattern according to which all creatures have been made, but that Christ is the vehicle through which God's act of creation is mediated to all creatures. Or, more accurately, that Christ is the vehicle through which all creatures depend on God.

In any case, the point here is that, as David Bentley Hart writes, "God is never without his [sic] Logos, the divine Wisdom, in and through whom the world is created, ordered, and sustained".[42] If "the word of God is the means by which we live in God . . . when God speaks, things come to be",[43] then the "word of God" is not just "formal" cause to all creatures, but "efficient" and "final" cause as well. That is, there is nothing that God does which God does not do through Christ: Christ is "the universal and *exclusive* agent of creation".[44]

---

[41]   John Bishop and Ken Perszyk, "The Divine Attributes and Non-personal Conceptions of God", *Topoi* 36 (2017), p. 614 (italics in original).

[42]   Hart, *The Experience of God*, p. 235.

[43]   Enzo Bianchi, *Praying the Word of God* (Kalamazoo, MI: Cistercian Publications, 1998), p. 24.

[44]   O'Collins, *Christology*, p. 302 (italics added).

Christ as mediator

If Christ as creator means that Christ "mediates" God's creative "activity", then this can be seen as a specific instance of a much "wider" belief in Christ as the mediator between God and creatures. Such a belief in Christ as mediator is necessary in order to explain how creatures could be related to God, who is completely transcendent of the universe and cannot be "brought into the subject–object structure of being".[45] Even if the relation between God and creatures is understood as a "mixed" relation there is still the problem of how creatures can be related to "something" so utterly and completely transcendent.

This tension between the transcendence of God and creatures' relation with God leads some to reject the transcendence of God in the first place. Keith Ward, for example, in a similar spirit to those "theistic personalist" theologians who deny atemporality and simplicity because neither permit God to be a conscious and/or purposive actor, argues that there is a "crucial difficulty" with "the relation of God, the necessary, eternal, perfect and immutable being, to a universe of contingent, and even free, beings".[46] By this, Ward means that "the truly contingent cannot arise from the wholly necessary", so that "if God is the creator or cause of a contingent world, he [sic] must be contingent and temporal; but if God is a necessary being, then whatever he causes must be necessary and changelessly caused".[47] Again, Ward restates the problem:

> If God is distinguished from the world, opposed to it as simple to complex, eternal to temporal, immutable to changing and infinite to finite, then as we have just seen it is extremely difficult to see how such a God can be related to the world at all.[48]

---

[45] Tillich, *Systematic Theology Vol. 1*, p. 172.

[46] Keith Ward, *Rational Theology and the Creativity of God* (Oxford: Basil Blackwell Ltd., 1982), p. 2.

[47] Ward, *Rational Theology and the Creativity of God*, p. 3.

[48] Ward, *Rational Theology and the Creativity of God*, p. 81.

Ward's answer to this difficulty is to argue that God is "both necessary and contingent", and that God must therefore be conscious,[49] sensitive,[50] and a "purposing mind",[51] all of which Ward sees as synonymous with "seeing the divine reality as a personal will".[52] Ward continues that this means that God is neither self-sufficient,[53] immutable, atemporal,[54] nor simple[55] and that "it is essential to [God's] being love that he [sic] can be changed and affected by what his own power permits to be".[56] In other words, God reacts to the world.[57]

It is clear that Ward is sympathetic with process theology (and so also with "theistic personalism") and so his solution to the problem, therefore, is to appeal to the "dipolar" nature of God which is characteristic of process theology. God (for Ward and process theology) has both a "primordial nature" and a "consequential nature",[58] so that "only if God is temporal, can he be a free creator of a universe of free creatures; only if he is eternal, can he possess that necessity which is the foundation of the intelligibility of the world; only if he is dipolar, can he be both".[59]

It should be clear that such a solution fundamentally contradicts the approach taken by this book. As has already been acknowledged in relation to the criticism of "theistic personalism", Ward takes a univocal view of personhood and sees its application to God as non-negotiable: if God is truly a "person", then God cannot exhibit those traditional attributes that were intended to emphasize God's transcendence. Nevertheless, what is important for the purposes of this chapter is that Ward correctly notes

---

49 Ward, *Rational Theology and the Creativity of God*, p. 102.

50 Ward, *Rational Theology and the Creativity of God*, p. 103.

51 Ward, *Rational Theology and the Creativity of God*, p. 107.

52 Ward, *Rational Theology and the Creativity of God*, p. 108; see also pp. 140–1.

53 Ward, *Rational Theology and the Creativity of God*, p. 147.

54 Ward, *Rational Theology and the Creativity of God*, p. 151.

55 Ward, *Rational Theology and the Creativity of God*, p. 216, p. 230.

56 Ward, *Rational Theology and the Creativity of God*, p. 151.

57 Ward, *Rational Theology and the Creativity of God*, p. 198.

58 Ward, *Rational Theology and the Creativity of God*, pp. 227–8.

59 Ward, *Rational Theology and the Creativity of God*, p. 230.

that the transcendence of God seems to be incompatible with God being the creator of a finite world.

Frances Young notes another way in which the transcendence of God is dealt with: Christ. Recasting the problem Ward explains in terms of the Hellenist context in which Christ was originally postulated as a solution, she writes that an "impassive" God who is "unaffected by anything external" and so "could have no history or development" meant that

> it was hard to relate God, or the One, with the multiplicity of things, the world of which he [sic] was supposed to be the source and ground of being. His utter transcendence meant his substantial irrelevance to the problem of which he had originally been the solution.[60]

The solution, for the Greek theologians, was not to postulate a complex, "process" God, who has both a transcendent and an immanent "pole", who is responsive and sensitive to the universe that God is supposed to have created (as Ward does), but to postulate a mediator, so that "Logos theology and Trinitarian doctrine made it possible for God to be involved" in the world. Young continues that

> the impassable, transcendent one, beyond being, was intellectually adequate and mystically inspiring, but could not elicit the faith and devotion of most ordinary mortals. The doctrines of the Logos and the Spirit made it possible to believe in a God who is both transcendent and immanent, however paradoxical that might seem to be.[61]

The doctrine of the Logos makes it possible to have a God that is utterly transcendent but to whom creatures can also be related. Thus, she writes that "the force of [New Testament interpretation of Christology] is to make Jesus the one intermediary through whom God is revealed and

---

[60] Frances Young, "A Cloud of Witnesses", in John Hick (ed.), *The Myth of God Incarnate* (London: SCM Press, 1977), p. 24.

[61] Young, "A Cloud of Witnesses", pp. 41–2.

can be approached with confidence".[62] In other words, Keith Ward is entirely correct in his conclusion that "only if God is temporal, can he be a free creator" and that "only if [God] is eternal, can he possess that necessity which is the foundation of the intelligibility of the world",[63] but the problem is that Ward narrowly sees that only if God has a "dipolar" nature can God be both. Ward seems to have entirely missed that Jesus Christ, who is both God and creature, can—and, indeed, already does— perform this function. God cannot be both only if God has a "dipolar" nature; God can be both, and indeed, is both, in the person of Jesus Christ.

John Macquarrie notes the prevalence of this belief in the early Church. Writing about Justin Martyr, he notes that:

> For Justin [Martyr], in accordance with the philosophy of the time, God was remote, nameless, unknowable. So he did not appear on earth or speak directly. "The ineffable Father of all neither comes to any place nor walks nor sleeps nor arises, but always remains in his [sic] place, acutely seeing or hearing, not with eyes or ears, but with power beyond description." When therefore the Old Testament speaks of God appearing on earth or speaking to patriarchs or prophets, this is the *Logos*.[64]

Whatever God is said to do, God does not do directly but through the mediatory Logos. However, the crucial question is, "How does this eternal *Logos* relate to the human Jesus?"[65] In other words, it is all very well to have a *logos* who mediates the creature/divine relation, but if the *logos* is still "just" the immaterial, incorporeal, eternal second person of the Trinity, how can this eternal *logos* perform the function of mediation?

---

[62]   Young, "A Cloud of Witnesses", p. 23.

[63]   Ward, *Rational Theology and the Creativity of God*, p. 230.

[64]   Macquarrie, *Jesus Christ in Modern Thought*, p. 152; see Justin Martyr, "Dialogue with Trypho", in Alexander Roberts and James Donaldson (eds), *Ante-Nicene Christian Library Vol. 2* (Edinburgh: T&T Clark, 1867), pp. 260–1.

[65]   Macquarrie, *Jesus Christ in Modern Thought*, p. 152.

Replacing the transcendent "infinite" Father with a transcendent "infinite" *Logos* does not address the concern.

One way would be to see the *logos* as being less than God, so that the *logos* occupies an ontologically mediatory position—not quite incorporeal, infinite, eternal God, but not quite corporeal, finite, temporal creature either. This would be Arianism and is obviously to be avoided. Alternatively, and more satisfactorily, one could say that the *logos* can *only* perform the function of a mediator as incarnate; that is, the *logos* can only be a mediator when that mediator has both an infinite nature and a finite nature. Thomas Aquinas is quite clear on this matter. He writes:

> It belongs to [Christ], *as man*, to unite men to God, by communicating to men both precepts and gifts, and by offering satisfaction and prayers to God for men. And therefore He is most truly called Mediator, *as man*.[66]

Emil Brunner[67] and Thomas Torrance[68] also appear to explicitly link Christ's mediatory role with his being both God and creature simultaneously. As Thomas Torrance writes, the incarnation "takes the form of a 'hypostatic union' between divine nature and human nature in his one Person, which is the immediate ground for all Christ's mediatory and reconciling activity in our human existence".[69] Peter Forrest therefore acknowledges that it is this "traditional devotion to Jesus as mediator between the purely divine and the purely human" that necessitates "the humanity of the exalted Christ".[70] The implication is that if Jesus were not human and divine simultaneously, he could not function as the mediator between them. John Macquarrie continues that "Jesus could only be Son, Word, Mediator, High Priest and so on if somehow he bridged the

---

[66] *ST* 3, 26, 2 (italics added).

[67] Emil Brunner, *The Mediator* (London: The Lutterworth Press, 1934), p. 309.

[68] Thomas Torrance, *The Mediation of Christ* (Edinburgh: T&T Clark, 1992), pp. 63–5.

[69] Torrance, *The Mediation of Christ*, pp. 64–5.

[70] Peter Forrest, "The Incarnation: A Philosophical Case for Kenosis", *Religious Studies* 36:2 (2000), p. 134.

gap between God and the human race, and that seems to demand that somehow he must belong to both sides".[71] Christ is a mediator *because* he is ontologically identical with both. This fact, Frances Young continues, makes Christ "the instrument through which God created and sustains the world and the mediator who reveals and displays providential love in his direction of the world and its history".[72]

It is particularly pertinent that Young calls Christ the "instrument" of God's creating, when Thomas Aquinas dismissed the notion that Christ can be the "instrument" of God, which he claims would seem to diminish Christ somewhat. This has led some to dismiss the language of "mediator" altogether. For example, Gerald Hiestand writes that "for Irenaeus, the relational and ontological unity between Father, Son, and Spirit is such that the creation of the world by the Father via the Son and the Spirit is not a mediated act of creation by the Father, but is the very means by which the Father himself creates directly".[73] This means, for Irenaeus, that "the Son and the Spirit do not merely work alongside the Father (as second and third independent creating agents), or serve as proxies or mediators of the Father's creative power, working on the Father's behalf. Instead, the Son and the Spirit must in some way be an extension and embodiment of the Father's personal creative will."[74] The spectre of Arianism (understandably) puts some people off using words like "mediator" to describe the role of Christ.

However, this should not be taken as criticism of the approach that this chapter takes. If "mediator" is understood as a "being" who is *ontologically intermediate* between God and creatures—and so is ontologically neither—then Hiestand and Irenaeus must be correct. Likewise with Aquinas' dismissal of the language of Christ as an "instrument". Yet, if Christ is mediator and instrument precisely because he is *ontologically*

---

[71]   Macquarrie, *Jesus Christ in Modern Thought*, p. 153.

[72]   Frances Young, *From Nicaea to Chalcedon* (London: SCM Press, 1983), p. 18.

[73]   Gerald Hiestand, "'And Behold it Was Very Good': St. Irenaeus' Doctrine of Creation", *Bulletin of Ecclesial Theology* 6:1 (2019), pp. 8–9.

[74]   Hiestand, "'And Behold it Was Very Good'", p. 9.

identical to both, then he can perform that function perfectly. As Ian McFarland evidences:

> In this way, Jesus mediates between Creator and creature not by standing in some imagined ontological space between God and the world (as Arius and other advocates of subordinationist Christologies believed), or by collapsing the distinction between them (as in modern Christologies from below), but by uniting in his person the being of God and humanity "without confusion or change, without division or separation."[75]

Thus, if Christ is the "one mediator between God and [creatures]",[76] "the actual mediator between God and man *and* man and God *in all things*",[77] so that "the gap between heaven and earth is only bridged definitively in the figure of Christ",[78] and that "without the personal self-manifestation of God that the incarnation brings" God is "separated from us by an infinite gulf",[79] then, as Jesus says, "no one comes to the Father except through [Christ]".[80] Moreover, it is the *incarnate* Son, and *only* the *incarnate* Son, who performs this role.[81] "Christ cannot be other than

---

[75] Ian McFarland, *The Word Made Flesh: A Theology of the Incarnation* (Louisville, KY: Westminster John Knox Press, 2019), p. 9.

[76] 1 Timothy 2:5.

[77] Thomas Torrance, *Space, Time, and Incarnation* (Oxford: Oxford University Press, 1978), p. 52 (italics added).

[78] Rupert Shortt, *God Is No Thing: Coherent Christianity* (London: Hurst & Company, 2016), p. 77.

[79] Gerald O'Collins, "The Incarnation: The Critical Issues", in Stephen Davis, Daniel Kendall and Gerald O'Collins (eds), *The Incarnation* (Oxford: Oxford University Press, 2002), p. 26.

[80] John 14:6.

[81] See Alexander Garton, "'Very truly I tell you, before Abraham was, I am': A Theological Treatise on the Concept of Time in John's Gospel", *Modern Theology* 35:4 (2019), p. 627.

the cause of all created actuality, and he is such not simply as the Logos, but as the Logos *incarnate*".[82]

Thus, David Bentley Hart might be entirely correct that "God is never without his [sic] Logos, the divine Wisdom, in and through whom the world is created, ordered, and sustained",[83] but this needs to be nuanced. It is not just the *logos* that God is never without; it is the human Jesus that God is never without; as Paul Helm writes, there is "no sense talking of the eternal Son of God apart from the incarnation".[84]

Incarnation and atemporality

So far, this chapter has made two claims: (1) Christ can only be creator as mediator; and (2) Christ can only be mediator as incarnate. That is, only when Christ is both divine and creature simultaneously can there be a relation of ontological dependence (i.e., participation/imitation) between creatures and God. However, there would appear to be a problem here: if Jesus can perform the function of mediator *only* when Jesus is incarnate, then this would seem to imply that Jesus is only the mediator for the thirty-odd years in which he was alive in the world. If God's divine activity cannot be temporally located, and Jesus is definitely temporally located, then this seems to create significant problems for atemporality. How is it that *all* creatures can participate in God through the *incarnate* Jesus Christ, if Christ is only walking the earth for a finite period? How is it that God is "*never*" without the human Jesus if Jesus is only human for a *finite* period?

Of all the issues that theologians identify as making divine atemporality problematic, the incarnation is perhaps the most compelling. Thomas Senor, for example, defends the argument that the incarnation and divine atemporality cannot be coherently held together. Essentially,

---

82   Donald Keefe, *Thomism and the Ontological Theology of Paul Tillich* (Leiden: Brill, 1971), p. 92 (italics added).

83   Hart, *The Experience of God*, p. 235.

84   Paul Helm, "Divine Timeless Eternity", in Gregory Ganssle (ed.), *God and Time: Four Views* (Downers Grove, IL: IVP Academic, 2001), p. 54.

Senor makes two distinct (but related) arguments: (a) the fact that the incarnation happens *in time*—i.e., that there is a before and after the birth of Jesus—seems to imply that there is a before and after in the experience of God; and (b) the fact that God is hypostatically united in the "person" of Christ seems to imply that the temporal succession and duration of Jesus' life is also experienced for God. The first of these essentially argues that (based on the scriptural account of the incarnation presented in Philippians 2) Christ "took on" the human "nature" and there is no way of understanding this "taking on" without there being an intrinsic change in the Son.[85] The second of these arguments claims that since temporal predicates apply to Christ, and Christ is God, then those temporal predicates must also apply to God. In this way, it is impossible to say that Christ "read in the synagogue" before "he carried his cross" and not also say that this applies to God.[86] While Senor acknowledges that there are complexities involving precisely how those two "natures" are related in Christ, he concludes that orthodox Christology holds that Christ was a "*single* dual-natured person", so the "person" to whom the temporal predicates are applied is also the same "person" who is truly God.[87] It appears impossible to hold that Christ experiences temporal succession without also holding that God also experiences this succession.

Yet not everyone agrees with this interpretation.[88] If "the relation between God and space is not itself a spatial relation",[89] then neither can the relation between God and time itself be a temporal relation. In

---

[85] Thomas Senor, "Incarnation and Timelessness", *Faith and Philosophy: Journal of the Society of Christian Philosophers* 7:2 (1990), pp. 156–7.

[86] Senor, "Incarnation and Timelessness", pp. 150ff.

[87] Senor, "Incarnation and Timelessness", p. 154.

[88] Gregory of Nazianzus, who held to a divine atemporality similar to the one held by Augustine, Boethius, and Anselm (and so similar to the one espoused in this chapter) (see Gregory of Nazianzus, "Oratio 38") , also appears to argue for the eternity of the incarnation when he writes that "the Flesh which the Only-begotten Son assumed in the Incarnation for the remodelling of our nature was no new acquisition, but that that carnal nature was in the Son from the beginning" (Gregory of Nazianzus, "Epistle 202").

[89] Torrance, *Space, Time, and Incarnation*, p. 2.

other words, the connection or relationship between atemporality (God) and temporality (creature) in Christ is not itself a temporal relationship, so there is no need to assume that there is a contradiction involved. Contra Senor, if the incarnation does not imply that God literally came *down* from heaven through space, then neither does it imply that God experiences time in becoming incarnate. Eleanore Stump and Norman Kretzmann are quite clear, therefore, that they do not see the incarnation as having temporal connotations. Specifically, they do not think that the incarnation introduces a *change* in God; that is, they do not think that the temporality of the historical creature Jesus means that at a specific point in time the second "person" of the Trinity "takes on" a new nature. Drawing on Boethius, they write that:

> the divine nature of the second person of the Trinity, like the divine nature of either of the other persons of the Trinity, cannot become temporal; nor could the second person at some time acquire a human nature he does not eternally have. Instead, the second person eternally has two natures; and at some temporal instants, all of which are . . . simultaneous with both these natures in their entirety, the human nature of the second person has been temporally actual. At those times and only in that nature the second person directly participates in temporal events . . . [thus, w]e hope simply to have pointed out that the doctrine of the Incarnation cannot be reduced to the belief that God became temporal and that, if it is understood as including the doctrine of the dual nature, it can be seen to have been constructed in just such a way as to avoid being reduced to that simple belief.[90]

While the paragraph is worth quoting at length, it is the comment that "the second person eternally has two natures" that is the most important.

---

[90] Eleonore Stump and Norman Kretzmann, "Eternity", *The Journal of Philosophy* 78:8 (1981), p. 453.

What they mean is that, while there was a time when Jesus was not born, there is no "time" when Christ is not incarnate.[91]

Stephen Theron understands the incarnation in the same way. He writes that "God is not now living in a time after the Incarnation, whereas once he lived in a time before it. One says the same, after all, about the act of creation, viz. that it entails no change in God."[92] The fact that Theron explicitly relates the incarnation to the "act of creation" is pertinent. Neither are understood as events that happen *in time*, and if they are not events that happen in time then they must be understood as *ontological* relations. Just as creation must be "an ontological relationship—a relationship in the order of being—with no reference to temporality",[93] then so must the incarnation. To say that "the second person eternally has two natures" is to say that the relationship between them is ontological, not temporal. Just as the Big Bang (i.e., a temporal origin to the universe) does not have any bearing on the atemporality of the "act" of creation, so the birth of Jesus (i.e., the temporal origin of Jesus) has no bearing on the atemporality of the "act" of the incarnation. If the origin (i.e., Big Bang) does not make creation a temporal event, so the birth (i.e., origin) of Jesus does not do the same for the incarnation. The incarnation is not a moment in the temporal life of God, but a hierarchical relation with the creaturely nature of Jesus. That Jesus is birthed *in time* no more makes the incarnation a temporal event than does the Big Bang make creation. That the universe begins does not mean that God starts to do something at that moment; that the universe begins does not mean that God does not create eternally, or that the relationship is not eternal for

---

91   See Helm, "Divine Timeless Eternity", p. 54; Ioan Mircea Ielciu, "Doctrinal Aspects in Evagrius Ponticus", *Revista Teologică* 99:1 (2017), p. 25.

92   Stephen Theron, "Creation *stricto sensu*", *New Blackfriars* 89:1020 (2008), p. 209. As Mivart writes, "there never was a time when God was thus in solitary Being, for time is, as we have seen, but an abstraction of an abstraction drawn from succeeding things, and till such things were created there could have been no 'time.'" (St. George Mivart, *On Truth: A Systematic Inquiry* (London: Kegan Paul, Trench and Co., 1889), p. 485).

93   Steven Baldner and William Carroll (tr.), *Aquinas on Creation* (Toronto: Pontifical Institute of Mediaeval Studies, 1997), p. 16.

God.[94] Likewise, that Jesus is born at a particular time does not mean that the incarnation (hypostatic union) is not eternal. There is a time (in history) when Jesus was not born, but there is not a "time" (in the life of God) when Christ is not incarnate.

Brian Leftow also disagrees that the incarnation and atemporality are mutually exclusive using the image of a scuba diver. He argues that

> scuba gear is intimately connected to the diver's body. Yet it keeps the diver disconnected from the water it touches; scuba gear lets one swim without getting one's feet wet. [The historical body of Jesus] is the Son's environment suit, letting him manoeuvre in time yet stay dry.[95]

The "environment suit" (or "temporal suit") allows the atemporal divine Son to move about in time (water) without becoming temporal (wet). Christ atemporally "wears" the "temporal suit", but this does not mean that the temporality of Jesus not being born at some times and being born at others is experienced by the atemporal Christ, who is left "dry" of any temporality.[96]

---

[94]   See Sergei Bulgakov, *The Bride of the Lamb* (Grand Rapids, MI: William B. Eerdmans, 2002), pp. 58–60.

[95]   Brian Leftow, "A Timeless God Incarnate", in Stephen Davis, Daniel Kendall and Gerald O'Collins (eds), *The Incarnation* (Oxford: Oxford University Press, 2002), p. 292. Further, while it does not feature as part of Leftow's argument, the "scuba gear" analogy works just as well for preserving divine simplicity as it does for atemporality. If the "scuba suit" keeps the atemporal God "dry" of time inside the suit despite there being temporal succession outside the suit, then the complexity on the outside of the suit does not mean that God must be complex inside the suit.

[96]   This analogy perhaps works better if one assumes a "four-dimensional block universe". In that way, that there are parts of the sea to which the diver never ventures does not mean that the diver is not genuinely in the sea and not genuinely dry. So, there might be spatiotemporal regions to which Jesus Christ does not venture, but this does not mean that he is not "always" in the "temporal suit" or that he is not genuinely "dry".

In this way, the "scuba gear" analogy becomes another image of the absence of a real relation. Just as Thomas could point to the animal that moves in relation to a pillar without the pillar experiencing movement, so the scuba diver can move about in the water without the diver himself experiencing the water. Outside of the suit there is change; inside the suit is unchanging and atemporal simplicity. Inside the "suit" the Son/Logos "remains" simple and atemporal with a single/simple/eternal will and energy, however, that single/simple/eternal will and energy is manifested in temporal succession and complex activity on the outside. Importantly, the Son does not "take on" the suit at a certain point; the Son "always", eternally, wears the "scuba suit". In other words, to use Stump and Kretzmann's language, time and complexity (i.e., multiplicity and difference) are *extrinsic* to the *logos*. There is an ontological relation or identity between the *logos* and Jesus, but time, complexity, and change are *extrinsic* to the *logos*.

One might also counter the argument that God must experience the temporal events of Jesus' life by pointing to Patripassianism; indeed, the early Fathers developed the doctrine of the Trinity precisely to deal with the fact that when Jesus died, God did not experience that death.[97] Certainly, Christ is united to God in a unique and personal way, and Senor is certainly correct, as Gerald O'Collins also writes, that "despite the duality of natures, there is only one subject of attribution",[98] but it does not follow from this that God experiences time any more than God experiences birth or death.

In this way, Stump and Kretzmann and Leftow can be seen to address Senor's arguments (although Senor considers Stump and Kretzmann's arguments in his paper and finds them inadequate). On the one hand, by emphasizing that Christ is eternally in two "natures", Stump and Kretzmann argue that the incarnation does not necessarily need to be an event in the atemporal life of God (so counter Senor's argument (a)). On the other hand, Leftow, argues that, despite being hypostatically united to Jesus in the "person" of Christ, the temporal events of Jesus' life need not

---

[97]   Leftow, "A Timeless God Incarnate", p. 289.

[98]   Gerald O'Collins, *Interpreting Jesus* (London: Mowbray, 1983), p. 183.

imply that God experiences those temporal events (so counter Senor's argument (b)).

The pre-existence of Christ: The incarnation as ontological relation

If the incarnation does not introduce time into God "then God's having an assumed human nature is not something characteristic of God at some times but not at others. It is something characteristic of God always", and so "God is never in the state of not having an assumed human nature".[99] Denis Edwards, drawing on the "deep incarnation" theology of Niels Henrik Gregersen, also writes that "from the perspective of the eternal divine life . . . there never was, and never will be, a disembodied Logos. Logos was always embodied and will always be embodied".[100] There is not a problem with the sentiment that these two quotations wish to convey, but there is a problem with the language with which they choose to present it. As Sergei Bulgakov recognizes, there is a problem with saying that this is "always" a characteristic of God, because "always" is a temporal designation and is problematic when applied to God.[101] One could say that God is *eternally* incarnate—as "eternally" "is not a very long time, nor an endless or infinite time. It is no time at all"[102]—but it is better to see it as an ontological rather than a temporal designation. That is, the incarnation is an ontological relation of identity between the second person of the Trinity and the human Jesus, not that the incarnation temporally extends for all time (i.e., always).

Importantly, this means that Christ's "pre-existence" must be re-thought; Christ cannot *temporally* "pre-exist" as an immaterial Word if Christ is *eternally* in two natures. The Son does not precede the incarnate Jesus temporally, so that Christ creates (in the beginning) *and then* becomes incarnate. Rather, the Son is "ontologically prior", or, better,

---

[99] Stump, *The God of the Bible and the God of the Philosophers*, p. 100.

[100] Denis Edwards, *Deep Incarnation: God's Redemptive Suffering with Creatures* (Maryknoll, NY: Orbis Books, 2019), p. 23.

[101] Bulgakov, *The Bride of the Lamb*, p. 58.

[102] Herbert McCabe, "Eternity", in Philip McCosker and Denys Turner (eds), *The Cambridge Companion to The Summa Theologiae* (Cambridge: Cambridge University Press, 2016), p. 110; see also Gregory of Nazianzus, "Oratio 38".

"ontologically more primary" to Jesus. Timothy Pawl, for example, writes that "one should be hesitant to interpret this 'pre-existence' as a temporal pre-existence, since Christ, in his divine nature, does not exist in time".[103] Niall Coll makes a similar observation. He writes that "what lies at the heart of the doctrine of Christ's pre-existence is the belief. . . that Christ's personal identity is that of the eternal Son of God and that his personal being did not originate when his earthly human history began".[104] Drawing on Gerald O'Collins, Coll agrees that it is better to speak of a "trans-existence" or "meta-existence" rather than a pre-existence, so as to avoid the inevitable but incorrect temporal implications.[105]

In other words, the Son is *ontologically* greater and more primary than Jesus, but the Son is eternally identified with Jesus. This leads Paul Helm to write that there is "no sense talking of the eternal Son of God apart from the incarnation".[106] Ian McFarland says much the same thing: "Although Christians will find themselves compelled to confess that the Word, as God, is eternal, they will find themselves equally constrained to acknowledge that they cannot speak of the Word apart from the flesh, not even as the one who is to become enfleshed."[107] Likewise, Paulo Gamberini puts it that "Jesus cannot be thought of without his relation to the Logos", by which he does not mean that *logos* is limited to Jesus or that the Son is "absorbed and exhausted in Jesus alone", but that it is necessary "to distinguish Jesus from the Christ" as Christ is "greater and prior to his disclosure in Jesus".[108]

---

[103] Timothy Pawl, *In Defence of Conciliar Christology: A Philosophical Essay* (Oxford: Oxford University Press, 2016), p. 15; in this way, it is utterly incoherent to "hypothesize that Jesus had some memories of his pre-incarnate state" (Forrest, "The Incarnation", p. 129).

[104] Niall Coll, *Christ in Eternity and Time* (Dublin: Four Courts Press, 2001), p. 175.

[105] Coll, *Christ in Eternity and Time*, p. 179; see O'Collins, *Christology*, p. 238.

[106] Helm, "Divine Timeless Eternity", p. 54.

[107] McFarland, *The Word Made Flesh*, p. 85.

[108] Paulo Gamberini, "The Concept of 'Person': A Dialogue with Contemporary Asian Theology", *Irish Theological Quarterly* 76:3 (2011), p. 265.

Instead, in the language that this book has found so helpful, the pre-existence should be taken as being essentially ordered to Jesus, not accidentally ordered. The incarnation is not an accidentally ordered event in the life of the Son, who pre-exists that event as incorporeal and *then* exists later as the corporeal Jesus. Rather, the incarnation is an ontological hierarchical relation that eternally exists between Jesus and the Son. The Son is never without that ontological relation with Jesus, but Jesus does not exhaust the ontology of the Son.[109]

Of course, while this chapter distinguishes between Christ/Son/Logos on the one hand, and Jesus on the other, and sees the Logos as having ontological priority over Jesus and is that which passes on being to Jesus from the Father, this is in no way intended to imply Nestorianism, that in Christ there are two persons—Christ and Jesus. There is one person, one subject of attribution, who is Jesus Christ, and it is *in* the one single, completely united person that this essentially ordered relation between Logos and Jesus occurs. The distinction is necessary to explain *how* Christ is the mediator—that Christ is both simultaneously—but it in no way implies a hypostatic distinction between the two; on the contrary, the distinction is made to make it even clearer that the two are hypostatically *united*. Christ can only function as mediator if the *Logos* and human Jesus are hypostatically united in one person.

This understanding of the pre-existence as "ontological relation"— so that the incarnation is thought of as an essentially ordered cause in the person of Christ, rather than an accidentally ordered cause—is connected in quite a profound way with the notion of Christ as the "first born of creation". As many commentators have noticed, the designation "first-born" "could mean the priority in time or rank, though most commentators prefer the latter, since temporal priority is hardly what

---

[109] This means that the most appropriate translation of the Niceno-Constantinopolitan creed is not "born of the Father *before all ages*", but "*eternally* begotten of the Father". The former may well be the more accurate translation of the original Greek "τὸν ἐκ τοῦ Πατρὸς γεννηθέντα πρὸ πάντων τῶν αἰώνων", but the latter is the more theologically accurate interpretation of the doctrine of Christ's pre-existence.

the author is trying to emphasize here".[110] Christ as "the firstborn of all creation . . . [who] himself is before all things"[111] does not indicate that Christ is the temporally first creature (the first in an accidentally ordered series of creatures that extends backwards in time), but rather indicates that Christ is the ontologically primary creature (the first in an essentially ordered hierarchy that extends "upwards" to God). Christ is *ontologically* first in an essentially ordered series—who mediates between those who are "above" and "below" him in that hierarchy—not *temporally* first in an accidentally ordered series. Thus, Edward Oakes can write that "while Adam holds a temporal priority over Christ in the history of salvation, Christ is ontologically prior".[112] Adam is accidentally prior to Jesus, but Adam depends upon and participates in Jesus.

The same might be said of the virgin birth. That is, the virgin birth does not give a literal biological fact about Jesus' birth, but is a theological motif that designates his being the ontologically first-born. Thus, John Robinson writes that

> the virgin birth story is not there to give information about gynaecology any more than the story of the Fall is there to give information about primitive anthropology. Its primary intention, as we have seen (though the New Testament writers were compelled to no such conscious antithesis), is not to assert discontinuity in the biological series (thus setting it directly against the genealogies that accompany it), but to make a positive statement at the level of spirit—to affirm the entire genesis of Jesus Christ as the act and initiative of God.[113]

Kallistos Ware draws attention to this point. He writes that the incarnation makes three important theological points. First, perhaps quite obviously, it "points always beyond his situation in space and time to his heavenly and eternal origin", that Christ "is within history

---

[110] Deane-Drummond, *Christ and Evolution*, p. 105.

[111] Colossians 1:15–17.

[112] Oakes, *A Theology of Grace in Six Controversies*, p. 131.

[113] John Robinson, *The Human Face of God* (London: SCM Press, 1973), p. 120.

but also above history".[114] Indeed, it is necessary for Christ to be both within history and beyond history for the hypostatic union to be genuine. Second, the virgin birth expresses theologically that "the incarnation did not involve the coming into being of a new *person*".[115] Third, and most importantly for present purposes, the virgin birth "indicates that his birth is to be ascribed in a unique manner *to the divine initiative*".[116] While Kallistos Ware does not mean exactly the same thing as outlined here, there is an important connection: the point is not that Jesus did not have a biological father, but that the divine activity in Christ must be primary; the divine initiative must have ontological priority. God does not rely on, depend on, or respond to anything in creation, but God's action is always primary. This does not mean temporally first—that God acts first and so builds in any response to creaturely acts (e.g., that God foresaw the fall and so foreordained the incarnation from eternity to deal with it)—but ontologically primary—that God does not depend upon any other action, and so cannot be a response to anything, even if it is an "anticipatory" response.

Incarnation as creation

All the necessary tools are now in place to show how it is that the incarnation is itself the "act" of creation; that is, if creation is a hierarchical relation between God and creatures through which all creatures participate for their being, then the incarnation is precisely that hierarchical relation. If Christ is the creator, then Christ is the creator as the mediator of this relationship. This mediation happens through the hypostatic union.

It has already been established that creation and incarnation are "typally" identical; what happens in creation also happens in the incarnation. This was necessary for Athanasius to claim that "it may be duly perceived that the renewal of creation has been the work of the

---

[114] Kallistos Ware, *The Orthodox Way* (Crestwood, NY: St. Vladimir's Seminary Press, 1979), p. 76.

[115] Ware, *The Orthodox Way*, p. 76 (italics added).

[116] Ware, *The Orthodox Way*, p. 76 (italics in original).

selfsame Word that made it at the beginning".[117] It was also necessary
for creation and incarnation to by typally identical for Thomas Aquinas
to claim that "the first creation of things was made by the power of God
the Father through the Word; hence the second creation ought to have
been brought about through the Word".[118] Understanding the incarnation
as an ontological hierarchy contributes to this understanding. Neither
creation nor incarnation are origins, both are creations: both creation
and incarnation are ontological hierarchies. Therefore, if it is already
established that creation and incarnation are "typally" identical, then all
that is being done now is claiming that they are "numerically" identical
as well: the incarnation is constitutive of the relationship that is creation,
not a continuation or repetition of it. There are not two speakings of the
word—one in creation and one in the incarnation—there is only one
eternal speaking:[119] the incarnation is not *in addition* to God as "ground
of being"; the incarnation is *how* God is the ground of being.

Correctly understanding the eternity of the incarnation further
cements this as a legitimate interpretation. If Stump is correct that "if God
is eternal, then God's having an assumed human nature is not something
characteristic of God at some times but not at others" so that "God is
never in the state of not having an assumed human nature",[120] then Helm
must likewise be correct that there is "no sense talking of the eternal
Son of God apart from the incarnation".[121] If it is impossible to "speak
of the Word apart from the flesh, not even as the one who is to become
enfleshed",[122] then Hart must likewise be correct that "God is never
without his [sic] Logos, the divine Wisdom, in and through whom the
world is created, ordered, and sustained",[123] with the exception that it is
not just that God is never without the *logos*, but that God is never without

---

[117] Athanasius, "On the Incarnation", p. 56.

[118] *ST* 3, 3, 8.

[119] cf. Bonaventure, *Breviloquium*, IV, 1, 2; Wand, *The Four Great Heresies*, p.
27.

[120] Stump, *The God of the Bible and the God of the Philosophers*, p. 100.

[121] Helm, "Divine Timeless Eternity", p. 54.

[122] McFarland, *The Word Made Flesh*, p. 85.

[123] Hart, *The Experience of God*, p. 235.

the historical Jesus. Further, if God is never without the historical Jesus, then the incarnation is not just the "supreme example of God's action in the world",[124] but simply *the sole* example of divine activity. Whatever God does, God "does" through the human Jesus, and so if "God's creative action *just is* creation's dependence on God for its existence",[125] then creation depends on God *through* Jesus. The incarnation is not coincident with the *origins* of the universe: the incarnation is the *creation* of the universe.

Ian McFarland puts this point slightly differently. Drawing on the theology of Karl Barth, he writes that "because the 'problem' that the incarnation addresses is overcoming the divide between Creator and creature, and because this divide is intrinsic to the very ontology of creation and is not a consequence of human sin, the Word's taking flesh is not dependent on and is thus logically prior to (*supra*) humanity's fall (*lapsus*)".[126] Thus, McFarland continues, "the existence of the world and the human beings within it depends on the incarnation rather than the other way around: the truth is not that God had to become flesh to save the world, but that the world's creation and consummation alike are rooted in God's will to be made flesh".[127] This means, McFarland notes, that the incarnation is not "a means to an end",[128] and so the incarnation is not thought of as "the solution to a problem, whether the problem is the incommensurability of finite and infinite or the destructive power of sin". Rather, crucially, "the incarnation is instead more appropriately understood as the ground of our being, such that these 'problems' are secondary".[129] In fact, McFarland goes so far as to claim that "to put it more sharply, creation happens because God wills to take flesh".[130] Thus, McFarland continues, "Christ is mediator not as a *tertium quid* positioned

---

[124]   Maurice Wiles, *God's Action in the World* (London: SCM Press, 1986), p. 82.

[125]   Bishop and Perszyk, "The Divine Attributes and Non-personal Conceptions of God", p. 614.

[126]   McFarland, *The Word Made Flesh*, pp. 9–10.

[127]   McFarland, *The Word Made Flesh*, p. 11.

[128]   McFarland, *The Word Made Flesh*, p. 11; See Karl Barth, *Church Dogmatics: Study Edition* (Edinburgh: T&T Clark, 2009), II, 2, p. 33.

[129]   McFarland, *The Word Made Flesh*, p. 12.

[130]   McFarland, *The Word Made Flesh*, p. 12.

between two *predefined realities*, but rather as the one in whom God and humankind acquire their identities in the first place, that is, the one in and through whom the distinction between Creator and creature is itself established".[131] That is crucial: God and creatures are not two *predefined realities* that Christ brings together, but the very distinction between God and creatures—that is, the very relation between them (a relation of ontological dependency)—is established and maintained in the hypostatic union.

Creation/incarnation as hierarchy

If the logic expressed here is correct, then if Christ is that in whom "all things in heaven and on earth were created", and in whom "all things hold together",[132] then that is not something that Christ does separate from or *before* the incarnation. It does not matter that the historical Jesus does not have temporal duration that lasts for the entire history of the universe because it "does not follow from the world's dependence on God at all times" that "God's creative activity [should] therefore be understood to be performed at all times";[133] Jesus (and the world through Jesus) is related to the Son as the circumference of a circle is related to its centre.[134] To use the image of the sun that was crucial to the doctrine of creation expounded in the previous chapter, creation happens "as light is produced in the air by the presence of the sun",[135] yet "just as the rays of the sun do not set fire

---

[131] McFarland, *The Word Made Flesh*, p. 12 (italics added).

[132] Colossians 1:15–17.

[133] Robin Attfield, *Creation, Evolution and Meaning* (Aldershot: Ashgate Publishing, 2006), p. 77.

[134] "'[T]he instantaneous and imperceptible moment of creation', to use Basil's phrase [*Hexaemeron* 1.6.], is 'equidistant', one could say, to all times, even as the center of a circle is equidistant to all points on the circumference" (Wolfgang Smith, *Teilhardism and the New Religion* (Rockford, IL: Tan Books and Publishers inc., 1988), p. 72).

[135] Marilyn McCord Adams, *What Sort of Nature? Medieval Philosophy and the Systematics of Christology* (Milwaukee, WI: Marquette University Press, 1999), p. 52; see also Gavin Kerr, "A Thomistic Metaphysics of Creation",

to anything by themselves, so God does not touch our souls with the fire of supernatural knowledge and experience without Christ".[136]

The image of the sun is an important image of creation. It was central to Pseudo-Dionysius' description of God's relation to the world. God "sends the rays of its undivided goodness to everything with the capacity, such as this may be, to receive it" and so "these rays are responsible for all intelligible and intelligent beings, for every power and every activity".[137] If that is the case, then the incarnation is these rays; the incarnation is the emanation of divine grace.

If the sun was central to how Pseudo-Dionysius understood creation, then so was hierarchy. In fact, arguably, Pseudo-Dionysius did not have a doctrine of creation that is not hierarchy. As Sarah Wear and John Dillon argue, hierarchy is the way that "God relates to his creation" and, therefore, "the activity of the hierarchy is the act of God's creation".[138] This does not mean that God creates *and then* establishes a hierarchy; hierarchy *is* creation. This hierarchy, Pseudo-Dionysius explains, functions because each individual within the hierarchy is tasked with "hand[ing] on to successor whatever of the divine light he has received and this, in providential proportion, is spread out to every being".[139] Thus, "predecessor hands on to successor whatever of the divine light he has received",[140] so "those closer to God should be the initiators of those less close by guiding them to the divine access, enlightenment, and communion".[141] This does not mean that creatures are expected to move

---

Religious Studies 48 (2012), pp. 345–7; and Matthew R. McWhorter, "Aquinas on God's Relation to the World", *New Blackfriars* 94:1049 (2013), pp. 3–19.

[136] Thomas Merton, *New Seeds of Contemplation* (London: Burns & Oates, 1961), p. 106.

[137] Pseudo-Dionysius, *The Divine Names* 4.1.

[138] Sarah Wear and John Dillon, *Dionysius the Areopagite and the Neoplatonist Tradition* (Aldershot: Ashgate, 2007), p. 51, p. 66.

[139] Pseudo-Dionysius, *The Complete Works* (Mahwah, NJ: Paulist Press, 1987), *The Celestial Hierarchy* 13.3.

[140] Pseudo-Dionysius, *The Celestial Hierarchy* 13.3.

[141] Pseudo-Dionysius, *The Celestial Hierarchy* 4.3.

"up" the hierarchy,[142] but through creatures, the ecclesiastical hierarchy, and the celestial hierarchy, that hierarchy reaches Jesus, who is at the end of every hierarchy.[143] Jesus then continues the essentially ordered ontological hierarchy through his hypostatic union to God, the source and ground of all being. The Father passes being to the Son who in turn, through the incarnation, passes on being to all creatures. This is what is meant by creation.[144] Interestingly, Marilyn McCord Adams notes the same idea in Thomas Aquinas: "As God is fontal source of natural being

---

[142] The function of hierarchy is "not that one should climb up to God, but that each should fulfil its role" (Louise Nelstrop, *Christian Mysticism: An Introduction to Contemporary Theoretical Approaches* (Farnham: Ashgate, 2009), p. 109), "that is, divinization occurs in the hierarchy not by moving up the hierarchy to achieve some final end, but rather existing in one's hierarchical rank (whether it be clerical or lay) (in a divinely ordained and divinely communicative way in relation to others". (Ashley M. Purpura, *God, Hierarchy, and Power: Orthodox Theologies of Authority from Byzantium* (New York, NY: Fordham University Press, 2018), p. 29) (see Chapter 6).

[143] Pseudo-Dionysius, *The Ecclesiastical Hierarchy* 5.5.

[144] One must be careful here. If creatures participate in—i.e., receive being from—Jesus as through an essentially ordered series, and so Jesus is a "link" in an essentially ordered hierarchy from God to all creatures, this does not mean that the Son participates in the Father, as participation would indicate ontological inferiority. Creatures have their being from the Son by participation, but the Son does not have his being from the Father by participation. Certainly, the Son has "being" from the Father—who is the "fountainhead" of divinity and who begets the Son—but this does not mean that the Son is not equal to the Father. Again, this chapter has used the Son and Jesus quite differently, but this should not be taken to mean Nestorianism. There is only one person, and that is the divine second person of the Trinity, truly and fully God. Christ is the mediator, who mediates being "down" the hierarchy through the incarnation, but that in no way should be taken to suggest that Christ is ontologically intermediate. The Son is truly God, equal to, and so in no way participates in, the Father, yet creatures participate in the Son. The Son receives being from the Father but has being necessarily; creatures receive their being from the Son, through Jesus (who

(*esse*) and goodness in creatures, so Aquinas envisions a cascading flow of grace: from Godhead into the human soul hypostatically united to it; from the soul of Christ into all the members of the body of which he is the head."[145] It is no secret that Thomas Aquinas was influenced heavily by Pseudo-Dionysius and so there is a connection here with the idea of creation as ontological relationship.

This means that, if creation is an ontological, hierarchical, essentially ordered relationship—not an accidentally ordered first event coincident with origins—then Jesus is the creator because Jesus occupies a mediatory position in that hierarchy. Jesus is the ontologically firstborn of creation (not temporally first born at the origin), through whom "being" descends from the Father—the "fontal source of natural being"—to all creatures. Yet, this does not make Jesus ontologically intermediate, but Jesus functions as a mediator between God and creatures because Jesus is both truly God and truly created. That is, Jesus represents part of an essentially ordered series from God to creatures. Jesus is the creator, not because Jesus is that which "pushes the first domino" or "lights the blue touch paper"; Jesus is creator because Jesus is the vehicle through which and in which "being" is participated. The hypostatic union literally *is* the essentially ordered cause that was described in Chapter 2 as being the content of the doctrine of creation and which is the single, uniform, "basic" divine will. That is, the incarnation is that which enables creatures to participate in God.

Incarnational deism

Creation is not an event that happens at the beginning of time, or before the beginning of time, or one that extends through the duration of the universe, gradually moulding and perfecting the world (through evolution), continually at work to bring about some end, but is a hierarchy, "an ontological relationship—a relationship in the order of being—with no reference to temporality".[146] Thus, the incarnation is not something

---

is the same identical person as the Son), but they do not have it necessarily, but contingently through participation.

[145] McCord Adams, *What Sort of Nature?*, p. 52.

[146] Baldner and Carroll, *Aquinas on Creation*, p. 16.

that operates only at a given moment, but is a hierarchical relationship. The birth (and death) of Jesus does happen in time (it *has* to if Jesus is truly the mediator between history and eternity), but the incarnation, the life of the historical creature Jesus Christ, is also essentially ordered to all creatures and all spatiotemporal points as the centre of a circle is to its circumference. To use Bulgakov's distinction between "cause" and "creator", Jesus is a "cause"—and so is a part of the nexus of cause and effect—as he must be in order to be a creature, but Jesus is also "creator"—above all other creatures in the ontological hierarchy and that through which they participate in that hierarchy.

Perhaps somewhat counter-intuitively, this means that, strictly speaking, there is no creation, only incarnation. To say that, strictly speaking, there is no creation does not mean that God is not that upon which ultimately all creatures depend, nor does it mean that the world can exist independently of God. Rather, it means that if creation is nothing more than an ontological relationship, if "God's creative action *just is* creation's dependence on God for its existence",[147] then that ontological relationship is found *only and uniquely* in the incarnation. That is, there is no creation and only incarnation, because the content of the doctrine of the creation is exhaustively explained by the incarnation; the relation of ontological dependency is constituted and maintained by the hypostatic union. The incarnation *is* the ontological relationship. The incarnation is not a *second* speaking of the word of God; the incarnation is the *only* speaking of the word—the eternal speaking of the word on which all creatures depend. (Remember that Paul, John, and Athanasius all explicitly moved from "Christ is the agent of re-creation" to "Christ must be the agent of creation". All that is being done here is to take this logical extrapolation to its next step: if the incarnation is the act of re-creation then the incarnation must be the act of creation. Furthermore, creation is not an event that "pre-dates" the incarnation, but is an ontological relationship, so one does not need to postulate two incarnations—two speakings of the word—and so creation can now be a relationship that is described by the incarnation.) Likewise, as identified above, God does

---

[147] Bishop and Perszyk, "The Divine Attributes and Non-personal Conceptions of God", p. 614.

not become incarnate *in order to* "*then*" create and establish a relationship, the incarnation *is* that creation/relationship. Thus, the single divine idea that is Jesus Christ *is* the single, uniform, "basic" divine will for creation. The "idea of Jesus" and "the will to create" are the same "thing". "All" God does is become incarnate, which establishes participation. (Precisely *how* the incarnation can establish participation will be explored in the examination of *kenosis* in the next chapter.)

Or, to put this differently, there is no creation, not because God is not ultimately responsible for the entire universe, which depends entirely and uniquely on God for its very being, but because "creation" is the result—or effect—of the hypostatic union, not a separate "act" or "event" that happens prior to it. (Of course, the use of causal language here is somewhat misleading, as has already been expounded at some length, the universe is the "effect" of the hypostatic union in an essentially ordered manner, not "more or less, what is usually meant by 'cause' in contemporary philosophy"[148] after the scientific revolution. As Bulgakov has already been quoted in support, language of "creation" is better than language of "cause"; nevertheless, the point is well made: creating is not something God "does", but is the essentially ordered "effect" of the hypostatic union.)

Admittedly, this is a novel and speculative suggestion, but it is nothing more than the bringing together of two very well-established ideas. On the one hand, "the question of creation has never simply concerned some event that may have happened 'back then', at the beginning of time, or some change between distinct physical states . . . but has always concerned the *eternal relation* between logical possibility and logical necessity, the contingent and the absolute, the conditioned and the unconditioned",[149] and, on the other hand, it is that "*eternal relation* of God to man [sic] which is manifest in the Christ",[150] who is Emmanuel.

If creation is understood as ontological relationship, rather than "story" of physical beginnings through to physical perfection, then the incarnation *is* that ontological relationship, precisely because a person

---

[148]   Feser, *Scholastic Metaphysics: A Contemporary Introduction*, p. 97.

[149]   Hart, *The Experience of God*, p. 304 (italics added).

[150]   Tillich, *Systematic Theology Vol. 2*, p. 96 (italics added).

who is *both* God and creature *simultaneously* is required to act as a "causal joint" (to borrow Austin Farrer's term) between the two; a person who is *both* God and creature *simultaneously* is required to explain how temporal, complex, and finite creatures can be related to a transcendent, atemporal, and simple God. Importantly, a "causal joint" is not needed to explain how God can influence the "motion" of the world (which would mean that "causality" is understood univocally and that there was a real relation between God and creatures), but is needed to explain how creatures can participate in God (which would mean divine "causality" is understood analogically and there is no real relation between God and creatures). Thus, Helen Oppenheimer writes that:

> The point of Incarnational Deism was precisely to locate some kind of body or "vehicle" for God, so that one could talk validly about His [sic] activity, without having to make flimsy assumptions or vague suppositions of His presence where one would find His presence convenient. Nothing could meet this need more directly than God the Son Incarnate if one can believe in Him.[151]

Oppenheimer has here articulated the thesis of this chapter. Incarnational deism allows one to maintain the transcendence of God, yet still have Christ as the "vehicle" of divine activity.

The deist claims that there is a single divine act, that God just creates and nothing more. But now it is claimed that there is no act, just a relationship, so the deist looks not for somewhere that a divine act has more obviously occurred, but somewhere that a divine relationship is more obviously occurring. That relationship is the incarnation. Thus, if the "traditional" deist (i.e., the deist of Isaac Newton) sees only the Big Bang, then the incarnational deist sees only the incarnation. The incarnation is that through which "being" is mediated to all creatures, and that is the only "thing" that God "does".

---

[151] Oppenheimer, *Incarnation and Immanence*, p. 88.

Hypostatic Union: The "physical" theory of the incarnation and the "corporate" nature of Christ's humanity

So far, it has been argued that Christ is the creator as a mediator, so that if creation is understood as a relation, then the hypostatic union is that relation. Jesus, precisely because he is eternally both God and creature, mediates "being" through a hierarchy from God and on to all other creatures. The fact that Jesus can perform this function even though he is only alive for thirty-odd years has been explained as a result of the fact that the incarnation is an ontological designation. Jesus can be that through which all creatures participate, even for those who were not around during the thirty-odd years in which Jesus was alive, because atemporality is understood as the relationship between the centre of a circle and its circumference. That is, all spatiotemporal points are present to God; God does not have to be present at every spatiotemporal point. In other words, Jesus does not need to be physically present at every spatiotemporal point to be that in which all creatures participate in God; Jesus needs to be that through which all spatiotemporal points are present to God. As Robin Attfield has already been quoted, it "does not follow from the world's dependence on God *at all times*" that "God's creative activity [should] therefore be understood to be performed *at all times*".[152] Therefore, the historical Jesus can still be that through which all creatures participate in God even though Jesus is no longer alive, because Jesus is eternally incarnate.

Likewise, the claim that creation and the incarnation are completely and utterly numerically identical should not destroy the historicity of the birth, death, resurrection and ascension of Jesus. So, claiming that creation and the incarnation are numerically identical does not lead to the conclusion that the literal, particular, historical body of Jesus Christ is completely and utterly numerically identical with the universe as a cosmic whole. That is, this does not lead to viewing the literal, particular, historical body/existence of Jesus Christ as a sort of theological motif in which the incarnation stands for and/or represents divine/creature

---

[152] Attfield, *Creation, Evolution and Meaning*, p. 77 (italics added).

relations. This does not lead to a demythologization of the historical Jesus in favour of a sort of abstract relation. Nor, in the language of Teilhard de Chardin, is the cosmos a "third nature" that sacrifices the historical particular for the cosmic universal. Quite the opposite. As John Macquarrie notes, "The Christian claim is not simply that there is an ideal laid up in the heavens or an archetype imprinted in the structure of reason."[153] There is an historical reality to that "ideal" and/or "archetype". Jesus *had* to be genuinely historical and genuinely divine to function as the mediator of being. Without a particular historical creature, there can be no real relation between historical reality and divine eternity.

The question then becomes: *how* does Jesus mediate "being" to each and every creature when those creatures have no "contact" with Jesus? Put differently, *how* can Jesus be that through which all spatiotemporal points are present to God? That is, it is clear how the Son mediates being to Jesus—and so the ontological relation that is creation is established and maintained in the person of Jesus—but it is not clear how Jesus mediates being to each individual creature. The answer can be found in imitation: the relation "extends" to all creatures through the imitation of Christ. In answering this question, two important Christological categories will be highlighted: the "physical" theory of the incarnation—that the incarnation is not efficacious because of anything that Jesus does *as* historical, but because in Jesus' person is the "sheer joining" of God and creatures—and the "corporate" nature of Jesus' body—that Jesus (and uniquely Jesus) is not *just* or *merely* a single particular historical body, but that Jesus assumes the whole of creation, recapitulated in the single body of a human.

The "physical" theory of the incarnation

The "physical" theory of the incarnation holds that human nature is "automatically deified in the incarnation"[154] or "derives the deification

---

[153] Macquarrie, *Jesus Christ in Modern Thought*, p. 349.

[154] J. N. D. Kelly, *Early Christian Doctrines* (London: Adam and Charles Black, 1965), p. 377.

... from its hypostatic union with the incarnate logos of God"[155] so that "the consequence of this hypostatic union in Christ of the two natures was the deification of the human nature he assumes".[156] The consequence of viewing the incarnation in this way is that it emphasizes as much as possible that what is important about the incarnation is not *what* Jesus does subsequent to being incarnate but *who* Jesus is *as* incarnate. What is efficacious about the incarnation is not what Jesus does *as* human, but *that* Jesus was God and human. It is the hypostatic union *itself* that is effective. Thus, Jeffrey Finch writes that "the human flesh which has become enslaved to corruption and death through sin was thought to be healed and immortalized through *mere contact* with divinity through the incarnation of the Logos, thus evacuating the need for Christ's atoning death".[157] That Jeffrey Finch calls the effect of the incarnation "mere contact" is crucial. What is effective about the incarnation is that it initiates and maintains a "mere contact". It is the very fact that there is a coming together and union of God and creatures in the one person that is effective. Anna Williams says much the same thing. She writes:

> The union of fallen human nature with the utterly holy divine nature necessarily changes the unholy ... it is not in the first instance what Christ does that saves us, but who he is ... it is the *sheer joining* of divinity and humanity in a single person, Jesus Christ, which renovates the nature sickened by the fall ... from this first moment of the union of divinity and humanity in the word newly conceived in a woman's womb, our nature is taken back to its newly minted state.[158]

---

[155] Georgios Mantzaridis, *The Deification of Man* (Crestwood, NY: St. Vladimir's Seminary Press, 1984), p. 29.

[156] Mantzaridis, *The Deification of Man*, p. 29.

[157] Jeffrey Finch, "Athanasius on the Deifying Work of the Redeemer", in Stephen Finlan and Vladimir Kharlamov (eds), *Theosis: Deification in Christian Theology* (Eugene, OR: Pickwick Publications, 2006), p. 106 (italics added).

[158] Anna Williams, "Nestorianism: Is Jesus Christ one person or does he have a split identity, with his divine nature separate and divided from his human

Again, Williams points to the "sheer joining" of creatures and God as being that which alone is effective. It is the hypostatic union, the coming together of God and creature in one person, the "contact" between divinity and creatures, that is effective.

Importantly, both Williams and Finch refer to the "mere contact" and "sheer joining" in relation to salvation, not creation. Likewise, Kelly and Mantzaridis expound the "physical" theory in relation to deification, not creation. Moreover, it is more than likely that the Patristic theologians who influenced these commentators saw this "mere contact" as being accidentally ordered. That is, they saw the incarnation as an event in salvation history before which the world was in need of salvation and after which the world was saved. That is, they saw the incarnation as the *renewal* of human nature—the repetition and/or continuation of *creatio originalis*—and that this was separate from the fact that "without their participation in the word, the entire universe would revert to the nothingness from which it came".[159]

However, if what has been said so far about divine activity is correct, if creation and deification are identical *for* God because both are *extrinsic* to God—that is, if God eternally "emanates grace" through the Son regardless of whether or not a universe actually obtains—then whether or not the creature experiences the bestowal of grace as deification or creation is entirely *extrinsic* to God. Therefore—and particularly given that Athanasius, Thomas Aquinas and others have already been quoted in support of the fact that the incarnation and creation are typally identical—if the "sheer joining" of God and creatures causes the deification of creatures, then the "sheer joining" of God and creatures causes the creation of creatures as well. The "sheer joining" of God and creatures in the person of Jesus Christ *is* creation. While Ian McFarland did not draw on this physical theory of the incarnation, he says much the same thing when he writes that "Christ is mediator not as a *tertium quid* positioned between two *predefined realities*, but rather as the

---

nature?", in Ben Quash and Michael Ward (eds), *Heresies and How to Avoid Them* (London: SPCK, 2007), p. 38 (italics added).

[159] Samuel Powell, *Participation in God* (Minneapolis, MN: Augsburg Fortress Press, 2003), p. 18.

one in whom God and humankind acquire their identities in the first place, that is, the one in and through whom the distinction between Creator and creature is itself established".[160] Christ can only function as a mediator as both God and creature, but this is not the "sheer joining" of two *predefined realities*; the hierarchy *is* the creation of the ontological relationship on which all creatures depend. The "sheer joining" *is* the creation of one by the other, because creation is a "certain relation" of dependence between one and the other.

The fact that the "physical" theory of the incarnation "was advanced by Irenaeus and further developed by Athanasius, Nyssa, etc. . . . thus becoming the common property of the Orthodox tradition"[161] means that this is not a novel suggestion. All that is being offered here is the suggestion that this "sheer joining" is not viewed as an accidentally ordered event that happens after the Big Bang and is (in a manner of speaking) the re-"origination" of the universe, but is rather viewed as an essentially ordered relationship that is the "creation" of the universe. After all, it has been argued that there was no temporally "pre-existent" Word to then "join" with humanity at some point after the Big Bang. This "mere contact", then, is essentially ordered to all creatures like the centre of a circle to its circumference; humanity is not *changed* by the "mere contact", but is that on which it depends for being. As Denis Edwards writes of Athanasius' theology, "Creation is an ongoing relation of participation, by which creatures exist securely because they partake of the Word of God," and, crucially, "it is the *presence* of the Word that enables creaturely existence",[162] that is, it is the *presence* of the Word that enables participation. Just as the "sheer contact" deifies, so the "sheer contact" creates. The distinction between the two is entirely *extrinsic* to God.

Two further questions are provoked by this. The first has been addressed previously in this book: how is it that the incarnation—which happened in first century Palestine—can be the "act" of creation when it occurs after the origin of the universe? Or, put differently, how can creation be a "contact" when there are not two "predefined realities"

---

[160] McFarland, *The Word Made Flesh*, p. 12 (italics added).

[161] Mantzaridis, *The Deification of Man*, p. 29.

[162] Edwards, *Deep Incarnation*, p. 58 (italics added).

to become contacted? The answer is that the basis of these questions reveals a mistaken assumption: one can only ask how "contact" can occur between two "realities" that are not predefined if one confuses "creation" and "origin". That is, this is nothing more than a restatement of the question of how creation can be a relationship if there is nothing that pre-exists that relationship that can then become related. As quoted from Thomas Aquinas, "By bestowing *esse*, God produces also that which receives the *esse*, and thus there is no need for him to operate out of something that was already in existence."[163] God does not create and *then* relate or come into contact with that creation; the contact *is* the creation.[164] The incarnation is not the origin of "motion", the incarnation is the source of "being". To quote Ian McFarland once again, "Christ is mediator not as a *tertium quid* positioned between two *predefined realities*, but rather as the one in whom God and humankind acquire their identities in the *first place*, that is, the one in and through whom the distinction between Creator and creature is *itself established*".[165]

The second question, building on this interpretation of the incarnation, asks that if "being" is donated to all creatures through an essentially ordered series that is established through the "mere contact" between God and creatures in the person of Jesus, then how is it that Jesus "hands on to successor whatever of the divine light he has received and . . . in providential proportion, is spread out to every being?"[166] How does "predecessor hand on to successor whatever of the divine light he has received",[167] so that "those closer to God should be the initiators of those less close by guiding them to the divine access, enlightenment, and communion"?[168] Or, to put this same point differently, how is it that God's "personal" presence in Christ can be seen as the source of God's "general"

---

[163] Thomas Aquinas, quoted in Cornelio Fabro, "The Intensive Hermeneutics of Thomistic Philosophy: The Notion of Participation", *The Review of Metaphysics* 27:3 (1974), p. 473.

[164] See Chapter 5 of my book *Incarnation and Neo Darwinism*.

[165] McFarland, *The Word Made Flesh*, p. 12 (italics added).

[166] Pseudo-Dionysius, *The Celestial Hierarchy* 13.3.

[167] Pseudo-Dionysius, *The Celestial Hierarchy* 13.3.

[168] Pseudo-Dionysius, *The Celestial Hierarchy* 4.3.

presence in all creatures as their participation? How is it that all creatures and spatiotemporal points are present to God *in* Jesus?

The "corporate" nature of Jesus' body

The relationship that donates being to the universe *is* the hypostatic union. However, this does not mean that Jesus' historical body is identical to the cosmos; the universe does not constitute the body of Christ. How, then, does Jesus perform his "cosmic" function? This was a problem for Teilhard de Chardin, who struggled to accept that the historical body of Jesus could have cosmic significance and so postulated a third Christological nature—Christ's "cosmic nature"—to explain how it is that the universe can be united with the divine. For Teilhard, there had to be another Christological nature in addition to Christ's divine and human nature in order for Christ's body to constitute the universe as a whole, in addition to Christ's body also being a particular discrete body that was *in* the universe. If, for Teilhard, "fundamentally—since all time and forever—but one single thing is being made in creation: the body of Christ",[169] and "in a real sense, only one man will be saved: Christ, the head and living summary",[170] then this cannot refer to Christ's "second" human nature because, quite clearly, such a nature does not represent the end of evolution or the fullness of creation. That is, one might say, Teilhard saw Christ's "second" nature as teleologically inferior to his "third" nature. Importantly, Teilhard does not hold that this "third" nature means that there must be more than one Christ. Rather, Richard Kropf explains, Teilhard "holds that the Incarnation of Christ is spread over the whole universe, both in space and time, in such a way that Christ needs to have been born, die and rise only once to affect the outcome of the whole process, quite independently, it would seem, from any knowledge of what is going on".[171] That is, Christ's "third nature" is

---

[169]   Pierre Teilhard de Chardin, *Christianity and Evolution* (London: Harvest, 1971), p. 74.

[170]   Pierre Teilhard de Chardin, *The Divine Milieu* (New York, NY: Harper & Row, 1968), p. 143.

[171]   Richard W. Kropf, "Teilhard de Chardin's Vision of Ultimate Reality and Meaning in the Light of Contemporary Cosmology", *Ultimate Reality and*

not a new or second incarnation, but is the culmination of the "second" nature in the incarnation.

While it is an interesting and novel idea, it has been roundly criticized for a number of reasons, none of which are important to consider here. What is important, however, is to understand the motive that led Teilhard to posit such a "third" nature. Teilhard read such Pauline sentiments such as that "He himself is before all things, and in him all things hold together"[172] and took them literally, that all creatures, taken together, literally constitute the body of Christ. When he saw this through the lens of progress that was so central to Teilhard's theology of evolution, it becomes understandable why he posited a "third" nature; that point in history when Christ quite literally is the universe.

However, it is entirely possible (and, as it will be argued, preferable) to interpret the claim that "in him all things hold together"[173] as meaning, not that the universe literally and physically constitutes that body of Christ, but something more like a "mystical imitation" or "participation". That is, the universe is not identical to the body of Christ—as in "third" nature of Christ—but the universe is "included" in the body of Christ through his assumption of a created nature. As Denis Edwards writes, "The Word assumes the creaturely humanity of Jesus with all its ecological and cosmic interconnections, and . . . these interconnections are by the divine intention co-constitutive of the Word incarnate."[174] Christ assumes a *particular* human nature, but this particular human nature includes the *universal* cosmos because it is "connected" to it.

This was a common feature of Patristic Christology. Norman Russell, for example, writes that "the unity of humankind, which Athanasius takes for granted, means that the whole human nature is deified in principle when the human nature which the logos assumed is deified in him".[175] J. N. D. Kelly also writes that "Athanasius' language often suggests that he

---

Meaning 23:3 (2000), pp. 252–3.

[172] Colossians 1:17.

[173] Colossians 1:17.

[174] Edwards, *Deep Incarnation*, p. 112.

[175] Norman Russell, *The Doctrine of Deification in the Greek Patristic Tradition* (Oxford: Oxford University Press, 2004), p. 172.

conceived of human nature, after the manner of platonic realism, as a concrete idea or universal in which all men participate . . . from assuming it Christ saves it and his divinizing force would be communicating to all mankind".[176] Jaroslav Pelikan also writes that "[the Logos had] not assumed some particular human being, but universal man, or the universal [human] nature, yet a nature that is seen in one individual" and so "Christ could be universal man only if his entire divine nature, with all its properties, was joined to a complete human nature, with all its properties, in a permanent and indissoluble union".[177] This is what is meant by "recapitulation", which Kelly describes as "Christ [being] representative of the whole race . . . just as all humans are present in Adam, they are present in the second".[178] The incarnation is relevant to all humans because Christ recapitulates all humanity in his person.

In the twentieth century, Henri de Lubac, drawing on the theology of Hilary of Poitiers, also writes that "the word did not merely take a human body; his incarnation was not a simple '*corporatio*', but, as St. Hilary says, a '*concorporatio*'." So, "in making a human nature, it is human nature that he united to himself, that he enclosed in himself, and it is the latter, whole and entire, that in some sort he uses as a body".[179] William Cavanaugh evidences this element of de Lubac's work, writing that "in the incarnation God takes on not simply an individual human body but human nature as such", therefore, "Christ is incorporated in a human body, but likewise humanity is saved by being incorporated into the body of Christ. The body of Christ is the locus of mutual participation of God in humanity and humanity in God".[180]

Others have noted that this "recapitulation" in Christ is not just a recapitulation of *humanity*, but extends to the *entirety of material*

---

[176]   Kelly, *Early Christian Doctrines*, p. 378.

[177]   Pelikan, *The Christian Tradition*, p. 84.

[178]   Kelly, *Early Christian Doctrines*, pp. 376–7.

[179]   Henri de Lubac, *Catholicism: Christ and the Common Destiny of Man* (San Francisco, CA: Ignatius Press, 1947), pp. 37–8.

[180]   William T. Cavanaugh, "The City: Beyond Secular Parodies", in John Milbank, Catherine Pickstock and Graham Ward (eds), *Radical Orthodoxy* (Oxford: Routledge, 1999), p. 184.

existence. Christ does not just stand for human nature, but for all created natures. Drawing on the opening of John's Gospel, Michael Lee writes that "when the Gospel of John says that the Word became *sarx* (John 1), it means that the presence of God reaches into the depths of material existence, not just to humans, but all of creation".[181] The incarnation is not Christ's assumption of humanity, it is the assumption of all creatures. It is also an important feature of Niels Henrik Gregersen's theology of "deep incarnation", which argues that "in [Jesus] God becomes human, and (by implication) foxes and sparrows, grass and soil".[182] Elsewhere, Gregersen writes that "in this context, the incarnation of God in Christ can be understood as a radical or 'deep' incarnation, that is, an incarnation into the very tissue of biological existence, and system of nature"[183] and so "the particular incarnation in Jesus of Nazareth go[es] the whole way down, from the particulars of his human personhood into the depths of biological and physical materiality".[184] It is this last quotation that is particularly illustrative. The incarnation is not just the incarnation of a particular individual human, it is not even the incarnation of a "general" humanity; Christ's incarnation certainly is this, but it is also so much more. In becoming incarnate, Jesus assumes the very "tissue of biological existence".

However, this emphasis on the "corporate" nature of Christ's humanity (creaturehood) does not "replace" or detract from the fact that Jesus was a particular male human, with specific and particular attributes and capacities. Jesus' individual and particular historical existence *is* a *genuine* individual and particular existence, but it is not *merely* a particular existence because in that historical body is the eternal relation between God and all creatures. Thus, John Robinson writes that "to be a

---

181 Michael E. Lee, "Historical Crucifixion: A Liberationist Response to Deep Incarnation", *Theological Studies* 81:4 (2020), p. 896.

182 Niels Henrik Gregersen, "Deep Incarnation: Why Evolutionary Continuity Matters in Christology", *Toronto Journal of Theology* 26 (2010), p. 182.

183 Niels Henrik Gregersen, "The Cross of Christ in an Evolutionary World", *Dialog: A Journal of Theology* 40:3 (2001), p. 205.

184 Niels Henrik Gregersen, "Deep Incarnation: From Deep History to Post-axial Religion", *HTS Teologiese Studies/Theological Studies* 72:4 (2016), p. 4.

'universal man' is not to have every human quality, but to be the sort of person of whom we recognize *in* the individual that which transcends the individual. We see in him what *each* of us could be—in his own unique way".[185] This is important. To call Jesus the "corporate" human—or, as we must in light of evolution, the "corporate" creature—does not mean that he exemplifies literally every possible way of being a creature, but that every possible way of being a creature is "recapitulated" in him. John Milbank, Catherine Pickstock, and Graham Ward also write that "[Jesus'] body is both actual and metaphorical: actually male and metaphorically both male and female. It is both individual and historically particular and historically extended through time",[186] to which must be added "actually human, but metaphorically human and non-human" etc.

This fact could be put differently, drawing yet again on the absence of a real relation. In much the same way that creatures can be said to be similar to God without God being in any way similar to creatures, or that God is atemporal because all spatiotemporal points are present to God, without God being present at every spatiotemporal point, then all creatures are imitations of Jesus, without Jesus having to exemplify every single creaturely attribute or capacity. That is, all creatures are really similar to Jesus, but Jesus is not really similar to all creatures; all creatures "look like" Jesus—they are made in the image of Jesus—but Jesus does not "look like" every creature. One can look at a mouse, or a tree, or a quark and see Jesus, but one cannot see mice, trees, or quarks when one looks at Jesus. This tension of the "absence of a real relation" or *analogia entis* is, like Przywara said, not just a particular doctrine, but the way that theology as a whole must be done. Only with *analogia entis* can each and every creature be an imitation of the human Jesus.

Christ's corporate nature and imitation
Imitation is very important for this interpretation of the corporate nature of Jesus. All creatures participate in Jesus—all creatures are

---

[185]   Robinson, *The Human Face of God*, p. 73 (italics in original).
[186]   John Milbank, Catherine Pickstock and Graham Ward, "Introduction", in John Milbank, Catherine Pickstock and Graham Ward (eds), *Radical Orthodoxy* (Oxford: Routledge, 1999), p. 13.

"recapitulated" in Jesus—because all creatures imitate Jesus. Thus, just as "all created natures are just ways of imperfectly imitating God",[187] so all created natures are just imperfect ways of imitating Jesus. If Jesus is God, then all creatures imitate God because they imitate Jesus. If "*Imitatio Christi* [is] based on the fact that the Christian participates in the life of Christ"[188] and "the logic [of participation and imitation] is the same" so that imitation of Christ is "just another way to express the central idea of participation",[189] then imitation of Christ is *how* creatures participate in God through Christ.

If that is the case, then it can be put quite simply that if "God's creative action *just is* creation's dependence on God for its existence",[190] and the incarnation is *how* creatures depend on God, then imitation of Jesus is *how* the incarnation can be creatures' dependence on God. To depend on God "looks like" imitation of Jesus. Of course, as it has already been argued, "*how* creatures imitate Jesus" (i.e., in what way creatures imitate Jesus, what particular imitation they are) is theologically irrelevant— God "let[s] be whatever would and could emerge from that freedom, and enjoy[s] *all* responses of *all* kinds as they have occurred from the beginning of time, with their various qualities, of which intelligence is only one"[191]—but "*that* creatures imitate Jesus" is that which makes them creatures. The definition of a creature is something that imitates Jesus.

When this idea is put together with the "physical" theory of the incarnation, then the idea of creation as a hierarchy in which Christ mediates "being" from the Father to all creatures becomes more understandable. The hypostatic union in the person of Christ becomes the "mere contact" between each and every creature and God because that which comes into contact with God in the hypostatic union is

---

[187] McCord Adams, *What Sort of Nature?*, p. 29.

[188] Susan Wood, *Spiritual Exegesis and the Church in the Theology of Henri de Lubac* (Edinburgh: T&T Clark, 1998), p. 141.

[189] Torstein Theodor Tollefsen, *Activity and Participation in Late Antique and Early Christian Thought* (Oxford: Oxford University Press, 2012), p. 163.

[190] Bishop and Perszyk, "The Divine Attributes and Non-personal Conceptions of God", p. 614.

[191] Ruth Page, *The Web of Creation* (London: SCM Press, 1996), p. 80.

the "recapitulation" of all creatures, a "recapitulation" that is achieved through creatures' imitation of Jesus. Creation is ontological relationship and ontological relationship is maintained through "contact" between God and creature in the hypostatic union; every creature participates in this "contact" through the imitation of Jesus.

Yet, this does not mean that the particular historical existence of Jesus is "swallowed" up by his cosmic function—this does not mean that Christ becomes what Teilhard would call a "third" or "cosmic" nature—because there absolutely *had* to be a real historical "pole" or real historical existence that Christ assumed. Jesus had to be really and truly particular and historical otherwise the particular and historical are not recapitulated in him. Yet, that real, historical existence is not "*merely*" historical; it is also that which eternally constitutes the ontological hierarchy/relation between God and creatures. In Christ, and through hierarchy, each and every creature comes into contact with God. The incarnation happened in time (which it *had* to do if it was to be the point at which the eternal, transcendent God comes into contact with the universe, and so establishes a relation on which all creatures depend for their being)—or, better, it has a temporal or historical "pole"—but it is chiefly a "vertical", hierarchical relation between God and creatures. The incarnation has to have a temporal and/or historical "pole" if it is to genuinely be the "bridge" that mediates between God and creatures (as Ward recognizes above), but it is first and foremost a hierarchical relation, related to each and every creature and each and every spatiotemporal point as the centre of a circle is related to its circumference. Jesus enters history at a specific point and is only present for thirty-odd years, but through him, all creatures become present to God by imitating his life. Jesus is not present to each and every creature at each and every spatiotemporal point (it "does not follow from the world's dependence on God *at all times*" that "God's creative activity [should] therefore be understood to be performed *at all times*"[192]). However, through imitation, each and every creature is present in Jesus and, through Jesus, in "contact" with God through an ontological hierarchy, like the circumference of a circle to its centre.

---

[192] Attfield, *Creation, Evolution and Meaning*, p. 77 (italics added).

Subsequent issues

It is important here to make explicit some connections that are implicitly demanded by this interpretation of the incarnation. If "God is never without his [sic] Logos",[193] and there is "no sense talking of the eternal Son of God apart from the incarnation",[194] then, it was argued, the incarnation becomes, not just the "supreme example of God's action in the world",[195] but simply *the sole* example of divine activity. In fact, it was suggested, there is no creation, there is no divine activity, there is just the incarnation, which establishes an ontological relation between God and creatures on which all creatures depend for their being. This obviously has important implications for how omnipotence, omniscience, etc. are understood. A few comments are necessary to expound those implications.

Omniscience

As omniscience was explicitly expounded in relation to the incarnation in the previous chapter, it is helpful to start with it here. Paul Tillich was quoted as arguing that "nothing is outside the centred unity of [God's] life; nothing is strange, dark, hidden, isolated, unapproachable",[196] and this means that "nothing falls outside the *Logos* structure of being".[197] Robert Barron said much the same thing, writing that:

> just as the Logos of the Father is the power through which all things are intelligible, so that same Word is the power through whom all things are known. Accordingly, it is in Christ and through Christ that even the simplest act of cognition takes place; "natural" reason is thoroughly Christological . . . what we know and how we know is conditioned by what was revealed in Jesus Christ.[198]

---

[193] Hart, *The Experience of God*, p. 235.

[194] Helm, "Divine Timeless Eternity", p. 54.

[195] Wiles, *God's Action in the World*, p. 82.

[196] Tillich, *Systematic Theology Vol. 1*, pp. 277–8.

[197] Tillich, *Systematic Theology Vol. 1*, pp. 277–8.

[198] See also Robert Barron, *The Priority of Christ: Towards A Postliberal Catholicism* (Grand Rapids, MI: Brazos Press, 2007), p. 148.

This can now be nuanced to say that omniscience means nothing less than that all things have their being through *imitatio Christi*. Omniscience is not the possession of all the data that it is possible to have, but is the affirmation that no datum is possible without the incarnation.

In this way, the incarnation does not become the "vehicle" or the "means" by which God acquires "new" knowledge, nor does it enable God to "exercise" knowledge that it would have been impossible for God to do so un-incarnate. For example, the incarnation is not necessary for God to "know" or to "learn" what fear, relief, suffering, etc. feels like.[199] This would obviously require God to be a person, who feels, thinks, and has desires etc., which this book has rejected.

Importantly, then, this interpretation also helps to answer questions about whether Jesus himself had special knowledge. That is, to say that Jesus was both limited in knowledge and omniscient does not mean that there is a contradiction positing that Jesus both "knew everything" and "did not know everything". To say that Jesus was omniscient does not mean that Jesus could not "[increase] in wisdom",[200] nor does it contradict the fact that Jesus did not know "that day or hour".[201] Rather, to say that Jesus was omniscient means that Jesus both had a limited creaturely knowledge of things based on what he could know through his senses *and* that he was also that in which all of those things were intelligible simultaneously. Jesus was omniscient because Jesus uniquely could always see and know things as they truly are, as imitations of himself, not because he had possession of every single possible datum.

Omnipotence

If "God's power is [God's] knowledge",[202] then this interpretation of omniscience works just as well for interpreting omnipotence. If

---

[199] E.g., Murray MacBeath and Paul Helm, "Omniscience and Eternity", *Proceedings of the Aristotelian Society, Supplementary Volumes* 63 (1989), pp. 71–2.

[200] Luke 2:52.

[201] Mark 13:32.

[202] Katherin Rogers, *Perfect Being Theology* (Edinburgh: Edinburgh University Press, 2000), p. 75.

omnipotence is not the perfect or maximal ability to do everything that it is possible (or impossible) to do, but is the "power" in which all things participate for their causal power, then it is the incarnation in which and through which this "power" is manifested. If all things are only intelligible in Jesus because "nothing falls outside the *Logos* structure of being",[203] then this "power" is only manifested in Jesus for the same reason. This "power" is not really "power" because "there is no prior category of causation in which both God and creatures both share"[204] and so (paraphrasing Palamas), "if God has power, then all else does not have power, but if every other things has power, then God does not have power".[205] This "power" is the "cause of being", and it is an essentially ordered cause that is only "exercised" or "manifested" through the incarnation.

As with omniscience, this does not mean that incarnation becomes the "vehicle" or "means" by which God acquires "new" power, nor does it enable God to "exercise" power that it would have been impossible for God to do so un-incarnate. Andrew Lore, for example, writes that "God *can* still make it possible that He chooses to do evil, by causing himself to take up a human nature (as in the incarnation) that allows Him to be exposed to desires to do evil (such as in situations of temptation). In such a scenario, after the incarnation God would have the ability to choose to do evil".[206] Yet, all this does is characterize divine activity as univocal with human activity and subject God to time and change, none of which conforms to how divine activity is understood in this book, which is clear that God can only "act" as an essentially ordered "cause"—i.e., *creatio*. The incarnation does not change God, nor allow God to exercise "powers" that God would be unable to without a body. The incarnation is not the means through which an un-personal and beyond-being God can become an individual person and thereby can be

---

[203] Tillich, *Systematic Theology Vol. 1*, pp. 277–8.

[204] Davison, *Participation in God*, p. 44.

[205] Gregory Palamas (tr. Robert Sinkewicz), *One Hundred and Fifty Chapters* (Toronto: Pontifical Institute of Mediaeval Studies, 1988), p. 78.

[206] Andrew Lore, "Divine Omnipotence and Moral Perfection", *Religious Studies* 14:4 (2010), p. 529.

said to have desires and wants and act in specific ways to realize them. The incarnation is not a way of retaining all those personal attributes that the "theistic personalist" wishes to retain for God (i.e., a way of explaining how an un-personal God can act in a personal way). Rather, the incarnation is the essentially ordered cause through which the "cause of being" is manifested, or, better, "emanated". The incarnation is how multiple, finite, temporal, and complex creatures can be related to one, infinite, atemporal, and simple God.

Thus, as was noted above, to say that Jesus is the "causal joint" of divine activity does not mean that God needs Jesus to initiate accidentally ordered causal chains, since that is not the content of divine "activity" (indeed, God does not act at all, whether through Jesus or not)—Jesus is not the *originator* of the universe, but its *creator*. Neither does God need Jesus in order to influence the outcome of a certain state of affairs in the material world—that is, God does not need Jesus to realize certain future ends. Rather, God needs Jesus to establish and maintain an essentially ordered ontological hierarchy between God and creatures on which all creatures depend as their "ground of being".

This also means that, again as with omniscience, this interpretation also helps to answer questions about whether Jesus himself had special powers. That is, to say that Jesus was both limited in power and omnipotent does not mean that there is a contradiction positing that Jesus both "could do everything it is possible (or impossible) to do" and "could not do everything". Just as with Rudolf Bultmann's "demythologization",[207] the miracles ascribed to Jesus in the Gospels do not attest to Jesus' possession of superpowers, but are theological or narrative motifs that explain Christ's divine status. Jesus' omnipotence does not mean that he was not limited in power, but explains that in the historical Jesus, and manifested in him, was the divine "cause of being".

Communicatio idiomatum

The *communicatio idiomatum* is obviously important here. As is often misunderstood, the *communicatio idiomatum* does not mean that

---

[207] Rudolf Bultmann, *New Testament and Mythology and Other Basic Writings* (Philadelphia, PA: Fortress Press, 1984).

the divine attributes can be applied to the creature and the creaturely attributes can be applied to God, but rather Christ's person had both simultaneously. As Richard Cross clarifies, *communicatio idiomatum* is not the "ascription of the properties of one nature to the other", which would mean that the divine nature *changes* and *becomes* created, but is "the ascription of divine and human properties to the person of the word".[208] That is, there is not an *exchange* of properties, nor is there a *confusion* of properties, but the person of Christ has both properties simultaneously.

If *communicatio idiomatum* is about "the ascription of divine and human *properties* to the person of the word",[209] then it must equally apply to the ascription of divine and human *activities*. As Aaron Riches acknowledges, "The Chalcedonian language of 'without separation' must apply to the energies of Christ as well [as the natures]."[210] As a result, István Perczel writes that because of *communicatio idiomatum* we can say that "[Christ] performs the divine deeds not as God but as man ... [and that] he performs the human deeds not as man, but as God".[211] Or, as Frederick Bauerschmidt puts it, "Christ, in all his actions, performed human actions divinely and divine actions humanly."[212] Thus, discussing the theology of Theodore of Mopsuestia, Frances Young writes that while "there remained two distinct natures, there was nevertheless one subject (*prosōpon*) to which all the actions of the saviour could be referred, one Son because of the union".[213] There are two "wills" and "energies", but there is only one person who does them both.

---

[208] Richard Cross, *The Metaphysics of the Incarnation* (Oxford: Oxford University Press, 2002), p. 184.

[209] Cross, *The Metaphysics of the Incarnation*, p. 184 (italics added).

[210] Aaron Riches, *Ecce Homo* (Grand Rapids, MI: William B. Eerdmans, 2016), p. 145.

[211] István Perczel, "The Christology of Pseudo-Dionysius: The Areopagite: The *Fourth Letter* in Its Indirect and Direct Text Traditions", *Le Muséon* 117:3–4 (2004), p. 422.

[212] Bauerschmidt, *Thomas Aquinas: Faith, Reason, and Following Christ*, p. 196; see *ST* 3, 19, 1.

[213] Young, *From Nicaea to Chalcedon*, p. 210.

However, just as *communicatio idiomatum* does not mean that Christ is at times divine and at times human, but must be *both* human *and* divine *simultaneously* at all "times", so the same must be said of the activities. There is not a sort of "switch" in the mind/person of Christ so that he is both God and creature, but only acts as one at any given time. There is not "a kind of alternation in Jesus Christ, who is now a divine being, now a human being"[214] but at all "times" Jesus Christ simultaneously exists and acts "theandrically":[215] "Christ did not do anything 'as God' or 'as man'. He did all things as the God–Man."[216]

This leads to an important implication. If divine activity is entirely recast as exclusively the essentially ordered "cause of being", so that omnipotence means that God is the "ground of being" for all things, not that God can do everything that it is possible (or impossible) to do, then this means that the fact that Jesus is divine adds nothing to the various creaturely acts that Jesus does as part of his creaturely, historical life. The incarnation does not "insert" into cosmic history a new, special chain of accidentally ordered events that transform the history of the world. Rather, the "mundane" or "normal" or "everyday" actions that Jesus performs as a creature are *simultaneously* those "activities" that "bridge" the ontological gap between God and creatures. Those "mundane", "normal", "everyday" actions are *simultaneously* the divine, essentially ordered "cause" through which all creatures participate in God. That is, being divine does not mean that a new range of activities is added to the limited range of activities that Jesus possesses as a result of being human, both of which are "theandrically" performed as both God and human simultaneously. Rather, it means that the limited range of activities that Jesus possesses as a result of being human is simultaneously the essentially ordered hierarchy that constitutes the eternal divine emanation. The limited range of activities that Jesus possesses as a result of being human

---

[214] Macquarrie, *Jesus Christ in Modern Thought*, p. 164.

[215] Tollefsen, *Activity and Participation in Late Antique and Early Christian Thought*, pp. 154–5; see Pseudo-Dionysius, *The Complete Works* (Mahwah, NJ: Paulist Press, 1987), *Letter Four*.

[216] Sergei Bulgakov, *The Lamb of God* (Grand Rapids, MI: William B. Eerdmans, 2008), p. 237.

are simultaneously those limited "mundane" activities *and* the "ground of being". The "limited" acts of Christ's human nature become the way that Christ is the "ground of being". Being God does not mean that Christ is able to do things that other creatures are incapable of doing; rather, being God means that the "limited" actions of the creature Jesus become "infused" with the ground of being.

This means that when Norman Wirzba writes that "the loving power that Jesus models in his feeding the hungry, healing the sick, exorcising the demon-possessed, and befriending the stranger and outcast is the *same* divine power that brings all creatures into being and that daily sustains and nurtures them",[217] he is essentially correct, but that claim requires nuancing. For Wirzba, this claim forms part of a doctrine of *creatio continua*, that Christ's "feeding the hungry, healing the sick, exorcising the demon-possessed, and befriending the stranger and outcast . . . communicate[s] that God's creating work is not solely completed at the beginning but is ongoing and revealed in fresh ways in the ministries of Jesus".[218] For Wirzba, Jesus' "feeding the hungry, healing the sick, exorcising the demon-possessed, and befriending the stranger and outcast" continues and/or completes the "divine power that brings all creatures into being" *in the beginning*, or is *another* instance of the "divine power that brings all creatures into being and that daily sustains and nurtures them". For Wirzba, the "feeding the hungry, healing the sick, exorcising the demon-possessed, and befriending the stranger and outcast" is a repetition of the accidentally ordered power that God exercises "in the beginning".

However, if what is being said in this chapter is correct, then the "the loving power that Jesus models in his feeding the hungry, healing the sick, exorcising the demon-possessed, and befriending the stranger and outcast" is not *another instance* of the "divine power that brings all creatures into being and that daily sustains and nurtures them", but is *the same instance* of the essentially ordered "divine power that brings all

---

[217] Norman Wirzba, "Creation *Through* Christ", in Andrew Torrance and Thomas McCall (eds), *Christ and the Created Order Vol. 2* (Grand Rapids, MI: Zondervan, 2018), p. 39 (italics added).

[218] Wirzba, "Creation *Through* Christ", p. 39.

creatures into being and that daily sustains and nurtures them". Or, to put this differently, "the loving power that Jesus models in his feeding the hungry, healing the sick, exorcising the demon-possessed, and befriending the stranger and outcast" *just is* "God's creative action" that "*just is* creation's dependence on God for its existence"[219] as an essentially ordered, ontological hierarchy. *Communicatio idiomatum* does not mean that Christ has two "sets" of activities that he does simultaneously; it means that Christ has one "set" of "mundane" activities that function both as "causes" in the intramundane spatiotemporal nexus *and* "creation" through the intermundane hierarchy *simultaneously*.

Analogy of being

Finally, if God is so transcendent of creation such that Christ is needed in order for a relation to exist between them, then this has important implications for the analogy of being. If Christ is that in which the ontological relation that is creation is established, then there is an analogy between God and creatures, not because of an abstract philosophical/ logical argument, but because Christ is both God and creature simultaneously. If the hypostatic union is responsible for creation, then it is also that which establishes the analogy of being. Creatures can be like God because Christ—the corporate creature, whom all creatures imitate—is God. Outside of Christ, there is no analogy between God and the creature. It is only because God and creatures are held together in unity in the "person" of Christ that there can be said to be an analogy of being between creatures and God. Creatures are analogous to God, because creatureliness is united to God in the "person" of Christ. Creatures imitate God because they are united to God in Christ as the source of their being; Christ as mediator is also Christ as analogy.

In this direction, it is pertinent that Erich Przywara writes that "the 'analogy of being' is certainly a bridge".[220] Analogy of being is a bridge between God and the creature, that which describes the ontological

---

[219]   Bishop and Perszyk, "The Divine Attributes and Non-personal Conceptions of God", p. 614.

[220]   Erich Przywara, *Analogia Entis* (Grand Rapids, MI: William B. Eerdmans, 2014), p. 236.

relationship between them. If it is a bridge, then Christ is that bridge, because "the gap between heaven and earth is only bridged definitively in the figure of Christ".[221] Hans Urs von Balthasar, who was heavily influenced by Przywara, also argued that Christology is "the condition for the possibility of analogy", so that "only in Christ is it possible then to understand the nature of the analogy of being: 'the divine Son who becomes man is the concrete *analogia entis*'".[222] Between God and creatures there is an *analogia entis* because God and creatures are united in Christ.

Conclusion

What has been said in this chapter might appear quite radical at first glance. However, it is nothing more than an exploration of what it means for Christ to be that "through which all things were made" if creation is understood as an ontological hierarchy/relation. The answer is that the hypostatic union is that in which and through which all creatures participate in God. This leads to the somewhat speculative conclusion that, strictly speaking, there is no creation; there is only incarnation. There is "something rather than nothing", because the Son took flesh and dwelt among us.

To put this differently, Christ is that which mediates "being" from the Father to all creatures. Creation is participation in God, but, because God is so utterly transcendent of and ontologically other to creation, so the incarnation is needed to explain how creatures can participate in God. Creation is participation in God, but participation in God "looks" like imitation of Jesus; all creatures participate in God through imitation of Jesus. In "*what*" way creatures are imitations of Jesus is determined by

---

[221] Shortt, *God Is No Thing*, p. 77.

[222] Graham Ward, "Kenosis: Death, Discourse and Resurrection", in Lucy Gardner, David Moss, Ben Quash and Graham Ward (eds), *Balthasar at the End of Modernity* (Edinburgh: T&T Clark, 1999), p. 43; see Hans Urs von Balthasar, *Theo-Drama II: Dramatis Personae: Man in God* (San Francisco, CA: Ignatius Press, 1992), p. 267.

their "origin", but "*that*" the creature imitates Christ at all is the reason "*that*" the creature exists at all.

Here, then, the basic thesis of this book is put forward. The first chapter argued that God is so utterly transcendent of and ontologically other to creatures that God is not a person who "does" things. The second chapter then argued that if God is not a person who "does" things, then creation is not a thing that God "does" but is a relation that creatures have with God, a relation that is the ground of their being. That relation is an essentially ordered ontological dependency called participation. The third chapter explored how that understanding of creation as participation can be used to interpret other questions of divine activity. This fourth chapter continues that, if God is so utterly transcendent of and ontologically other to creatures, then something else is needed to explain how it is that creatures participate in God. That is, if God is so utterly transcendent of and ontologically other to creatures that there cannot be a real relation between God and creatures (hence the need to emphasize to such an extent that all creation is *extrinsic* to God), then something "else" must be needed to explain how there can be a relation/imitation between creatures and God. The incarnation explains how it is that creatures participate in (have a relation to) God; creatures participate in God through imitation of Jesus: "Christ is the ultimate center of what is and what is known".[223]

---

[223]   Joshua C. Benson, "Structure and Meaning in St. Bonaventure's '*Quaestiones Disputatae de Scientia Christi*'", *Franciscan Studies* 62 (2004), p. 90.

5

Cross

The last chapter argued that the incarnation, as the coming together and "sheer joining" of God and creatures, is identical to, and so constitutes, the "certain relation"[1] of ontological dependence that is creation. The hypostatic union is that on which creatures depend for their being. All creatures participate in that union through imitation of Christ. Thus, creatures are "something rather than nothing" because, through imitation of Christ, they participate in the hypostatic union. The question that necessarily follows from this claim is what this means for the cross, which early in Church history became the symbol around which all theology and liturgy orbits. If what Jesus achieves is achieved by the very fact of his being born—or, for some, "from the moment of [Christ's] conception in the womb of Mary"[2]—then, why did he go to Jerusalem to be crucified?

Martin Kähler once remarked that the Gospel of Mark is a "passion narrative with an extended introduction".[3] That observation could well be made of any of the synoptic Gospels, if not of John's Gospel as well. The passion of Jesus Christ is not just an unfortunate end to the story of Jesus' incarnation; the passion *is* the story of Jesus Christ, the preceding ministry (and infancy stories) being merely introductory preambles to set the scene. Yet, this presents us with the complete opposite of what was called the "physical" theory of the incarnation, which emphasized

---

[1] *ST* i, 45, iii.

[2] Maximos Aghiourgoussis, "Orthodox Soteriology", in J. Meyendorff and R. Tobias (eds), *Salvation in Christ: A Lutheran–Orthodox Dialogue* (Minneapolis, MN: Augsburg Fortress, 1992), p. 41.

[3] Martin Kähler, *The So-called Historical Jesus and the Historic, Biblical Christ* (Philadelphia, PA: Fortress Press, 1964), p. 80, n. 11.

that "the human flesh which has become enslaved to corruption and death through sin was thought to be healed and immortalized through mere contact with divinity through the incarnation of the Logos" to such a degree that it led to an "evacuati[on of] the need for Christ's atoning death".[4]

Thus, Christology can be delineated along two main avenues: one in which the incarnation is a means to the cross, and one in which the incarnation is an end in itself. Oliver Quick designates these different Christologies as "Pauline" and "Johannine". On the one hand, from a "Pauline" perspective:

> The atonement, as God's redeeming act for man's salvation, [is] the centre and starting-point. The incarnation is seen as the method of the atonement; and the end, of which the incarnation is the means, is found in the fulfillment of God's saving work in the life of the world to come.[5]

In this way, the incarnation is only considered as a means to an end in the crucifixion. Contrastingly, from a "Johannine" perspective:

> The doctrine of the incarnation is the centre and starting-point of Christian theology. The atonement is derivative from it, and the eschatological doctrines concerning the ultimate of the human soul tend to appear, as it were, on the circumference of Christian theology.[6]

Here, the incarnation itself is efficacious and so is an end in and of itself.[7]

---

[4]   Jeffrey Finch, "Athanasius on the Deifying Work of the Redeemer", in Stephen Finlan and Vladimir Kharlamov (eds), *Theosis: Deification in Christian Theology* (Eugene, OR: Pickwick Publications, 2006), p. 106.

[5]   Oliver Quick, *Doctrines of the Creed* (London: Nisbet & Co., 1938), p. 189.

[6]   Quick, *Doctrines of the Creed*, p. 189.

[7]   "Certain heterodox theologians like to associate Roman Catholicism with the apostle Peter, Protestantism with the apostle Paul, and Orthodoxy with the apostle and evangelist John" (Savvas Agourides, "The Social Character

Anna Marmodoro and Jonathan Hill helpfully describe this distinction slightly differently. They distinguish between those who see the incarnation as "conditions that Christ had to meet in order to be able to save", and those who "thought that meeting these conditions was what salvation consisted in, at least in part".[8] It is clear that an identical tension is operative. Either the incarnation is a means to an end, a condition which Christ must meet in order to be able to save (i.e., "Pauline"), or the incarnation is an end in itself, the condition that itself constitutes what salvation is (i.e., "Johannine"). Chul Won Suh also delineates Christology along identical lines, but, again helpfully, does so using slightly different language by concentrating on the motivation behind the incarnation. Distinguishing between what he calls "elevation-line" theology and "restitution-line" theology, he notes that the former "seeks the motive and ground of the incarnation in the glorification or elevation of the creation or man" (i.e. "Johannine"), whereas the latter "presents sin as the sole, or at least primary, motive and cause of the incarnation of the Son of God" (i.e. "Pauline").[9] Regardless of the language used, however, the distinction between the two Christologies is the same.

It should be clear from what was argued in the previous chapter that this book assumes that the "Johannine" category is preferred: the incarnation is itself the divine act in which and through which creatures receive their being and participate in God through imitation of Jesus. There is nothing controversial about this fact; plenty of theologies take precisely this approach. However, while there is nothing controversial about supporting this position, it does still leave the question of how the theologian deals with the cross. As Jeffrey Finch so succinctly

---

of Orthodoxy", in A. J. Philippou (ed.), *The Orthodox Ethos: Studies in Orthodoxy Vol. 1* (Oxford: Holywell Press, 1964), p. 209). In this way (although Agourides himself clearly disagrees with the characterization), the former could be seen as representative of western theology and the latter of eastern theology.

8   Anna Marmodoro and Jonathan Hill, "Modeling the Metaphysics of the Incarnation", *Philosophy & Theology* 20:1/2 (2008), pp. 99–100.

9   Chul Won Suh, *The Creation-Mediatorship of Jesus Christ* (Amsterdam: Rodopi, 1982), p. 8.

and clearly puts the problem: if "the human flesh which had become enslaved to corruption and death through sin was thought to be healed and immortalized through mere contact with divinity through the incarnation of the Logos", then this surely leads to "evacuating the need for Christ's atoning death".[10] If the incarnation itself achieves everything that God might wish to "do"—a claim that is strengthened considerably when this book explicitly seeks to situate such a claim within deism—then what possible need is there for the crucifixion? Does Christianity's most enduring and undeniably central symbol become consigned to the rubbish heap?

The short answer is "no". This chapter will argue that, despite the fact that it has been argued that the incarnation is creation, the cross can, and should, retain its central position. It will do this by "extending" the logic that made the incarnation relevant to the deist. If the incarnation can be relevant to the deist—despite the fact that commentators have claimed that deism and the incarnation are incompatible—then the cross can be relevant for a Johannine Christology—despite the fact that commentators see Johannine Christologies as relegating the cross. If the previous chapter moved from the idea that creation and incarnation are typally identical—that the incarnation is a "re-doing" of creation—to the idea that creation and incarnation are numerically identical—the incarnation is not a re-doing of creation, it *is* that creation itself—then this chapter will make exactly the same move. If there is a fundamental connection between creation and incarnation—because "both are acts of condescension"[11]—then there is also a fundamental connection between creation, incarnation, and crucifixion—because "after the incarnation, [Christ's] human will completes the self-stripping; it accepts the death on the cross"[12]—so that the death of Christ "takes the incarnation to a

10   Finch, "Athanasius on the Deifying Work of the Redeemer", p. 106.
11   Celia Deane-Drummond, *Christ and Evolution* (London: SCM Press and Minneapolis, MN: Fortress Press, pp. 114–15.
12   Ferdinand Prat, *The Theology of St Paul: Vol. 1* (London: Burns, Oates & Washbourne, 1945), p. 319.

new depth".[13] If the crucifixion is typally identical to the incarnation and creation, then it can also be seen as numerically identical with them.

That is, if the incarnation recapitulates creation, then the cross recapitulates the incarnation. Or, if "God is never without his [sic] Logos, the divine Wisdom, in and through whom the world is created, ordered, and sustained",[14] and the Logos "is never in the state of not having an assumed human nature",[15] or there is "no sense talking of the eternal Son of God apart from the incarnation",[16] then to this can be added that the incarnate Logos is always the crucified Christ. Or, if the human Jesus is identified as the creator, then "we preach [a] Christ crucified"[17]—"The universe assumes the form of Christ—but, O mystery! the man we see is Christ crucified".[18] The Son is "never" without the human Jesus, and the human Jesus is always the crucified.

In making this argument, this chapter will make four main claims: (a) while the previous chapter clearly endorses a Scotist-esque Christology, in which the incarnation is seen in a much wider paradigm of creation, this chapter will claim that Scotus' theology of the cross is deficient; (b) while many see the cross as being normative for divine activity, this chapter will argue that such activity must be seen as relationship, not activity—in other words, the situation is "reversed", the cross does not reveal what divine activity is about, but the cross must be seen within the context of "creation as relationship"; (c) this leads to a reinterpretation of *kenosis*, in which the self-emptying is not a literal self-emptying, but becomes an image of, and synonym for, participation; and (d) this means that, just as the incarnation recapitulates creation so the cross

---

[13] Deane-Drummond, *Christ and Evolution*, p. 148.

[14] David Bentley Hart, *The Experience of God: Being, Consciousness, Bliss* (London: Yale University Press, 2013), p. 235.

[15] Eleonore Stump, *The God of the Bible and the God of the Philosophers* (Milwaukee, WI: Marquette University Press, 2016), p. 100.

[16] Paul Helm, "Divine Timeless Eternity", in Gregory Ganssle (ed.), *God and Time: Four Views* (Downers Grove, IL: IVP Academic, 2001), p. 54.

[17] 1 Corinthians 1:23.

[18] Pierre Teilhard de Chardin, *Writings in the Time of War* (London: Collins, 1968), p. 208.

recapitulates the incarnation. If the incarnation exhausts what is meant by creation, then crucifixion exhausts what is meant by incarnation; there is no creation, there is no incarnation, there is just the eternal crucifixion.

Cross and John Duns Scotus

It is clear that, while commentators have rightly identified that this "Johannine" Christology is more prevalent in the Greek Patristic tradition,[19] to western theology at least, John Duns Scotus' theology of the primacy of Christ is the most obvious starting place. For Scotus, sin could never be the context in which Christology is done, as this significantly lessens and diminishes the greatness of what God did/is doing in the incarnation. Instead, Christ must be seen within the context of revealing the greatness of God, not with redeeming humans. As Georges Florovsky writes, "The main emphasis of Duns Scotus was on the unconditional and primordial character of the divine decree of the incarnation, seen in the total perspective of creation."[20] For Scotus, the incarnation is much greater when it is seen as always part of God's intentions for creation, rather than a response to sin. Thus, Scotus famously disagreed with Augustine and Thomas Aquinas and affirmed that Christ would have become incarnate regardless of whether Adam sinned or not. Whereas for Aquinas "it is quite conceivable, in the abstract, to consider creation without redemption and incarnation, but not the incarnation without the redemption", for "Duns Scotus, who cannot conceive the creation without the incarnation" it is entirely possible to consider "the incarnation without the redemption".[21] The incarnation is about creation, not redemption. Scotus offers two interesting and compelling reasons for

---

[19]   E.g., Bogdan G. Bucur, "The Theological Reception of Dionysian Apophatism in the Christian East and West: Thomas Aquinas and Gregory Palamas", *The Downside Review* 125:439 (2007), pp. 131–46.

[20]   Georges Florovsky, *Creation and Redemption* (Belmont, MA: Norland Publishing Company, 1976), pp. 165–6.

[21]   Francis Klauder, *Aspects of the Thought of Teilhard de Chardin* (North Quincy, MA: The Christopher Publishing House, 1971), p. 80.

this: (a) if sin is the context in which the incarnation occurs, then Adam has been "rewarded" for his sin; and (b) the incarnation must be a more ontologically "primary" act than Adam's sin.

Scotus writes that the incarnation is the crowning glory of creation "because the glory of all creation is not as great in intensity as is the glory of Christ",[22] and so could not accept that such a crowning glory could be so dependent on human transgression. He continues that "the fall was not the cause of Christ's predestination. In fact, even if no man or angel had fallen . . . Christ would still have been predested this way".[23] It is easy to be sympathetic with Scotus' thinking. Such a divinely agapic outpouring was always the intention of creation, and nothing that humanity could do, including (perhaps somewhat ironically) *not* sinning, could frustrate that. Thus, Scotus writes that "it seems very absurd to claim that God would have left so great a work [i.e., the incarnation] undone on account of a good deed performed by Adam, such as Adam's not sinning".[24] It simply makes no sense for the quintessential divine act to be rendered unnecessary because Adam "failed" to sin. Surely, following Scotus' train of thought, it makes more sense to claim that Adam's sin made humanity unworthy of the incarnation, not that Adam's failure to sin would make him "too worthy" of it. Thus, Scotus writes that "the incarnation of Christ was not foreseen as something occasioned [by sin]", rather, "it was foreseen by God from all eternity".[25]

However, while Scotus argued for the primacy of Christ on the basis that it seems hardly logical to punish Adam's impeccability by withholding the most loving and intimate divine act, he also argued

---

22 John Duns Scotus, *Opus Parisiense, Lib III, d.7, q.4*, quoted in Maximillian Mary Dean, *A Primer on the Absolute Primacy of Christ: Blessed John Duns Scotus and the Franciscan Thesis* (New Bedford, MA: Franciscans of the Immaculate, 2006), p. 38.

23 John Duns Scotus, *Opus Parisiense, Lib III, d.7, q.4*, quoted in Dean, *A Primer on the Absolute Primacy of Christ*, p. 37.

24 John Duns Scotus, *Opus Parisiense, Lib III, d.7, q.4*, quoted in Dean, *A Primer on the Absolute Primacy of Christ*, p. 38.

25 John Duns Scotus, *Ordinatio, III, d.7, q.3*, quoted in Dean, *A Primer on the Absolute Primacy of Christ*, p. 35.

for it on the basis of the "ontological" priority of divine activity. For Scotus, the incarnation takes "ontological precedence" to Adam and Adam's actions, so the incarnation must occur regardless of Adam; if Christ is the "highest good of creation", then it does not follow that God would have predestined Adam to glory before Christ.[26] That is, this does not mean that the incarnation, or at least the "foreknowledge" of the incarnation, must *temporally* precede Adam's sin, but it means that the incarnation as a divine "act" is of far greater ontological precedence, so that God—who is atemporal—must have "predestined" the incarnation first, "before" Adam had a chance to sin. Scotus continues that "it [is not] likely that [God] predestined Adam to such good before He predestined Christ".[27] Duns Scotus argued that, in a "most orderly manner", God first "wills himself" and then the soul and glory of Christ "before any merit or demerit" on the part of humanity, "therefore, the entire process [of predestination] concerning Christ was foreseen prior to the fall and to all demerit".[28] Elsewhere, Scotus puts it differently, writing that "the positive act of the divine will regarding the predestined in common precedes all the acts of His will concerning either the reprobate or the

---

[26] Scotus appears to follow the Augustinian "dual-predestination" in that God "predestined some to glory" and "concerning some he had a negative act by not predestining" (Scotus, *Ordinatio*, III, d.7, q.3); there is no universal salvation. Christ's incarnation may not depend upon, or be caused by, the sin of Adam, but this does not mean that all will benefit from it. In many ways, this is far more stark and depressing than Augustine's version. At least for Augustine the predestination to damnation was the result of the fall, such that no one can complain of being predestined to damnation because "the rest of the race . . . deserve the (various degrees of) punishment they will receive" (H. Wheeler Robinson, *The Christian Doctrine of Man* (Edinburgh: T&T Clark, 1926), p. 190). Yet, for Scotus, the predestination "precedes" the fall, and thus seems to provoke the conclusion that God damns those God sees fit to without any reason.

[27] John Duns Scotus, *Ordinatio, III, d.7, q.3*, quoted in Dean, *A Primer on the Absolute Primacy of Christ*, p. 35.

[28] John Duns Scotus, *Opus Parisiense, Lib III, d.7, q.4*, quoted in Dean, *A Primer on the Absolute Primacy of Christ*, p. 38.

fall of anyone whatever"[29] and, similarly, that God wished humanity's "various degrees of perfection before He foresaw sin or the punishment for sinners".[30] Thus, God wills glory and grace "for every other soul . . . before He foresees those things which are the opposite of these habits [i.e. sin or damnation]"; and so the glory of Christ (i.e. the incarnation) is greater than the glory of redemption.[31]

For Duns Scotus, then, the incarnation must be primary for two reasons: (a) it makes no sense to reward Adam's not-sinning with the withholding of the "glory of Christ", which is greater than the "glory of all creation"; and (b) the "predestination of Christ" is more primary than the response to sin.[32] The first of these two reasons is more or less logically obvious; it requires no further analysis to explain why it is that Scotus finds it odd that Adam's sin should be rewarded and Adam's not-sinning should be punished. The second reason deserves more commentary, and it can be seen as being demanded by divine immutability, impassability, and aseity.

The rejection of redemption

Although she ultimately rejects the notion, Eleonore Stump also gives expression to the primacy of divine activity. Drawing on Reginald Garrigou-Lagrange, Stump writes that if God is immutable and unchanging then God cannot be acted upon (i.e., God is not passable), and so this seems to suggest that God cannot "will something because of something creatures do", which would seem to add "another sort of passivity in God, namely, in God's will". Thus, if "God's will is a cause of everything in creation", then God's will "does not depend on anything in creation".[33] That is, God cannot depend on anything that creatures do, nor

---

[29] John Duns Scotus, *Reportatio Barcinonensis, II, d.7, q.3*, quoted in Dean, *A Primer on the Absolute Primacy of Christ*, p. 40.

[30] John Duns Scotus, *Ordinatio, III, d.7, q.3*, quoted in Dean, *A Primer on the Absolute Primacy of Christ*, p. 35.

[31] John Duns Scotus, *Ordinatio, III, d.7, q.3*, quoted in Dean, *A Primer on the Absolute Primacy of Christ*, p. 34.

[32] See also Suh, *The Creation-Mediatorship of Jesus Christ*, pp. 23–6.

[33] Stump, *The God of the Bible and the God of the Philosophers*, pp. 24–5.

can God respond to anything that creatures do, because this ontologically relegates God to the level of creatures. It is not a case of saying that God "foresees" everything from eternity; this would be a sort of "temporal" independence, in which God does not have to depend on the temporal flow of cause, effect, and response because God transcends it.[34] Rather, what is referred to is an "ontological" independence; God cannot will something because of something creatures do because this relegates the ontological primacy of the divine act.[35] To use Thomas' language, God cannot will something because of something creatures do because this introduces potential into the divine act, when God is "*actus purus*".[36] It is clear how Garrigou-Lagrange's reasoning mirrors Scotus. If God is "pure actuality", with no potential whatsoever, and God is ontologically primary, then it is clear that these ideas are mutually supporting.[37]

Yet, Stump concludes, Garrigou-Lagrange's interpretation is ultimately incorrect and, while she affirms that God has no passivity/potential, she claims that this does not mean that God cannot respond to creatures

---

[34] Christopher Knight suggests something similar when he argues that God's act of creation has "fixed instructions" of "if/then" like statements (e.g., see Christopher C. Knight, "Divine Activity: A Neo-Byzantine Model", *International Journal for Philosophy of Religion* 58:3 (2005), p. 186; see also Christopher C. Knight, *The God of Nature: Incarnation and Contemporary Science* (Minneapolis, MN: Fortress Press, 2007), pp. 114–5; Paul Fiddes, *The Creative Suffering of God* (Oxford: Clarendon Press, 1988), p. 58; Delmas Lewis, "Timelessness and Divine Agency", *International Journal for Philosophy of Religion* 21:3 (1987), p. 144).

[35] See Gabriel Allegra, *My Conversations with Teilhard de Chardin on the Primacy of Christ* (Chicago, IL: Franciscan Herald Press, 1971), p. 94.

[36] Garrigou-Lagrange's rejection of all passivity in God can also be seen to support the interpretation of deism offered in Chapter 2. If there is no passivity in God—because God is "*actus purus*", or pure actuality—then God cannot "respond" to anything that occurs in time (including any "built in response", as Knight argues (see above)).

[37] Bishop Kallistos Ware was quoted making the same arguments in relation to the virgin birth in the previous chapter (Kallistos Ware, *The Orthodox Way* (Crestwood, NY: St. Vladimir's Seminary Press, 1979), p. 76).

or to act because of something that a creature does.[38] She reaches this conclusion because, as already acknowledged, according to her analysis, Thomas Aquinas allows for God to be both "*a*" being and the "ground of being". As God is *a* being, even though God is eternal and so God's acting does not "happen" either before or after anything, this does not prohibit God from acting as a result of something that a creature does. As a result, she believes that her interpretation is more faithful to Thomas Aquinas than is Garrigou-Lagrange's.

Whether or not Stump's or Garrigou-Lagrange's interpretation is the more faithful to Thomas' thought is not important here. What is important is that Garrigou-Lagrange's interpretation is more consistent with the theology presented in this book, and provides further support for Scotus' Christology. Nothing that God "does" is in response to, or dependent upon, anything that creatures do; divine activity is eternally ontologically primary. In this way—taking Garrigou-Lagrange and Scotus as the preferred Christology—the idea of "redemption"—i.e., that God "*responds*" to the sin of Adam through the incarnation as the re-creation and/or renewal of the universe, even if God "foresaw" that sin and "built in" a response to it in the eternal divine activity—must be wholly rejected.

Not only that, but increasing biological and geological investigation is leading theologians to become increasingly sure that there can be no historical event on which to pin the need for redemption in the first place. Evolution has made theologians rethink the idea of an original couple and this greatly affects the idea of whether humans (or any creatures) require salvation. This is further compounded by ongoing literary investigation of the Bible. Patricia Williams, drawing on the work of Harold Bloom, writes that "scholars agree that the idea that a fall occurs in Genesis 3 is found nowhere in the Hebrew scripture. Nor is it prominent in the New Testament."[39] Quite the contrary, Bloom "notes that the text explicitly says Adam and Eve become more like gods after they eat the fruit of the

---

[38]   Stump, *The God of the Bible and the God of the Philosophers*, pp. 93ff.

[39]   Patricia Williams, *Doing Without Adam and Eve* (Minneapolis, MN: Fortress Press, 2001), p. 38.

tree of knowledge".[40] This also shows that theologians need to rethink the idea that humanity is in need of redemption.

However, not only is the idea of redemption rightly dismissed on the grounds that philosophical (Scotus/Garrigou-Lagrange), biological (evolution), and literary (Bloom) endeavour has cast significant doubt on where such a need can or should be located and whether or not God could respond to such need, but there are significant *theological* problems with the idea as well. These problems are not new. Gregory of Nazianzus questioned to whom the sacrifice of the cross was addressed. If to the "Evil One", then "fire upon the outrage!", as this does nothing but legitimize the "tyranny" with which the "Evil One" held humanity and suspiciously points to a dualist outlook on the world in which history is a cosmic battle between good and evil. Yet, if it is addressed to the Father, then this seems to suggest that it was the Father by whom "we were being oppressed" and provokes the question of why God would have asked for such a sacrifice when God "would not receive even Isaac".[41]

It is easy to be sympathetic to Gregory's concerns here. Despite the fact that biblical theology and popular spirituality attribute evil and suffering in the world to evil spirits and/or Satan, it is clear that monotheistic theology cannot tolerate the idea that God is joined in the heavens by further "omnipotent" beings, or other "spirits" who can frustrate the will of God. Not only does this question the ontological primacy of God—and, as Gregory notes, legitimize Satan's tyranny—but it also seems to reduce God to a sort of Greek Pantheon god, whose activity in the world is in competition with the accidentally ordered activity of another equally powerful deity. It turns God into "*a*" being, who is in a subject/object relation with the world, rather than the essentially ordered "ground of being".

The second of Gregory's reasons also rightly rejects redemption, not for legitimizing Satan's tyranny, but for legitimizing God's "tyranny".

---

[40]   Williams, *Doing Without Adam and Eve*, p. 37.

[41]   Gregory of Nazianzus, "Oratio 45", in Philip Schaff and Henry Wace (eds), *Nicene and Post-Nicene Fathers Vol. 7* (New York, NY: The Christian Literature Company, 1894), 22; see also Paul Tillich, *Systematic Theology Vol. 2* (London: SCM Press, 1978), pp. 168–70.

John Macquarrie dismisses this latter picture (which Aulén called "Latin" theory) by criticizing its "tyrannical" view of God as deficient. Moreover, he contends that the idea of atonement to which it points is also deficient: atonement becomes escaping punishment, not new life.[42] Others have criticized it for similarly seeing God's activity in the context of "justice" rather than "love".[43]

Somewhat ironically, given the fact that Anselm is popularly seen as the characteristic example of the "Latin" view in which the incarnation is seen within the context of assuaging, appeasing, or satisfying divine wrath, Anselm has already been quoted as seemingly agreeing with Garrigou-Lagrange and Gregory of Nazianzus. Anselm is clear that God is not genuinely merciful, not because he is genuinely angry rather than merciful, but because the experience of mercy is *extrinsic* to the divine act. Thus, Anselm asks:

> How, then, are You merciful and not merciful, O Lord, unless it be that You are merciful in relation to us and not in relation to Yourself? In fact, You are [merciful] according to our way of looking at things and not according to Your way. For when You look upon us in our misery it is we who feel the effect of Your mercy, but You do not experience the feeling.[44]

God is not genuinely merciful; creatures experience God's act as mercy because of the particular context in which they experience that eternal immutable act. Thus, despite the fact that the "Latin" theory of

---

[42] John Macquarrie, *Jesus Christ in Modern Thought* (London: SCM Press, 1990), p. 401.

[43] See Gustaf Aulén, *Christus Victor* (London: SPCK, 1931), p. 130; Oliver Crisp, "Salvation and Atonement: On the Value and Necessity of the Work of Jesus Christ", in Ivor Davidson and Murray Rae (eds), *God of Salvation: Soteriology in Theological Perspective* (Farnham: Ashgate, 2011), p. 118; John Stott, *The Cross of Christ* (Leicester: InterVarsity Press, 1986), p. 115; F. Noel Palmer, *The Cross in History and Experience* (London: Church Book Room Press Ltd, 1949), pp. 19–20.

[44] Anselm, *Proslogion* 8.

atonement—which is more often than not characterized as a temporal God who first changes to become angry with creatures and then changes again to become assuaged—is ascribed to Anselm, it is in fact Anselm's quotation—taken as an example of the absence of a real relation—that shows most clearly why the "traditional theist" cannot subscribe to this theory of redemption either. God can neither be ontologically equal with any other being, such as the devil, nor does God demand restitution from humanity, nor can God change from angry to merciful.

Cross as creation

In this way, significantly, Scotus seems to be vindicated when he writes that while the crucifixion might be a fitting revelation of God's love, it is largely unnecessary. Scotus writes that:

> I hold, therefore, that whatever has been done by Christ for our Redemption became necessary only because it had been so decreed by the divine will, and thus it became necessary for Christ to suffer only by reason of that decree ... We are therefore greatly indebted to him. Indeed, since man could have been redeemed otherwise, but nevertheless he [Christ] chose to redeem him in that way by an act of his free will, we are greatly indebted to him, and even more so than if it had been necessary for us to be redeemed that way and not otherwise. I believe he did that chiefly to impel us to love him and because he wanted man to love him and because he wanted man to be more closely bound to God.[45]

Scotus seems clear on this issue. The cross is not necessary, it happens because God eternally decreed it to happen, but it could have been otherwise. Thus, Hans Urs von Balthasar writes that the Scotists "describe the Passion as an accidental addition in terms of the principle aim of the incarnation, the glorification of the Father by the Son who unites all

---

[45]   John Duns Scotus, *Opus Oxon., III, d.20, q.1*, quoted in Allegra, *My Conversations with Teilhard de Chardin on the Primacy of Christ*, p. 93.

things in himself".[46] Chul Won Suh also evidences this Scotist approach to redemption. He writes that, for Scotus:

> The suffering of Christ is not necessarily combined with redemption because of its own meritoriousness. His suffering and death is not the only way to salvation of man, but rather is one of many other possible ways. The divine acceptance of His suffering has made it meritorious; the suffering was not meritorious in itself.[47]

The suffering and cross of Christ are not necessary; "The merit of the suffering of Christ consists only in the fact that God has accepted it."[48] That Christ's suffering is redemptive is certainly "foreseen", but it is only an "afterthought" or of secondary importance. Thus, "we can say with Scotus, then, that the Incarnation itself is more meritorious than the suffering of Christ in His assumed nature".[49] This is a crucial statement, the force of which should not be lost: it is the incarnation that is absolutely paramount and necessary; the cross is a largely unnecessary extra.

However, while it is easy to follow Scotus' train of thought and understand why he reached the position that the cross is largely unnecessary, it is not the only way to express the logic of his position. In taking the position that he did—i.e., that the cross is largely unnecessary because what God did was achieved in the incarnation—Scotus implicitly accepts a connection between "atonement" and "cross". That is, for Scotus, the cross is essentially linked with the need for redemption, rather than with the incarnation. In this way, the need for a crucifixion is positively correlated with the need for redemption, so that, the more one downplays the need for redemption, the more one downplays the role of the crucifixion. In fact, one might speculate that it is possible to say that, for Scotus, if the need for redemption is completely rejected,

---

[46] Hans Urs von Balthasar, *Mysterium Paschale* (Edinburgh: T&T Clark, 1990), p. 11.

[47] Suh, *The Creation-Mediatorship of Jesus Christ*, p. 14.

[48] Suh, *The Creation-Mediatorship of Jesus Christ*, p. 27.

[49] Suh, *The Creation-Mediatorship of Jesus Christ*, p. 27.

then the crucifixion becomes completely superfluous; Christ could die in old age without any change to theology whatsoever. This, at least, is the logic behind Scotus' train of thought: no atonement, no cross. For Scotus, incarnation is always necessary, but crucifixion is not.

Yet, this seems to have the connection in the wrong place. Rather than seeing the connection between "atonement" and "cross", one should see the connection between "incarnation" and "cross". In this way, the crucifixion should be positively correlated with the incarnation, not "atonement", or, better, the cross is an essential "part" of the incarnation: there can be no incarnation without a cross. That is, the crucifixion does not achieve "atonement", rather it achieves whatever it is that the incarnation achieves and is an important part of it. If the incarnation is always necessary, then the cross is always a necessary part of the incarnation.

To put this differently, is the cross necessary as part of the incarnation or is it necessary as part of atonement? Or, differently again, does the cross happen because of the incarnation or because of atonement? If the cross is essentially linked with atonement, then the crucifixion takes place only in a world in which atonement is required; it recognizes the possibility of an incarnation without a crucifixion (i.e., in a world in which there is no fall, Christ will still come but not be crucified). However, if the cross is essentially linked with the incarnation, then the crucifixion takes place in every world in which the incarnation happens, regardless of whether it requires salvation or not; it recognizes the impossibility of an incarnation without a crucifixion. Whatever the motive is for the incarnation, and whatever it achieves, the crucifixion is an integral, essential part of it. There is no incarnation without crucifixion, not because the incarnation is the means to the crucifixion, but because the crucifixion is part of the incarnation. Thus, the crucifixion is not an added extra, but is precisely what God does as part of the creative incarnation. The whole life of Jesus is taken as the conditions of "effectiveness" and the motive of those "conditions" is "the glorification of creation".

Thus, the cross is not God's redemptive response to sin; the cross is part of God's "act" of creation in the incarnation. Ilia Delio writes that "the Incarnation represents not a divine response to a human need for salvation but instead the divine intention from all eternity to raise human nature to the highest point of glory by uniting it with divine nature".[50] Torstein Theodor Tollefsen agrees: "The historical incarnation is God's eternal purpose . . . motivated by the divine will to communion".[51] What Christ does in the incarnation is not redemption, but creation. Ilia Delio continues that:

> Christ's redemptive work relates to the overcoming of sin, but it does so in a way that brings God's creative action in the world to completion. This notion of redemption-completion, underscoring the primacy of Christ, allows for a broader view of salvation, one focused not on sin but on the primacy of love. In this respect, redemption is creative; it is that healing of the brokenness within humanity and Creation that enables the cosmic process to be completed, in which completion itself is a dynamic process of continuous Creation that is oriented toward the new Creation. Redemption, therefore, is not being "saved from" but rather being made "whole for" the healing and wholeness of God's Creation, and this wholeness is ultimately the transformation of created reality through the unitive power of God's creative love.[52]

Whether one agrees with Delio that the language of "redemption" can be retained as long as one significantly redefines what is meant by "redemption" or whether one completely rejects the language of

---

[50] Ilia Delio, "Revisiting the Franciscan Doctrine of Christ", *Theological Studies* 64 (2003), p. 9.

[51] Torstein Theodor Tollefsen, *Activity and Participation in Late Antique and Early Christian Thought* (Oxford: Oxford University Press, 2012), p. 148. The implication is that without Christ, God is "not with us", and if God is "not with us", then the ontological relationship on which all creatures depend for their being and existence is not present (see Steven Baldner and William Carroll (tr.), *Aquinas on Creation* (Toronto: Pontifical Institute of Mediaeval Studies, 1997), p. 16 and Andrew Davison, *Participation in God* (Cambridge: Cambridge University Press, 2019), p. 26).

[52] Delio, "Revisiting the Franciscan Doctrine of Christ", p. 18.

"redemption" altogether is largely irrelevant here. The point is that God comes in the incarnation to create.

However, this book has argued that creation has a particular meaning: an eternal, ontological hierarchy/relation with God. If that is the case, then to say that the cross is "creative" in the theological sense of the word—i.e., the cross is creation rather than origins—then the cross must be that in which and through which creatures participate in God; the cross must "enable" and/or "facilitate" the participation of all creatures in God.

Kenosis

If the cross is to be seen within the wider paradigm of the incarnation, so that it is seen as being inherently linked with the incarnation, not atonement, then there must be a fundamental connection between the cross and incarnation. Many theologians, while not taking the specific path that this chapter takes, have suggested that it is *kenosis* that provides this fundamental connection between the incarnation and the cross. That is, both incarnation and cross are examples of *kenosis*.

There are two ways of doing this.[53] Some, such as Michael Gorman, see the incarnation and crucifixion as two distinct "instances" of the same "type" of act, so that "the pre-existent Christ's self-emptying, self-lowering incarnation/enslavement" and "the human Jesus' self-humiliation, self-lowering obedience to the point of death by crucifixion" are "parallel action".[54] Others, such as Ferdinand Prat, see the incarnation and crucifixion as two "parts" of the same act, so that "after the incarnation, the human will completes the self-stripping; it accepts the death on the

---

[53] Importantly, these are the same two ways that were identified in the last chapter as being exemplified by Duns Scotus and eastern theology on the one hand, and Athanasius and Thomas Aquinas on the other. That the last chapter dismissed both and argued for a third is illustrative of the conclusion to this chapter as well.

[54] Michael Gorman, *Inhabiting the Cruciform God* (Grand Rapids, MI: William B. Eerdmans, 2009), p. 17.

cross".[55] Celia Deane-Drummond, too, writes that "Christ's descent into Hell can be compared with the first descent in the womb of the Virgin Mary" and thus is "kenotic self-emptying taken to its ultimate extent. In other words, it takes the incarnation to a new depth."[56] For Prat and Deane-Drummond, the incarnation and the crucifixion are not "parallel" or two distinct instances of the same "type" of act; the incarnation and the crucifixion together form the one act. Christopher Mooney, following this train of thought, concludes that this means that "the incarnation, therefore, is already redemptive in a true sense of the word, since it involves a 'kenosis into matter'".[57]

It is clear that such a connection is discernible from Paul's epistle to the Philippians. In what is commonly called the "Philippian hymn", Paul describes what Christ does as "*kenosis*"—that is, "empties"—and, importantly, Paul himself connects this *kenosis* with both the incarnation and crucifixion. Gordon Fee, for example, notes that the language and structure of the two halves of the Philippian hymn directly mirror each other, indicating that they were intended to be identical acts; what happens in one, happens in the other.

Though he was in the form of God, [he] did not regard equality with God as something to be exploited, but emptied himself, taking the form of a slave,	And being found in human form,
being born in human likeness.	he humbled himself and became obedient to the point of death— even death on a cross.[58]

---

[55] Prat, *The Theology of St. Paul: Vol. 1*, p. 319.

[56] Deane-Drummond, *Christ and Evolution*, p. 148.

[57] Christopher Mooney, *Teilhard de Chardin and The Mystery of Christ* (London: Collins, 1966), p. 122.

[58] Philippians 2:6–8.

The "emptied himself" and "being born in human likeness" are directly mirrored by "humbled himself" and "death on a cross".[59]

That the word "*kenosis*" can be used to describe what Christ does in *both* the incarnation *and* the crucifixion, and that such a connection can be used to support the idea that, at the very least, these are two instances of the same act, if not two "parts" of the very same single act, is beyond dispute. However, what is precisely meant by the word "*kenosis*" requires further exposition. That is, it is clear that the incarnation and the cross are both "emptyings", but what exactly does it mean for Christ to "empty"?

Kenosis: An historical survey

Quite clearly, *kenosis*, as a Christological doctrine, has biblical and historical authority. However, the term was very seldom used when discussing either the incarnation or the crucifixion until relatively recently.[60] In the nineteenth century, when the term was first used with a very particular and technical meaning, its purpose was to deal with the problem of the apparent contradiction that the Chalcedonian definition contained. Theologians such as German Lutheran Gottfried Thomasius and English Anglican Charles Gore were concerned that the Chalcedonian definition meant that if Christ had to be God and human simultaneously, then Christ also had to have both divine and human attributes simultaneously, which implied a contradiction. It meant, for example, that God was both omniscient and limited in knowledge, or, to put it bluntly, that Christ both knows every single datum and does not know every single datum, which would be incoherent. Likewise for power,

---

59   Gordon Fee, "St Paul and the Incarnation: A Reassessment of the Data", in Stephen Davis, Daniel Kendall, and Gerald O'Collins (eds), *The Incarnation* (Oxford: Oxford University Press, 2002), pp. 80–1.

60   For a history of *kenosis*, see Robert Stackpole, *The Incarnation: Rediscovering Kenotic Christology* (Langley, British Columbia: The Chartwell Press, 2019); C. Stephen Evans (ed.), *Exploring Kenotic Christology* (Oxford: Oxford University Press, 2006); Isaak Dorner, *Divine Immutability: A Critical Reconsideration* (Minneapolis, MN: Fortress Press, 1994), pp. 49–81; David Williams, *Kenōsis of God* (Bloomington, IN: iUniverse, 2009).

it supposedly meant that Christ could both do everything it was possible (or impossible) to do, and that Christ could not do everything that it was possible to do. These theologians postulated *kenosis*, and argued that the contradiction is solved by removing the "simultaneously" element from the Chalcedonian definition.[61] Christ was both God and human, but Christ "emptied" himself of those divine attributes and so did not possess those divine attributes for the period in which he was a human on earth. Thus, David Brown writes that whereas the Chalcedonian theory is "the view that Jesus was simultaneously God and man", *kenosis* is "the view that God became man and subsequently became God again".[62] C. Stephen Evans understands *kenosis* as describing "a being [that] was omnipotent and omniscient, temporarily lost these properties, and then regained them"[63] so that Stephen Davis, therefore, writes that the idea of the "logos as kenotically incarnate was only true from about 4 BC until about 29 AD, and indeed is now no longer true".[64] Accordingly, Brown continues that acceptance of a *kenotic* theory of the incarnation means abandoning divine immutability, atemporality, and impassibility.[65]

It might also be necessary for Christ to have relinquished divine attributes, not only so as to solve the apparent contradiction these theologians thought they saw in the Chalcedonian definition, but also for Christ to be truly human; one cannot be *truly* and *genuinely* human if one also has omnipotence and omniscience. Thus, in order to be "fully human" coherently, Christ had to have relinquished or divested himself of certain divine attributes. Thus, Charles Gore writes,

---

[61] This book acknowledged the same problem in the previous chapter but argued that it occurs because of a misunderstanding of what "omnipotence" or "omniscience" mean, not that the "simultaneously" has to be sacrificed.

[62] David Brown, *The Divine Trinity* (London: Duckworth, 1985), pp. 102–3.

[63] C. Stephen Evans, "The Self-Emptying of Love: Some Thoughts on Kenotic Christology", in Stephen Davis, Daniel Kendall, and Gerald O'Collins (eds), *The Incarnation* (Oxford: Oxford University Press, 2002), p. 254.

[64] Stephen Davis, "The Metaphysics of Kenosis", in Jonathan Hill and Anna Marmodoro (eds), *The Metaphysics of the Incarnation* (Oxford: Oxford University Press, 2011), pp. 118–19.

[65] Brown, *The Divine Trinity*, p. 257.

"in order for a true humanity to take shape in the Incarnate Logos a limitation of consciousness must take place; this is the only way a really human experience is made possible".[66] For these English and German theologians, it was logically impossible to be both God and human simultaneously and so Christ had to literally give up his divinity in order to assume humanity.

Perhaps as expected, commentators have understood this idea differently. Gottfried Thomasius, concerned with the same issues that led others to affirm *kenosis*, differentiated between essential divine attributes and non-essential divine attributes. Thomasius argues that what are called "omni" attributes—such as omnipotence or omniscience—are non-essential divine attributes because they require a creation over which God can wield those attributes, and creation is not "essential". Since omnipotence requires there to be a universe over which God can exercise that omnipotence, and creation is not necessary (it is possible for God not to create), then omnipotence is not an essential attribute because there is a possible world (i.e., one in which God did not create) "in which God is not omnipotent".[67] For Thomasius, *kenosis* involves the emptying of these non-essential divine attributes only. Others argue instead for what David Williams calls *krypsis*—the Greek for "hidden", as opposed to *kenosis* ("empty")—in which Christ does not relinquish the divine attributes, but instead simply does not exercise them.[68] Thus, there are a spectrum of ideas that come under the heading of "*kenosis*", which, one way or another, understand it as God giving something up, and it was the appearance that Chalcedon contained a contradiction that led them to embrace this idea.

---

[66] Charles Gore, *The Incarnation of the Son of God* (London: John Murray, 1891), p. 150.

[67] Gottfried Thomasius, "Christ's Person and Work Part II: The Person of the Mediator", in Claude Welch (ed.), *God and Incarnation in Mid-Nineteenth Century German Theology* (Oxford: Oxford University Press, 1965), pp. 25–101.

[68] David Williams, "Kenosis and the Nature of the Persons in the Trinity", *Koers* 69:4 (2004), p. 628; see also William Walker, *The Incarnation and Kenosis* (Self-published, 2015).

However, it is not clear that the Chalcedonian definition *does* contain a contradiction. First, as has been keenly argued in the previous two chapters, to suppose that "omniscience" and "limited knowledge" are two instances of the same "thing"—the former a "maximal" or "perfect" instance of the latter—fundamentally treats God and creatures as univocal. If "omniscience" and "limited knowledge" are deemed to be a contradiction, then one is defining omniscience as an infinite or unlimited version of the knowledge that creatures have. Yet, "omniscience", as it has already been suggested, is not about the possession of data, but is that in which each datum has intelligibility. As noted in the previous chapter, the fact that Christ is both omniscient and limited in knowledge only means that Christ "possessed" a particular set of data (consonant with his being alive in first century Palestine), and that Christ was also that in which all data is intelligible. Thus, the contradiction that is supposed to exist in the Chalcedonian definition does not exist. Christ can be limited in knowledge and omniscient *simultaneously* without contradiction.

Second, the suggestion that Christ can be God, then human, then God again, inherently introduces time into the divine life. As expounded in the previous chapter, the "pre-existence" of Christ is not a temporal designation indicating that the Son experienced incorporeal existence at some "time"; rather, it is an ontological designation indicating that while the Son is eternally "linked" with or "related" to the historical Jesus this does not exhaust the Son's ontology. Thus, the incarnation is not an *event* that happens in the life of Christ, but an ontological *relation*. Hence, in precisely the same way that the Big Bang and creation are not coincident, so the birth of Christ and the incarnation are in no way coincident; one is an "origin" and the other is "an ontological relationship—a relationship in the order of being—with no reference to temporality".[69] If the incarnation is not an *event*, then it makes no sense to talk about a "before" and "after" of it.

Thus, while *kenosis* has been offered as an alternative to Chalcedon, the problem for which it is proposed as a solution is not a problem. However, *kenosis* need not be understood as a literal emptying of the divine "nature" or "attributes", and so there are some who see *kenosis* not

---

Baldner and Carroll, *Aquinas on Creation*, p. 16.

as being an alternative to Chalcedon, but as being a complement to it, i.e., a way of interpreting what Chalcedon means. Hilary of Poitiers, for example, writes of the incarnation that God "contract[s] himself even to conception, to the cradle, to infancy; without departing from the power of God".[70] More recently, Karl Barth criticizes Lutheran theologians (such as Thomasius), and understands *kenosis* to consist "in a renunciation of His being in the form of God *alone*".[71] Christ, Barth continues, "was not committed to any such 'only'", so his self-emptying is not a "ceasing to be Himself as man", but is a "taking upon Himself to be Himself in a way quite other".[72] Christ does not divest himself of being God; he divests himself of being *only* God. Thus, Bruce McCormack notes that, for Barth, "*kenosis* ... is by addition and not by subtraction. Nothing proper to deity is 'left behind' when the 'Son' takes on the form of a servant. To put off the 'form of God' is simply to add the 'form of a servant'".[73] *Kenosis* is the idea that God takes on another way of being, not an emptying of certain attributes.

Sergei Bulgakov also defends a Chalcedonian definition of *kenosis* in his book *The Lamb of God*. He writes that "in becoming man, God does not stop being God; even after descending from heaven, he remains in heaven".[74] Bulgakov recognizes the contradiction in claiming that "without ceasing to be God, God ceases to be God",[75] but nevertheless affirms this interpretation. Moreover, Bulgakov connects the *kenosis* of the Son with the Son's intertrinitarian relations, so that "Sonhood is

---

[70] Hilary of Poitiers, "On the Trinity", in Henry Bettenson (ed.), *The Later Christian Fathers* (Oxford: Oxford University Press, 1982), p. 50.

[71] Karl Barth, *Church Dogmatics: Study Edition* (Edinburgh: T&T Clark, 2009), IV.1, pp. 59, 1 (italics added).

[72] Barth, *Church Dogmatics*, IV.I, 59, 1.

[73] Bruce McCormack, "Karl Barth's Christology as a Resource for a Reformed Version of Kenoticism", *International Journal of Systematic Theology* 8:3 (2006), p. 248.

[74] Sergei Bulgakov, *The Lamb of God* (Grand Rapids, MI: William B. Eerdmans, 2008), p. 220; see also pp. 225–9.

[75] Bulgakov, *The Lamb of God*, p. 221.

already *eternal kenosis*".[76] *Kenosis* then becomes for Bulgakov the way that "being" is "passed on"; the *kenosis* of the Son from the Father is how the *Logos* receives "being" from the Father. This seems to imply that the *kenosis* is, likewise, how Christ mediates that being from the Father to creatures. As Bulgakov continues:

> What is needed is a mediation, an ontological bridge to effect this union [between God and creatures]—a ladder on which this ascent–descent can be accomplished. The conventional opinion is that there can be no mediation between God and the creature ... But in reality there is such a mediation between God and the creature ... Sophia, the true wisdom of God, eternal and creaturely.[77]

This "sophia", perhaps *the* central concept that ties Bulgakov's theology together, Bulgakov identifies with the Son.[78] This is nothing more than what was argued in the previous chapter regarding Christ as creator through mediation. Crucially, then, he writes that not only is *kenosis* compatible with Chalcedon, but that without *kenosis*, Chalcedon leads to "either doceticism or to monophysitism".[79] For Bulgakov, *kenosis* is not just one possible way of complementing Chalcedon; *kenosis* is the "fundamental idea tacitly implied by the Chalcedonian dogma".[80]

Hans Urs von Balthasar also defends a Chalcedonian interpretation of *kenosis*, and draws on Hilary of Poitiers, Karl Barth, and Sergei Bulgakov in doing so. In the preface to *Mysterium Paschale*, von Balthasar criticizes the tendency in modern theology to either deny the impassibility and immutability of God or (the other extreme) reduce the suffering of Christ only to his human nature, which he argues would lead to Nestorianism or Monophysitism. "The only way which might avoid the two opposed and incompatible extremes" (of divine mutability and Nestorianism) is to

---

76 Bulgakov, *The Lamb of God*, p. 99.

77 Bulgakov, *The Lamb of God*, pp. 200–1.

78 Bulgakov, *The Lamb of God*, p. 224.

79 Bulgakov, *The Lamb of God*, p. 236.

80 Bulgakov, *The Lamb of God*, p. 239.

relate the *kenosis* of the Son to the "eternal 'super-Kenosis'" of the Father. What is absolutely crucial about this (although von Balthasar does not add any further exposition or analysis) is that von Balthasar explicitly links this with creation. He writes that "the inner-divine processions are the condition of the possibility for a creation", by which he means that the "super-*kenosis*" of the Father—the procession of the Son from the Father—is that which makes creation—by implication, the *kenosis* of the Son of God—possible.[81] It is important to ensure that the procession of the Son is different from creation (creatures participate in God, but the Son *is* God), but there is a sense here in which the Son receives being from the Father through *kenosis* and the Son then "passes on" being through the *kenosis* of the incarnation.[82]

This means (as already noted in relation to Barth) that *kenosis* is actually about "addition" rather than "subtraction". Sarah Coakley writes that "one could more truly say that kenosis involves gain rather than loss".[83] Coakley takes exception to what she sees as a narrowness in feminist theology, which criticizes *kenosis*, along with most theologies of the cross, because they see it as legitimizing patriarchal societies that expect women (and other marginalized members of society) to be subservient. Christ's own submission to authority, these criticisms claim, has given those in

---

[81]   von Balthasar, *Mysterium Paschale*, pp. vii–ix; see also Hans Urs von Balthasar, *Theo-Drama II: Dramatis Personae: Man in God* (San Francisco, CA: Ignatius Press, 1992), p. 154; Aristotle Papanikolaou, "Person, *Kenosis* and Abuse: Hans Urs von Balthasar and Feminist Theologies in Conversation", *Modern Theology* 19:1 (2003), p. 48; Graham Ward, "Kenosis: Death, Discourse and Resurrection", in Lucy Gardner, David Moss, Ben Quash and Graham Ward (eds), *Balthasar at the End of Modernity* (Edinburgh: T&T Clark, 1999), p. 45.

[82]   See Giles Emery, "Trinity and Creation", in Rik Van Nieuwenhove and Joseph Wawrykow (eds), *The Theology of Thomas Aquinas* (Notre Dame, IN: University of Notre Dame Press, 2005), p. 59; there are also significant links with Pseudo-Dionysius (see below).

[83]   Sarah Coakley, "Kenosis: Theological Meaning and Gender Connotations", in John Polkinghorne (ed.), *The Work of Love: Creation as Kenosis* (Grand Rapids, MI: William B. Eerdmans, 2001), p. 195.

power a way of convincing those who don't have power to accept their lot in the spirit of cultivating spiritual treasures. However, while there is certainly some legitimacy to these criticisms, Coakley contends that these feminists are too narrow and one-dimensional. Against those who see in *kenosis* an unhelpful legitimizing of (especially female) submission to (mainly male) abusive power, Coakley argues that *kenosis* need not refer to a divestment, but can be seen as a "making room for the other".[84] Coakley connects this sense of *kenosis* to earlier ideas that see *kenosis* not as a "divestment" but as a revelation of "power-in-vulnerability".[85] This sort of "vulnerability", she argues, "is not about asking for unnecessary and unjust suffering . . . nor is it a 'self-abnegation'", but is a "special self-emptying" that "is not a negation of the self, but the place of the self's transformation and expansion into God".[86] Thus, Coakley provides yet further evidence that it is possible to understand *kenosis* as being complementary to Chalcedon, rather than opposing it; it is possible to understand "emptying" as a way of explaining how Christ takes on *another* nature, not his divestment of one.

In this way, Edwin Chr. van Driel must be entirely incorrect when he claims that there is a distinction between the "classical theologian" who "thinks about the Incarnation in terms of an *addition*" and the *kenotic* theologian who "understands the Incarnation in terms of a *divestment*".[87] While this might be true of Thomasius, Gore et al., it is definitely not true of Barth, Bulgakov, von Balthasar, and Coakley. *Kenosis* is not about "emptying"; it is about "making room for the other"; it is about "addition", not "subtraction". When Chalcedon is seen through this sense of *kenosis*, *kenosis* becomes a "mechanism" for *how* God "*becomes*" incarnate, not

---

84   Sarah Coakley, "*Kenosis* and Subversion: On the Repression of 'Vulnerability' in Christian Feminist Writing", in Daphne Hampson (ed.), *Swallowing a Fishbone: Feminist Theologians Debate Christianity* (London: SPCK, 1996), pp. 107–9.

85   Coakley, "*Kenosis* and Subversion", p. 110.

86   Coakley, "*Kenosis* and Subversion", p. 108.

87   Edwin Chr. van Driel, "The Logic of Assumption", in C. Stephen Evans (ed.), *Exploring Kenotic Christology* (Vancouver: Regent College Publishing, 2006), pp. 265–6.

a "mode" of being incarnate. To put it differently, for Thomasius et al., *kenosis* is not a way of God becoming incarnate, but is a condition that Christ must meet before he can become incarnate. However, for Bulgakov et al., *kenosis* is the way that God takes on another nature. *Kenosis* is how Christ "makes room" for the created nature, not a solution to the (apparent) contradictions in claiming that Christ was both God and creature. To borrow Marmodoro and Hill's distinction,[88] *Kenosis* for Thomasius, Gore et al. understands "emptying" as "conditions that Christ had to meet in order to be able to save", as a condition that Christ had to meet before he could become incarnate, whereas, for Barth, Bulgakov, von Balthasar, and Coakley, "emptying" "was what salvation consisted in"; it is what the incarnation consists of.

In this way, one might claim that Thomasius and the non-Chalcedonians are using *kenosis* as an adjective, that Christ can only be incarnate in a *kenotic* way; Christ assumes a human nature, but that assumption can only occur after a divestment of divinity. On the other hand, Bulgakov and the Chalcedonians are using *kenosis* as a verb: *kenosis* is not a condition that must be met before an assumption can take place, but is the mechanism through which Christ assumes. For Bulgakov and the Chalcedonians, the created nature of Christ is the "*effect*" of *kenosis*, *not* how the divine and created natures are related *after* the incarnation (i.e., once Christ is human). In other words, drawing on the physical theory of the incarnation, the *kenosis* is how "contact" takes place. Or, as Ian McFarland implies (although he does not refer to *kenosis*), *kenosis* is not the relation "between two *predefined realities*", but rather describes how "the distinction between Creator and creature is itself established".[89] *Kenosis* is not a relation between two predefined realities—one of which must be divested before the other can be assumed—but is the way in which one of those realities is *created* (remembering that creation is not the *origin* of one of those realities, but the dependence of one of those realities on God for its being), and it is created in the person of Christ.

---

[88]   Marmodoro and Hill, "Modeling the Metaphysics of the Incarnation", pp. 99–100.

[89]   Ian McFarland, *The Word Made Flesh: A Theology of the Incarnation* (Louisville, KY: Westminster John Knox Press, 2019), p. 12 (italics added).

Between these two understandings of *kenosis* (one non-Chalcedonian and the other Chalcedonian), therefore, is a distinction between accidentally ordered and essentially ordered; the first sees *kenosis* as introducing a change, the second sees *kenosis* as a description of the hierarchical dependence of one on the other.

Kenosis and divine activity

The theologians considered in the previous section were expounding *kenosis* as a Christological doctrine; *kenosis* explains something that happens to Christ. However, there are some who apply *kenosis* more widely than this Christological context and see it as a more general theological doctrine about divine activity.

If some theologians have identified a fundamental or "typal" identity between the incarnation and the cross in that both can be described by *kenosis*, then—drawing on the conclusion of the last chapter that there is a typal identity between incarnation and creation—it is possible to extend this identity to include creation as well. Others have noted this connection and have explicitly identified *kenosis* with creation. Celia Deane-Drummond, for example, writes that "there are similarities between the incarnation and the creation of the world in that both are acts of condescension", the difference between them being that in creation the "logos is imprinted in the world in a general sense", whereas in the incarnation the logos becomes "in-humanized".[90] David Williams also sees *kenosis* as a connection between creation and incarnation,[91] and, in a similar way, Javier Monserrat also connects the "kenosis of Christ" with the "kenosis of God".[92]

That one can move from particular comments about the work of the Son in the incarnation (and the cross) to general comments about the work of God is a generally accepted and well-trodden move. Denis Edwards writes that "what we know about the nature of God comes from

---

[90]   Deane-Drummond, *Christ and Evolution*, pp. 114–15.

[91]   Williams, *Kenōsis of God*, p. 95.

[92]   Javier Monserrat, "Kenosis: Towards a New Theology of Science", *Pensamiento* 63:238 (2007), p. 657.

the Christ event".[93] Michael Gorman, likewise, writes that since "Christ crucified is the image and glory of God", so "God is like Christ crucified",[94] and that "to be fully human is to be Christlike and thus Godlike in this kenotic and cruciform sense".[95] Gregory Collins also writes that "[Christ's] entire life was marked by a kenotic movement from his descent into the womb of the Virgin through his baptism, ministry of mercy, betrayal, humiliation, crucifixion and burial". Collins continues that "th[is] *kenosis* of Christ on Calvary is a window opened out by God, revealing the *kenosis* going on eternally 'within' the life of the Holy Trinity. Christ's earthly cross points us beyond itself towards the 'cross' of undying love set up eternally within the heart of God."[96] Bulgakov and von Balthasar have made similar comments. Thus, if *kenosis* is an accurate description of what is happening in the incarnation and the cross, then it must be an accurate description of what God does, particularly in creation.

John Polkinghorne's volume *The Work of Love: Creation as Kenosis* is another example of understanding creation as *kenosis*.[97] The authors that contribute to this volume (whilst they have important disagreements) seem to agree with the idea that *kenosis* as a doctrine of creation does not describe *how* God creates but, rather, it explains how the world can possess genuine freedom *after* it has been created. Thus, the authors that contribute to this volume understand *kenosis* in exactly the same way that the "non-Chalcedonians" understood *kenosis*: that is, just as

---

93   Denis Edwards, *How God Acts: Creation, Redemption, and Special Divine Action* (Minneapolis, MN: Fortress Press, 2010), p. 64, p. 50; see also Monserrat, "Kenosis: Towards a New Theology of Science", p. 657; Stephen Pardue, "Kenosis and its Discontents: Towards an Augustinian Account of Divine Humility", *Scottish Journal of Theology* 65:3 (2012), p. 280.

94   Gorman, *Inhabiting the Cruciform God*, pp. 120–1.

95   Gorman, *Inhabiting the Cruciform God*, p. 36.

96   Gregory Collins, *Meeting Christ in His Mysteries* (Dublin: The Columba Press, 2010), pp. 284–5.

97   See also Thomas Senor, "Drawing on Many Traditions: An Ecumenical Kenotic Christology", in Jonathan Hill and Anna Marmodoro (eds), *The Metaphysics of the Incarnation* (Oxford: Oxford University Press, 2011), pp. 109–10.

the "non-Chalcedonians" saw omnipotence and limited power as a contradiction and so postulated *kenosis* as a way of relating the divine and human natures in Christ *after* the incarnation, so the authors that contribute to this volume see omnipotence and creaturely freedom as a contradiction and so postulate *kenosis* as a way of relating divine providence/governance of the world and creaturely freedom *after* creation. Again paraphrasing Marmodoro and Hill, *kenosis* becomes for them a "condition that [God] had to meet in order [for creatures to have genuine freedom]".[98] That these theologians are understanding creation as "origin"—so that it is coherent to talk about "*after* creation"—is also pertinent.

For example, in John Polkinghorne's essay within that volume, he offers a *kenotic* divine activity as an alternative to a Thomistic divine activity, clearly setting *kenosis* opposite classic ideas of God as impassible and immutable.[99] Creatures have genuine freedom because God freely relinquishes God's power to act in the world, or at the very least freely chooses not to wield it. Drawing on the concerns put forward by Process Theologians, Polkinghorne reiterates the concern that the Thomistic God is "so remote and insulated from creation as to put in question the fundamental Christian conviction that 'God is love'".[100] Thus, Polkinghorne writes that "while all that happens is permitted by God's general providence, not all that happens is in accordance with God's will

---

[98] Marmodoro and Hill, "Modeling the Metaphysics of the Incarnation", pp. 99–100.

[99] See also Craig Boyd and Aaron Cobb, "The Causality Distinction, Kenosis, and a Middle Way: Aquinas and Polkinghorne on Divine Action", *Theology and Science* 7:4 (2009), pp. 391–406; in a similar way, Javier Monserrat argues that "the God in whom it is possible to believe from current scientific culture is a kenotic God" (Monserrat, "Kenosis: Towards a New Theology of Science", p. 638), indicating that science is possible because God refrains from acting.

[100] John Polkinghorne, "Kenotic Creation and Divine Action", in John Polkinghorne (ed.), *The Work of Love: Creation as Kenosis* (Grand Rapids, MI: William B. Eerdmans, 2001), p. 92.

or brought about by special divine providence".[101] Rather, as the history of evolution shows, God allows creation the space to "make itself".

In the same work, Arthur Peacocke and Jürgen Moltmann offer similar interpretations of *kenosis*. However, both their and Polkinghorne's contributions appear to suffer from the same problem that this book has argued plagues Process Theology (see Chapter 1). That is, all three seem to understand divine activity as univocal with creaturely activity and so not only see them in competition with each other—and so, like the non-Chalcedonians, need a theory of *kenosis* to explain how they are not in competition with each other—but also see God "sharing" in the suffering of creatures in the evolutionary processes of the world, and so God suffers in the same way that creatures suffer.[102] God, they argue (as did Lucas, Plantinga, and others) must exhibit those capacities that humans do, or God is only a "deistic bystander" and not worthy of worship. That Polkinghorne explicitly contrasts his *kenotic* God with the God of "classic theology"[103] shows quite clearly that he does not subscribe to the God for which this book has apologized. In this way, Nicole Hoggard Creegan suggests that *kenosis* becomes a "partial answer to theodicy: God's temporary and temporal absence accounts for evil".[104]

For these theologians, *kenosis* as divine absence/limitation is an alternative to traditional concepts of divine activity in precisely the same way that *kenosis* as absence/limitation is an alternative to traditional

---

[101] Polkinghorne, "Kenotic Creation and Divine Action", p. 102.

[102] Arthur Peacocke, "The Cost of New Life", in John Polkinghorne (ed.), *The Work of Love: Creation as Kenosis* (Grand Rapids, MI: William B. Eerdmans, 2001), p. 38; see also Jürgen Moltmann, "God's *Kenosis* in the Creation and Consummation of the World", in John Polkinghorne (ed.), *The Work of Love: Creation as Kenosis* (Grand Rapids, MI: William B. Eerdmans, 2001), pp. 137–51.

[103] See also Keith Ward, "Cosmos and *Kenosis*", in John Polkinghorne (ed.), *The Work of Love: Creation as Kenosis* (Grand Rapids, MI: William B. Eerdmans, 2001), p. 152.

[104] Nicola Hoggard Creegan, "A Christian Theology of Evolution and Participation, *Zygon: Journal of Religion and Science* 42:2 (2007), p. 502.

interpretations of Chalcedon.[105] Thus, there are precisely the same problems with Polkinghorne, Peacocke, and Moltmann as there with Thomasius, Gore, and others. Both groups of theologians (a) suppose that omniscience or omnipotence is understood as a "maximal" or "perfect" version of the knowledge and power that creatures possess; (b) suppose that God is omnipotent, then not omnipotent, and then (supposedly) omnipotent again, i.e., that God is temporal and mutable; (c) suppose that creation is an origin; and (d) drawing on (a), (b) and (c), presume (whether explicitly or not) "theistic personalism" (i.e., they suppose that God is a person who does things, rather than the "ground of being"). Both groups of theologians see *kenosis* as an adjective that describes the relation that exists between two persons: God can only act in a *kenotic* way, otherwise creaturely freedom is impossible. For both, *kenosis* is the origin of an accidentally ordered "cause of motion" after which creatures have freedom or Christ can be human. Yet, for those who see creation as an ontological relation and *kenosis* as an interpretation of Chalcedon, none of these problems occur. Rather, *kenosis* is an essentially ordered "cause of being" through which that which is ontologically contingent depends on what is ontologically necessary. *Kenosis* is how "being" is "passed on" down the hierarchy.

On the one hand, the non-Chalcedonians see the incarnation as the origin of Christ and use *kenosis* to describe how the divine and created natures of Christ can be related *after* the birth of Christ. On the other hand, the theistic personalists see creation as the origin of the universe and use *kenosis* to describe how divine activity and creaturely freedom can be related *after* the origin of the universe. However, if creation is understood as essentially ordered hierarchy, then *kenosis* must be a description, not of origins, but of participation.

---

[105] Although, interestingly, Balthasar also links the *kenosis* of God with creaturely freedom (See Hans Urs von Balthasar, *Theo-Drama IV: The Action* (San Francisco, CA: Ignatius Press, 1994), pp. 328–31), which (if the argument presented here is accurate) represents a contradiction in his thinking. Sergei Bulgakov, too, speaks of the *kenosis* as a genuine limitation of God (see Bulgakov, *The Bride of the Lamb*, p. 236; see also p. 112).

Kenosis and participation

Drawing on the same sorts of criticisms that this chapter has levelled at Thomasius, Gore, Polkinghorne and others who share their theology, Andrew Davison dismisses the idea that *kenosis* (and the related idea of *tzimtzum*)[106] could be a theologically legitimate position on the basis that,

---

[106] Originally espoused by medieval Rabbi Isaac Luria, *tzimtzum* is described by Hans Jonas, a twentieth-century Jewish philosopher, as "contraction, withdrawal, self-limitation". He explains that "to make room for the world ... [God] had to contract himself so that, vacated by him, empty space could expand outside of him: the 'nothing' in which and from which God could then create the world" (Hans Jonas, *Mortality and Morality: A Search for God after Auschwitz* (Evanston, IL: Northwestern University Press, 1996), p. 134, p. 142). Daniel Horwitz describes *tzimtzum* in a similar way, however, absolutely crucially, Horwitz clarifies that "certain terms such as 'before' and 'after,' or 'above' and 'below,' are not meant to be taken literally; all this activity presumably takes place outside of what we understand to be time and space" (Daniel Horwitz, *A Kabbalah and Jewish Mysticism Reader* (Philadelphia, PA: Jewish Publication Society, 2016), p. 230). God is not above and before the world, so the "emptying" is an atemporal or eternal emptying. Crucially (supporting the interpretation offered above), Horwitz does not see this "withdrawal" as leading to an absence. Rather, "the light" that has contracted to leave a "space" returns and is that which forms the world in the "vacuum" (Hayyim Vital, quoted in Horwitz, *A Kabbalah and Jewish Mysticism Reader*, p. 231). Thus, Horwitz notes that *tzimtzum* also has the meaning of "concentration" (Horwitz, *A Kabbalah and Jewish Mysticism Reader*, pp. 224–5), so that "*tzimtzum* is not only the withdrawal of Divinity, but its concentration into the spark where that vitality is most keenly felt" (Horwitz, *A Kabbalah and Jewish Mysticism Reader*, p. 235), which Horwitz continues is comparable to panentheism. (Although by panentheism, Horwitz certainly does not mean that "process theism" type of panentheism in which, because God "contains" the world, so God is temporal, mutable and passable (see Michael Brierley, "Naming a Quiet Revolution: The Panentheistic Turn in Modern Theology", in Philip Clayton and Arthur Peacocke (eds), *In Whom We Live and Move and Have Our Being: Panentheistic Reflections on God's Presence in a Scientific World* (Grand Rapids MI: William B. Eerdmans,

2004), pp. 1–15)) In this way, *tzimtzum* does not lead to divine absence (in many ways, the opposite), but is a way that God creates. Indeed, Horwitz notes, one cannot speak of a literal *tzimtzum* because "God is not a physical being"; rather it is a way of God making room for the other (Horwitz, *A Kabbalah and Jewish Mysticism Reader*, p. 238).

Rabbi Shai Held similarly writes that the *tzimtzum* is how God can be present while making space (Shai Held, "Being Present While Making Space", *The Heart of Torah, Volume 1: Essays on the Weekly Torah Portion: Genesis and Exodus* (Philadelphia, PA: Jewish Publication Society, 2017), pp. 184–8). He argues that the original meaning of the word *tzimtzum* was not how God withdraws God's presence, but how God "contracts" that presence so as to fill a created vessel on earth (in relation to Exodus 25:2, 8). Thus, "for the [Rabbinic] sages, then, *tzimtzum* explains how a vast and uncontainable God can dwell in a finite space" (Held, "Being Present While Making Space", p.185). It is difficult to overemphasize the importance of this claim as a criticism of *kenosis* above: self-emptying leads to *presence not absence*.

It is understandable why *tzimtzum* is not widely explored in Christian theology (it is not even widely explored in Jewish theology), but it is not entirely unknown to Christian theology. Jürgen Moltmann has famously extolled the virtues of *tzimtzum* and incorporates it into his own theology, situating this discussion within the context of "an understanding of God's presence and activity in the cosmos" (Moltmann, "God's *Kenosis* in the Creation and Consummation of the World", p. 137). In the same volume—*The Work of Love*—Arthur Peacocke explicitly links *kenosis* and *tzimtzum*, writing that "Christian theology has long attributed self-limitation to God in the very notion of God creating something other than Godself", which "has been depicted by the idea of God 'making a space' (*zimzum*) for the created order" and, in a later essay, he (like Horwitz) explicitly links it with panentheism (Arthur Peacocke, "Articulating God's Presence in and to the World Unveiled by the Sciences" in Philip Clayton and Arthur Peacocke (eds) *In Whom We Live and Move and Have our Being: Panentheistic Reflections on God's Presence in a Scientific World* (Grand Rapids, MI: William B. Eerdmans, 2004), pp. 145–6). Importantly, Peacocke explicitly links this with the biblical idea of the "birth pangs" of new creation (Romans 8:19–22) and of a suffering God, so that "creation may in one sense be said to exist *through* suffering:

on the one hand, "its fundamental image is of God and creatures coming under some shared designation"[107] and, on the other hand, that it leads to a "truncated" God.[108] *Kenosis* and *tzimtzum*, Davison argues, seem to imply that creatures have a "part *of*" God,[109] and *kenosis* means that (to use Holmes Rolston III's language) creatures "share" God—which "has the Old English and Germanic root *sker*, to cut into parts"[110]—rather than participate in God. In other words, for Davison, *kenosis* seems to imply that God and creatures are in a zero-sum relationship, in which Christ is *more* human the *less* divine that he is, and creatures are *more* free the *less* that God acts.

Thus, Davison concludes, neither *kenosis* nor *tzimtzum* are compatible with a Thomistic participatory paradigm and are the "antithesis" of a participatory understanding.[111] For Davison, *kenosis* and participation are mutually exclusive ways of doing theology. If *kenosis* is understood in the way that Thomasius, Gore, and Polkinghorne understand it, then Davison is entirely correct in criticizing these impoverished interpretations of *kenosis*, which do seem to be contrary to a participatory theology. However, Davison appears to miss that *kenosis* does allow for a fuller interpretation. *Kenosis* does not necessarily mean that creatures share "part *of*" God; it can take the meaning that creatures take "part *in*" God.[112] *Kenosis* does not necessarily mean that God "shares" and can very well mean that creatures "participate".[113]

---

for suffering is recognized to have creative power when imbued with love" (Peacocke, "The Cost of New Life", pp. 38–9).

[107] Davison, *Participation in God*, p. 137.

[108] Davison, *Participation in God*, p. 212.

[109] Davison, *Participation in God*, p. 136.

[110] Holmes Rolston III, "*Kenosis* and Nature", in John Polkinghorne (ed.), *The Work of Love: Creation as Kenosis* (Cambridge MA: William B. Eerdmans, 2001), p. 48.

[111] Davison, *Participation in God*, p. 137.

[112] Davison, *Participation in God*, p. 136.

[113] There is a connection here with *epektasis*: the inexhaustibility of God in terms of an ever-greater potential for more and closer participation in God is mirrored in God's ever-greater "ability" to "make room" for the other in

In this way, when *kenosis* is said—as Coakley does—to "make room for the other", this does not mean that God has to "move out"; rather, it is nothing but another way of saying that the universe participates in God as the "ground of being". The "self-emptying" is analogical. God does not literally "self-empty". Rather, *kenosis* is a "symbol" or "image" that points to participation. Davison therefore looks at *kenosis* from the wrong perspective; *kenosis* is not a "pushing out" of divinity, but a "letting in" (or "letting be") of creatures—a "letting in" that is the ground of their being and *how* creatures depend on God for their being. *Kenosis* should be seen as a direct synonym for participation. If "analogy, imitation, and participation thus form a continuum rather than express radically different kinds of relationship",[114] then *kenosis* should be added to that list. If "imitation" is "just another way to express the central idea of participation [since to] imitate God is to participate in God",[115] then *kenosis* is just another way as well. All three—"*kenosis*", "imitation", and "participation"—should rightly be seen as exact synonyms, with one crucial exception: whereas "imitation" is what it means for creatures to participate—creatures participate through imitation—"*kenosis*" is what it means for God to be participated in—God is participated in through *kenosis*. God *kenotes* and creatures imitate. Both are describing precisely and exactly the same participation in God as the "ground of being", but one (*kenosis*) describes it from the divine side and the other (imitation) describes it from the created side. *Kenosis* is not an accidentally ordered "event", after which God has changed, or after which God has been "portioned out" among creatures who "share" in God's being. Rather, *kenosis* should be understood as an essentially ordered "relationship", in which and through which creatures participate in God and depend on God for their being.

---

kenosis. God descended that we might ascend; God became a creature that we might become God; God (in Christ) self-empties that we might participate in God (through Christ).

[114] Norman Russell, *The Doctrine of Deification in the Greek Patristic Tradition* (Oxford: Oxford University Press, 2004), p. 2.

[115] Tollefsen, *Activity and Participation in Late Antique and Early Christian Thought*, p. 163.

However, before more is said about how this interpretation of *kenosis* should apply to what Jesus does on the cross, two further comments are needed to more fully understand how *kenosis* can be seen as a synonym for participation: (a) the distinction between "motion" and "being"; and (b) the role of hierarchy.

Kenosis and being

If the distinction between accidentally ordered and essentially ordered can be traced exactly onto the distinction between "motion" and "being"—so that all "cause" is accidentally ordered and all "creation" is essentially ordered—then it is clear that *kenosis* should be seen as referring exclusively to "being": *kenosis* is a "cause of being", not a "cause of motion". Here, again, is yet another reason why Thomasius, Polkinghorne et al. are incorrect in their interpretation of *kenosis* as a literal emptying: it turns "creation" into an "origin"—i.e., the first in an accidentally ordered series of motion. If *kenosis* were a "giving up of motion", then God would be treated univocally with creatures, who would "share" in God's being and power. Rather, *kenosis* is about ontological participation, and ontological dependence. *Kenosis* is "how" God donates being; not by emptying Godself, but, in and through the incarnation (and cross), making ontological room for the other. *Kenosis* is a "letting the other participate".

In this way, *kenosis* is not the giving of *freedom*—a way to explain how God and creatures can both act—but the giving of *being*—a way to explain how God creates. *Kenosis* is an end in itself, not as a way of making possible another end(s)/further act(s). *Kenosis* does not oblige the theologian to see Christ (or God) as giving up divine attributes, but "making room" for the other (i.e., creating). *Kenosis* is the "mechanism" of creation; it is how God creates the creaturely nature of Christ and how God creates the universe.

Kenosis and hierarchy

If *kenosis* is an essentially ordered "cause of being" and not an accidentally ordered "cause of motion", then *kenosis* is an ontological hierarchy. The *kenotic* theology of Bulgakov and von Balthasar is crucial here. It is important to link the explicit connection that Bulgakov and von Balthasar make between the *kenosis* of the incarnation and the Son's procession from the Father with Pseudo-Dionysius' theology of hierarchy, a theology that was important for understanding the incarnation expounded in the previous chapter. Ashley Purpura, for example, writes that "the self-emptying activity of divine communication within the hierarchy is reflective of divine condescension", so that "the activity of divine love is communicating divinity to others through self-condescension".[116] Bulgakov and von Balthasar postulate a *kenosis* between Father and Son, and explicitly link this with the *kenosis* of the Son. Thus, within the Trinity—*ad intra*—there is a *kenosis* of the Father, who gives "being" to the Son and the Spirit, and outside the Trinity—*ad extra*—there is a *kenosis* of the Son, who gives "being" to all creatures. The *kenosis* of the Father is that which gives being to the Son, and the Son's comparable *kenosis* is that which permits creatures' participation in God through the Son. Once again, although there is no explicit mention of it, there is a fundamental connection with creation. *Kenosis* is not an "emptying"; it is a "creating". *Kenosis* is not about God giving something up, but about enabling others to participate in God.

Of course, extreme care is required. If *kenosis* is a synonym for participation, then this cannot be taken to mean that the Son participates in the Father. Certainly, creatures participate in God as the "ground of being", and, certainly, the human nature of Jesus participates in the divine nature of the Son as the "ground of being", and both of these are correctly described as *kenosis*. However, if there is a *kenosis* of the Father, then this cannot be taken to mean that the Son participates in the Father. As it has already been noted, "Participation necessarily requires a relation between two things that are unequal and that remain unequal and distinct in the act of the one participating in the other."[117] If the Son participates in the Father, then there would be an inequality between the Son and the Father,

---

[116] Ashley M. Purpura, *God, Hierarchy, and Power: Orthodox Theologies of Authority from Byzantium* (New York, NY: Fordham University Press, 2018), p. 24

[117] Daniel Keating, *Deification and Grace* (Naples, FL: Sapientia Press, 2007), p. 97.

or, to put this differently, this would make the Son a creature. Such a conclusion is obviously problematic.

The Son is God and God does not "have" being; God *is* being. Therefore, the Father does not "donate" being to the Son, nor does the Son participate in the Father. However, this does not mean that the Father is not "above" the Son in the hierarchy, nor that the Father is not the source of the Son's divinity. The Son does not "have" being or participate in being, but this does not mean that the Father does not "beget" the Son, who has his divinity through the Father. Thus, this does not mean that the relationship between the Father and the Son is not *kenosis*. The hierarchy of "being" can genuinely be seen to move from the Father—who is the source of divinity, the *arche anarchos*—to the Son, and from the Son through the incarnation to all creatures, however, the *kenosis ad intra* must be distinguished from the *kenosis ad extra*. Failure to do so would make the procession of the Son and the Spirit from the Father a creation and would therefore make the Son and the Spirit ontologically equal to creatures.

Kenosis as incarnation and cross

Creation, incarnation, and the cross are the same type of act: all three are *kenosis*. *Kenosis* is a synonym for participation, an essentially ordered hierarchy in which what is above "passes on" "being" and what is below depends entirely and completely on what is above. Thus, what Jesus does on the cross is no different from what Jesus does in the incarnation: the cross is how creatures participate in God. What does it mean to say that the cross establishes a participation of creatures in God?

First, the fact that the incarnation and crucifixion are "typally" identical means that the two "events" must be seen through the lens of the other. This means that the incarnation illuminates what the cross is. If the incarnation is God "making room for the other", then the cross must likewise be a "making room". This might seem like a somewhat strange statement, but it is not a novel suggestion. For example, in *Mysterium Paschale*, Hans Urs von Balthasar writes that with the doctrine of *kenosis*, "the incarnation takes on the quality of the Passion from the very start".[118] This, Graham Ward writes, means that "the doctrine of *kenosis* makes the descent into death inseparable from the incarnation",[119] and so leads von Balthasar to call the incarnation the "first result" of the "mystery of the *kenosis*".[120] Of course, this does not mean that the crucifixion is *another* incarnation—even the resurrection is not Jesus taking on *another* body. Rather, it means that the incarnation and the cross both have the same "result". If that is participation, then the result of the cross is participation.

This also means that the cross illuminates what the incarnation is. In his original and influential book, *The Lamb of God*, Bulgakov expounds the incarnation as *kenotic* and cruciform. He writes:

> To apply the text concerning humiliation solely to Christ's earthly condition is to impoverish and weaken the most acute thought of this text, its most audacious antithesis between divine grandeur and voluntary self-humiliation which results in the obedience until death.[121]

Thus, he concludes, it is not possible to "separate in Christ His earthly, human humiliation from his heavenly, divine *kenosis*, which is the descent from heaven and the incarnation itself".[122] In a crucial use of imagery, Bulgakov continues that this means that "in the cross of the earthly path is realized the cross of the heavenly *kenosis*".[123] The incarnation, writes Bulgakov, is a "heavenly cross". Bulgakov continues to deepen this imagery, writing that "the *kenosis* of the incarnation is the *metaphysical* Golgotha of the self-crucifixion of the *Logos* in time. The *historical* Golgotha was only a *consequence* of the metaphysical one . . . voluntary, so to speak, dying of the second hypostasis and his burial in

---

[118]   von Balthasar, *Mysterium Paschale*, p. 12.

[119]   Ward, "Kenosis: Death, Discourse and Resurrection", p. 23.

[120]   von Balthasar, *Mysterium Paschale*, p. 90.

[121]   Bulgakov, *The Lamb of God*, p. 215.

[122]   Bulgakov, *The Lamb of God*, p. 215.

[123]   Bulgakov, *The Lamb of God*, p. 217.

time.”[124] The crib in Bethlehem, the manger in which the newborn Jesus is placed and adored, is the tomb of the incarnation. The image of the "metaphysical Golgotha" is clear; the incarnation is cruciform. What happens in the cross has already happened (is already happening) in the incarnation. Or, more explicitly, the *historical kenosis is the metaphysical kenosis*. Thus, Bulgakov continues, "the Son, the Lamb of God, is pre-eternally 'sacrificed' in the creation of the world".[125] Here Bulgakov has already made explicit this *communicatio idiomatum* of the incarnation and the cross: the incarnation is itself a "sacrifice" and the "sacrifice" is the "creation of the world". What can be said of the incarnation can also be said of the crucifixion and *vice versa*. In history, these events might be marked by the birth and death of Jesus respectively, but ontologically they are identical; both are the condition of the world's participation in God.

It is clear that Bulgakov is influenced by biblical sentiments such as "the Lamb that was slaughtered from the foundation of the world".[126] The cross becomes creation; the crucifixion of the Son is that through which all creatures participate in God. Thus, if creation is an ontological relationship, then the crucifixion is that which establishes that relation. Creatures have "being" because Jesus dies on the cross. Frances Young also gives expression to this idea that the cross itself is the divine act of creation. She writes that:

> God has emptied himself. This means that both the creation and the incarnation are included in the passion . . . God's creative love which maintains us in existence is not merely superabundance of generosity, it is also renunciation and sacrifice. Not only the

---

[124] Bulgakov, *The Lamb of God*, p. 232 (italics in original).

[125] Bulgakov, *The Lamb of God*, p. 129.

[126] Revelation 13:8; although another interpretation could be "everyone whose name has not been written from the foundation of the world in the book of life of the Lamb that was slaughtered", which points to an ambiguity in the English translation of the passage.

> passion but the creation itself is a renunciation and sacrifice on
> the part of God.[127]

Yet, this cannot mean that the cross *completes* what was started in creation and incarnation because nothing was *started* in the *creatio originalis* and the incarnation. Moreover, that would make the creation and incarnation accidentally ordered to one another and the cross. It would mean that the creation is not a relation, but is an act of construction and formation, which requires completion at a later point in time.

In fact, the previous chapter argued that strictly speaking there is no act of creation, there is only incarnation; there is only a single, essentially ordered relation that obtains because the Son assumed flesh. The incarnation, it was argued, "recapitulates" creation. Now, this logic must be extended. In the last chapter, three understandings of Christ as creator were given, i.e., three understandings for how the *creatio originalis* and the incarnation can be related: either (a) the incarnation is a repetition of creation; (b) the incarnation is a continuation of creation; or (c) the incarnation *is* creation. This chapter now makes the same move with *kenosis*: either (a) the cross is a repetition of the incarnation (another instance of *kenosis*); (b) the cross is a continuation of the incarnation (the same, continuing instance of *kenosis*); or (c) the cross *is* the incarnation (the *kenosis* of the cross just is the *kenosis* of the incarnation). In that case, this means that the cross recapitulates the incarnation. There is no creation, because it turns out that the content of the doctrine of creation is exhaustively explained by the incarnation—that is, a relationship of ontological dependency that is constituted and maintained by the hypostatic union. So, in the same way, there is no incarnation, because it turns out that the content of the doctrine of incarnation is exhaustively explained by the crucifixion—an eternal *kenosis*, in which the Son eternally ontologically self-empties, a self-emptying that is exactly numerically identical to all creatures' participation. In other words, there is no creation because that ontological relation can now be described by the hypostatic union, but there is no incarnation either because the

---

[127] Simone Weil, quoted in Frances Young, *Can These Dry Bones Live?* (London: SCM Press, 1982), p. 57.

hypostatic union can itself now be described by the crucifixion, precisely because all three are *kenosis* and the crucifixion is the *kenotic* "act" of God. Creation is the ontological dependence of creatures on God through the hypostatic union and the hypostatic union is nothing more than the eternal *kenosis* of the Son.

There is no incarnation and creation, not because God does not become incarnate or is not ultimately responsible for the entire universe, which depends entirely and uniquely on God for its very being, but because the universe is the result—or effect—of the hypostatic union, which in turn is the result—or effect—of the eternal cruciform *kenosis*, not because "incarnation" and/or "creation" are separate identifiable acts/events/causes themselves. (Again, the use of "causal" language here is misleading. The eternal cruciform *kenosis* does not "cause" the hypostatic union, which in turn does not "cause" the universe, in "what is usually meant by 'cause' in contemporary philosophy"[128] after the scientific revolution, but as in an essentially ordered series, which is better described as "creation" rather than by "cause".)

If the incarnation is not linked to the birth of Christ—that is, if the incarnation is an ontological relation that explains the participation of the historical nature in the divine nature, with no reference to the birth of Christ (in precisely the same way that creation is an ontological relation with no reference to the Big Bang)—then recapitulating the incarnation into the crucifixion makes no more difference to the birth of Christ than does recapitulating creation into the incarnation. In other words, if creation is not about the origin of the universe, but about its essentially ordered participation in God, and the incarnation is not about the birth of Christ but about the eternal hypostatic union, then the cross is not about the death of Christ but is about the eternal *kenosis* of the Son. That eternal *kenosis* is identical to the eternal hypostatic union, which, in turn, describes and establishes the "certain relation" that is all creatures' participation in God. If the incarnation is not linked to the birth of Christ, then the crucifixion is not linked to the death of Christ. Both are ontological relations, and neither are coincident with a specific part of the historical life of Jesus. Thus, the crucifixion is just as much responsible for

---

[128] Feser, *Scholastic Metaphysics: A Contemporary Introduction*, p. 97.

the birth of Jesus as it is the death of Christ, because the crucifixion is that which—through *kenosis*—"mediates" "being" from God to all creatures. The cross, then, is the point in the ontological hierarchy that has (up until now) been called creation and/or incarnation; the cross is the point in the hierarchy where the Son *kenotes* and "causes" creatures to participate.

The eternal cross
The incarnation is an ontological cross, which makes the cross God's single act of creation. John Behr has also suggested something similar. Behr starts from the hypostatic union, from the fact that there are not two different subjects in Christ, but rather there is one subject that is both properly human and properly divine.[129] This means, Behr continues, that "we can, therefore, no longer contemplate the exalted 'man' as in any way separate, distinguished by the lowly properties, from the Right Hand of God".[130] As one would expect, Behr points to the *communicatio idiomatum* to evidence this "identity".[131] That is, "contemplated by themselves, the properties of divinity and flesh remain distinct", but "because of the contact and union the [proper attributes] are each common to both".[132] This book has already quoted John Macquarrie, who writes that there is not "a kind of alternation in Jesus Christ, who is now a divine being, now a human being".[133] This is crucial: it is not just that the properties are common to both—or, more accurately, that the properties of both are common to the person of Jesus—but that they are simultaneous in Jesus.

This simultaneity means that Behr can say that "this identity achieved through the Passion means, in turn, that neither can we contemplate the one who brought all things into being as distinct from the crucified and

---

[129] John Behr, *The Mystery of Christ: Life in Death* (Crestwood, NY: St. Vladimir's Seminary Press, 2006), p. 36.

[130] Behr, *The Mystery of Christ*, p. 37.

[131] Behr, *The Mystery of Christ*, p. 38.

[132] Behr, *The Mystery of Christ*, p. 38; quoting Gregory of Nyssa, "Against Eunomius", in Philip Schaff and Henry Wace (eds), *Nicene and Post-Nicene Fathers Vol. 5* (Peabody, MA: Hendrickson Publishing, 1995), 5.5.

[133] Macquarrie, *Jesus Christ in Modern Thought*, p. 164.

exalted one".[134] It is always the crucified Christ who is the creator. Here, then, Behr makes his point explicit:

> The transcendent power of the eternal, timeless God, manifest in the Passion of Christ, is the same power that upholds all creation, so that the Cross is, indeed, the *axis mundi*, the still, eternal or timeless, axis around which the world rotates.[135]

It is worth repeating the crucial point: the power of the cross *is the same power that upholds all creation*. One could interpret that as meaning that the cross is *another* instance of this creating power. Athanasius and Thomas Aquinas, who both see God recreating in Christ, would do so. Norman Wirzba—who was quoted in the previous chapter arguing that "the feeding the hungry, healing the sick, exorcising the demon-possessed, and befriending the stranger and outcast is the *same* divine power that brings all creatures into being and that daily sustains and nurtures them"[136]—would presumably do the same and see the power of the crucifixion as *another instance* of the power of creation. However, Behr does not take that interpretation. Behr is clear that the creating power in the cross *is* identical to creation. He continues that:

> Theologically speaking, creation and its history begins with the Passion of Christ and from this "once for all" work looks backwards and forwards to see everything in this light, making everything new. Christian cosmology, elaborated as it must be from the perspective of the Cross, sees the Cross as impregnated in the very structure of creation: *stat crux dum volvitur orbis*— the Cross stands, while the earth revolves. The power of God

---

[134] Behr, *The Mystery of Christ*, p. 37.

[135] Behr, *The Mystery of Christ*, p. 37.

[136] Norman Wirzba, "Creation *Through* Christ", in Andrew Torrance and Thomas McCall (eds), *Christ and the Created Order Vol. 2* (Grand Rapids, MI: Zondervan, 2018), p. 39 (italics added).

revealed in and through the Cross brought creation into being
and sustains it in existence.[137]

Just in case one was left in any doubt about what he means here, Behr
pushes the point home even further, writing that "just as the date of the
Passion of Christ in antiquity was considered to be 25 March (which
. . . was the basis for calculating the date of his nativity, nine months
later), so also in antiquity 25 March was considered to be the very date
of creation, the Creation which revolves around the axis of the eternal,
immovable Cross".[138] Thus, Behr concludes, "as paradoxical as it might
sound, one can say, theologically, that *creation and salvation were effected
simultaneously on that day, 25 March,* AD *33,* when Christ gave himself
for the life of the world".[139] That Behr notes that the "connection between
the tomb and the womb seems to have been behind the calculation for
the date of the celebration of the Nativity . . . so in the liturgical calendar,
the Passion of Christ was followed, nine months later, by the birth of
Christ"[140] only serves to underline that—even in the early Church (Behr
quotes Augustine)—the incarnation *is* a crucifixion, the incarnation is
kenosis. It is only a small move to go from "the incarnation is *a* crucifixion"
to "the crucifixion is *the* incarnation".

Maintaining that the cross is God's manifestation of God's creating
power requires a particular understanding of time. So, Behr continues,
today "we tend to think in linear, historical terms, beginning with God
having brought creation into being", through the first humans, fall, and
sin, and then followed by the gradual preparation of sin "culminating

---

[137] Behr, *The Mystery of Christ*, p. 90.

[138] Behr, *The Mystery of Christ*, p. 91.

[139] Behr, *The Mystery of Christ*, p. 91 (italics added).

[140] Behr, *The Mystery of Christ*, p. 135; Maximos Aghiourgoussis similarly writes
that "humanity was already saved and deified, from the moment of [Christ's]
conception in the womb of Mary" (Aghiourgoussis, "Orthodox Soteriology",
p. 41). What is important is the conception of Christ in the womb, not the
birth of Christ. Thus, the descent into the world is identified with the descent
into the womb.

in the Incarnation of Christ".[141] Rather, Behr tells his reader, "a properly theological cosmology and 'history of salvation' ... begins with the Passion of Christ, and from this vantage point looks backwards and forwards to see everything in this light".[142] Oscar Cullmann said much the same thing: "The mid-point [i.e., Christ event] is also the starting point of primitive Christian understanding ... the divine plan of salvation opened up in both a forward and backward direction".[143] It is clear from what Behr claims (although he quite clearly uses very different language) that, rather than thinking in "linear, historical terms", one should think more in what this book has termed "hierarchical, ontological terms".

The use of the image of the earth revolving around the cross—*stat crux dum volvitur orbis*—points not only, quite obviously, to the eternity of the cross—time and space moves around the cross which is eternally in the centre—but, in doing so, also points to an image that has been central to this book: that of the relationship of God to the universe as the centre of a circle to its circumference. God is not sempiternal—endless duration—but eternal—time*less*—so God is not present at all spatiotemporal points, but all spatiotemporal points are present to God. The cross, now, takes the place of the centre of the circle. It is the cross through which the world is related to God; it is the cross which "makes ontological room for the other", through which all creatures are able to participate in God; it is the cross which stands at the centre of a four-dimensional spatiotemporal sphere, equidistant from all creatures. It is the cross that is Jesus' *kenosis* through which all creatures can participate in God as the ground of their being.

To use another image, the cross is "Jacob's ladder", that which "connects" God and creatures. The cross is Jacob's ladder, which is a *kenosis* down and a participation up. The cross is a hierarchical Jacob's ladder, essentially ordered to all events in spatiotemporal history, ontologically prior to history, and that through which everything participates. If Christ is the "one mediator between God and [creatures]",[144] if "the gap

---

[141] Behr, *The Mystery of Christ*, p. 77; see also p. 174.

[142] Behr, *The Mystery of Christ*, p. 178.

[143] Oscar Cullmann, *Christ and Time* (London: SCM Press, 1962), p. 107.

[144] 1 Timothy 2:5.

between heaven and earth is only bridged definitively in the figure of Christ",[145] so that "without the personal self-manifestation of God that the incarnation brings" God is "separated from us by an infinite gulf",[146] then it is specifically the cross that mediates between God and creatures. If "God is never without his [sic] Logos, the divine Wisdom, in and through whom the world is created, ordered, and sustained",[147] then "O mystery! the man we see is Christ crucified".[148] God never "acts" as essentially ordered cause without the *logos*, and the *logos* is always the crucified Jesus.

The cross as historical event

As much as the cross is an eternal "event", this does not diminish the fact that it is an historical event. The cross, like the Big Bang and the birth of Christ, did literally occur in history, and as a result of occurring in history the three events are genuinely accidentally ordered to one another. However, the cross is more than the historical cross; it is also the ontological *kenosis* that establishes the ontological hierarchy that is creation. Certainly, undeniably, Jesus' death is accidentally ordered to Jesus' birth, and so to other events within the spatiotemporal causal nexus; this is not an attempt to argue that the death of Christ is somehow a non-historical event. However, regardless of whether it is temporally related to other events in the spatiotemporal causal nexus, it is also ontologically more primary than all other events and, so, is that on which all other events depend for their being.

Indeed, the same was said in the last chapter regarding the incarnation. If Jesus does not need to have the same temporal duration as the universe to be that through which all spatiotemporal points and creatures are present to God, then it does not matter that the birth itself has a particular

---

[145] Rupert Shortt, *God Is No Thing: Coherent Christianity* (London: Hurst & Company, 2016), p. 77.

[146] Gerald O'Collins, "The Incarnation: The Critical Issues" in Stephen Davis, Daniel Kendall and Gerald O'Collins (eds), *The Incarnation* (Oxford: Oxford University Press, 2002), p. 26.

[147] Hart, *The Experience of God*, p. 235.

[148] Teilhard de Chardin, *Writings in the Time of War*, p. 208.

spatiotemporal location. That it occurs at a specific spatiotemporal point no more prohibits the birth (and now the death) from being that in which all creatures and spatiotemporal points are present to God than is the circumference of a circle prohibited from being present to its centre.

Likewise, it is important to re-emphasize that if "creation" is not "origin", then the Big Bang is not coincident with it. If this is the case, then neither is the birth of Christ coincident with the incarnation and so neither is the death of Christ coincident with the crucifixion. That is, it is quite possible to say that Christ is eternally crucified because, if crucifixion is understood, like incarnation, to be a relationship, then there is no reason why it should be limited to a specific spatiotemporal event. Thus, just as the birth of Christ being an event that happens at a particular point in space-time does not preclude the incarnation from also being an eternal aspect of Christ, neither does the fact that the crucifixion happens at a particular point in space-time preclude it from also being, or primarily being, an eternal aspect of Christ. Like the incarnation, this makes the crucifixion not an event in the historical life of God, but an ontological relationship, an atemporal, essentially ordered relationship in which God makes room for the other. In other words, what is being claimed here is that the cross, by being the defining event of Christ's life, and so becoming the defining event of the incarnation, is that which constitutes that relationship. The incarnation is "the *metaphysical* Golgotha of the self-crucifixion of the *Logos* in time"[149] and that *metaphysical* Golgotha is the "[pre-eternal] '[sacrifice]' in the creation of the world".[150] The crucifixion is all there is; from the Father, through the Son, through Jesus, there is just one eternal cross, which is the *kenosis* that constitutes the ontological hierarchy through which all creatures participate in the "ground of being".

What has been suggested here is quite novel, and it turns on the fact that "origins" and "creation" are entirely separate terms referring to entirely separate ideas. It also requires that this distinction is mirrored in the difference between "birth of Jesus" and "incarnation", and similarly between "death of Jesus" and "cross". The origin of the universe, the birth

---

149 Bulgakov, *The Lamb of God*, p. 232 (italics in original).

150 Bulgakov, *The Lamb of God*, p. 129.

of Jesus, and the death of Jesus are all *separate, distinct events* that take place within the accidentally ordered spatiotemporal nexus. However, creation, incarnation, and crucifixion are all *the same, identical essentially ordered relationship* that from the divine side looks like *kenosis* and from the created side looks like participation. Certainly, the "birth of Jesus" is entirely necessary for a relationship between creatures and God to be established and maintained, but that birth is itself the manifestation of the eternal cross of the Son, whose self-emptying (*kenosis*) from the father eternally "continues" through to creaturely death. Thus, there is only one essentially ordered divine activity through which creatures depend entirely on God for their being, and that essentially ordered cause is cruciform.

Something similar was said regarding the "pre-existence" of Christ. The "pre-existence" is not a temporally prior incorporeal existence, but is an ontological relation. Designating the pre-existence as ontological means that one can maintain that the Son is not exhausted by the historical Jesus, but is never without him either. The Son is eternally incarnate, but is ontologically greater than the historical Jesus. So the crucifixion, as eternal, is not "absorbed and exhausted" by the cross alone. That historical cross is the most explicit revelation of, and also constitutes, what the incarnation *is*, which makes it the most explicit revelation of the ontological relationship between God and creatures: the historical death of Christ becomes the point in history that shows the eternal crucifixion in and of the second person of the Trinity—an eternal crucifixion that constitutes the ontological relationship on which all creatures depend.

The Cross and the hypostatic union

This chapter has now come full circle. It started by affirming a Scotist view of the incarnation, which, at least on the face of it, relegates the cross quite significantly. In many ways, as Jeffrey Finch writes, it "evacuat[es] the need for Christ's atoning death"[151] completely. It has now reversed this outlook, affirming quite forcefully that the cross retains its central place in theology. In fact, not only does the cross retain its place in theology,

---

[151] Finch, "Athanasius on the Deifying Work of the Redeemer", p. 106.

but it has become all that theology is about: there is no creation; there is no incarnation; there is only the cross.

However, this does not mean one is forced to reverse the support for a Johannine Christology and maintain that, if there is no incarnation and only cross, the theology is forced to defend a "Pauline" Christology in which the incarnation is just the means to an end. In other words, just because it is now claimed that the cross constitutes the relation between God and creatures on which all creatures depend for their being, this does not mean that the incarnation is now relegated to what Anna Marmodoro and Jonathan Hill call "conditions that Christ had to meet in order to be able to save".[152] This does not, somewhat counter-intuitively, place the cross as the centre of the story to the detriment of the incarnation, as it seems to have done for the "Pauline" account. Rather, this only serves to underline that a *true* "Johannine" Christology must see the incarnation itself as efficacious, but only in connection with the cross: there cannot be an incarnation without a crucifixion. The incarnation and crucifixion are the same event, one is not the preliminary of the other or an additional extra.

Michael Lee offers a similar interpretation of the cross in relation to "deep incarnation", writing that "the incarnation is not subordinate to crucifixion (Jesus came to die), but . . . the crucifixion expresses the fullest sense of the incarnation (Jesus died because he came)".[153] In other words, perhaps what has been done here is to see Kähler and Finch's claims as being mutually influential. That is, the Christology that saw the "mere contact" as being efficacious has now been centred on the cross. Or, differently, the Gospels absolutely are passion narratives with extended introductions, but only because the passion becomes the central event of "mere contact". The passion becomes "how" there can be "mere contact".

Such a suggestion is likely to be contested by many and rejected as incoherent. Admittedly, it is a long way from the story of Jesus coming to die for the sins of the many. However, it does nothing more than build

---

[152]   Marmodoro and Hill, "Modeling the Metaphysics of the Incarnation", pp. 99–100.

[153]   Michael E. Lee, "Historical Crucifixion: A Liberationist Response to Deep Incarnation", *Theological Studies* 81:4 (2020), p. 898.

slightly further on what was claimed in the last chapter. If creation is not an "event" but a relationship, then this relationship can be seen as identical with, and constituted by, the incarnation. That is, the hypostatic union is nothing more than the "contact" between God and creatures, which is that on which all creatures depend—in an essentially ordered series—for their being. The hypostatic union *is* the point in the ontological hierarchy where creatures can be related to God, through Jesus, and so participate in God's being precisely because Christ is both fully God and fully human and so mediates "being" hierarchically between both. This chapter does nothing more than claim that the hypostatic union (the incarnation), while it is a contact between God and creatures, is actually a crucifixion. That is, if *kenosis* is a making room, and the crucifixion is a *kenosis*, then the hypostatic union—which is an ontological making room for creatures in the person of Christ—must be a crucifixion. The crucifixion in the person of Christ is that which makes room for the other and thereby eternally "initiates" contact. The incarnation is not different from the crucifixion, because the two are exactly the same "act"—making room for the other—but just given a different name (with one traditionally identified with the birth of Jesus and the other traditionally identified with the death of Jesus, but nevertheless precisely the same). Thus, Ian McFarland's quotation (that has proved central to this idea) that Christ does not mediate between "between two *predefined realities*", but whose mediation is "the one in whom God and humankind acquire their identities in the first place, that is, the one in and through whom the distinction between Creator and creature is itself established",[154] can be nuanced; it is the cross in which and through which the distinction between Creator and creature is itself established. The eternal ontological crucifixion of the Son is *how* the Son functions as mediator (and so creator). There is no creation; there is no incarnation; there is only the eternal crucifixion of the Son.

The birth of Christ and the death of Christ are (obviously) spatiotemporally separate, but the incarnation and the crucifixion are ontologically and numerically identical. The cross of the human Christ *is* identical to the eternal cross of the Son. The cross is the Son both

---

[154] McFarland, *The Word Made Flesh*, p. 12 (italics added).

becoming flesh and dying. In the one cross, space-time and eternity meet. There is just one *kenosis*; that cross is the incarnation of the Son and how creatures participate in God.

Final remarks

This chapter began by outlining that it would be considering four distinct but related points: (a) the deficiency in Scotus' theology of the cross, which unnecessarily downplays the role of the cross; (b) a reminder that if the cross is creative, it is creative as a relationship of dependency, so that the cross must not dictate what divine activity should be like, but that the cross should be seen in the context of essentially ordered "causality"; (c) a necessary reinterpretation of *kenosis*, in which Christ does not literally self-empty, but becomes a synonym for participation; and (d) the cross "recapitulates" the incarnation, so if there is no creation, only incarnation, then now it must be that there is neither creation nor incarnation, only crucifixion.

In the last chapter, on incarnation, it was argued that what was said in the previous chapter, on creation, can be summarized, or recapitulated, in the incarnation. The creation—the relationship of dependency—is meaningless unless it is seen through the lens of the incarnation. The incarnation exhausts the content of the doctrine of creation. Now, the same is said again, what is said about the incarnation is meaningless unless it is seen through the lens of the cross. The cross recapitulates the incarnation as the incarnation recapitulates the creation. The cross exhausts the content of the doctrine of the incarnation. There is only one single divine act. On the side of God, there is just one thing that God does: crucifixion. On the side of the universe that one thing that God does—crucifixion—is responsible for everything. There is an absence of a real relation: God eternally crucifies; the multiple and diverse effects of that crucifixion are extrinsic to it. The cross is not related to anything— the cross is the divine "emanation" of grace—but all and everything is related to the cross. That single divine act is like a column which moves from being "on the right" to "on the left", without the column moving or changing whatsoever: it is the animal that moves and changes in relation to the column, not the column itself. Except, now it is not a column, it is the cross, which remains eternally still, while all spatiotemporal history revolves and moves around it.

Or, differently, for the deist, all God does is create and nothing more. For the traditional deist (who sees divine activity as accidentally ordered), origin is all there is and there is no incarnation. For the incarnational deist, creation is not an event (i.e., it is not an origin) but an ontological relationship; that relationship is identical to the incarnation, i.e., the hypostatic union. For the incarnational deist, that hypostatic union is cruciform. It is the historical person of Jesus—in first century Palestine—in whom is the eternal relation of God to creatures. He occupies a specific spatiotemporal point, and that specific spatiotemporal point is essentially ordered like the centre of a four-dimensional sphere to its circumference. Yet, that historical person is eternally the crucified one; that historical person is eternally crucified at the foundation of the world. That eternal crucified person mediates the ontological hierarchy; the *kenosis* of the Son from the Father to his death in time is identical to, constitutive of, all creatures' participation in, and dependence on, God.

As already quoted from Teilhard de Chardin, "The universe assumes the form of Christ—but, O mystery! the man we see is Christ crucified."[155] If everything is only intelligible through Christ, then it is the crucified Christ through which all things are intelligible. *Stat crux dum volvitur orbis.*

---

[155] Teilhard de Chardin, *Writings in the Time of War*, p. 208.

6

The Fulfilment of Creation

With the conclusion of the previous chapter comes the thesis of this book: the eternal crucifixion of the Son, which eternally creates an ontological space for all creatures in the person of Jesus (i.e., the hypostatic union, the sheer joining of creature and God in Jesus), is for all creatures the donation of being on which they depend entirely for their being through imitation, and this is "all" that God "does". This is deism, but not a deism in which God leaves unactualized potential activity; it is a deism in which creatures' participation in God does not imply that God can influence the particular course of the history of the universe. In this interpretation, the incarnation and crucifixion are not subsequent to creation; the incarnation and crucifixion *are* creation. In fact, strictly speaking, there is no creation or incarnation; there is only the eternal crucifixion of the Son, which establishes the hypostatic union through which all creatures participate in God.

However, Christianity (in fact most religions) is not just a religion that has something to say about where the universe came from; it is also a religion that has something to say about *why* there is a universe. For many people, the question of *why* there is a universe is inherently connected with the question of what might, could, or will happen to that universe in the future. As was noted in the Introduction, even traditional deists might want to point to a future life bringing rewards and punishments, despite rejecting any and all ideas of providence.[1] However, that connection between "why" and "future" is not necessary. This book has eagerly emphasized Tillich's claim that the reason for creation is nothing

---

[1]   John Macquarrie, *Jesus Christ in Modern Thought* (London: SCM Press, 1990), p. 24.

more than an exercise of God's creativity and it has equally eagerly expounded that creativity in an atemporal, *inter*mundane (as opposed to an *intra*mundane), vertical, essentially ordered paradigm, alluding that the "fulfilment" of that creativity must likewise be a "vertical" fulfilment. In this way, one does not need to appeal to a future (or past) situation to explain why there is a present and what meaning that present should take.

This book has also sought to validate this way of thinking by suggesting that a literal and strong emphasis on atemporality and simplicity should lead to the conclusion that creation is about ontological relationship, rather than something akin to human construction or generation. As a result, the characteristic deist rejection of providence (if providence is understood as God's rule over and guidance of the history of the universe) can be supported and embraced, without that rejection of providence leading to the need to sacrifice important Christological doctrines of the incarnation and the cross. One simply needs to see those Christological doctrines in a different light, not abandon them.

However, even the most casual of readers will have noticed that nothing has yet been said about the resurrection. Traditionally, the crucifixion only takes on its definitive meaning because it is seen in the light of the resurrection. It is important to make a few comments on how and why this book essentially stops with the crucifixion. Similarly, it would surely be lacking if this book did not say something, however brief, about how one might understand the Christian doctrines of "the last things". It is all very well to say that *creation* is a relationship, but what does/should one say about *deification* in this paradigm? As already hinted at in Chapter 3, if creation is a "vertical" or hierarchical relationship, then the fulfilment of creation cannot be thought of as the future attainment of a perfect state of affairs or aggregation of atoms, but what does this mean?

Essentially, it means that the relation between nature and grace must be entirely subjective. In other words, as already argued in Chapter 4 on the incarnation, if the very fact that the universe obtains at all entails no change in God, then the deification of the individual creature should likewise entail no change in God. If the idea of God as *actus purus* means that God cannot be changed by creation—i.e., that God does not "do" anything in creation—then this idea of God as *actus purus* must also mean that God cannot be changed by deification.

Nature and grace

Traditionally, "the consequence of th[e] hypostatic union in Christ of the two natures was the deification of the human nature he assumes".[2] The incarnation was traditionally understood as *re*-creating. Traditionally, the incarnation is either a continuation of what was started "in the beginning", or it is a repetition of what was done "in the beginning". If historically and traditionally the incarnation is about re-creation, then it is about deification.

However, drawing on atemporality, simplicity, and the single divine "act", the chapter on incarnation (and crucifixion) argued that it is possible—indeed, necessary—to posit a third option: the incarnation *is* creation. This makes it necessary to move from the idea that the incarnation deifies to the idea that the incarnation creates. If God is atemporal and simple, then there cannot be two creations; there can only be one single divine "act". Moreover, that single divine act cannot be extended in time, begun in a *creatio originalis* and completed (or at least continued) in the incarnation. Thus, if God deifies (i.e., re-creates) all creatures through the "sheer joining" in the hypostatic union, and there is only one divine "act", and the incarnation and creation are identical "acts", then the incarnation creates. When creation is understood as an ontological relation, not an event that is coincident with the first moment in time, then the incarnation must be that which creates, because creation is an ontological relationship, and that relationship requires the mediation of one who is both God and creature.

This interpretation has assumed, but has not made explicit, that if creation and deification are both "effects" of the incarnation then they must be *extrinsic* effects of the incarnation. If the origin of the universe does not bring about a change in God—i.e., the move/change from a potential universe to an actual universe is *extrinsic* to God—so that "even in worlds in which [God] does not create, [God's] act of being, by which creation is produced, is no different in these otherwise empty worlds than

---

[2] Georgios Mantzaridis, *The Deification of Man* (Crestwood, NY: St. Vladimir's Seminary Press, 1984), p. 29.

in worlds chock-full of contingent beings of every order",[3] then, likewise, the move from a "created" world to a "deified" world must also be entirely *extrinsic* to God. If creation is like the move of the pillar from the right to the left of the creature, then deification must similarly be like the move of the pillar again. If creation is just a relation in the creature (not in God), then deification is likewise a relation in the creature.

This seemingly has the remarkably counter-intuitive (and, many might think, Pelagian) conclusion that if creation is nothing more than a certain relation that the creature has with the cross of Christ, then deification is nothing more than another certain relation that the creature has with Christ. If "God is no different whether [God] creates or does not create and . . . the difference between these two alternatives lies wholly in the created being",[4] then the same must be said of the distinction between "creation" and "deification". Deification, then, is nothing more than a particular way in which the creature relates to God through the cross. As controversial as that claim might be, it is nothing more than the logical extrapolation of Thomas Aquinas' doctrine of creation and is less controversial than the claim that God has some unrealized potential that is actualized subsequent to God's act of creation. (Although, of course, the "theistic personalists" would not find it controversial at all.) If one accepts that God is the *actus purus*, then deification cannot be other than a certain relation that the creature has with God.

As much as this conclusion might seem controversial, it is found in Pseudo-Dionysius, upon whom this book has drawn heavily, and who "does not seem to distinguish clearly between the gracious generosity of God in creating and what the Scholastics will call habitual or sanctifying grace".[5] However, as much as it might seemingly be necessitated by an extrapolation of Thomas' logic, and as much as it might seemingly be a

[3]   William Lane Craig, "Timelessness, Creation, and God's Real Relation to the World", *Laval théologique et philosophique* 56:1 (2000), p. 109.

[4]   Craig, "Timelessness, Creation, and God's Real Relation to the World", p. 109.

[5]   William Riordan, *Divine Light* (San Francisco, CA: Ignatius Press, 2008), p. 154; see also Robert F. Scuka, "Resurrection: Critical Reflections on a Doctrine in Search of Meaning", *Modern Theology* 6:1 (1989), pp. 77–95.

position that is found in Pseudo-Dionysius, it is not often appreciated in discussions on the relationship between "nature" and "grace".

Nature, grace, and "extrinsicism"

It is perhaps not too much of an exaggeration to claim that no controversy in twentieth century Roman Catholic theology has attracted more comment than whether one should see "grace" as being *extrinsic* or *intrinsic* to "nature". That is, whether grace comes to humanity from "outside"—in which case it is *extrinsic* to nature—or whether grace is "necessary" for humanity to be human—in which case it is *intrinsic* to nature.

To a certain extent, the debate over whether "grace" was *extrinsic* or *intrinsic* to "nature" was nothing more than an argument over the correct interpretation of Thomas Aquinas' theology. For many, the question was not so much a normative one—assessing all of the relevant issues to reach a particular position—but an historical one. For some—such as Henri de Lubac (and others who might be termed *nouvelle théologie*)—the question was more about whether or not there was an over-reliance on Thomas Aquinas in modern theology (as a result of Pope Leo XIII's encyclical *Aeterni Patris*, which effectively determined that Catholic theology was either Thomistic or it was not Catholic theology) and whether or not there was the need for a rediscovery of Augustine of Hippo and other Patristic sources. However, for most, the question was about what Thomas Aquinas really meant. Yet, for all that the participants in the debate quarrelled over what Thomas Aquinas meant (or whether there was an over-reliance on his theology), the side on which one fell in that debate (like all theological questions!) had far-reaching doctrinal implications.

To understand this debate properly, it must be seen within its historical context. At the turn of the twentieth century, a number of theologians were becoming increasingly dissatisfied with the direction in which Catholic theology was being taken. While those who were becoming concerned were primarily academics (although most of them were members of Religious Orders), their dissatisfaction was not so much an academic quibble over correct interpretation, which had no real impact on the lives of the laity; rather, it was with the fact that theology had no real impact on the lives of the laity to begin with. Jürgen Mettepenningen writes that these theologians, in particular the French Dominican Yves Congar, "[lament] the lack of interest among theologians for the cares and activities of real life, the life of the factory worker, for example, and his wife and children", and as a result, "theology tended to circle around itself rather than around the narrative God is writing or desires to write with his people".[6] As Mettepenningen continues, Congar and his colleagues saw this as "the central reason behind the growth in secularization", because the Church "was far too focused on itself" and so "people were more and more inclined to set faith to one side in search of happiness in life".[7] As a result, thought Congar, the "closed scholasticism" of the current Church needed to be abandoned. In other words, theologians such as Congar saw theology becoming increasingly supportive (however inadvertently) of a separation of Church and state; the more the Church became increasingly insular, the more the laity could quite happily live their lives without troubling themselves with the Church and what it said.

The problem was with Thomism, or, at least with Thomism as they saw it. Medieval theology had interpreted Thomas Aquinas in such a way that "nature" had become entirely separated from "grace". That is to say, it was entirely possible for "nature" to be fulfilled, or for "nature" to achieve a "purely natural" end, entirely separate from the role of "grace". This is not to say that one can fulfil "nature" without God, as Lawrence Feingold writes, "in either case [i.e., with or without grace], man's end lies in the contemplation of God", rather, "the difference between the connatural and the supernatural end lies in the way God is contemplated: *by our natural powers* ... [or] *by the light of glory*".[8] There is no end to "nature" that is not the contemplation of God; however, the supernatural contemplation of God "by the light of glory" through the influence of grace is infinitely

---

6   Jürgen Mettepenningen, *Nouvelle Théologie—New Theology: Inheritor of Modernism, Precursor of Vatican II* (London: T&T Clark International, 2010), p. 45.

7   Mettepenningen, *Nouvelle Théologie—New Theology*, p. 45.

8   Lawrence Feingold, *The Natural Desire to See God According to St. Thomas Aquinas and his Interpreters* (Naples, FL: Sapientia Press, 2010), p. 2 (italics in original).

superior. In many ways, it is precisely *because* theologians saw it as so much superior to the contemplation of God "by our natural powers" that they saw "grace" as so separate from "nature".

For Congar and his colleagues, the Church's increasing "disinterest" in the lives of the laity led to an increasing separation of Church and state; the pursuit of "grace" became irrelevant to the laity. Central to this separation is a desire to protect the gratuitousness of "grace" and to emphasize its radical difference from "nature". If "grace" were necessary for the contemplation of God—and so the fulfilment of "nature"—then the theologian would be in a position of having to suggest either that God is constrained to bestow grace on creatures or that God could freely refrain from bestowing on humanity that which it needs for its fulfilment. In order to take these concerns seriously, theologians argued that there was a "purely natural" end to "nature"—which was "inherent in [humanity's] nature"—and another end—the beatific vision or supernatural end—which was "bestowed on him gratuitously".[9] If "grace" was not necessary for the "natural" end that was "inherent" in "nature", then the Church became increasingly irrelevant. If there was a "purely natural" end to "nature" that did not require "grace", then humanity didn't need the Church to come to God.

The crucial theological issue that underpinned all of these concerns was a phobia of constraining God in some way. If "grace" was necessary for the fulfilment of "nature", then God was seen as being constrained by "nature" to bestow "grace". In other words, if "nature" required a subsequent bestowal of "grace" for it to be fulfilled, then God would be *passable* because it would mean that God's will was dependent on something in creation.[10] If humanity is incomplete without "grace", then God's act of creation impinges upon the freedom of God in some way. That is, because God has created in the past, so God's freedom is constrained in the future: God is not freely able to withhold grace without leaving God's creation incomplete or unfulfilled. If "nature"

---

9   Edward Oakes, *A Theology of Grace in Six Controversies* (Grand Rapids, MI: William B. Eerdmans, 2016), p. 26.

10   Eleonore Stump, *The God of the Bible and the God of the Philosophers* (Milwaukee, WI: Marquette University Press, 2016), pp. 24–5.

requires the addition of "grace", then God is not free to withhold "grace" (at least without eternally frustrating "nature"). If "nature" requires the addition of "grace" for its fulfilment, then God is constrained by creation.

Henri de Lubac (one of Congar's colleagues who is critical of this position) evidences this phobia, writing that "one of the chief motives that have led modern theology to develop its hypothesis of 'pure nature' … has been the anxiety to establish the supernatural as being a totally free gift".[11] There is such a thing as "pure nature"—i.e. "nature" that can exist entirely independently and without "grace"—because if "nature" could not be "pure", then "grace" could not be truly "free"; God would be constrained by—and so acted upon by—"nature". If there was no "pure nature", then this would introduce another sort of passivity in God.

Theologians call this position "extrinsicism", by which is meant that grace is "extrinsic" to nature. That is, grace comes to nature from the outside. Thus, as Andrew Swafford writes, "extrinsicism emphasizes the distinction of nature and grace for the purpose of preserving the supernatural and transcendent gratuity of grace".[12] The reason why theologians emphasize that "grace" is *extrinsic* to "nature"—and argue that this is what Thomas Aquinas held—is because these theologians are concerned more than anything else to maintain the gratuity and radicality of grace.[13] If the *extrinsicity* of grace is not upheld, then God is constrained by creation, i.e., a passivity is introduced into God.

---

[11]   Henri de Lubac, *The Mystery of the Supernatural* (New York, NY: The Crossroad Publishing Company, 1998), p. 53.

[12]   Andrew Dean Swafford, *Nature and Grace: A New Approach to Thomistic Ressourcement* (Cambridge: James Clarke & Co., 2015), p. 6.

[13]   "Extrinsic" has already been used quite extensively in this book as a way of explaining the absence of a real relation—all motion and change (including generation) is entirely *extrinsic* to God. While it is important to recognize the difference between the two uses of "extrinsic", the use of "extrinsic" in relation to the transcendence of God (i.e., as a description of the absence of a real relation) can help to elucidate the use of "extrinsic" in relation to the gratuitousness of grace. If "extrinsic" when used in relation to the absence of a real relation means that the effect is "extrinsic" to the "cause" (although, strictly speaking, God does not act as a cause at all), this does not point to a

Theologians have also referred to this "extrinsic" relationship between "nature" and "grace" as the *obediential potency*, which is contrasted with the *natural potency*. Andrew Swafford describes this *obediential potency* as "the capacity of a creature to 'obey' the creator, since the finite creature is always susceptible to being elevated or transformed by divine omnipotence".[14] In other words, if a "natural potency" is a thing's potential for something due to its own nature, then an "obediential potency" is a thing's potential for something due to the action of something acting upon it. Perhaps the best example of what this means is to consider a block of marble. It would be odd to suggest that the block of marble remains incomplete or unfulfilled if it is not carved into a statue, and yet the block of marble always remains capable of being so carved. The carving of a statue is not a *natural potency* of the marble—because it would be odd to suggest that marble has not fulfilled its "nature" if it failed to be so carved—but the marble has the potential to undergo such a change. As Lawrence Feingold puts it, "Marble does not have a natural agency to carve itself into a statue ... but it has a natural aptitude to undergo such action on the part of a higher natural agent."[15] The marble cannot be incomplete if it is not carved into a statue, nor can it cause itself to be so carved, yet the potential for the marble to become carved into a statue is always there to be actualized by another agent acting upon it.

Thus, when theologians refer to the relationship between "nature" and "grace" as "extrinsic", they mean that "nature" has an *obediential potential* for grace, not a *natural potential*. In the same way that one cannot look at the block of marble and move from it to the statue, so extrinsicists claim that one cannot look at "nature" and move from it to the beatific visions, i.e., "grace". If "grace" is held apart from "nature" to such an extent that "pure nature" (i.e., "nature" without "grace") is possible, and so a "purely natural" end or fulfilment to "nature" is also

---

similar relationship between "nature" and "grace". Rather, it means that while "grace" can (and does) transform and perfect "nature", "grace" is by no means implied by, or arrived at, through "nature".

[14] Swafford, *Nature and Grace*, p. 15.

[15] Feingold, *The Natural Desire to See God According to St. Thomas Aquinas and his Interpreters*, p. 149.

possible, then it can be said differently that humanity has an *obediential potential* for the beatific vision. If creatures cannot achieve the beatific vision without divine assistance, and if that divine assistance is not "obliged", then the beatific vision can only be an *obediential potential*. In this way, even though the beatific vision is "the highest good possible for human nature", "there is no need for God ever to realize it",[16] or, perhaps better, there is no *obligation* for God ever to realize it. As "nature" can exist coherently without "'grace" (like the marble can exist without being made into a statue) so the supernatural end is an *obediential potential*. It is, to put it rather bluntly, an unessential added extra, or, as J. M. H. Quenum puts it, grace becomes an "arbitrary something extra".[17] An infinitely great "end" no doubt, but not necessary for the contemplation of God.

Nature, grace, and "intrinsicism"

The desire to follow the "extrinsic" path is entirely understandable: (a) it emphasizes the radical "otherness" of grace; (b) it protects the gratuitousness of grace; (c) it prevents having to affirm divine passability—that God is affected by creation, which constrains God; all of which can be summed up by saying that (d) "nature" has an obediential potential for "grace". Such considerations are further nuanced when they are seen in the light of original sin and the need for salvation; if one thinks that original sin has blemished humanity, then the need to protect the otherness and gratuity of grace—and deny a "natural potency"—is all the more important.

However, even without the lens of original sin and the need for salvation, the desire to protect the gratuity and radicality of grace is a laudable position to take. God cannot be constrained by anything, including God's own act—God's act of creating nature cannot oblige or constrain God to bestow grace. However, despite the fact that the

---

[16]   Feingold, *The Natural Desire to See God According to St. Thomas Aquinas and his Interpreters*, p. 134.

[17]   J. M. H. Quenum, "Is Divine Grace really beyond human comprehension? An exploration of the theology of Henri de Lubac", *Testamentum Imperium* 3 (2011), p. 6.

intentions behind taking this "extrinsic" position are laudable, one must be cognizant of what this position leads to (even if unwittingly or inadvertently). Despite the very laudable intentions that might lead someone to take this "extrinsicist" view, both Yves Congar and Henri de Lubac were ultimately critical of it. As already outlined, they argued that if one wishes to emphasize the gratuity and radicality of grace, then one is obliged to hold to what commentators have called "pure nature", that is, one is obliged to hold that nature is a "closed and self-sufficient whole",[18] and so there is a "recognition of the intrinsic value and worth of the natural created order".[19] This means, Principe continues, that once one affirms the "intrinsic value" of nature, which is a "closed and self-sufficient whole", then nature becomes "asserted more strongly" and is given an autonomy and independence "in relation to the sacred and in particular to the Church". As already noted, emphasizing "pure nature" leads to a separation between the sacred and the secular, between the Church and the state.[20] Lawrence Feingold is even bleaker in his outlook than Principe, writing that this "extrinsic" position on the relationship between "nature" and "grace" is the "harbinger of modern naturalism and atheism".[21] Once one accepts that "nature" does not need "grace" for its fulfilment, then it is logical that religion itself is eventually rejected as irrelevant.

It is easy to see why the so-called "new theologians"—*nouvelle théologie*—like Yves Congar were so concerned about the direction in which theology was heading. The relationship between "nature" and "grace" might have been something with which only those interested in theology as an academic pursuit concerned themselves, but it had a very

---

[18] Feingold, *The Natural Desire to See God According to St. Thomas Aquinas and his Interpreters*, p. 81.

[19] Walter Principe, "Aquinas' Spirituality for Christ's Faithful Living in the World", in Thomas F. O'Meara (tr.), *Exploring Thomas Aquinas: Essays and Sermons* (Chicago, IL: New Priory Press, 2017), p. 91.

[20] Principe, "Aquinas' Spirituality for Christ's Faithful Living in the World", p. 91.

[21] Feingold, *The Natural Desire to See God According to St. Thomas Aquinas and his Interpreters*, p. 81.

real impact on the laity. If grace was not necessary for humanity to live "complete" and "fulfilled" lives, then the desire for grace, and the role of the Church in the lives of those who did not have a particular desire for grace, became increasingly marginal issues. Once it is affirmed that one can lead a perfectly acceptable life without the need for grace and the Church, then the Church becomes increasingly irrelevant to the laity, and becomes relevant only to those who have a particular desire for the beatific vision. If grace is *extrinsic* to nature, then one can live a perfectly fulfilled life outside of the Church. Indeed, one can see quite easily how this move can lead to "naturalism" and "atheism", as Feingold warns. Once the Church becomes an irrelevance to the laity, then it is only a short step from being irrelevant to being wrong or, worse, nefarious. One might be protecting the gratuity of grace and impassibility of God, but one is also making the Church entirely irrelevant to the laity.

Henri de Lubac, as a representative of those who reacted against this position, argued that grace is not "*extrinsic*" to nature, but "*intrinsic*". As one might expect, this means that, for de Lubac, grace is not entirely and completely outwith nature—so that nature is a "closed and self-sufficient whole"[22]—but requires grace for its fulfilment; without grace, nature would be continually and eternally frustrated. Whole libraries could be written on the complexities of this debate, and space prevents a full discussion of de Lubac's theology and the relative merits of this reaction against the "extrinsic" position. Nevertheless, a few comments are necessary.

The crux of the issue for de Lubac is that humanity has a "desire to see God". Importantly, this desire to see God "is not some 'accident' ... [but is] a result of [their] belonging to humanity" and, further, this "desire" or "call" is "constitutive" of "nature", so that the "finality, which is expressed by this desire, is inscribed upon [their] very being as it has been put into this universe by God". For de Lubac, precisely because humanity participates in God for its being, so a desire for God must be constitutive of what it means to be human. Karl Rahner agrees, noting that precisely because humanity depends on God for its very existence, so it cannot

---

22   Feingold, *The Natural Desire to See God According to St. Thomas Aquinas and his Interpreters*, p. 81.

ever be in a position, whether accepted or not, whether acknowledged or not, in which its life is not directed towards God;[23] that is, if humanity depends on God for its very being, if humanity imitates God for its very being, then humanity must have a *natural* desire for God.[24] This means, de Lubac argues, that the desire to see God "cannot be permanently frustrated without an essential suffering" and, moreover, "a good and just God could hardly frustrate [humanity], unless [they], through [their] own fault, turn away from him by choice".[25] "Grace", for de Lubac, is not a superfluous added extra, a luxury granted to those chosen few whom God deems worthy. Rather, because the desire for God is *natural*—i.e., the desire for God is *constitutive* of "nature"—so the failure to fulfil this desire results in a very real suffering for humanity.

It was this possibility of a real suffering that de Lubac saw as the real content of the doctrine of *epektasis*. For de Lubac, Gregory of Nyssa's notion of "eternal progress" is "deceptive" because the creature makes no real progress. If the creature can never arrive at God, if the creature can never find true rest but is always—eternally—moving further and further towards God, then this is as good as saying that the creature makes no progress at all—the creature never actually gets closer to God if eternal progress is possible. In fact, de Lubac argues, is not this notion of "eternal progress" the very definition of eternal frustration? Writing of a "real dynamism and real advance", which means that "the further forward one goes towards an inaccessible goal, the closer one in fact gets to it", de Lubac compares this "real advance" to "the agony which must surely be the lot of a being whose endless pursuit, spurred on by an ever more vehement desire, never really gets anywhere at all".[26] *Epektasis*, for de Lubac, is not (as has been outlined in Chapter 1) a necessary implication of the *analogia entis* (necessary because it describes the infinite ontological gulf that separates the creature from the creator), but is that which describes the frustration that must characterize the

---

[23]   Karl Rahner, *The Foundations of Christian Faith: An Introduction to the Idea of Christianity* (New York, NY: Crossroad, 1978), pp. 77–8.

[24]   Rahner, *The Foundations of Christian Faith*, p. 298.

[25]   de Lubac, *The Mystery of the Supernatural*, pp. 54–5.

[26]   de Lubac, *The Mystery of the Supernatural*, p. 201.

creature who has a natural desire for grace which is constantly and eternally frustrated.

For de Lubac, therefore, "grace" must be *intrinsic* to "nature" because the *desire* for God must be constitutive of "nature". If the desire for grace is constitutive of what it means for a creature to be a creature, then the failure to obtain grace must result in an eternal frustration and suffering.

Yet, as much as grace must be *intrinsic* for de Lubac, he was clear that this did not make "grace" certain. Henri de Lubac was critical of the "extrinsic" position, but this does not mean that he was not sympathetic to their intentions. As much as grace must be "intrinsic" to nature as its fulfilment (because the desire for grace is constitutive of nature), de Lubac is just as keen to stress that "the created nature is no kind of divine seed ... it is not even the promise of it".[27] Likewise, de Lubac continues to emphasize, there is "no kind of metaphysical necessity" so that "just as creation is no kind of necessary consequence of something which 'preceded' it within God, so the gift ... of the supernatural is no mere consequence of creation".[28] If there is nothing within God that compels God to create, nothing that constrains God to create, then the fact that God creates in the first place does not constrain God to bestow grace subsequently. The act of creation—"the first thing"—"does not necessarily imply" the "call"—"the second" thing—nor the beatific vision—"the third" —as that would "inhibit God's utter independence".[29] Thus, de Lubac concludes that this must mean that "God could have refused to give himself to his creatures", and such a refusal would result in the eternal frustration and suffering of creatures. Even after creation, grace "remains gratuitous at every stage of preparation for the gift, and at every stage of the giving of it". There is, reiterates de Lubac, "no 'disposition' in creatures [that] can ever, in any way, bind the creator".[30] That creatures have been created does not oblige God to bestow on them that which they desire as the very constitution of their nature. As much as de Lubac disagrees with the tendency to see grace as "extrinsic" to nature, he is

---

[27]   de Lubac, *The Mystery of the Supernatural*, p. 84.

[28]   de Lubac, *The Mystery of the Supernatural*, p. 82.

[29]   de Lubac, *The Mystery of the Supernatural*, p. 81.

[30]   de Lubac, *The Mystery of the Supernatural*, pp. 236–7.

absolutely clear that the bestowal of grace must still be distinct from the "act" of creation, so as to retain the freedom of God; no matter how the relationship is characterized, the fact of creation, the fact that God has "already" created, cannot constrain or oblige God to bestow grace. God could frustrate creation if God so wished.

Arguably, therefore, it is this point that can be seen as the crucial difference between the "extrinsicists" and the "intrinsicists". Whereas the "extrinsicists" could not accept that God would create "nature" that could ultimately be left to frustration and suffering—and so postulated a "purely natural" end to nature to ensure that, even without grace, nature would not be left frustrated—the "intrinsicists" accepted that this is precisely what the logic of the position dictated: there could never be a "purely natural" contemplation of God, but God could still freely withhold the "supernatural light of glory" that was necessary for this contemplation. In other words, de Lubac was sympathetic to the motives that led "extrinsicists" to make the claims they did, but he was also cognizant that following the separation of "nature" and "grace" to the extent they did led to the irrelevance of the Church and the absurd notion that humans can lead a genuinely fulfilling life without the Church. Thus, de Lubac distinguishes between the *desire* for God and the *attainment* of grace: the former is natural, the latter is *super*natural. De Lubac writes that "the desire is not to be defined by its effect but rather by its cause; therefore it will be called natural not because man could naturally elicit it, but because nature has placed it in him".[31] This is crucial. By arguing for the *intrinsicity* of "grace", de Lubac was absolutely not arguing for a *natural potency* for grace; rather, he was affirming that "grace" has to be *intrinsic* because that "grace" is constitutive of humanity's relationship with God.

The difference between the "extrinsic" position and the "intrinsic" position, then, might be put differently as a difference of emphasis. Those who subscribe to the "extrinsic" position are possessed of an "anxiety to establish the supernatural as being a totally free gift"[32] and so are happy to affirm the possibility of "pure nature" and a "purely natural" contemplation

---

[31]   Henri de Lubac, *Augustinianism and Modern Theology* (London: Geoffrey Chapman, 1969), p. 137.

[32]   de Lubac, *The Mystery of the Supernatural*, p. 53.

of God in order to emphasize "the distinction of nature and grace for the purpose of preserving the supernatural and transcendent gratuity of grace".[33] Without that gratuity, the radical distinction between God and creatures is weakened and God and creatures become more or less univocal, and so "grace" becomes different from "nature" only by degree. If the radical distinction between "nature" and "grace" is not upheld—if the complete gratuity of the beatific vision is not emphasized—then the complete otherness of God is lost. On the other hand, those who subscribe to the "intrinsic" position are concerned that this means that grace becomes "so irrelevant to the most fundamental longings of the human heart that God's offer of salvation can easily be shrugged off".[34]

On the one hand, emphasizing the gratuity and radical otherness of grace seems to lead to the possibility that grace becomes irrelevant to the creature, who can "shrug off" the offer of salvation and relegate the Church from the life of the laity. On the other hand, emphasizing the natural desire for God (as opposed to the natural attainment of grace) and placing that desire at the very constitution of what it means to be a creature—precisely because all creatures participate in God as the "ground of being"—seems to make God and creatures univocal and leads to the possibility that God could wilfully frustrate creatures by withholding grace, or at the very least that God is constrained by creation to bestow grace as its fulfilment. Either God is irrelevant to all but the most ardent of worshippers ("extrinsicism") or God is passable ("intrinsicism").

Nature and grace and the single divine activity

Yet, for all that the "intrinsic" and "extrinsic" positions are opposite ways of looking at the relationship between "nature" and "grace", they are in agreement regarding a particular element of the question: for the "intrinsicist" and the "extrinsicist" alike, the bestowal of grace is an entirely distinct act *for* God—i.e., the creation of nature and the bestowal of grace are two distinct acts *for* God. If God can freely withhold the bestowal of grace—something that *both* the "extrinsicist" and "intrinsicist" keenly affirm—then the bestowal of grace becomes a potential that may

---

[33]   Swafford, *Nature and Grace*, p. 6.

[34]   Oakes, *A Theology of Grace in Six Controversies*, p. 8.

or may not be actualized by God subsequently. That is, if God can freely withhold grace—*after* or in addition to creation—then God is neither *actus purus*—because there is a potential (i.e., the bestowal of grace) that God could leave unactualized—nor simple—because the bestowal of grace means that God is really related to the world differently at different spatiotemporal points. Regardless of whether or not the "extrinsicist" position or the "intrinsicist" position accurately represents Thomas Aquinas' thinking, for present purposes, the real issue lies in whether the relationship between "nature" and "grace" adequately takes account of the idea of creation as an ontological relationship. To a certain extent, it does not matter what motives lead the theologian to affirm that "grace" is either "extrinsic" or "intrinsic" to "nature"; neither position is compatible with the theology presented in this book. Both positions seem to assume that creation is an event that has happened in the past, and that the bestowal of grace is something additional that God can do subsequent to creating in the future. Both positions assume that God experiences time and is really related to different spatiotemporal points differently.

Neither the "extrinsicist" position nor the "intrinsicist" position can be correct (at least in relation to the theology presented in this book) if neither of them takes seriously the absence of a real relation. Neither position can be correct if the distinction between "nature" and "grace" is real *for* God. If God is genuinely simple and is genuinely *actus purus*, and if "viewed from God's point of view the bestowal of grace is uniform",[35] so that the difference between creation and deification is *extrinsic* to God, and is *only* real for creatures (like the distinction between "right" and "left" for the creature who moves in relation to a column), then neither the "extrinsic" nor the "intrinsic" position can be correct if both take seriously the notion that "God could have refused to give himself to his creatures".[36] The problem is with the idea that God could have created *and then* withheld grace, as if the "creating" and the "bestowing" are two separate acts *for* God. It seems that if God can refuse to give

---

[35] Philip McCosker, "Grace", in Philip McCosker and Denys Turner (eds), *The Cambridge Companion to The Summa Theologiae* (Cambridge: Cambridge University Press, 2016), p. 216.

[36] de Lubac, *The Mystery of the Supernatural*, p. 236.

"grace"—having *already* created—then "grace" must be separate and distinct from God's act of creating: that is, "nature" and "grace" must be two distinct acts. If that is the case, then it would appear that there is possibility and potential in God, and so God can neither be the *actus purus* nor be genuinely simple. Differently, if God can refuse to give grace, then there is a real possibility of God relating differently to different creatures and different spatiotemporal points (i.e., it seems that grace is not uniform).

Participants in this debate do seem to have noted this problem about reconciling the relationship between "nature" and "grace" with the notion that "there is only one activity in God".[37] Writing about the single divine activity, Henri de Lubac quotes with approval Juan Alfaro and Frances de Sales:

> God decreed all that exists in the indivisibility of a single act of his sovereign liberty; the distinctions which may be introduced into that divine act by the imperfection of our understanding can only be justified by the created connection that exists between created things and that divine decree.
>
> God then has no need of several acts since a single act of his almighty will suffices to produce all the variety of his works, because of his infinite perfection.[38]

---

[37] Thomas Aquinas, *Selected Writings* (London: Penguin, 1998), *Disputed Questions on the Power of God* 7.

[38] Juan Alfaro and Francis of Sales, quoted by de Lubac, *The Mystery of the Supernatural*, p. 81.

Such sentiments have already been quoted at length in this book, particularly in relation to how Thomas Aquinas[39] and Bonaventure[40] understood the act of creation: God creates everything in one single act; all diversity, difference, change, and multiplicity are *extrinsic* to God's act. However, de Lubac is also quick to clarify his position. Immediately after quoting with approval these sentiments on the singularity of the divine act, de Lubac writes that "we must be careful to distinguish two instances of gratuitousness [and] two divine gifts" such that "if creation can in a real sense be called a 'grace', then the call to see God is another one".[41] Even if creation is "*gratuitous*"—i.e., "of grace"—then, for de Lubac, there must be two types of grace; one that creates and the other that calls creatures to the beatific vision. There might be a single divine act, but there are genuinely two "parts" or "elements" to that single act.

Others have already been quoted making a similar distinction. Edward Oakes, for example, writes that "God's power to create and sustain the universe in being is not the same as his power to become incarnate".[42] Likewise, Karl Rahner has also already been quoted writing that "we can understand creation and Incarnation as two moments and two phases of the *one* process of God's self-giving and self-expression, although it is an *intrinsically differentiated* process".[43] Again, creation and the bestowal of grace in the incarnation are different *for* God; creation and deification

---

[39] See Frederick Bauerschmidt, *Thomas Aquinas: Faith, Reason, and Following Christ* (Oxford: Oxford University Press, 2013), pp. 114–5; Eleonore Stump and Norman Kretzmann, "Absolute Simplicity", *Faith and Philosophy: Journal of the Society of Christian Philosophers* 2:4 (1985), p. 354; Craig, "Timelessness, Creation, and God's Real Relation to the World", p. 109.

[40] See Joshua C. Benson, "Structure and Meaning in St. Bonaventure's 'Quaestiones Disputatae de Scientia Christi'", *Franciscan Studies* 62 (2004), p. 74; Junius Johnson, "The One and the Many in Bonaventure Exemplarity Explained", *Religions* 7:144 (2016), p. 12; see also Katherin Rogers, *Perfect Being Theology* (Edinburgh: Edinburgh University Press, 2000), p. 27.

[41] de Lubac, *The Mystery of the Supernatural*, p. 82.

[42] Oakes, *A Theology of Grace in Six Controversies*, p. 38.

[43] Rahner, *The Foundations of Christian Faith*, p. 97 (italics added).

are *intrinsically differentiated*, not *extrinsically differentiated* (i.e., not like the movement in relation to the pillar).

Moreover, if "nature" and "grace" are separate and distinct *for* God, so that "creation" and "deification" must be two distinct acts *for* God, then they must be two events in an accidentally ordered series. If "grace" (i.e., deification) is a separate act to "nature" (i.e., creation), such that the latter does not imply or oblige the former, then it becomes impossible to think of "creation" and "deification" in any other way than as two distinct *events* that happen at specific points in time. It becomes impossible to conceive of "creation" (nature) and "deification" (grace) as anything other than two pearls together on a string. If "creation" (nature) becomes nothing more than the first event in a series that (potentially) includes "deification" (grace), which completes "nature", then, regardless of whether the latter is "extrinsic" or "intrinsic" to the former, neither can be understood as an essentially ordered hierarchy through which creatures participate in God. Instead, creation becomes—for the "extrinsicist" and "intrinsicist" equally—one part of a much wider whole, a process that is started at one point and finished at another. "Creation" ("nature") becomes synonymous with "origin", and fulfilment ("grace") becomes synonymous with "end".

If what has been said in this book is correct, then all discussions of the relationship between "nature" and "grace" are problematic. This book has argued that "creation" is an ontological hierarchy through which creatures participate in God, and so this means that "grace" cannot be something that God does subsequently to that "act" and which "perfects" or fulfils it. Yet, of course, this is in no way intended to be taken as a rejection of the category of "grace", as if the theology presented in this book must reject "grace" as being useful or relevant for theology. Nor is it a suggestion that there cannot be any difference between "nature" and "grace" *for creatures* in their relationship to and with God. Neither does it suggest that God is constrained to bestow grace on nature. Rather, it affirms that there is a real need for reinterpretation or nuance of the categories of "nature" and "grace" in order to take seriously this theological problem: if one takes seriously divine atemporality, simplicity, divine impassability, and God as *actus purus*, if one wishes to uphold a single divine act (which is an essentially ordered relationship) then one cannot also maintain either the "extrinsicist" or "intrinsicist" position regarding the relationship between "nature" and "grace".

The question, then, is: how does the incarnational deist who takes the Thomist doctrine of creation as an essentially ordered ontological relation genuinely accept a doctrine of "deification" or "fulfilment of creation" without either discarding the idea of "grace" entirely or compromising those theological concerns and anxieties that troubled those who took a side in the debate over "extrinsicism" or "intrinsicism"? Differently, how can one accept a doctrine of the fulfilment of creation without having to subscribe to a doctrine of providence, or of God's "continuing" involvement and guidance of history?

Grace and deism

In attempting to affirm and emphasize the gratuity and radical otherness of grace, Henri de Lubac contrasts the beatific vision with creation, writing that "between nature as it exists and the supernatural ... the distance is as great, the difference as radical, as that between non-being and being".[44] Indeed, de Lubac has already been quoted making similar comparisons between "the first thing" (creation), "the second" thing (the "call") and "the third" (the beatific vision).[45] Likewise, he has already been quoted calling the beatific vision "another" grace if "creation can in a real sense be called a 'grace'".[46] However, the explicit reference to the distinction between "non-being" and "being"—and the explicit comparison of this distinction to the difference between "nature" and "grace"—immediately points to an important fact that it appears none of the participants in the debate over the relationship between "nature" and "grace" have even acknowledged, let alone paid due attention to: the difference between "non-being" and "being" is a hierarchical, ontological relationship, not a temporal, accidentally ordered origin. Not only that, but it is a relationship that is *extrinsic* to God. Indeed, it was precisely the fact that the difference between "non-being" and "being" is a relationship that is *extrinsic* to God—so that God remains unchanged regardless of

---

44 de Lubac, *The Mystery of the Supernatural*, p. 83.

45 de Lubac, *The Mystery of the Supernatural*, p. 81.

46 de Lubac, *The Mystery of the Supernatural*, p. 82.

whether there is a universe or not—that lay at the heart of William Lane Craig's criticism of Aquinas' doctrine of the absence of a real relation. This is what Richard Cross would call a "weak" account of creation, meaning that it denies that "creation" is an identifiable discrete act that God does, and which differs from conservation: that is, it denies that "creation" is in any way comparable to, or coincident with, "origins". For Thomas Aquinas, creation is a "certain relation" of dependence, not an event. Or, differently, God does not *do* anything to create "nature"; creation is about an essentially ordered, hierarchical relation.

This leads to one of two conclusions: either (a) Henri de Lubac thinks that creation is not a relationship, but is instead synonymous with the "origin" of the universe; or (b) Henri de Lubac is incorrect in his claim that the distinction between "nature" and "grace" is comparable to the distinction between "non-being" and "being". Or, to put the same distinction differently, either (a) the bestowal of grace cannot be a *second* act, because there is not a *first* act; or (b) if de Lubac is correct that the difference between "nature" and "grace" is comparable to the difference between "being" and "non-being", then the difference between "nature" and "grace" must likewise be *extrinsic* to God. In this way, the fulfilment of creation cannot be identified with or be coincident with a future state of affairs in which the universe becomes perfected and incorruptible. The fulfilment of creation cannot be about the attainment of a perfect state of affairs that characterizes the physical constitution of the universe, but, rather, it is to be understood as a metaphysical, ontological relationship.

However, if the distinction between "nature" and "grace" is *extrinsic* to God, how does this avoid Pelagianism? How can the distinction between "nature" and "grace" be *extrinsic* to God while maintaining the gratuity of grace? Quite clearly, the issue for both the "intrinsic" and the "extrinsic" position is the emphasis on the gratuity of grace. As already argued, it is the gratuity of grace that moves exponents of both positions to affirm that God's first act of creation cannot oblige or constrain God's second act of creation (i.e., deification). The difference between them is the extent to which they emphasize the radicality of grace: "extrinsicists" emphasize that the radicality of grace means that there can only be an *obediential potential*; "intrinsicists" emphasize that there is a *natural desire* for God. It is easy to see why there is a preoccupation with the gratuity of God. It is difficult to explicitly reject those Augustinian heresies—Pelagianism, Jansenism, and Baianism—that have been so influential on western thought and not perceive that one's hands are tied on the issue of gratuity. That is, if grace is *necessary* for creatures, then one seems to be open to the criticism that one affirms a form of Baianism—that humanity is so pathetic that they are owed grace—and/or Jansenism—that humanity is so pathetic that they cannot freely accept grace if it is freely given. That is, if one downplays the gratuity of grace, then it seems that one is arguing that in some way grace is "owed" to creatures, that there is a *debitum naturae*, or debt to nature: i.e., because God has created "nature", so God owes grace. Once one de-emphasizes the gratuity of grace, then one seems obliged to affirm one or other of the Augustinian heresies.

Yet, if it is easy to be sympathetic to these concerns, they are nothing more than those concerns that lie at the heart of criticisms of the "sun" analogy for creation as "emanation". That is, just as theologians are keen to stress the gratuity of grace, so they are keen to stress the gratuity of creation in the first place. As already quoted from de Lubac, "Just as creation is no kind of necessary consequence of something which 'preceded' it within God, so the gift ... of the supernatural is no mere consequence of creation";[47] the gratuity of grace mirrors the gratuity of creation. Thus, if creation is like the rays of the sun, which "exercises no rational process, no act of choice, and yet by the very fact of its existence it gives light to whatever is able to partake of its light, in its own way",[48] then this seems to be incompatible with the idea of God as a thinking, willing, deciding, and acting person, who freely chooses to create and could just as well have not created. In other words, if creation is an "emanation" then this seems to impinge upon the freedom of creation.

However, understandable as these concerns are, one does not need to sacrifice the gratuity of creation in the "sun analogy" in order to affirm its appropriateness. That is, despite the fact that creation as "emanation" seems to lead to the conclusion that God exercises "no act of choice",[49] this does not lead to the conclusion that creation is *necessary*. "Freedom"

---

[47] de Lubac, *The Mystery of the Supernatural*, p. 82.

[48] Pseudo-Dionysius, *The Divine Names* 4.1.

[49] Pseudo-Dionysius, *The Divine Names* 4.1.

and "necessity" are not mutually opposed, as if the loss of freedom leads to necessity. Sergei Bulgakov argues this point with some clarity. In his book *Bride of the Lamb*, Bulgakov criticizes Thomas Aquinas and other western theologians for unwittingly "anthropomorphizing" God by distinguishing between "freedom" and "necessity" for God. What he means by this is that any theology that sees "necessity" as an opposite to, and violation of, "freedom" *for God*, relegates God to the realm of creation and so treats God as univocal with creatures. Rather, in relation to God, necessity does not impinge upon and/or destroy the freedom of God.[50] Certainly, Bulgakov admits that such a distinction between "necessity" and "freedom" is "permissible for creaturely limitedness", but in God such a distinction "brings into divinity the element of accident and arbitrariness".[51] To say that God could have refrained from creating is to postulate in God an anthropomorphic will.[52]

The question of time and eternity is central to this issue. Bulgakov writes that "eternity belongs to creation, and therefore the world for God is co-eternal with Him",[53] so that, "if God created the world, this means that he *could not have refrained from creating it*".[54] In other words, *that* there is a world that has been created is all the evidence one needs that God has created, and if God is eternal and immutable, then it could not have been any different. This does not mean that creation is necessary, or that God is constrained or obliged to create; God could have not created, but God has created, and if God is atemporal and immutable then this must eternally have been the case.

Despite the fact that Bulgakov explicitly sees his dismissal of the distinction between "freedom" and "necessity" as a reaction against what he perceives to be anthropomorphism in Thomas Aquinas, there is a connection with Thomas Aquinas' doctrine of the absence of a real relation. That the universe obtains at all does not introduce a change

[50]   Sergei Bulgakov, *The Bride of the Lamb* (Grand Rapids, MI: William B. Eerdmans, 2002), p. 30.

[51]   Bulgakov, *The Bride of the Lamb*, p. 31.

[52]   Bulgakov, *The Bride of the Lamb*, p. 31.

[53]   Bulgakov, *The Bride of the Lamb*, p. 59.

[54]   Bulgakov, *The Bride of the Lamb*, p. 31 (italics in original).

in God; even if there were no universe, God would still "do" the same. That is, the fact that the universe exists at all is a change on the part of the creature and so is *extrinsic* to God. In other words, the "decision" to create is not something that God does or does not do. God eternally remains the same, and God is eternally creative. This does not mean that God is constrained or obliged to "do" something particular because those categories misrepresent "what" God is; those categories bring God into the realm of "being" and "personhood" and make God univocal with creatures. Of course, Bulgakov and Aquinas held very different theologies (despite the connections that this book has suggested exist between them), and so it is irresponsible to suggest that there is an absolute identity between what they are claiming, but the general principle is the same: if God is eternal and immutable, then God could not have not created, because there is a universe.

To say that "eternity belongs to creation", so that the world is "co-eternal with God" might sound odd to many, particularly as it is so often assumed that the eternity of creation/matter is in direct opposition to the doctrine of God as creator. Indeed, it was the supposition that "eternity of matter" and "creation" are directly opposed that led Hawking and others to proclaim confidently (but entirely mistakenly) that once one has removed a beginning to the universe one has removed the need for a creator. As Aquinas was clear, it is not philosophically and/or theologically incoherent to hold *both* that the world has infinite temporal duration *and* is created. It is entirely possible for the world to be eternal and created because creation has nothing to do with the beginning of the universe and is about its dependence on God (i.e., it is about an essentially ordered series). "Eternity" of creation holds that the world extends temporally "backwards" infinitely without termination, and "act" of creation holds that the world extends ontologically "upwards" finitely, terminating in God. Thus, to say that creation is "co-eternal with God" is nothing more than another way of saying the same thing: that creation is about "vertical" dependency, not physical and/or temporal beginnings.

In other words, whether one calls this "co-eternal with God" or "the absence of a real relation" the conclusion is the same: the real issue is not about "freedom" and "necessity" but about "dependence". It is not heretical to say that God lacks the freedom not to create (or bestow grace) because that assumes that creation is an accidentally ordered cause concerned with beginnings and that God is an anthropomorphic "super-human" who can deliberate and choose to leave some accidentally ordered potential unactualized. If God "lacks" freedom, this does not make the universe *necessary* because even if God could not "not create", that creation that God did not have the freedom to refrain from "doing" *still depends entirely* on God for its being. Even if God lacked the freedom not to create, creation would still be contingent. In other words (and this is Bulgakov's point), it is not "freedom" that is the opposite of "necessity", but "dependence". Thus, if the "sun analogy" is an appropriate image for creation, then one can make the same response to the same concern about the gratuity of grace. If creation does not need to be "freely" done—so that God could have chosen not to create—then grace does not need to be "freely" given. To put this differently, the worry over the gratuity of grace—while completely understandable—is entirely misplaced. The question, then, is not about whether God bestows grace gratuitously or not, but whether God is a person who can deliberate and decide not to create, or that, after God has decided to create, God can then decide not to fulfil that creation.

For the "traditional theist", the setting up of a tension between "first" and "second" acts of God and a tension between "freedom" and "necessity" is just a false dichotomy. Here, the difference between "nature" and "grace" and between "creation" and "deification" is identical to the "Thomistic column". Just as "right" and "left" are genuinely different positions, but only subjectively real for the person who is standing in relation to the pillar, which itself does not move, so creation—the difference/change between "non-being" and "being"—is a genuinely real distinction, but it is only subjectively real for the creature in relation to the "eternal emanation" of God's creative "ground of being". Likewise, just as "right" and "left" are genuinely real, so "nature" and "grace" are genuinely distinct and different ways of relating to God, but they do not change God; God does not do anything different. Thus, "non-being", "nature", and "grace" are all just different ways of relating to God's eternal emanation. In other words, the difference between (what de Lubac would call) the "eternal frustration" of the creature and the "fulfilment" of the creature's life in the beatific vision are entirely identical to God; the difference between "frustration" and "fulfilment" is only a subjectively real difference for the creature.

This means that "grace" is not bestowed on the creature in a distinct and separate act from the bestowal of "being"; "grace" is the individual creature's realization that they already participate in God and imitate Christ. "Grace" is not something that can be withheld from creatures and bestowed on them at some point in time as determined by a God who acts in complete freedom. The creature is always under the influence of grace; the difference between "creation" and "deification" is in the creature who realizes that the world already participates in and imitates Christ. Grace is like a gestalt; grace is looking at the same universe but realizing that it is cruciform, that the very same universe has the form of Christ.

In many ways, then, this chapter completes the chapter on providence and confirms that if providence is understood as "the purpose of God unfolding itself in the development of the cosmos and of human history",[55] then it seems inevitable that the deist cannot support providence; hence the characteristic deist denial of providence. However, if providence is understood in the way that Tillich does (which is an acceptable if not the obvious interpretation of Thomas' own doctrine of providence) and if creation is understood as an ontological relationship—participation—that the creature has with God, then the deist is not forced to reject providence. Providence for the Thomist-deist is each creature finding their ontological end in God, not the ordering of history towards a perfect future end-time.

Deism, then, does not lead to a "detached and impotent God,"[56] who "certainly has no specific interest in human affairs";[57] that would be a "theistic personalist" God, whose relationship to the world is conceived only in terms of univocality of causality and whose "interest" in and love of the world is conceived entirely correlated with God's capacity to influence the history of the world. Rather, if God is seen through the lens of Thomas' doctrine of creation, then God's "failure" to influence the history of the world in any way does not lead to an uninterested God, but

---

55   Gilkey, "The Concept of Providence in Contemporary Theology", p. 171.

56   Saunders, *Divine Action & Modern Science*, p. 100.

57   Dawkins, *The God Delusion*, pp. 39–40.

a God whose "interest" in and relationship with the world is conceived wholly differently, not in the sense that God "respects" the freedom of the world and so refrains from getting involved, but in the sense that divine activity is about ontology.

Grace and Eastern Orthodoxy
Neither the "extrinsic" position nor the "intrinsic" position can be correct. Both are phobic of any sort of relationship that compromises the "freedom" of God and, in being so, cannot present an adequate understanding of "grace" in which God is not a "person" who makes decisions and does things and in which deification is not a distinct and separate act *for* God. Perhaps, then, the whole western understanding of "grace" is incompatible with the theology presented in this book; perhaps a different understanding of "grace" is required. An eastern orthodox view of grace may be more amenable.

Russian Orthodox theologian Vladimir Lossky, for example, is emphatic in this regard. He writes that the Eastern Church "knows nothing of 'pure nature' to which grace is added as a supernatural gift. For [Eastern Orthodoxy], there is no natural or 'normal' state, since grace is implied in the act of creation itself."[58] What this means is that, for Orthodox theologians, what is important is not that God does something specific at a specific time in order to transform/perfect humanity, but that humanity submits itself more and more to the influence of the grace that is already effective in the world as the very basis of their "being" in the first place. Thus, for the Eastern Church, it is "synergia" that is more important, not anything that God does or does not do.

This caricature of the difference between eastern and western theology is well documented. For western theologians—influenced as they were by Augustine, a comparable figure to which does not occur in the east—the story of salvation history was one of a *restitutio in integrum*: a second act of God was entirely necessary in order to restore creatures to their former standing. However, for eastern theologians—who were more influenced by Irenaeus—the story of salvation history was one of growth from infant

---

58   Vladimir Lossky, *The Mystical Theology of the Eastern Church* (Cambridge: James Clarke & Co., 1957), p. 101.

to spiritual maturity. There was much more room for (what to western eyes looked like a semi-Pelagian) emphasis on humanity's response to God's act of creation, rather than the need for God to restore it.

Importantly, this is not an unwitting affirmation of the univocality of being. It might be tempting to see "synergia" as indicating that God and creatures are equal, that God and creatures both contribute something different and so "grace" requires something equally of creatures as it does God. This would be incorrect. "Synergia" does not mean that "grace" is brought about through a conjunction of divine and creaturely causality. One might see Philip Hefner's notion of "created co-creators" or Austin Farrer's notion of "double causality" as this sort of synergia. For Hefner and Farrer, God and creatures do roughly the same sort of thing, but one—God—has a greater range of powers to an infinitely greater degree than the other. In other words, synergia does not mean that God and creatures are both accidentally ordered causes that work in conjunction to bring something about. Rather, synergia is about submission. As Anna Williams writes, "Synergia [is] not so much the cooperation of God and humanity considered as equals but ... the process whereby human persons offer their wills to God's sanctifying action."[59] That is, she continues, "[it is] not whether sanctification is God's work or ours but whether our sanctification can be accomplished against our will or without our wills."[60]

Thus, "submission to God" does not mean something like "allowing God to act", as if submission to the divine will is about human "inaction", just as one might submit to the rule of a monarch, or as Jesus submitted to the will of Pontius Pilate. This clearly would mean that God and creatures are univocal, that divine activity and creaturely activity are in competition so that the influence of the divine requires creatures to refrain from acting. This, again, would assume (however unwittingly) that divine activity is about the accidentally ordered movement of the world to a specific state of affairs. Submitting to God's will does not mean constraining one's activity in order to permit God to control one's activity

---

[59]   Anna Williams, *The Ground of Union: Deification in Aquinas and Palamas* (Oxford: Oxford University Press, 1999), p. 133.

[60]   Williams, *The Ground of Union*, p. 130.

to greater degrees. Indeed, drawing on the conclusion to Chapter 2, divine activity has nothing to do with "motion" or with causing specific things to occur at specific moments. Divine creation and deification are about "being". Submission to God, then, is nothing more than this dependence on God—in an essentially ordered series—for one's very being and causal power. Submission to God is the recognition that one depends on God at all moments. Creation itself, as a relationship, is inherently gracious. Grace, then, the grace of Jesus Christ bestowed in the incarnation, is as much that which is responsible for creation as it is deification. Grace, understood as a submission to God, is about the creature's realization that they depend on God for their very "being". If deification is recast as the realization that the world already participates in and imitates Christ so that "grace" is like a gestalt, then this "submission to God" must be about the recognition that one is entirely dependent on God as the very basis of their "being".

No doubt, there will be some who find this "subjective" interpretation of deification unacceptable. No doubt there will be those who argue that if deification is about creatures submitting to the grace that is already present in God's creating, God is not really doing anything at all. Critics might then suggest that, if God is not doing anything, then humanity is, and so this inevitably leads to Pelagianism. Of course, it is easy to be sympathetic to these concerns. Precisely because of the lasting legacy of Augustine, one cannot do theology in the west without being constantly concerned about any theology that might see deification as being something that is brought about by humanity or, at the very least, as something that God is constrained to bestow. However, eastern theology did not have a comparable figure to that of Pelagius so has never been anywhere near as phobic of postulating that humanity can "contribute" in some way. Likewise, eastern theology did not have comparable figures to that of Cornelius Jansen and Michael Baius, and so have not been anywhere near as phobic of talking about "necessity" in relation to God, as Bulgakov evidences.

Thus, it would be a mistake to think that a subjective view of grace is heretical. Not because Pelagianism must be re-evaluated, but because the issues that lead theologians to Pelagianism are just not relevant to eastern theology. One can only arrive at Pelagianism if one sees divine activity and created activity as univocal—so that humanity is doing what is the prerogative of God—and/or if one sees the need for salvation as being a return to a past perfection that requires a re-creation. Yet, for the eastern theories of grace, humanity does not require a return to a past perfection that requires re-creation (which is the sole prerogative of God); even if it did, those eastern theories do not argue that humanity's contribution to synergia is "creation" in the same way that God "creates". They cannot be Pelagian, then, because they do not think of humanity as doing something that is the sole prerogative of God. Thus, it becomes much easier to see "grace" as being the submission of humanity to a dependence on God that makes one more open to the influence of grace and therefore genuinely related to God in a new and more "fulfilling" way. God does not change, nor does God do anything new—God is impassable and immutable—but humanity is genuinely transformed by submitting to and depending upon God in a more profound and deeper way. The issue, as Anna Williams puts it, is not whether deification is God's work or humanity's (such a question assumes that divine activity and created activity are univocal), but whether creatures—whose very "being"' is already defined through a participation in an ontological, hierarchical relation to God—realize their dependence on God and submit to it, allowing the transforming influence of grace—which is already constitutive of their "ground of being" and reaches out to all creatures like the rays of the sun—to fulfil their "being".

In this way, focusing on whether "*grace*" is "extrinsic" or "intrinsic" to "*nature*" completely misses the real question: whether any *distinction between* "nature" and "grace" is "extrinsic" or "intrinsic" *for* God. Once one accepts this latter question, then the former becomes somewhat irrelevant. The important issue is that the difference between "nature" and "grace" can only be real for creatures, and so the move from "nature" to "grace" can only be because of a change in the creature in relation to God, not a change in God in relation to the creature. The creature is not bringing about their own salvation—as if the creature is introducing a new passivity into God, who bestows grace to the creature because of something they do—but, because "grace" is nothing more than a "gestalt" recognition that one is, always has been and always will be, dependent on God for being and causal power, so the creature's salvation is genuinely brought about by their submission to the grace of God that is the basis of their very being in the first place.

Resurrection?

To western readers, such a theology is hard to stomach. It seems too much like Pelagianism and Jansenism. Either humanity is the cause of their own deification or God is "forced" to bestow grace. However, there is another reason why such a theology might be hard to stomach. If there is not a "new" divine act, then it seems to imply that there is no resurrection. On the face of it, failure to accommodate the resurrection might seem to be a death knell for a theology, but this need not be the case.

Robert Scuka, in his critical reflections on the resurrection, seems to agree with the theology presented here, in which the distinction between "frustration" and "fulfilment" is a distinction only for the creature. He writes that "God's grace has never been absent. The problem was not God's 'silence', but the people's blindness, a blindness that was based on a misconception concerning the nature of divine grace".[61] Grace is always operative, always present, not because there is no distinction between "nature" and "grace", nor because God is not free to "withhold" grace, but because the difference is only real for the creature, not God. Thus, for Scuka, "grace is given in and with the conditions of human existence".[62] This is almost exactly what Lossky argued: creation is itself gracious. Scuka continues that

> for [the Hebrews], the promise and fullness of life is to be experienced here and now, by "living in right relationship to God". What more could one want, the ancient Hebrews implicitly argued, than to live one's life in right relationship to God, and what greater gift could possibly be given us than the gift of life itself. Life, the ancient Hebrews recognized, is not a means to some other end; it instead is an end unto itself, with all the potential richness one can imagine.[63]

---

[61] Robert F. Scuka, "Resurrection: Critical Reflections on a Doctrine in Search of Meaning", *Modern Theology* 6:1 (1989), p. 86.

[62] Scuka, "Resurrection", p. 95, n. 26.

[63] Scuka, "Resurrection", p. 88.

Grace/deification is not a future state, it is not a future reality that is characterized by physical perfection and closer relationship with God, rather, it is the realization that one already has a relationship with God in the here and now and that such a relationship is the best that one could hope for. This leads Scuka to "conflate" the various "types" of grace. He writes that:

> God's prevenient grace is already a salvific or justifying grace in the sense that it is what enables any individual to live life and to respond to God in a faithful way. Thus, God's grace, whether prevenient or salvific, constitutes the condition of, and has the effect of making possible, the very living of life itself . . . [therefore] the traditional distinction between the prevenient and the salvific grace of God is called into question, for the notion of an *additional and distinct* salvific grace is superfluous insofar as it makes no sense to suppose that human sinfulness could somehow render the salvific efficacy of God's (prevenient) grace inoperative. Rather, to be meaningful at all, the notion of divine grace must in principle designate something that is universally present and preveniently efficacious, without even the possibility of this efficaciousness being compromised. Thus, what is termed salvific grace is *not something additional* to prevenient grace, but instead designates the salvific efficaciousness of the one divine grace that functions universally and preveniently. Properly understood, then, "salvific" and "prevenient" do not designate two distinct kinds of grace. They instead designate two dimensions of one and the same divine grace—a grace that in its universal presence is both preveniently and salvifically efficacious.[64]

One would add to this last sentence that if they do "designate two dimensions of the one and same divine grace", then these two dimensions are only real for creatures because, "on the part of the doer, there is only

---

[64] Scuka, "Resurrection", p. 83 (italics added).

one activity in God . . . but considered on the side of what is done, there are indeed different activities".[65]

There is nothing in this quotation that this book has not already supported in relation to the doctrine of divine simplicity. Philip McCosker, for example, was quoted saying that "we must avoid thinking of Thomas' distinctions between different kinds of grace as divisions between different kinds of stuff, different kinds of godly goo which do this or that".[66] There are not different types of grace that are used in different situations. Rather, "Thomas' distinctions are ways of highlighting the way God's constant gracious action appears to us in different contexts."[67] That is, it is the "recipient" of grace who determines what that grace "does"—whether "creation" or "deification"—depending on how or in what way that creature is related to God. God does not do anything differently; it is the creature's relation to what God "does" that changes. Thus, endorsing what has been said above, Scuka writes:

> What salvation properly designates, on these terms, is the acceptance of the conditions that are given in and with human existence itself and which make the very living of life possible. It of course is possible to forsake these conditions in such a way that the living of life becomes, at best, difficult and burdensome. And this properly is what is meant by sin. But acknowledging this in no sense requires one to conclude that our non-acceptance of the possibility of salvation in any way qualifies the efficaciousness of divine grace.[68]

If deification is about "right relationship in the here and now", then this leaves very little room (if any at all) for a doctrine of the resurrection, understood as a future reality in which the believer rises from the dead into a perfect body that enables greater and deeper relation with God. Scuka recognizes this, and is quite clear about the need for

---

[65] Thomas Aquinas, *Disputed Questions on the Power of God* 7.

[66] McCosker, "Grace", p. 210.

[67] McCosker, "Grace", p. 210.

[68] Scuka, "Resurrection", pp. 83–4.

demythologizing the resurrection. Questioning the seemingly obvious statement that "it appears quite reasonable to claim, as an historical argument, that the evangelical success of early Christianity was a function of its resurrection message", Scuka argues that it is actually not clear that it was the resurrection of Jesus that provoked and gave credence to the Apostles' evangelization attempts. He continues: "It is plausible to argue, however, that this is to get the historical relationship backwards; that it rather was the Christian's actual experience of new life in the Spirit and liberation from bondage that was the basis for the elaboration of the story about Jesus' resurrection."[69] The resurrection of Jesus is not an event that precedes and so provokes the Apostles' life in the Spirit; the resurrection of Jesus is retrospectively posited as a way of describing the Apostles' experience. Patricia Williams has made the same argument in relation to the crucifixion. She writes that, when the Apostles experienced Jesus' crucifixion, "they believed they had received atonement, they thought Jesus had made an atonement when he was crucified, and they looked for a catastrophe to explain his death".[70] In this way, "Christians were convinced Jesus' terrible crucifixion made atonement, and they sought a horrific historic catastrophe to explain the cross".[71] The apostles did not think they were living in sin and were on the lookout for an atoning event; they believed they had been atoned by Christ and so sought an event that would explain their need for salvation. Scuka makes the same point regarding the resurrection: the apostles believed they were living in a new spiritually profound reality and needed to find something that caused such a reality.

In this way, the resurrection is not an objective event that happens in the life of Jesus, and which provokes the apostles to evangelize. Rather, Scuka continues:

> The resurrection—indeed, the resurrection of Jesus—signifies
> for Paul that Christian disciple's own experience of new life in

---

[69]   Scuka, "Resurrection", p. 78.

[70]   Patricia Williams, *Doing Without Adam and Eve* (Minneapolis, MN: Fortress Press, 2001), p. 31.

[71]   Williams, *Doing Without Adam and Eve*, pp. 80–1.

the Spirit . . . Likewise, when the liturgy says "The Lord is Risen! The Lord is Risen indeed!", this is not to be understood as a claim about the personal destiny of Jesus. Rather, it is a way of acknowledging the participant's own experience of the life-giving power of the Spirit that is understood to derive from Jesus.[72]

The resurrection is not an event that happens in the life of Jesus; it is a motif that explains and describes the apostles' new-found proximity to God. "Properly understood, all elements of the Christian proclamation—including that of Jesus' resurrection—have as their purpose this proclamation of the universal presence of divine grace."[73]

Importantly, however, while it might leave little room for a doctrine of resurrection, this does not *preclude* there being a future raising of the body to perfection; a future raising to perfection and ontological fulfilment are not mutually exclusive. Rather, as Oliver Quick claims, "[t]he object of ultimate hope is communion with the eternal God, and not any prolongation of human lives as such".[74] It's not that there absolutely isn't a future perfect reality, it's that "communion with the eternal God" cannot be a temporal category. Communion with the eternal God is about a "vertical" essentially-ordered participation, not an accidentally-ordered future end to time.

Resurrection and Johannine Christology
If the reader is concerned about this "demythologization" of the resurrection, then it might be suggested that it has more in common with a "Johannine" Christology than might at first be appreciated. In the previous chapter, a "Johannine" Christology was defined as one in which "the doctrine of the incarnation is the centre and starting-point of Christian theology" with everything else being "derivative from it, and the eschatological doctrines concerning the ultimate of the human soul tend to appear, as it were, on the circumference of Christian theology".[75]

---

[72]   Scuka, "Resurrection", p. 79.

[73]   Scuka, "Resurrection", p. 87.

[74]   Quick, *Doctrines of the Creed*, p. 262.

[75]   Oliver Quick, *Doctrines of the Creed* (London: Nisbet & Co., 1938), p. 189.

The incarnation itself constitutes the Christ-event, rather than it being a mere preliminary condition that must be met in order for Christ to "perform" the Christ-event in the cross. It was then argued that, far from "evacuating the need for Christ's atoning death",[76] this actually *reinforces* the central place that the cross occupies. The "eternal" cross actually becomes that which *is* the incarnation; indeed, there is no incarnation, only the eternal crucifixion of the Son (or, the incarnation is exhausted by the cross).

As many have noticed, this centrality of the cross is also an important characteristic of John's theology, so much so that, for John, the cross seems to exceed the resurrection in importance. John Macquarrie, for example, recognizes that what sets John apart from the synoptics (among the numerous obvious differences between them) is that, in John, "there is no series of mysteries spread over several weeks, as there is in Luke and in the conventional ending. Rather, everything is packed into one decisive happening".[77] What John does, Macquarrie continues, is to compare Christ's crucifixion with Moses' lifting up of the serpent in the wilderness. Macquarrie writes that "the allusion is to a story in the Old Testament of a plague which afflicted Israel, until Moses fashioned a serpent which he raised on a pole, and which healed the people when they looked toward it". Thus, for John, "Jesus' exaltation *is* the cross! His exaltation *is* his humiliation! After this, a separate ascension into heaven would be an anti-climax."[78]

Hans-Ruedi Weber says much the same thing, writing that "most studies of John's passion story, therefore, interpret the crucifixion narrative wholly in the light of passages that proclaim his being raised up and glorified: Christ's execution was his enthronement, the cross became his throne, and the passion was the Revealer's [i.e., Christ's]

---

76 Finch, "Athanasius on the Deifying Work of the Redeemer", in Stephen Finlan and Vladimir Kharlamov (eds), *Theosis: Deification in Christian Theology* (Eugene, OR: Pickwick Publications, 2006), p. 106.

77 Macquarrie, *Jesus Christ in Modern Thought*, p. 413.

78 Macquarrie, *Jesus Christ in Modern Thought*, p. 413 (italics in original).

triumphant return to heaven".[79] John Behr also agrees that "the images throughout the early Christian period depicting the Crucifixion ... consistently depict the crucified Christ with an upright body and eyes wide open, not because of an inability to depict a dead corpse, but precisely because the crucified one is the triumphant Lord: the Cross itself is taken simultaneously as a reference to the Crucifixion and to the risen Christ".[80] For John, the resurrection is an after-event, an epilogue to the main narrative; the Christ event is complete with the raising up of Jesus on the cross. Just as for John the incarnation is not a "condition that Christ had to meet in order to be able to save", but rather salvation consisted in meeting that condition,[81] so the cross is not a condition that Christ had to meet in order to become resurrected, but rather the cross itself is the condition of salvation.

There will undoubtedly be those who will always remain sceptical of any theology that seeks to "replace" the resurrection (understood as a future reality characterized by the possession of a perfect body that enables greater and more profound relationship with God) with a sort of subjective account of resurrection as correct relationship with God in the here and now. No doubt it will be those who are determined to subscribe to "theistic personalism" and to maintain that creation is a doctrine about the origin of the universe that are likewise determined to see "grace" as a separate, distinct, freely chosen "act" of God, which transforms creatures in the future. On the other hand, it should also be fairly clear that, if one is committed to the *analogia entis* of "traditional theism", committed to seeing a single divine activity understood as an essentially ordered relationship, committed to understanding distinctions in divine activity in the context of the absence of a real relation, then it seems clear that one is also committed to seeing "grace" as being a change in the creature's relationship with God, not *vice versa*.

---

[79]   Hans-Ruedi Weber, *The Cross: Tradition and Interpretation* (London: SPCK, 1979), p. 132.

[80]   John Behr, *The Mystery of Christ: Life in Death* (Crestwood, NY: St. Vladimir's Seminary Press, 2006), p. 28.

[81]   Anna Marmodoro and Jonathan Hill, "Modeling the Metaphysics of the Incarnation", *Philosophy & Theology* 20:1/2 (2008), pp. 99–100.

Final cause: fulfilment is not an "end"

It is worth pausing here to summarize what has been said thus far. First, exponents of both the "extrinsic" and "intrinsic" positions towards the relationship between "nature" and "grace"—irrespective of the differences between them—are eager to emphasize that the gratuity of grace—i.e., the freedom of God not to bestow grace—must be protected at all times. However, such a preoccupation with the gratuity of grace misses two important implications. First, there can only be one, single, divine activity that is "done" from all eternity, which, as many commentators of Thomas Aquinas and Bonaventure recognize, means that all diversity and change—including the distinction and change between "nature" and "grace"—must be *extrinsic* to God. Second, the dichotomy of "freedom" and "necessity" is a false dichotomy, meaning that—as commentators on Thomas Aquinas' doctrine of creation as "emanation" recognize—denying God the freedom not to bestow grace does not mean that creation is necessary. God can only be "free" if God is a person who can choose to act or not to act; if God is not a person, then God cannot be free. This does not mean that creation or grace are necessary—both only have an *obediential potential* like the statue and the marble—but it does mean that the difference between them—like the difference between "non-being" and "being"—is a relationship that the creature has with God, and which is *extrinsic* to God: creatures are really related to God, but God is not really related to creatures. While this might sound suspiciously Pelagian, Jansenian, or Baian to western ears, it sounds perfectly reasonable to eastern ears. For Eastern Orthodox theologians, "grace is given in and with the conditions of human existence"[82] and deification consists in "the acceptance of the conditions that are given in and with human existence itself and which make the very living of life possible",[83] which means submission to the influence of grace. The difference between "nature" and "grace" is genuinely real—it is a genuinely different, more profound relationship with God—but it is not different *for* God.

This can be put differently. Ernan McMullin has already been quoted explaining how "widespread misunderstanding of the notion of final

---

[82] Scuka, "Resurrection", p. 95, n. 26.

[83] Scuka, "Resurrection", pp. 83–4.

causality"[84] leads to a "confusi[on of] two of the four causes or types of explanation listed by Aristotle, [and] the critics [of teleology] suppose that postulating a 'final' cause implies a sort of backward efficient causality, somehow causing, in an agency sense of that term, a process already in the past",[85] adding that "citing the goal of a living activity is one way (Aristotle would add: the best way) to understand that activity but in no way ought this be taken to endorsing a counter-intuitive sort of backward-in-time efficient causal action".[86] Thus, final cause is not that to which the efficient cause is heading, as if the efficient cause pushes and the final cause pulls all "transitions of energy [and] movements of mass"[87] from origin to end. Rather the final cause gives meaning to the efficient cause and what it accomplishes.

Étienne Gilson agrees with McMullin's analysis. Gilson writes that "the finalism of Aristotle is an attempt to give a reason for the very existence of this organism",[88] and so "Aristotle concludes that if one asks which cause is primary, the material or mechanical cause, or the final cause, the response must be, 'plainly, however, that cause is the first which we call the final one'".[89] The point is that it being called "*final* cause" has perhaps confused thinkers into seeing it as something in the future, a sort of "backward efficient causality" as McMullin puts it, pulling everything towards a *final* state, rather than pushing everything forward from a beginning. This is not what "final cause" means. The final cause of the universe is not a future point, but the reason behind everything. The final cause is not a future point to which everything is heading, but is nothing more

---

84   Ernan McMullin, "Could Natural Selection Be Purposive?", in Joseph Seckbach and Richard Gordon (eds), *Divine Action and Natural Selection* (Singapore: World Scientific, 2008), p. 118.

85   McMullin, "Could Natural Selection Be Purposive?", p. 118.

86   McMullin, "Could Natural Selection Be Purposive?", p. 119.

87   David Bentley Hart, *The Experience of God: Being, Consciousness, Bliss* (London: Yale University Press, 2013), p. 103.

88   Étienne Gilson, *From Aristotle to Darwin and Back Again: A Journey in Final Causality, Species and Evolution* (San Francisco, CA: Ignatius Press, 2009), p. 6.

89   Gilson, *From Aristotle to Darwin and Back Again*, p. 10.

than the meaning of it. The final cause has no reference to any time and "mechanical" movement in time. In this way, God can be the final cause of the universe, not because God is that which pulls creation towards a future point that is characterized by closer relationship, but because God is that which gives the universe its meaning. The final cause, then, is essentially ordered to creation, not the last in an accidentally ordered series.

There is also an important connection with what was concluded in the chapter on creation. If creation is not about "origins", then its fulfilment cannot be about "ends". The "origin" and "end" of the universe (assuming the universe does have a finite beginning and end) are nothing more than boundaries that define the universe; they have no further metaphysical meaning than that. In this way, the temporal boundaries of the universe are no more important than the spatial boundaries; if the fact that the universe is not spatially infinite has no metaphysical meaning, then neither does the fact that the universe is not temporally infinite.

This depends on a particular understanding of time in which it is seen as similar to space. That is, time is like what John McTaggart would call a "b-series", not an "a-series".[90] In a "b-series", time functions as subjective pointers rather than objective indices. In this way, just as there can be no objective "here"—"here" means something entirely different for each individual creature—so there can be no objective "now". To put this differently, no point in time is more "existent" than any other; just as King Charles III and Pope Francis still exist, but in different spatial locations, so Pope Francis and Pope Peter still exist, but in different temporal locations.[91] Most modern physicists, following Albert Einstein's

---

[90] J. M. E. McTaggart, *The Nature of Existence, Vol. II* (Cambridge: Cambridge University Press, 1927), p. 10; see H. Nelson, "Time(s), Eternity, and Duration", *International Journal for Philosophy of Religion* 22:1/2 (1987), pp. 14–15.

[91] William Lane Craig writes that for these philosophers "the spatial indexical 'here' is entirely parallel to the temporal indexical 'now' ... 'here' is just a subjective perspective on a world which exists in space independently of such perspectives. The same is true of 'now' and temporal tenses." (William Lane Craig, *Time and Eternity: Exploring God's Relationship to Time* (Wheaton,

theory of relativity, agree that this is an accurate depiction of the universe. For them, the universe does not exist in three dimensions that move through time from beginning to end; rather, the universe exists in four dimensions, including all three spatial dimensions and one temporal. All creatures equally exist together in one "eternal now", but just with varying temporal and spatial boundaries and relations. Such is this the case, that Albert Einstein famously wrote to a friend's sister on the occasion of his friend's death, writing that "Michele has left this strange world a little before me. This means nothing. People like us who believe in physics, know that the distinction made between past, present and future is nothing more than a persistent, stubborn illusion."[92] The death of Michele does not mean that Michele no longer exists; it means that the temporal boundaries of Michele and Einstein are not in perfect alignment and overlap one another. Creatures might experience time as a linear movement that can only be in one direction, but this is not true to what it really is.

If the "origin" and the "end" of the universe are nothing more than temporal boundaries, then "birth" and "death" are likewise nothing more than temporal boundaries. Just as each creature will have spatial boundaries (which, for most people in the modern world, with fast travel, is the spatial boundaries of the planet earth), so each creature will have temporal boundaries (which, likewise, for most people in the modern world with modern medicine, are much wider than ever before). There is nothing special about either of those boundaries, but they define the life of those who possess them. Ian McFarland says much the same thing. Discussing the biblical idea that God "has made everything beautiful

---

IL: Crossway, 2001), p. 127.) In this way, "the difference between past, present, and future is merely a subjective matter of human consciousness" (Craig, *Time and Eternity: Exploring God's Relationship to Time*, p. 264), which means, so Carlo Rovelli writes, that "the 'present' does not exist in an objective sense any more than 'here' exists objectively" (Carlo Rovelli, *Seven Brief Lessons on Physics* (London: Penguin, 2015), p. 60).

92   Rovelli, *Seven Brief Lessons on Physics*, p. 58.

in its time",[93] and the fact that human lives are extremely varied in length seemingly without any reason, McFarland asks why it is that we question that extreme variety and think of dying young as some sort of evil. He asks, "Is it more reasonable to say that a human being should be expected to live to a certain minimum age than that one should grow to a certain minimum height?"[94] Importantly, McFarland draws on Ruth Page to support the rejection that the failure to live to a certain age is seen as something of an evil. He continues that "although the idea that all creatures should live to the full age attainable by their species has a certain appeal, it arguably buys into a prejudicial sort of teleology, according to which life as lived now in the present moment is less than fully good." Ruth Page's "Teleology Now!", McFarland writes, "provides a valuable corrective to the urge to equate creaturely flourishing with a given creature's achievement of any particular outcome (e.g., a ripe old age), since such an equation subverts the fundamental principle of a properly Christian theology of creation, namely, God's joy in the sheer existence of creatures at every point of their existence."[95] Death is not an "evil force" that runs counter to "grace" and stands in ontological opposition to God and participation in God; indeed, Gregory of Nazianzus has already been quoted outlining the problems for strict monotheism that

---

[93] Ian McFarland, *The Word Made Flesh: A Theology of the Incarnation* (Louisville, KY: Westminster John Knox Press, 2019), p. 64; see Ecclesiastes 3:11.

[94] McFarland, *The Word Made Flesh*, p. 64.

[95] McFarland, *The Word Made Flesh*, p. 64. What is interesting about McFarland's observation that it is no more reasonable to say that humans should attain a certain height than they should attain a certain age is that (whether consciously or not) it draws on the idea (which this book accepts) that space and time are more or less the same. That is, McFarland directly compares a temporal "problem"— "longevity"—with a spatial "problem"— "tallness". That is, just as there is no evil in one having smaller spatial "boundaries" than any other creature, so there is no evil in one having smaller temporal "boundaries" than any other. Similarly, the same way that the absence of certain (mental, rational, or any other) capacities does not represent an evil, so having a smaller temporal boundary does not represent an evil.

such a view creates.[96] Rather, death is nothing more than one boundary that defines the creature's life in the same way that birth or the various spatial boundaries define one's life.

Much like Page, McFarland might have issues with the language with which this book has attempted to expound the very same idea, but it is nothing more than what is presented here. If God is atemporal and simple, and if creation is a hierarchical, ontological relationship—in and through Jesus—then the fulfilment of that relationship cannot have anything to do with future achievement. In other words, ultimate meaning cannot be defined by whatever might happen in the future; ultimate meaning has nothing to do with "*what*" a creature is or could become, but with *that* it is. Thus, those spatial and temporal boundaries that define "*what* something is" have absolutely no impact whatsoever on "*that* something is". Birth and death are part of the "*what* something is", not "*that* something is". In other words, God determines *that* a particular creature *is*, but God does not determine *when* and for *how long* that creature *is*, and neither aspect has any theological relevance. The *when* and *how long* are part of the *what*. Death has no more theological relevance than does birth. If creation is not coincident with beginnings and origins, then fulfilment/deification cannot be coincident with ends. If birth is not understood as creation, then neither is death (and resurrection) understood as fulfilment. Time and history must form part of the fulfilment of creatures—creatures are inherently spatiotemporal so they must find that fulfilment in time and space—but this does not mean that time is a process through which creatures must pass in order to arrive at fulfilment. Tillich said the same about providence: "This fulfilment does not lie in an eventual time-and-space future."[97]

The final cause, the creature's fulfilment of its own "*that* it is", has no reference whatsoever to "*what* it is" (which, it was argued in Chapter 3, is defined by its origin) or "*for how long* it is". That is, it has no reference whatsoever to the "horizontal" accidentally ordered series of events that make up its life. It is a "vertical", essentially ordered, hierarchical category.

---

[96]   Gregory of Nazianzus, "Oratio 45", p. 22.

[97]   Paul Tillich, *Systematic Theology Vol. 1* (Chicago, IL: The University of Chicago Press, 1957), p. 267.

This is not to say that nothing a creature does in this life has an impact on it, but the point is that there is no coincidence between the temporal life of a creature and its fulfilment. That is, the fulfilment of a creature's life is the realization that they participate in God and imitate Christ, not the completion of a process that coincides with an "end".

In this way, there is a sort of analogue to Stephen Hawking's confusion of "creation" with "origins". Just as Hawking (and the many others who share his thinking) thought that "so long as the universe had a beginning, we could suppose it had a creator. But if the universe is really completely self-contained . . . [w]hat place, then, for a creator?"[98]—and so thought that the absence of a beginning to the universe meant that there was no more need to postulate a creator of the universe—so it can be said that the absence of a "last day" or future "day of resurrection" does not mean that there is no deification or "fulfilment" to creation. The absence of a "day of resurrection" does not mean that there is no fulfilment of creation in participation in God. Just as one should not confuse "origin" with "creation", so one should not confuse "end" with "fulfilment". If creation is about hierarchical relationship, then resurrection should mean the fulfilment of that relationship. Of course, being temporal, that fulfilment must work itself out in space and time, but this does not mean that fulfilment has any spatiotemporal connotations.

Christ as the only source of grace

One final comment is necessary here, particularly in light of the fact that grace is now seen not as distinct from creation, but as being that which is responsible for creation just as much as it is responsible for deification—and that is that Christ is the only source of grace. J. Quenum writes that "Jesus Christ is the source of God's grace in the world", so that "divine grace as a free gift is introduced in human history when the Son of God, Jesus Christ, assumed human nature by being born as a man".[99] Celia Deane-Drummond, drawing on the theology of Karl

---

[98]   Stephen Hawking, *A Brief History of Time* (London: Transworld Publishers, 1988), pp. 140–1.

[99]   Quenum, "Is Divine Grace really beyond human comprehension?", p. 7.

Rahner, also writes that "the incarnation is a singular moment in the universal bestowal of grace".[100]

No doubt such sentiments are made with reference to a theology in which Christ is incarnate as an atonement, specifically to deal with sin. No doubt, those sentiments draw on Paul's epistle to the Romans, in which he writes that "the abundance of grace and the free gift of righteousness exercise dominion in life through the one man, Jesus Christ".[101] No doubt, especially in relation to Quenum's claim that grace is "introduced in human history", such sentiments are made in a context in which God, a maximally powerful and knowing person, is seen as acting at a specific point in time as part of an accidentally ordered series that leads to a future state in which creatures are brought to perfection. Yet, it is also possible to understand such sentiments in relation to what has already been argued in Chapter 4. That is, the hypostatic union—the "mere contact" and "sheer joining" of the universe with God in the second person of the Trinity—is that which bestows grace and so is the source of grace in the universe. That "grace", which "is given in and with the conditions of human existence",[102] is as much responsible for the "being" of the universe as it is the "deification" of the universe. That "grace" is that which "breathes fire into the equations and makes a universe for them to describe",[103] just as much as it is that which enables the supernatural vision of God. That "grace" is not something "super-added" to "nature"; it is that upon which all creatures depend and that in which all creatures participate as their very "ground of being". Whether that "grace" is responsible for creation or deification depends entirely upon how the creature relates to God. The bestowal of that grace is the only "thing" that God does, through the eternal *kenosis* of the Son in the eternal crucifixion, through which there is ontological space for all creatures to participate in the being of God by the imitation of Jesus.

---

[100] Celia Deane-Drummond, *Christ and Evolution* (London: SCM Press and Minneapolis, MN: Fortress Press, 2009), p. 42.

[101] Romans 5:17b.

[102] Scuka, "Resurrection", p. 95, n. 26.

[103] Hawking, *A Brief History of Time*, p. 174.

Bibliography

Abbruzzese, John, "The Coherence of Omniscience: A Defense",
   International Journal for Philosophy of Religion 41 (1997), pp.
   25–34.

Aghiourgoussis, Maximos, "Orthodox Soteriology", in John
   Meyendorff and R. Tobias (eds), *Salvation in Christ: A Lutheran–
   Orthodox Dialogue* (Minneapolis, MN: Augsburg Fortress, 1992),
   pp. 35–57.

Agourides, Savvas, "The Social Character of Orthodoxy", in A. J.
   Philippou (ed.), *The Orthodox Ethos: Studies in Orthodoxy Vol. 1*
   (Oxford: Holywell Press, 1964), pp. 209–20.

Alanen, Lilli, "Descartes, Duns Scotus and Ockham on Omnipotence
   and Possibility", *Franciscan Studies* 45 (1985), pp. 157–88.

Allegra, Gabriel, *My Conversations with Teilhard de Chardin on the
   Primacy of Christ* (Chicago, IL: Franciscan Herald Press, 1971).

Anscombe, G. E. M. and Geach, Peter, *Three Philosophers* (Ithaca, NY:
   Cornell University Press, 1976).

Anselm of Canterbury, *Collected Works* (Oxford: Oxford University
   Press, 1998).

Aquinas, Thomas, *Summa Theologiae* (New York, NY: Benziger
   Brothers, 1948).

Aquinas, Thomas, *Quaestiones Disputatae de Potentia Dei*
   (Westminster, MD: The Newman Press, 1952).

Aquinas, Thomas, *Quaestiones Disputatae De Veritate* (Chicago, IL:
   Henry Regnery Company, 1952).

Aquinas, Thomas, *De Aeternitate Mundi*, in Thomas Gilby (tr.),
   Philosophical Texts (Durham, NC: The Labyrinth Press, 1982).

Aquinas, Thomas, *Selected Writings* (London: Penguin, 1998).

Aquinas, Thomas, *Commentary on John* (Albany, NY: Magi Books,
   Inc., 1998).

Aquinas, Thomas, *Summa Contra Gentiles* (London: Burns & Oates, 2005).

Aquinas, Thomas, *Commentary on Colossians* (Naples, FL: Sapientia Press, 2009).

Ashworth, E. J., "Suárez on the Analogy of Being: Some Historical Background", *Vivarium* 33:1 (1995), pp. 50–75.

Athanasius, "On the Incarnation", in Hardy, Edward (tr.), *Christology of the Later Fathers* (London: Westminster John Knox Press, 1954).

Attfield, Robin, *Creation, Evolution and Meaning* (Aldershot: Ashgate Publishing, 2006).

Aulén, Gustaf, *Christus Victor* (London: SPCK, 1931).

Ayres, Lewis, *Nicaea and its Legacy: An Approach to Fourth-Century Trinitarian Theology* (Oxford: Oxford University Press, 2004).

Balashov, Yury, "On the Evolution of Natural Laws", *The British Journal for the Philosophy of Science* 43:3 (1992), pp. 343–70.

Baldner, Steven and Carroll, William (tr.), *Aquinas on Creation* (Toronto: Pontifical Institute of Mediaeval Studies, 1997).

Barbour, Ian, *Religion in an Age of Science* (San Francisco, CA: Harper, 1990).

Barron, Robert, *The Priority of Christ: Towards A Postliberal Catholicism* (Grand Rapids, MI: Brazos Press, 2007).

Barron, Robert, *Exploring Catholic Theology* (Grand Rapids, MI: Baker Academic, 2015).

Barth, Karl, *Church Dogmatics: Study Edition* (Edinburgh: T&T Clark, 2009).

Bauerschmidt, Frederick, *Thomas Aquinas: Faith, Reason, and Following Christ* (Oxford: Oxford University Press, 2013).

Behe, Michael, *Darwin's Black Box* (New York, NY: Simon & Schuster, 1998).

Behr, John, *The Mystery of Christ: Life in Death* (Crestwood, NY: St. Vladimir's Seminary Press, 2006).

Benson, Joshua C., "Structure and Meaning in St. Bonaventure's 'Quaestiones Disputatae de Scientia Christi'", *Franciscan Studies* 62 (2004), pp. 67–90.

Betz, John, "Translator's Introduction", in Erich Przywara, *Analogia Entis* (Grand Rapids, MI: William B. Eerdmans, 2014), pp. 1–115.

Bianchi, Enzo, *Praying the Word of God* (Kalamazoo, MI: Cistercian Publications, 1998).

Birch, Charles, "Participatory Evolution: The Drive of Creation", *Journal of the American Academy of Religion* 40:2 (1972), pp. 147–63.

Bishop, John and Perszyk, Ken, "The Divine Attributes and Non-personal Conceptions of God", *Topoi* 36 (2017), pp. 609–21.

Bonaventure, *Breviloquium* (Paterson, NJ: At. Anthony Guild Press, 1963).

Boyd, Craig and Cobb, Aaron, "The Causality Distinction, Kenosis, and a Middle Way: Aquinas and Polkinghorne on Divine Action", *Theology and Science* 7:4 (2009), pp. 391–406.

Brierley, Michael, "Naming a Quiet Revolution: The Panentheistic Turn in Modern Theology", in Philip Clayton and Arthur Peacocke (eds), *In Whom We Live and Move and Have Our Being: Panentheistic Reflections on God's Presence in a Scientific World* (Grand Rapids, MI: William B. Eerdmans, 2004), pp. 1–15.

Brooke, John Hedley, *Science and Religion: Some Historical Perspectives* (Cambridge: Cambridge University Press, 1991).

Brooke, John Hedley, "Science, Religion, and Historical Complexity", *Historically Speaking* 8:5 (2007), pp. 10–13.

Brown, David, *The Divine Trinity* (London: Duckworth, 1985).

Brown, David O., *Incarnation and Neo-Darwinism: Evolution, Ontology, and Divine Activity* (Durham: Sacristy Press, 2019).

Brown, David O., "Creation as Participation: Essentially-Ordered Series, 'Spontaneous Creation', and the Rejection of Divine Efficient Causality", *Angelicum* 98:2 (2021), pp. 273–306.

Brunner, Emil, *The Mediator* (London: The Lutterworth Press, 1934).

Bucur, Bogdan G., "The Theological Reception of Dionysian Apophatism in the Christian East and West: Thomas Aquinas and Gregory Palamas", *The Downside Review* 125:439 (2007), pp. 131–46.

Bucur, Bogdan G., "Foreordained from All Eternity: The Mystery of the Incarnation According to Some Early Christian and Byzantine Writers", *Dumbarton Oaks Papers* 62 (2008), pp. 199–215.

Bulgakov, Sergei, *The Bride of the Lamb* (Grand Rapids, MI: William B. Eerdmans, 2002).

Bulgakov, Sergei, *The Lamb of God* (Grand Rapids, MI: William B. Eerdmans, 2008).

Bultmann, Rudolf, *New Testament and Mythology and Other Basic Writings* (Philadelphia, PA: Fortress Press, 1984).

Burns, Robert, "The Divine Simplicity in St. Thomas", *Religious Studies* 25:3 (1989), pp. 271–93.

Byrne, Celia, "The Role of Essentially Ordered Causal Series in Avicenna's Proof for the Necessary Existent in the Metaphysics of the Salvation", *History of Philosophy Quarterly* 36:2 (2019), pp. 541–55.

Cabasilas, Nicholas, *The Life in Christ* (Crestwood, NY: St. Vladimir's Seminary Press, 1974).

Castelli, Elizabeth, *Imitating Paul: A Discourse of Power* (Louisville, KY: Westminster John Knox Press, 1991).

Cavanaugh, William T., "The City: Beyond Secular Parodies", in John Milbank, Catherine Pickstock and Graham Ward (eds), *Radical Orthodoxy* (London: Routledge, 1999), pp. 182–200.

Chaberek, Michael, *Catholicism and Evolution: A History from Darwin to Pope Francis* (Kettering, OH: Angelico Press, 2015).

Clarke, W. Norris, *Explorations in Metaphysics: Being-God-Person* (Notre Dame, IN: University of Notre Dame Press, 1994).

Clarke, W. Norris, *The Philosophical Approach to God: A New Thomistic Perspective* (New York, NY: Fordham University Press, 2007).

Clayton, Phillip, *God and Contemporary Science* (Edinburgh: Edinburgh University Press, 1997).

Coakley, Sarah, "*Kenosis* and Subversion: On the Repression of 'Vulnerability' in Christian Feminist Writing", in Daphne Hampson (ed.), *Swallowing a Fishbone: Feminist Theologians Debate Christianity* (London: SPCK, 1996), pp. 82–111.

Coakley, Sarah, "Kenosis: Theological Meaning and Gender Connotations", in John Polkinghorne (ed.), *The Work of Love: Creation as Kenosis* (Grand Rapids, MI: William B. Eerdmans, 2001), pp. 192–210.

Cobb, John B. and Griffin, David Ray, *Process Theology: An Introductory Exposition* (London: The Westminster Press, 1976).

Cohoe, Caleb, "There must be a First: Why Thomas Aquinas Rejects Infinite, Essentially Ordered, Causal Series", *British Journal for the History of Philosophy* 21:5 (2013), pp. 838–56.

Cole-Turner, Ron, "New Perspectives on Human Origins: Three Challenges for Christian Theology", *Theology and Science* 18:4 (2020), pp. 524–36.

Coll, Niall, *Christ in Eternity and Time* (Dublin: Four Courts Press, 2001).

Collins, Gregory, *Meeting Christ in His Mysteries* (Dublin: The Columba Press, 2010).

Copan, Paul and Craig, William Lane, *Creation out of Nothing: A Biblical, Philosophical, and Scientific Exploration* (Grand Rapids, MI: Baker Academic, 2004).

Craig, William Lane, "Divine Timelessness and Personhood", *International Journal for Philosophy of Religion* 43:2 (1998), pp. 109–24.

Craig, William Lane, "Creation and Conservation Once More", *Religious Studies* 34:2 (1998), pp. 177–88.

Craig, William Lane, "Timelessness, Creation, and God's Real Relation to the World", *Laval théologique et philosophique* 56:1 (2000), pp. 93–112.

Craig, William Lane, *Time and Eternity: Exploring God's Relationship to Time* (Wheaton, IL: Crossway, 2001).

Creegan, Nicola Hoggard, "A Christian Theology of Evolution and Participation", *Zygon: Journal of Religion and Science* 42:2 (2007), pp. 499–518.

Crisp, Oliver, "Salvation and Atonement: On the Value and Necessity of the Work of Jesus Christ", in Ivor Davidson & Murray Rae (eds), *God of Salvation: Soteriology in Theological Perspective* (Farnham: Ashgate, 2011), pp. 105–20.

Cross, Richard, *Duns Scotus* (Oxford: Oxford University Press, 1999).

Cross, Richard, *The Metaphysics of the Incarnation* (Oxford: Oxford University Press, 2002).

Cross, Richard, *Duns Scotus on God* (Aldershot: Ashgate Publishing, 2005).

Cross, Richard, "The Eternity of the World and the Distinction between Creation and Conservation", *Religious Studies* 42:4 (2006), pp. 403–16.

Cullmann, Oscar, *Christ and Time* (London: SCM Press, 1962).

Cunningham, Conor, *Darwin's Pious Idea* (Grand Rapids, MI: William B. Eerdmans, 2010).

Davies, Brian, "Aquinas On What God is Not", *Revue Internationale de Philosophie* 52:204 (1998), pp. 207–25.

Davies, Brian, *An Introduction to the Philosophy of Religion* (Oxford: Oxford University Press, 2004).

Davies, Brian, *The Reality of God and the Problem of Evil* (London: Continuum, 2006).

Davies, Paul, "Introduction", in Werner Heisenberg, *Physics and Philosophy* (London: Penguin, 1989), pp. vii–xvii.

Davies, Paul, "Teleology without Teleology: Purpose Through Emergent Complexity", in Philip Clayton and Arthur Peacocke (eds), *In Whom We Live and Move and Have Our Being: Panentheistic Reflections on God's Presence in a Scientific World* (Grand Rapids. MI: William B. Eerdmans, 2004), pp. 95–108.

Davies, Paul, "The Day Time Began", in Jeremy Webb (ed.), *Nothing* (London: Profile Books, 2013).

Davis, Stephen, "The Metaphysics of Kenosis", in Jonathan Hill and Anna Marmodoro (eds), *The Metaphysics of the Incarnation* (Oxford: Oxford University Press, 2011), pp. 114–33.

Davison, Andrew, "Looking Back Towards the Origin: Scientific Cosmology as Creation *ex nihilo* Considered 'From the Inside'", in Gary A. Anderson and Markus Bockmuehl (eds), *Creation Ex Nihilo: Origins, Development, Contemporary Challenges* (Notre Dame, IN: University of Notre Dame Press, 2018), pp. 367–89.

Davison, Andrew, *Participation in God* (Cambridge: Cambridge University Press, 2019).

Dawes, Gregory, *Theism and Explanation* (New York, NY: Routledge, 2014).

Dawkins, Richard, *River Out of Eden: A Darwinian View of Life* (London: Phoenix, 1996).

Dawkins, Richard, *A Devil's Chaplain* (London: Phoenix, 2003).

Dawkins, Richard, *The God Delusion* (London: Black Swan, 2006).

Dawkins, Richard, *The Selfish Gene* (Oxford: Oxford University Press, 2006).

Dean, Maximillian Mary, *A Primer on the Absolute Primacy of Christ: Blessed John Duns Scotus and the Franciscan Thesis* (New Bedford, MA: Franciscans of the Immaculate, 2006).

Deane-Drummond, Celia, *Christ and Evolution* (London: SCM Press and Minneapolis, MN: Fortress Press, 2009).

Delio, Ilia, "Revisiting the Franciscan Doctrine of Christ", *Theological Studies* 64 (2003), pp. 3–23.

Delio, Ilia, *The Unbearable Wholeness of Being* (Maryknoll, NY: Orbis Books, 2013).

de Lubac, Henri, *Catholicism: Christ and the Common Destiny of Man* (San Francisco, CA: Ignatius Press, 1947)

de Lubac, Henri, *Augustinianism and Modern Theology* (London: Geoffrey Chapman, 1969).

de Lubac, Henri, *The Mystery of the Supernatural* (New York, NY: The Crossroad Publishing Company, 1998).

Dodds, Michael, "Science, Causality, and God: Divine Action and Thomas Aquinas", *Angelicum* 91:1 (2014), pp. 13–36.

Dorner, Isaak, *Divine Immutability: A Critical Reconsideration* (Minneapolis, MN: Fortress Press, 1994).

Edwards, Denis, *How God Acts: Creation, Redemption, and Special Divine Action* (Minneapolis, MN: Fortress Press, 2010).

Edwards, Denis, *Deep Incarnation: God's Redemptive Suffering with Creatures* (Maryknoll, NY: Orbis Books, 2019).

Einstein, Albert, *Out of my Later Years* (Westport, CT: Greenwood, 1970).

Emery, Giles, "Trinity and Creation", in Rik Van Nieuwenhove and Joseph Wawrykow (eds), *The Theology of Thomas Aquinas* (Notre Dame, IN: University of Notre Dame Press, 2005), pp. 58–76.

Eriugena, *De Divina Praedestinatione liber*, ed. G. Madec, *Corpus Christianorum Continuatio Mediaevalis* 50 (Turnhout: Brepols, 1978).

Evans, C. Stephen, "The Self-Emptying of Love: Some Thoughts on Kenotic Christology", in Stephen Davis, Daniel Kendall, and Gerald O'Collins (eds), *The Incarnation* (Oxford: Oxford University Press, 2002), pp. 246–72.

Evans, C. Stephen (ed.), *Exploring Kenotic Christology* (Oxford: Oxford University Press, 2006).

Fabro, Cornelio, "The Intensive Hermeneutics of Thomistic Philosophy: The Notion of Participation", *The Review of Metaphysics* 27:3 (1974), pp. 449–91.

Farrer, Austin, *Faith and Speculation* (Edinburgh: T&T Clark, 1988).

Fee, Gordon, "St. Paul and the Incarnation: A Reassessment of the Data", in Stephen Davis, Daniel Kendall and Gerald O'Collins (eds), *The Incarnation* (Oxford: Oxford University Press, 2002), pp. 62–92.

Feingold, Lawrence, *The Natural Desire to See God According to St. Thomas Aquinas and his Interpreters* (Naples, FL: Sapientia Press, 2010).

Feser, Edward, *Scholastic Metaphysics: A Contemporary Introduction* (Heusenstamm: editiones scholasticae, 2014).

Feuerbach, Ludwig, *The Essence of Christianity* (New York, NY: Harper Torchbooks, 1957).

Fiddes, Paul, *The Creative Suffering of God* (Oxford: Clarendon Press, 1988).

Finch, Jeffrey, "Athanasius on the Deifying Work of the Redeemer", in Stephen Finlan and Vladimir Kharlamov (eds), *Theosis: Deification in Christian Theology* (Eugene, OR: Pickwick Publications, 2006), pp. 104–21.

Flores, Juan Carlos, "Accidental and Essential Causality in John Duns Scotus' Treatise 'On the First Principle'", *Recherches de théologie et philosophie médiévales* 67:1 (2000), pp. 96–113.

Florovsky, Georges, *Creation and Redemption* (Belmont, MA: Norland Publishing Company, 1976).

Ford, Lewis S., "Tillich and Thomas: The Analogy of Being", *The Journal of Religion* 46:2 (1966), pp. 229–45.

Forrest, Peter, "The Incarnation: A Philosophical Case for Kenosis", *Religious Studies* 36:2 (2000), pp. 127–40.

Freddoso, Alfred, "Introduction", in Alfred Freddoso (ed.), *On Creation, Conservation, and Concurrence* (South Bend, IN: St. Augustine Press, 2002), pp. xi–cxxiii.

Gamberini, Paulo, "The Concept of 'Person': A Dialogue with Contemporary Asian Theology", *Irish Theological Quarterly* 76:3 (2011), pp. 259–77.

Garton, Alexander, "'Very truly I tell you, before Abraham was, I am': A Theological Treatise on the Concept of Time in John's Gospel", *Modern Theology* 35:4 (2019), pp. 617–37,

Geach, Peter T., "Omnipotence", *Philosophy* 48:183 (1973), pp. 7–20.

Gilkey, Langdon, "The Concept of Providence in Contemporary Theology", *The Journal of Religion* 43:3 (1963), pp. 171–92.

Gilkey, Langdon, "Cosmology, Ontology, and the Travail of Biblical Language", in Owen Thomas (ed.), *God's Activity in the World: The Contemporary Problem* (Chico, CA: Scholars Press, 1983), pp. 29–43.

Gilson, Étienne, *From Aristotle to Darwin and Back Again: A Journey in Final Causality, Species and Evolution* (San Francisco, CA: Ignatius Press, 2009).

Gilson, Étienne, *Medieval Essays* (Eugene, OR: Cascade Books, 2011).

Gore, Charles, *The Incarnation of the Son of God* (London: John Murray, 1891).

Gorman, Michael, *Inhabiting the Cruciform God* (Grand Rapids, MI: William B. Eerdmans, 2009).

Grayling, Anthony, "Introduction", in *The Britannica Guide to the Ideas that Made the Modern World: The People, Philosophy, and History of the Enlightenment* (London: Robinson, 2008), pp. ix–xxix.

Greene, John C. and Ruse, Michael, "On the Nature of the Evolutionary Process: The Correspondence between Theodosius Dobzhansky and John C. Greene", *Biology and Philosophy* 11 (1996), pp. 445–91.

Gregersen, Niels Henrik, "The Cross of Christ in an Evolutionary World", *Dialog: A Journal of Theology* 40:3 (2001), pp. 192–207.

Gregersen, Niels Henrik, "Deep Incarnation: Why Evolutionary Continuity Matters in Christology", *Toronto Journal of Theology* 26 (2010), pp. 173–88.

Gregersen, Niels Henrik, "Deep Incarnation: From Deep History to Post-axial Religion", *HTS Teologiese Studies/Theological Studies* 72:4 (2016), pp. 1–12.

Gregory of Nazianzus, "Oratio 28", in Philip Schaff and Henry Wace (eds), *Nicene and Post-Nicene Fathers Vol. 7* (New York, NY: The Christian Literature Company, 1894), pp. 288–301.

Gregory of Nazianzus, "Oratio 45", in Philip Schaff and Henry Wace (eds), *Nicene and Post-Nicene Fathers Vol. 7* (New York, NY: The Christian Literature Company, 1894), pp. 422–34.

Gregory of Nyssa, *The Life of Moses* (Mahwah, NJ: Paulist Press, 1978).

Gregory of Nyssa, "Against Eunomius", in Philip Schaff & Henry Wace (eds), *Nicene and Post-Nicene Fathers Vol. 5* (Peabody, MA: Hendrickson Publishing, 1995).

Gregory Palamas (tr. Robert Sinkewicz), *One Hundred and Fifty Chapters* (Toronto: Pontifical Institute of Mediaeval Studies, 1988).

Grigg, Richard, "Religion, Science, and Evolution: Paul Tillich's Fourth Way", *Zygon: Journal of Religion and Science* 38 (2003), pp. 943–54.

Grünbaum, Adolf, "The Pseudo-Problem of Creation in Physical Cosmology", *Philosophy of Science* 56:3 (1989), pp. 373–94.

Hagan, Anette, "Divine Sovereignty and Human Freedom: Divine Providence in the Theology of Friedrich Schleiermacher", *Testamentum Imperium* 2 (2009), pp. 2–31.

Hall, Alex, "Confused Univocality", *Proceedings of the Society for Medieval Logic and Metaphysics* 7 (2007), pp. 18–31.

Harrison, Peter, "Introduction", in Peter Harrison (ed.), *The Cambridge Companion to Science and Religion* (Cambridge: Cambridge University Press, 2010), pp. 1–17.

Harrison, Peter, "Science, Eastern Orthodoxy, and Protestantism", *Isis* 107:3 (2016), pp. 587–91.

Hart, David Bentley, *The Experience of God: Being, Consciousness, Bliss* (London: Yale University Press, 2013).

Haught, John, *God after Darwin* (Boulder, CO: Westview Press, 2000).

Haw, Christopher, "The Human Soul and Evolution: A Mimetic Perspective", *New Blackfriars* 102:1097 (2021), pp. 41–74.

Hawking, Stephen, *A Brief History of Time* (London: Transworld Publishers, 1988).

Hawking, Stephen, *The Grand Design* (London: Bantam Press, 2010).

Hayes, Zachary, "Christology and Metaphysics in the Thought of Bonaventure", *The Journal of Religion* 58 (1978), pp. S82–S96.

Hefner, Philip, *The Human Factor* (Minneapolis, MN: Augsburg Fortress, 1993).

Held, Shai, "Being Present While Making Space", in *The Heart of Torah, Volume 1: Essays on the Weekly Torah Portion: Genesis and Exodus* (Philadelphia, PA: Jewish Publication Society, 2017).

Heller, Michael, "Scientific Rationality and Christian Logos", in Robert Russell, William Stoeger and George Coyne (eds), *Physics, Philosophy, and Theology* (Vatican City: Vatican Observatory, 1988), pp. 141–50.

Helm, Paul, "Divine Timeless Eternity", in Gregory Ganssle (ed.), *God and Time: Four Views* (Downers Grove, IL: IVP Academic, 2001), pp. 28–60.

Hiestand, Gerald, "'And Behold it Was Very Good': St. Irenaeus' Doctrine of Creation", *Bulletin of Ecclesial Theology* 6:1 (2019), pp. 1–27.

Hill, Scott, "Giving up Omnipotence", *Canadian Journal of Philosophy* 44:1 (2014), pp. 97–117.

Hoekema, Anthony, *Created in God's Image* (Grand Rapids, MI: William B. Eerdmans, 1994).

Holland Jr., Richard, *God, Time, and the Incarnation* (Eugene, OR: Wipf & Stock, 2012).

Holt, Jim, *Why Does the World Exist?* (London: Profile Books, 2013).

Horwitz, Daniel, *A Kabbalah and Jewish Mysticism Reader* (Philadelphia, PA: Jewish Publication Society, 2016).

Houser, R. E., "Avicenna, 'Aliqui', and Thomas Aquinas' Doctrine of Creation", *Recherches de théologie et philosophie médiévales* 80:1 (2013), pp. 17–55.

Hume, Basil, *Searching for God* (York: Ampleforth Abbey Press, 2002).

Ielciu, Ioan Mircea, "Doctrinal Aspects in Evagrius Ponticus", *Revista Teologică* 99:1 (2017), pp. 18–30.

Isham, Chris, "Creation of the Universe as a Quantum Process", in Robert J. Russell, William Stoeger and George Coyne (eds), *Physics, Philosophy, and Theology* (Vatican City: Vatican Observatory, 1988), pp. 375–408.

John Duns Scotus (tr. Evan Roche), *De Primo Principio* (St. Bonaventure, NY: The Franciscan Institute, 1949).

John Duns Scotus, *Ordinatio*, in Allan Wolter (tr.), *Philosophical Writings* (Edinburgh: Thomas Nelson and Sons, 1962).

John of Damascus, *An Exact Exposition of the Orthodox Faith* (New Delhi: Isha Books, 2013).

Johnson, Junius, "The One and the Many in Bonaventure Exemplarity Explained", *Religions* 7:144 (2016), pp. 1–16.

Jonas, Hans, *Mortality and Morality: A Search for God after Auschwitz* (Evanston, IL: Northwestern University Press, 1996).

Jordan, Mark, "The Intelligibility of the World and the Divine Ideas in Aquinas", *The Review of Metaphysics* 38:1 (1984), pp. 17–32.

Justin Martyr, "Dialogue with Trypho", in Alexander Roberts and James Donaldson (eds), *Ante-Nicene Christian Library Vol.2* (Edinburgh: T&T Clark, 1867), pp. 85–278.

Kähler, Martin, *The So-called Historical Jesus and the Historic, Biblical Christ* (Philadelphia PA: Fortress Press, 1964).

Keating, Daniel, *Deification and Grace* (Naples, FL: Sapientia Press, 2007).

Keefe, Donald, *Thomism and the Ontological Theology of Paul Tillich* (Leiden: Brill, 1971).

Kelly, J. N. D., *Early Christian Doctrines* (London: Adam and Charles Black, 1965).

Kerr, Gavin, "A Thomistic Metaphysics of Creation", *Religious Studies* 48 (2012), pp. 337–56.

Kirkpatrick, Frank, *The Mystery and Agency of God: Divine Being and Action in the World* (Minneapolis, MN: Fortress Press, 2014).

Kittle, Simon, "God is (Probably) a Cause among Causes: Why the Primary/Secondary Cause Distinction Doesn't Help in Developing Noninterventionist Accounts of Special Divine Action", *Theology and Science* 20:2 (2022), pp. 247–62.

Klauder, Francis, *Aspects of the Thought of Teilhard de Chardin* (North Quincy, MA: The Christopher Publishing House, 1971).

Knight, Christopher C., "Divine Activity: A Neo-Byzantine Model", *International Journal for Philosophy of Religion* 58:3 (2005), pp. 181–99.

Knight, Christopher C., *The God of Nature: Incarnation and Contemporary Science* (Minneapolis, MN: Fortress Press, 2007).

Knight, Christopher C., "Divine Action and the Laws of Nature: An Orthodox Perspective on Miracles", in Daniel Buxhoeveden and Gayle Woloschak (eds), *Science and the Eastern Orthodox Church* (Abingdon: Routledge, 2016), pp. 41–51.

Koperski, Jeffrey, *Divine Action, Determinism, and the Laws of Nature* (Abingdon: Routledge, 2020).

Krauss, Lawrence, *A Universe from Nothing* (London: Simon & Schuster, 2012).

Kropf, Richard W., "Teilhard de Chardin's Vision of Ultimate Reality and Meaning in the Light of Contemporary Cosmology", *Ultimate Reality and Meaning* 23:3 (2000), pp. 238–59.

La Croix, Richard, "The Impossibility of Defining 'Omnipotence'", *Philosophical Studies: An International Journal for Philosophy in the Analytic Tradition* 32:2 (1977), pp. 181–90.

Lane, Dermot, *The Reality of Jesus* (London: Sheed & Ward, 1975).

Lash, Nicholas, "Observation, Revelation, and the Prosperity of Noah", in Robert J. Russell, William Stoeger, and George Coyne (eds), *Physics, Philosophy, and Theology: A Common Quest for Understanding* (Vatican City: Vatican Observatory, 1988), pp. 203–15.

Lee, Michael E., "Historical Crucifixion: A Liberationist Response to Deep Incarnation", *Theological Studies* 81:4 (2020), pp. 892–912.

Leftow, Brian, *Time and Eternity* (Ithaca, NY: Cornell University Press, 1991).

Leftow, Brian, "A Timeless God Incarnate", in Stephen Davis, Daniel Kendall and Gerald O'Collins (eds), *The Incarnation* (Oxford: Oxford University Press, 2002).

Leidenhag, Joanna, "God, Consciousness, and Conjunctive Explanations", in Diarmid A. Finnegan, David H. Glass, Mikael Leidenhag and David N. Livingstone (eds), *Conjunctive Explanations in Science and Religion* (New York: Routledge, 2023), pp. 121–46.

Lewis, Delmas, "Timelessness and Divine Agency", *International Journal for Philosophy of Religion* 21:3 (1987), pp. 143–59.

Lombardo, Nicholas, "What God Cannot Do: Divine Power, the Gratuity of Grace, and Henri de Lubac", *Modern Theology* 37:1 (2021), pp. 114–38.

Lore, Andrew, "Divine Omnipotence and Moral Perfection", *Religious Studies* 14:4 (2010), pp. 525–38.

Lossky, Vladimir, *The Mystical Theology of the Eastern Church* (Cambridge: James Clarke & Co., 1957).

Lossky, Vladimir, *In the Image and Likeness of God* (New York, NY: St. Vladimir's Seminary Press, 1974).

Louth, Andrew, "The Cosmic Vision of Saint Maximos the Confessor", in Philip Clayton and Arthur Peacocke (eds), *In Whom We Live and Move and Have Our Being* (Grand Rapids, MI: William B. Eerdmans, 2004), pp. 184–96.

Lucas, J. R., "The Temporality of God", in Robert Russell, Nancey Murphy and Chris Isham (eds), *Quantum Cosmology and the Laws of Nature: Scientific Perspectives on Divine Action* (Vatican City: Vatican Observatory, 1993), pp. 235–46.

MacBeath, Murray and Helm, Paul, "Omniscience and Eternity", *Proceedings of the Aristotelian Society, Supplementary Volumes* 63 (1989), pp. 55–87.

Macquarrie, John, *Jesus Christ in Modern Thought* (London: SCM Press, 1990).

Mantzaridis, Georgios, *The Deification of Man* (Crestwood, NY: St. Vladimir's Seminary Press, 1984).

Marion, Jean-Luc, *God without Being* (Chicago, IL: The University of Chicago Press, 2012).

Markus, Arjan, "Divine Timelessness", *Sophia* 43:2 (2004), pp. 29–48.

Marmodoro, Anna and Hill, Jonathan, "Modeling the Metaphysics of the Incarnation", *Philosophy & Theology* 20:1/2 (2008), pp. 99–128.

Maryniarczyk, Andrzej, "Philosophical Creationism: Thomas Aquinas' Metaphysics of *Creatio ex Nihilo*", *Studia Gilsoniana* 5:1 (2016), pp. 217–68.

McCabe, Herbert, "Creation", *New Blackfriars* 61:724 (1980), pp. 408–15.

McCabe, Herbert, "Eternity", in Philip McCosker and Denys Turner (eds), *The Cambridge Companion to The Summa Theologiae* (Cambridge: Cambridge University Press, 2016), pp. 102–16.

McCord Adams, Marilyn, *What Sort of Nature? Medieval Philosophy and the Systematics of Christology* (Milwaukee, WI: Marquette University Press, 1999).

McCormack, Bruce, "Karl Barth's Christology as a Resource for a Reformed Version of Kenoticism", *International Journal of Systematic Theology* 8:3 (2006), pp. 243–51.

McCosker, Philip, "Grace", in Philip McCosker and Denys Turner (eds), *The Cambridge Companion to The Summa Theologiae* (Cambridge: Cambridge University Press, 2016), pp. 205–21.

McDonough, Sean, *Christ as Creator: Origins of a New Testament Doctrine* (Oxford: Oxford University Press, 2009).

McFarland, Ian, *The Word Made Flesh: A Theology of the Incarnation* (Louisville, KY: Westminster John Knox Press, 2019).

McMullin, Ernan, "Could Natural Selection Be Purposive?", in Joseph Seckbach and Richard Gordon (eds), *Divine Action and Natural Selection* (Singapore: World Scientific, 2008), pp. 93–103.

McMullin, Ernan, "Cosmic Purpose and The Contingency of Human Evolution", *Zygon: Journal of Religion and Science* 48:2 (2013), pp. 338–63.

McTaggart, J. M. E., *The Nature of Existence, Vol. II* (Cambridge: Cambridge University Press, 1927).

McWhorter, Matthew R., "Aquinas on God's Relation to the World", *New Blackfriars* 94:1049 (2013), pp. 3–19.

Merton, Thomas, *New Seeds of Contemplation* (London: Burns & Oates, 1961).

Mettepenningen, Jürgen, *Nouvelle Théologie—New Theology: Inheritor of Modernism, Precursor of Vatican II* (London: T&T Clark International, 2010).

Metz, Thaddeus, "Could God's Purpose Be the Source of Life's Meaning?", *Religious Studies* 36:3 (2000), pp. 293–313.

Meyendorff, John, *A Study of Gregory Palamas* (London: The Faith Press, 1964).

Milbank, John, Pickstock, Catherine and Ward, Graham, "Introduction", in John Milbank, Catherine Pickstock and Graham Ward (eds), *Radical Orthodoxy* (Oxford: Routledge, 1999), pp. 1–20.

Mivart, St. George, *Contemporary Evolution* (London: Henry S. King & Co., 1876).

Mivart, St. George, *On Truth: A Systematic Inquiry* (London: Kegan Paul, Trench & Co., 1889).

Mix, Lucas and Masel, Joanna, "Chance, Purpose, and Progress in Evolution and Christianity", *Evolution* 68:8 (2014), pp. 2441–51.

Moltmann, Jürgen, "God's *Kenosis* in the Creation and Consummation of the World", in John Polkinghorne (ed.), *The Work of Love: Creation as Kenosis* (Grand Rapids, MI: William B. Eerdmans, 2001), pp. 137–51.

Monserrat, Javier, "Kenosis: Towards a New Theology of Science", *Pensamiento* 63:238 (2007), pp. 637–58.

Montagnes, Bernard, *The Doctrine of Analogy of Being According to Thomas Aquinas* (Milwaukee, WI: Marquette University Press, 2004).

Mooney, Christopher, *Teilhard de Chardin and The Mystery of Christ* (London: Collins, 1966).

Morewedge, Parviz, *The Metaphysics of Avicenna* (London: Routledge, 1973).

Moritz, Joshua M., "Rendering unto Science and God: Is NOMA Enough?", *Theology and Science* 7 (2009), pp. 363–78.

Mortensen, John, *Understanding St. Thomas on Analogy* (Rome: Pontifical University of the Holy Cross, 2006).

Moulder, James, "Is a Chalcedonian Christology Coherent?", *Modern Theology* 2:4 (1986), pp. 285–307.

Murphy, Francesca, "The Sound of the 'Analogia Entis' Part 1", *New Blackfriars* 74:876 (1993), pp. 508–21.

Murphy, Nancey, "Human Nature: Historical, Scientific, and Religious Issues", Warren Brown, Nancey Murphy and H. Newton Malony (eds), *Whatever Happened to the Soul: Scientific and Theological Portraits of Human Nature* (Minneapolis, MN: Augsburg Fortress Press, 1998), pp. 1–29.

Murphy, Nancey, "Emergence, Downward Causation, and Divine Action", in Robert Russell, Nancey Murphy and William Stoeger (eds), *Scientific Perspectives on Divine Action: Twenty Years of Challenge and Progress* (Vatican City: Vatican Observatory Foundation, 2008), pp. 111–31.

Nelson, H., "Time(s), Eternity, and Duration", *International Journal for Philosophy of Religion* 22:1/2 (1987), pp. 3–19.

Nelstrop, Louise, *Christian Mysticism: An Introduction to Contemporary Theoretical Approaches* (Farnham: Ashgate, 2009).

Nestlehutt, Mark S. G., "Chalcedonian Christology: Modern Criticism and Contemporary Ecumenism", *Journal of Ecumenical Studies* 35:2 (1998), pp. 175–96.

Nicolaidis, Efthymios, *Science and Eastern Orthodoxy: From the Greek Fathers to the Age of Globalisation* (Baltimore, MD: The Johns Hopkins University Press, 2011).

Nielsen Jr., Niels C., "Przywara's Philosophy of the 'Analogia Entis'", *The Review of Metaphysics* 5:4 (1952), pp. 599–620.

Noone, Timothy B., "The Originality of St. Thomas's Position on the Philosophers and Creation", *The Thomist: A Speculative Quarterly Review* 60:2 (1996), pp. 275–300.

Oakes, Edward, *A Theology of Grace in Six Controversies* (Grand Rapids, MI: William B. Eerdmans, 2016).

O'Collins, Gerald, *Interpreting Jesus* (London: Mowbray, 1983).

O'Collins, Gerald, *Christology: A Biblical, Historical, and Systematic Study of Jesus* (Oxford: Oxford University Press, 1995).

O'Collins, Gerald, "The Incarnation: The Critical Issues", in Stephen Davis, Daniel Kendall & Gerald O'Collins (eds), *The Incarnation* (Oxford: Oxford University Press, 2002), pp. 1–28.

O'Connor, Timothy, "Scotus on the Existence of a First Efficient Cause", *International Journal for Philosophy of Religion* 33:1 (1993), pp. 17–32.

Ogden, Schubert, "What Sense Does it Make to Say, 'God Acts in History'?", in Owen Thomas (ed.), *God's Activity in the World: The Contemporary Problem* (Chico, CA: Scholars Press, 1983), pp. 77–100.

Oppenheimer, Helen, *Incarnation and Immanence* (London: Hodder and Stoughton, 1973).

Oppenheimer, Helen, *Christian Faith for Handing On* (Cambridge: James Clarke & Co., 2014).

Page, Ben, "Wherein Lies the Debate? Concerning whether God is a Person", *International Journal for Philosophy of Religion* 85 (2019), pp. 297–317.

Page, Ruth, *The Web of Creation* (London: SCM Press, 1996).

Palmer, F. Noel, *The Cross in History and Experience* (London: Church Book Room Press LTD., 1949).

Papanikolaou, Aristotle, "Person, *Kenosis* and Abuse: Hans Urs von Balthasar and Feminist Theologies in Conversation", *Modern Theology* 19:1 (2003), pp. 41–65.

Pardue, Stephen, "Kenosis and its Discontents: Towards an Augustinian Account of Divine Humility", *Scottish Journal of Theology* 65:3 (2012), pp. 271–88.

Passmore, John, *The Perfectibility of Man* (London: Duckworth, 1970).

Pawl, Timothy, *In Defence of Conciliar Christology: A Philosophical Essay* (Oxford: Oxford University Press, 2016).

Peacocke, Arthur, *Theology for a Scientific Age* (Minneapolis, MN: Fortress Press, 1993).

Peacocke, Arthur, "The Cost of New Life", in John Polkinghorne (ed.), *The Work of Love: Creation as Kenosis* (Grand Rapids, MI: William B. Eerdmans, 2001), pp. 21–42.

Peacocke, Arthur, *Paths from Science Towards God* (Oxford: OneWorld, 2001).

Peacocke, Arthur, "Articulating God's Presence in and to the World Unveiled by the Sciences", in Philip Clayton and Arthur Peacocke (eds), *In Whom We Live and Move and Have Our Being: Panentheistic Reflections on God's Presence in a Scientific World* (Grand Rapids, MI: William B. Eerdmans, 2004), pp. 137–54.

Pelikan, Jaroslav, *The Christian Tradition: The Spirit of Eastern Christendom (600–1700)* (Chicago, IL: University of Chicago Press, 1977).

Perczel, István, "The Christology of Pseudo-Dionysius: The Areopagite: The *Fourth Letter* in Its Indirect and Direct Text Traditions", *Le Muséon* 117:3–4 (2004), pp. 409–46.

Peters, Ted, "On Creating the Cosmos", in Robert J. Russell, William Stoeger and George Coyne (eds), *Physics, Philosophy, and Theology: A Common Quest for Understanding* (Vatican City: Vatican Observatory, 1988), pp. 273–96.

Pidel, Aaron, "Erich Przywara on Nature–Grace Extrinsicism: A Parallax View", *Modern Theology* 37:4 (2021), pp. 865–87.

Pike, Nelson, *God and Timelessness* (New York: Schocken Books, 1970).

Pius XII, *Humani generis* (Vatican City, 1950).

Plantinga, Alvin, *Does God Have a Nature?* (Milwaukee, WI: Marquette University Press, 1980).

Polkinghorne, John, *Science and Providence* (London: SPCK, 1989).

Polkinghorne, John (ed.), *The Work of Love: Creation as Kenosis* (Grand Rapids, MI: William B. Eerdmans, 2001).

Polkinghorne, John, "Kenotic Creation and Divine Action", in John Polkinghorne (ed.), *The Work of Love: Creation as Kenosis* (Grand Rapids, MI: William B. Eerdmans, 2001), pp. 90–106.

Poon, Wilson, "Science as the Foolishness of God: Twenty-Eight Theses and *Scholia* on 'Science and Religion'", in Andrew Torrance and Thomas McCall (eds), *Christ and the Created Order Vol. 2* (Grand Rapids, MI: Zondervan, 2018), pp. 253–71.

Pope, Stephen J., "Does Evolution Have a Purpose? The Theological Significance of William Stoeger's Account of 'Nested Directionality'", *Theological Studies* 78:2 (2017), pp. 462–82.

Pouivet, Roger, "Against Theistic Personalism: What Modern Epistemology Does to Classical Theism", *European Journal for Philosophy of Religion* 10:1 (2018), pp. 1–19.

Powell, Samuel, *Participation in God* (Minneapolis, MN: Augsburg Fortress Press, 2003).

Prat, Ferdinand, *The Theology of St. Paul: Vol. 1* (London: Burns, Oates & Washbourne, 1945).

Principe, Walter, "Aquinas' Spirituality for Christ's Faithful Living in the World", in Thomas F. O'Meara (tr.), *Exploring Thomas Aquinas: Essays and Sermons* (Chicago, IL: New Priory Press, 2017), pp. 83–106.

Przywara, Erich, *Analogia Entis* (Grand Rapids, MI: William B. Eerdmans, 2014).

Pseudo-Dionysius, *The Complete Works* (Mahwah, NJ: Paulist Press, 1987).

Purpura, Ashley M., *God, Hierarchy, and Power: Orthodox Theologies of Authority from Byzantium* (New York, NY: Fordham University Press, 2018).

Quenum, J. M. H., "Is Divine Grace really beyond human comprehension? An exploration of the Theology of Henri de Lubac", *Testamentum Imperium* 3 (2011), pp. 1–20.

Quick, Oliver, *Doctrines of the Creed* (London: Nisbet & Co., 1938).

Quinn, Philip, "Divine Conservation, Secondary Causes, and Occasionalism", in Thomas Morris (ed.), *Divine and Human Action: Essays in the Metaphysics of Theism* (Ithaca, NY: Cornell University Press, 1988), pp. 50–73.

Rahner, Karl, *The Trinity* (London: Burns & Oates, 1970).

Rahner, Karl, *The Foundations of Christian Faith: An Introduction to the Idea of Christianity* (New York, NY: Crossroad, 1978).

Reichard, Joshua, "Beyond Causation: A Contemporary Theology of Concursus", *American Journal of Theology & Philosophy* 34:2 (2013), pp. 117–34.

Riches, Aaron, *Ecce Homo* (Grand Rapids, MI: William B. Eerdmans, 2016).

Riordan, William, *Divine Light* (San Francisco, CA: Ignatius Press, 2008).

Ritchie, Sarah Lane, "Dancing around the Causal Joint: Challenging the Theological Turn in Divine Action Theories", *Zygon: Journal of Religion and Science* 52:2 (2017), pp. 361–79.

Robinson, H. Wheeler, *The Christian Doctrine of Man* (Edinburgh: T&T Clark, 1926).

Robinson, John, *The Human Face of God* (London: SCM Press, 1973).

Rogers, Katherin, "Eternity Has No Duration", *Religious Studies* 30:1 (1994), pp. 1–16.

Rogers, Katherin, *Perfect Being Theology* (Edinburgh: Edinburgh University Press, 2000).

Rogers, Katherin, "Anselm on Eternity as the Fifth Dimension", *The Saint Anselm Journal* 3:2 (2006), pp. 1–8.

Rolston III, Holmes, "*Kenosis* and Nature", in John Polkinghorne (ed.), *The Work of Love: Creation as Kenosis* (Cambridge, MA: William B. Eerdmans, 2001), pp. 43–65.

Ross, Robert R. N., "The Non-Existence of God: Tillich, Aquinas, and the Pseudo-Dionysius", *The Harvard Theological Review* 68:2 (1975), pp. 141–66.

Rovelli, Carlo, *Seven Brief Lessons on Physics* (London: Penguin, 2015).

Ruse, Michael, *Darwin and Design: Does Evolution Have a Purpose?* (Cambridge, MA: Harvard University Press, 2003).

Russell, Norman, *The Doctrine of Deification in the Greek Patristic Tradition* (Oxford: Oxford University Press, 2004).

Russell, Robert John, "The Relevance of Tillich for the Theology and Science Dialogue", *Zygon: Journal of Religion and Science* 36:2 (2001), pp. 269–308.

Sarot, Marcel, "Omniscience and Experience", *International Journal for Philosophy of Religion* 30:2 (1991), pp. 89–102.

Saunders, Nicholas, *Divine Action and Modern Science* (Cambridge: Cambridge University Press, 2002).

Schleiermacher, Friedrich, *The Christian Faith* (Berkeley, CA: Apocryphile Press, 2011).

Scruton, Roger, *Green Philosophy* (London: Atlantic Books, 2013).

Scuka, Robert F., "Resurrection: Critical Reflections on a Doctrine in Search of Meaning", *Modern Theology* 6:1 (1989), pp. 77–95.

Seife, Charles, *Zero: The Biography of a Dangerous Idea* (London: Souvenir Press, 2000).

Senor, Thomas, "Incarnation and Timelessness", *Faith and Philosophy: Journal of the Society of Christian Philosophers* 7:2 (1990), pp. 149–64.

Senor, Thomas, "Drawing on Many Traditions: An Ecumenical Kenotic Christology", in Jonathan Hill and Anna Marmodoro (eds), *The Metaphysics of the Incarnation* (Oxford: Oxford University Press, 2011), pp. 88–113.

Sherrard, Philip, *Christianity: Lineaments of a Sacred Tradition* (Edinburgh: T&T Clark, 1998).

Shortt, Rupert, *God Is No Thing: Coherent Christianity* (London: Hurst & Company, 2016).

Silva, Ignacio, "Revisiting Aquinas on Providence and Rising to the Challenge of Divine Action in Nature", *The Journal of Religion* 94:3 (2014), pp. 277–91.

Silva, Ignacio, "Divine Action and Thomism: Why Thomas Aquinas's Thought is Attractive Today", *Acta Philosophica* 25:1 (2016), pp. 65–84.

Silva, Ignacio, "Thomas Aquinas and William E. Carroll on *Creatio ex Nihilo*: A Response to Joseph Hannon's 'Theological Objections to a Metaphysicalist Interpretation of Creation'", *Theology and Science* 19:2 (2021), pp. 91–99.

Simoni, Henry, "Omniscience and the Problem of Radical Particularity: Does God Know How to Ride a Bike?", *International Journal for Philosophy of Religion* 42 (1997), pp. 1–22.

Smith, Barry, *The Oneness and Simplicity of God* (Eugene, OR: Wipf & Stock, 2014).

Smith, James, "Our Chalcedonian Moment", in Andrew Torrance and Thomas McCall (eds), *Christ and the Created Order Vol. 2* (Grand Rapids, MI: Zondervan, 2018), pp. 179–93.

Smith, James K. A., *Thinking in Tongues: Pentecostal Contributions to Christian Philosophy* (Grand Rapids, MI: Eerdmans, 2010).

Smith, Wolfgang, *Teilhardism and the New Religion* (Rockford, IL: Tan Books and Publishers inc., 1988).

Smolin, Lee, *The Life of the Cosmos* (London: Weidenfeld & Nicolson, 1997)

Soskice, Janet, "Knowledge and Experience in Science and Religion: Can We Be Realists", in Robert J. Russell, William Stoeger and George Coyne (eds), *Physics, Philosophy, and Theology: A Common Quest for Understanding* (Vatican City: Vatican Observatory, 1988), pp. 173–84.

Southgate, Christopher, *The Groaning of Creation* (Louisville, KY: Westminster John Knox Press, 2008).

Southgate, Christopher, "Re-reading Genesis, John and Job: A Christian Response to Darwinism", *Zygon: Journal of Religion and Science* 46:2 (2011), pp. 370–95.

Stackpole, Robert, *The Incarnation: Rediscovering Kenotic Christology* (Langley, British Colombia: The Chartwell Press, 2019).

Stoeger, William, "Contemporary cosmology and its implications for the science–religion dialogue", in Robert J. Russell, William Stoeger and George Coyne (eds), *Physics, Philosophy, and Theology: A Common Quest for Understanding* (Vatican City: Vatican Observatory, 1988), pp. 219–47.

Stoeger, William, "Conceiving Divine Action in a Dynamic Universe", in Robert Russell, Nancey Murphy and William Stoeger (eds), *Scientific Perspectives on Divine Action: Twenty Years of Challenge and Progress* (Vatican City: Vatican Observatory Foundation, 2008), pp. 225–47.

Stoeger, William, "God, Physics, and the Big Bang", in Peter Harrison (ed.), *The Cambridge Companion to Science and Religion* (Cambridge: Cambridge University Press, 2010), pp. 173–89.

Stott, John, *The Cross of Christ* (Leicester: InterVarsity Press, 1986).

Stump, Eleonore and Kretzmann, Norman, "Eternity", *The Journal of Philosophy* 78:8 (1981), pp. 429–58.

Stump, Eleonore and Kretzmann, Norman, "Absolute Simplicity", *Faith and Philosophy: Journal of the Society of Christian Philosophers* 2:4 (1985), pp. 353–82.

Stump, Eleonore, *The God of the Bible and the God of the Philosophers* (Milwaukee, WI: Marquette University Press, 2016).

Suh, Chul Won, *The Creation-Mediatorship of Jesus Christ* (Amsterdam: Rodopi, 1982).

Swafford, Andrew Dean, *Nature and Grace: A New Approach to Thomistic Ressourcement* (Cambridge: James Clarke & Co., 2015).

Swinburne, Richard, "Omnipotence", *American Philosophical Quarterly* 10:3 (1973), pp. 231–7.

Swinburne, Richard, *The Coherence of Theism* (Oxford: Clarendon Press, 1993).

Swinburne, Richard, "Causation, Time, and God's Omniscience", *Topoi* 36 (2017), pp. 67–84.

Tabaczek, Mariusz, "An Aristotelian Account of Evolution and the Contemporary Philosophy of Biology", *Dialogo* 1:1 (2014), pp. 57–69.

Tabaczek, Mariusz, "Thomistic Response to the Theory of Evolution: Aquinas on Natural Selection and the Perfection of the Universe", *Theology and Science* 13:3 (2015), pp. 325–44.

Tabaczek, Mariusz, "What Do God and Creatures Really Do in an Evolutionary Change? Causal Analysis of Biological Transformism from the Thomistic Perspective", *American Catholic Philosophical Quarterly* 93:3 (2019), pp. 445–82.

Tabaczek, Mariusz, "The Metaphysics of Evolution: From Aquinas's Interpretation of Augustine's Concept of *Rationes Seminales* to the Contemporary Thomistic Account of Species Transformism", *Nova et vetera* 18:3 (2020), pp. 945–72.

Tabaczek, Mariusz, "Does God Create Through Evolution? A Thomistic Perspective", *Theology and Science* 20:1 (2022), pp. 46–68.

Teilhard de Chardin, Pierre, *The Divine Milieu* (New York, NY: Harper & Row, 1968).

Teilhard de Chardin, Pierre, *Writings in the Time of War* (London: Collins, 1968).

Teilhard de Chardin, Pierre, *Christianity and Evolution* (London: Harvest, 1971).

Theron, Stephen, "Creation *stricto sensu*", *New Blackfriars* 89:1020 (2008), pp. 194–213.

Thomasius, Gottfried, "Christ's Person and Work Part II: The Person of the Mediator", in Claude Welch (ed.), *God and Incarnation in Mid-Nineteenth Century German Theology* (Oxford: Oxford University Press, 1965), pp. 31–101.

Tillich, Paul, *Systematic Theology Vol. 1* (Chicago, IL: The University of Chicago Press, 1957).

Tillich, Paul, *Systematic Theology Vol. 2* (London: SCM Press, 1978).

Tollefsen, Torstein Theodor, *Activity and Participation in Late Antique and Early Christian Thought* (Oxford: Oxford University Press, 2012).

Tomkinson, J. L., "Divine Sempiternity and Atemporality, *Religious Studies* 18:2 (1982), pp. 177–89.

Torrance, Thomas, *Space, Time, and Incarnation* (Oxford: Oxford University Press, 1978).

Torrance, Thomas, *The Mediation of Christ* (Edinburgh: T&T Clark, 1992).

Tracy, Thomas, "Divine Action, Created Causes, and Human Freedom", in *The God Who Acts* (University Park, PA: The Pennsylvania State University Press, 1994), pp. 77–102.

Trakakis, Nick, "The Absolutist Theory of Omnipotence", *Sophia* 136:2 (1997), pp. 55–78.

Tromans, Oliver, "The 'Divine Names' and the 'Attributes of Deity': On the (Infinite) Analogical Interval in Forty-Six Aphorisms", *Modern Theology* 36:3 (2020), pp. 629–40.

Turner, Denys, *The Darkness of God: Negativity in Christian Mysticism* (Cambridge: Cambridge University Press, 1998).

van Driel, Edwin Chr., "The Logic of Assumption", in C. Stephen Evans (ed.), *Exploring Kenotic Christology* (Vancouver: Regent College Publishing, 2006), pp. 265–90.

Verschuuren, Gerard, *Aquinas and Modern Science* (Kettering, OH: Angelico Press, 2016).

Vogel, Lawrence, "Introduction", in Hans Jonas, *Mortality and Morality: A Search for God after Auschwitz* (Evanston, IL: Northwestern University Press, 1996), pp. 1–40.

von Balthasar, Hans Urs, *Mysterium Paschale* (Edinburgh: T&T Clark, 1990).

von Balthasar, Hans Urs, *Theo-Drama II: Dramatis Personae: Man in God* (San Francisco, CA: Ignatius Press, 1992).

von Balthasar, Hans Urs, *Theo-Drama IV: The Action* (San Francisco, CA: Ignatius Press, 1994).

Walker, William, *The Incarnation and Kenosis* (Self-published, 2015).

Wand, J. W. C., *The Four Great Heresies* (London: Mowbray, 1961).

Ward, Graham, "Kenosis: Death, Discourse and Resurrection", in Lucy Gardner, David Moss, Ben Quash and Graham Ward (eds), *Balthasar at the End of Modernity* (Edinburgh: T&T Clark, 1999), pp. 15–68.

Ward, Keith, *Rational Theology and the Creativity of God* (Oxford: Basil Blackwell Ltd., 1982).

Ward, Keith, "Cosmos and *Kenosis*", in John Polkinghorne (ed.), *The Work of Love: Creation as Kenosis* (Grand Rapids, MI: William B. Eerdmans, 2001), pp. 152–66.

Ware, Kallistos, *The Orthodox Way* (Crestwood, NY: St. Vladimir's Seminary Press, 1979).

Wawrykow, Joseph, "Aquinas and Bonaventure on Creation", in Gary Anderson and Markus Bockmuehl, *Creation ex nihilo: Origins, Development, Contemporary Challenges* (Notre Dame, IN: University of Notre Dame Press, 2018), pp. 173–94.

Wear, Sarah and Dillon, John, *Dionysius the Areopagite and The Neoplatonist Tradition* (Aldershot: Ashgate, 2007).

Weber, Hans-Ruedi, *The Cross: Tradition and Interpretation* (London: SPCK, 1979).

Wildman, Wesley, "The Divine Action Project, 1988–2003", in Robert Russell, Nancey Murphy and William Stoeger (eds), *Scientific Perspectives on Divine Action: Twenty Years of Challenge and Progress* (Vatican City: Vatican Observatory Foundation, 2008), pp. 131–75.

Wiles, Maurice, *God's Action in the World* (London: SCM Press, 1986).

Williams, Anna, *The Ground of Union: Deification in Aquinas and Palamas* (Oxford: Oxford University Press, 1999).

Williams, Anna, "Nestorianism: Is Jesus Christ one person or does he have a split identity, with his divine nature separate and divided from his human nature?", in Ben Quash and Michael Ward (eds), *Heresies and How to Avoid Them* (London: SPCK, 2007), pp. 32–40.

Williams, David, "Kenosis and the Nature of the Persons in the Trinity", *Koers* 69:4 (2004), pp. 623–40.

Williams, David, *Kenōsis of God* (Bloomington, IN: iUniverse, 2009).

Williams, Patricia, *Doing Without Adam and Eve* (Minneapolis, MN: Fortress Press, 2001).

Williams, Rowan, *Wrestling with Angels: Conversations in Modern Theology* (London: SCM Press, 2007).

Williams, Rowan, *Christ the Heart of Creation* (London: Bloomsbury Continuum, 2018).

Wirzba, Norman, "Creation *Through* Christ", in Andrew Torrance and Thomas McCall (eds) *Christ and the Created Order Vol. 2* (Grand Rapids, MI: Zondervan, 2018), pp. 35–54.

Wittgenstein, Ludwig, *Tractatus Logico-Philosophicus*, tr. C. K. Ogden (London: Routledge & Kegan Paul, 1933).

Wood, Rega, "Distinct Ideas and Perfect Solicitude: Alexander of Hales, Richard Rufus, and Odo Rigaldus", *Franciscan Studies* 53 (1993), pp. 7–31.

Wood, Susan, *Spiritual Exegesis and the Church in the Theology of Henri de Lubac* (Edinburgh: T&T Clark, 1998).

Worthing, Mark William, *God, Creation, and Contemporary Physics* (Minneapolis, MN: Fortress Press, 1996).

Wright, N. T., "Jesus' Self-Understanding", in Stephen Davis, Daniel Kendall and Gerald O'Collins (eds), *The Incarnation* (Oxford: Oxford University Press, 2002), pp. 47–61.

Young, Frances, "A Cloud of Witnesses", in John Hick (ed.), *The Myth of God Incarnate* (London: SCM Press, 1977), pp. 13–47.

Young, Frances, *Can These Dry Bones Live?* (London: SCM Press, 1982).

Young, Frances, *From Nicaea to Chalcedon* (London: SCM Press, 1983).

Index of Names

Ingram Content Group UK Ltd.
Milton Keynes UK
UKHW022253010523
421049UK00015B/793